MW00657833

FROM BYTOWN
— TO THE —
BIG LEAGUES

150 YEARS OF AMERICA'S PASTIME IN CANADA'S CAPITAL
OTTAWA BASEBALL FROM 1865 TO 2025

Edited by Steve Rennie and Bill Nowlin

Associate editors Frank McDonald,
Philippe Cousineau, and Carl Riechers

Society for American Baseball Research, Inc.
Phoenix, AZ

From Bytown to the Big Leagues: 150 Years of America's Pastime in Canada's Capital
Ottawa Baseball from 1865 to 2025

Edited by Steve Rennie and Bill Nowlin
Associate editors Frank McDonald, Philippe Cousineau, and Carl Riechers

Design: Gilly Rosenthol

Front cover photograph: Courtesy of Timothy Austen.
Back cover images: Courtesy of the City of Ottawa Archives.

978-1-960819-32-1 (ebook)
978-1-960819-33-8 (paperback)
Library of Congress Control Number: 2024926254

Copyright © 2025 Society for American Baseball Research, Inc.
All rights reserved. Reproduction in whole or in part without permission is prohibited.

Cronkite School at ASU
555 N. Central Ave. #406
Phoenix, AZ 85004
Phone: (602) 496-1460
Web: www.sabr.org
Facebook: Society for American Baseball Research
X: @SABR

FROM BYTOWN
— TO THE —
BIG LEAGUES

150 YEARS OF AMERICA'S PASTIME IN CANADA'S CAPITAL
OTTAWA BASEBALL FROM 1865 TO 2025

TABLE OF CONTENTS

OTTAWA LYNX (1993 – 2007)

TWENTY-FIRST CENTURY

HOMETOWN HEROES

FOREWORD

BY MARK SUTCLIFFE

IT WAS A TIME OF hopes and dreams. When the Ottawa Lynx played their first home game on April 17, 1993, baseball was on the ascendancy in Canada. The Toronto Blue Jays had just won the first of two consecutive World Series. The Montreal Expos, the parent team of the fledgling Lynx, were climbing the standings, a year away from having the best team and the best record in baseball.

For the players arriving in Ottawa that spring, it was less about the launch of a franchise and more the hopeful start of a new season and the penultimate step to stardom. A Triple-A prospect is always only an injury, a trade, or a prolonged slump by a major leaguer away from a phone call and a ticket to The Show. Future major leaguers including Matt Stairs and Tim Laker arrived in Ottawa with a sense that their moment had almost arrived. A few solid months in Ottawa and they would soon be with the Expos.

For the fans, it was a new chapter in a love affair with baseball and the Expos. For a generation, busloads of residents had made regular trips to Jarry Park and Olympic Stadium to watch Rusty Staub, Gary Carter, Andre Dawson, and Tim Raines. For Ottawa to not only have a Triple-A team but to affiliate with the Expos was perceived as nothing short of a match made in baseball heaven. Ottawa fans eagerly embraced the chance to follow the Expos of tomorrow and cast eyes on visiting prospects, including future Hall-of-Famers from Derek Jeter to Jim Thome, to join the fraternity of professional baseball towns, to relish spring and summer evenings in a brand-new ballpark.

And for a 24-year-old aspiring broadcaster, it was a dream come true. Raised on the voices of Dave Van Horne and Duke Snider carried over the airwaves and onto the portable radio I kept under my pillow and brought to my grandparents' house for Sunday afternoon games, I was desperate to take a spot at the microphone and spin my own lyrical tales of green grass and fresh young faces, of stolen summer nights and stolen bases. I auditioned for and earned a spot on the part-time broadcast team, announcing games on both radio and television.

The arrival of the Triple-A Lynx was a new beginning, but also the continuation of a story of professional baseball in Ottawa dating back to the nineteenth century. In 1898, Ottawa played in the Eastern League. The Ottawa Senators existed in a variety of forms in the first half of the twentieth century. Ottawa had a stint in the International League in the 1950s, as affiliates of the New York Giants and the Philadelphia Athletics playing at Lansdowne Park.

But nothing matched the excitement of the arrival of the Lynx. Though it ended in a semifinal loss and not a championship, the inaugural season was close to perfect. Dozens of games were sold out as Ottawa broke a decades-old International League attendance record. Large groups of fans gathered in the picnic area down the left-field line or watched from the restaurant next to the press box. A local country musician, Gail Gavan, recorded the team's theme song, "The Lynx Are on the Prowl." The field was immaculate, considered one of the best-maintained in the minors. The crowds welcomed a new mascot, Lenny the Lynx, a cat with an attitude. In between innings, the umpires had water delivered in a tiny replica of an *Ottawa Citizen* newspaper truck.

The team was a delight to follow. Within a few weeks of opening day there was a combined no-hitter. Flashy outfielders Cliff Floyd and Rondell White were called up from Double A. A fast-working 22-year-old left-hander from Illinois named Kirk Rueter arrived en route to a 13-year career in the majors. Curtis Pride won the hearts of fans with his compelling story of perseverance; when the minor-league season ended, he became the first deaf player in almost half a century to play in the big leagues.

And of course, there was the ultimate fan favorite, F.P. Santangelo. Santangelo was scrappy and energetic, played multiple positions, gave a great interview, and appeared in all but a handful of games for the Lynx. And when Lenny the Lynx was officially introduced, he stole the mascot's ATV and drove it around the warning track.

Such was the magic of Triple-A baseball in Ottawa in 1993. It was light, it was fun, it was entertaining. It was everything that minor-league baseball promised to be. It filled the long spring and summer nights while Ottawa's main professional sports franchise, the NHL's Senators, were still losing like an expansion team and a few years away from extending their season beyond the first week of April. Ottawa became the darling of the International League.

Little did we know that the magical summer of 1993 was the crescendo rather than the opening act. The following August, the players' strike ended not only the finest season in Expos history, it precipitated the decline and eventual demise of the franchise and with it a downward spiral in interest in the sport in Eastern Canada. The Expos went from World Series favorites to an abandoned, ownerless franchise that would eventually play some of its games in Puerto Rico. The Lynx went from hosting superstars such as Larry Walker and Moises Alou at their annual exhibition game to being joined at the hip with the worst franchise in professional sports.

After the record-setting inaugural season, the attendance for the Lynx declined steadily. At first, it seemed like a normal rationalization after the honeymoon of the first season. But the free fall never stopped. An anemic Canadian dollar didn't help the business model, with Ottawa and other minor-league clubs north of the border having to pay most of their expenses in US funds.

Before the team's fateful destiny became apparent, there were a few more shining moments. For the final few weeks of the 1994 season, with no major-league games to broadcast, the baseball world's attention shifted to the minors and Van Horne covered the Lynx nightly along with his latest broadcast partner Ken Singleton. It was a small silver lining to what would become the longest work stoppage in baseball history. And in 1995, when the strike mercifully ended, a club made up of prospects and would-be replacement players captured the team's only championship, winning the Governors Cup in front of the home crowd.

For the diehard fans who continued to follow the team during the decline of the Expos and when Ottawa eventually aligned with Baltimore and then Philadelphia, there were future stars including José Vidro, Orlando Cabrera, Michael Barrett, and J.A. Happ. But the magic of sold-out crowds and feeding the Expos' future ambitions was over. Once lost, the magic of minor-league baseball is almost impossible to reclaim. The Lynx dwindled, other Canadian cities lost their Triple-A teams, and the inevitable finally occurred in 2007 when the team moved to Pennsylvania, never to be heard from in these parts again.

In the years that have followed, a series of semi-professional and independent baseball teams have called Ottawa home, including the Rapidz, the Fat Cats, the Champions, and now in 2024 the Ottawa Titans. There was a brief effort to bring a Double-A team to Ottawa, but that opportunity fizzled.

Like many stories that begin with hopes and dreams, the saga of the Ottawa Lynx has a melancholy ending. Nothing lasts forever. But it's better to have witnessed the minor miracle than missed it altogether. We will always have F.P., Lenny, the summer of 1993, and a lifetime of baseball memories. And hope remains for big crowds and hot prospects in Ottawa's future.

INTRODUCTION

BY TIM HARPER

SPRING IN OTTAWA TAUNTS. It teases and tantalizes, offering its charms in unexpected bursts, only to pull back its promise with cruel wintry blasts that test endurance and resilience. In January, spring is merely a concept, but as the days come off the calendar, there is cause for hope, perhaps distant, but hope, nonetheless.

There is but one sound, however, that can definitively prove that renewal is at hand. Well, a few sounds actually—the crack of the bat, the pop of the mitt, and the shouts of "let's turn two."

It has been thus in the nation's capital for more than 150 years, even as much of the world thinks of this northern post as a town consumed by hockey, or, intermittently, Canadian football. Baseball's formal appearance, like early spring, has sometimes come in intermittent bursts, but baseball has been woven into the fabric of the city and, while professional players and teams have come and gone, quality hardball has always been played here, the combatants lionized and celebrated in the local press for years. A more pedestrian quality of ball continues to be played out in sandlots named Hampton (nestled behind a Food Basics), Brewer, Britannia, and Clarington. A parade of pros have come and gone through the years, but the amateurs have consistently kept the love alive.

Just don't expect to be sliding into second during April, at least without first clearing away the remnants of stubborn, grey snowbanks and other undesirable winter detritus that may litter the basepaths late into the month. In fact, the city in 2024 asked teams to stay *off* the playing surface of local diamonds until May 15.[1]

But, oh, it's worth the wait. History has proven that the wait has always borne fruit in Ottawa. History has also shown that while Montreal and Toronto have hit the big leagues,[2] Ottawa is no poor cousin when it comes to homegrown baseball enthusiasm, even though it has never received a promotion from Triple A. Yes, early-season rain and late-season frost were unwelcome features of an Ottawa baseball season, but fans simply endured rainouts in April and May and donned heavy coats for September playoffs. Premiers, prime ministers, future prime ministers, and visiting royalty all turned up for various opening days, and Ottawans embraced their local baseball heroes, even though for much of the twentieth century that embrace was good only Monday-Saturday. Ottawa voters were determined that Sunday was no day for home runs or double plays, or sports of any kind, for that matter.

The city has witnessed extraordinary baseball skill, even if the likes of Bill Metzig, Urban Shocker, Frank "Shag" Shaughnessy, and F.P. Santangelo are today little remembered. Metzig had two major-league hits, filling his stat sheet with a single run scored and batted in,[3] but excelled in Ottawa as a player-manager. Shaughnessy was simultaneously player-manager of the Ottawa Senators of the Canadian Baseball League Class-B entry, coached the McGill University football team to a championship, and was the business manager for the Ontario Hockey Association. He hit .340 for the Senators in 1913[4] and would go on to be president of the International League from 1936 to 1960. Shocker racked up 39 wins in Ottawa in two years before graduating to fame with the New York Yankees and St. Louis Browns, while Santangelo became an icon of the Triple-A Lynx over four years and 347 games, taking the team's first at-bat in 1993 and scoring its first run, and winning over fans with his blue-collar style of play, becoming the first Lynx player to have his jersey retired.[5] When he finally graduated to the parent Montreal Expos in 1996, he finished fourth in Rookie of the Year balloting.[6]

Baseball in Ottawa got off to a rather rough start, to be sure. The first nine an Ottawa side ever sent over the white lines did not particularly distinguish themselves, falling to a team from Ogdensburg in Upstate New York in 1867 by a count of 141-20.[7] The Senators debuted in Ottawa as the first professional team when the Rochester, New York, Eastern League team relocated to the capital midway through the 1898 season and lost their first home game on July 15 by a score of 8-1. Nearly 2,500 enthusiastic fans filled the grandstand, "many of them ladies."[8] But the Senators finished last and decamped from the capital in November of that year, making Ottawa's first professional foray one that could be counted in weeks. They lost 14 of their final 15 games, despite the efforts of "Quiet" Joe Knight, a .338 hitter from Port Stanley, Ontario, who went to hit .312 for the 1890 Cincinnati Reds and is enshrined in the International League Hall of Fame.[9]

In 1906, the Northern Independent League, an outlaw circuit which operated outside the National Association of Professional Baseball Leagues, became a five-team loop with the addition of Ottawa as its only Canadian entrant. Again, the professional experience in the national capital was brief and the Ottawans folded after 34 games, citing debts of at least $5,000, claiming losses of $700 per week.[10] Yet fans were able to watch some extremely high caliber baseball with catcher "Red" Murray and center fielder Ray Demmitt leading the way among five future major leaguers on its roster. Murray bolted for the St. Louis Cardinals midseason.[11]

Another quick exit sparked a local debate: was Ottawa really a lacrosse town, not a baseball town? The debate had fierce adherents on either side, and both sides often competed for field space and playing time. But, perhaps baseball had a leg up when it came to the fanaticism of its hard core "cranks," who go temporarily insane during the season (but they do recover).[12] Still, with two very brief forays into professional baseball both over in a blink, another attempt, this time with the Ottawa Senators of the Canadian League in 1912, was greeted with some skepticism—but not by the local newspaper. "Ottawa Has Never Fallen Down as a Good Baseball 'Town,'" the Ottawa Citizen proclaimed, as it assessed the prospects for the Senators.[13]

This time the operators had invested $5,000 in the team and expected to spend $2,500 per month, "a big outlay" as the paper noted. But those who pointed to the Eastern and Northern League failures were wasting their energy, the unbylined story protested. Everyone knew Ottawa was a lacrosse town when the 1898 Senators moseyed into town from Rochester, but still baseball drew well. The author argued the Ottawa outlaw team was a victim of incompetent management that couldn't draw crowds on the road. This time, they would not have to pay any player more than $300, compared to the outrageous $700 in salaries in the Independent League and besides "there is a big baseball boom in Ottawa just now and the city is far more advanced in a sporting sense than it was five years ago."[14]

Hopes were high. Thousands were expected to attend the Canadian League opener in 1912, with fireworks and an automobile parade scheduled, and the players were invited to a theatre opening, a horse show and a civic lunch, all part of Ottawa's baseball "epidemic."[15] "I have been in professional baseball nine years and it has never been my good fortune to come in contact with such a gentlemanly lot of players," manager Louie Cook declared of his Class-D squad on the eve of the opener in St. Thomas, Ontario.[16] Whether it was their gentlemanly demeanor or their diamond skills, Cook was correct. This iteration of the Senators went 63-35 in its first year and only got better from there during its four-year run, winning four championships, even after the league graduated to Class-B status in 1914.

Such was the popularity of the Senators that Opening Day 1914 was attended by Prime Minister Robert Borden and the former prime minister Wilfrid Laurier. Their season opener in St. Thomas, Ontario, was attended by the Duke of Connaught.[17] The Senators were led by their dominant spitballer Urban Shocker who won 39 games over the 1914-15 seasons before joining the New York Yankees and becoming an elite major-league pitcher who won 27 games in 1921 for the St. Louis Browns and became a member of two Yankees World Series champions, including the legendary 1927 team. He did not pitch in that World Series, but he won 18 games for the team while pitching through serious health concerns and tragically he died of heart disease the following year at the age of 37.

The 1914 season had been clouded by war and the Senators' exploits were eclipsed by events of more mortal foreboding. A scaled-back league operated in 1915 and the Senators easily won their fourth consecutive pennant but when the 1916 league was suspended during World War I, the league, and that iteration of the Senators, never operated again.

In the ensuing years, professional baseball was played in Ottawa by teams called (again) the Senators (1922 Class B) and the Canadiens (with almost all home games played in Montreal, 1923[18]), the Ottawa-Hull Senators of the Quebec-Ontario-Vermont League (1924), again the Senators of the Canadian-American League (1936), the Braves (1937-38), again the Senators (1939), and the Ottawa-Ogdensburg (New York) Senators in the 1940 Can-Am League.

Success was often elusive. The 1936 team had fallen $4,500 in the red and the team had to be disbanded on the account of the players' hefty salaries, said manager Clair Forster.[19] Forster scouted and signed 15 players and kept the former Senators in the Canadian-American League, now reconstituted as the Braves, and their first workout of the season, on May 3, 1937 was attended by a couple hundred curious onlookers.[20] They didn't draw much more than that during the season, an average of 298 per game to see the Braves finish last with a record of 32-75. The following year, they went 38-83 and entertained 410 per game (at 30 cents per adult admission, tax included).[21] As many as 1,500 attended a late May doubleheader, but the Braves were shut out twice by Oswego dropping to last place and the newspaper predicted a swift drop off in attendance if the team could not turn things around. They couldn't.[22]

By December of 1939, the owners of the Ottawa entrant in the Canadian-American League were preparing to move the team to Oneonta, New York, for play the following season. Although they promised to protect the Ottawa "identity" in the league and potentially play a handful of 1940 games there, they cited a lack of playing grounds in Ottawa, the "international situation," and the exchange rate as reasons for the move.[23] The plan was further revised to split games between Ottawa and Ogdensburg, New York, and the team stormed to the pennant, but drew only 718 per game in Ottawa, playing in a Lansdowne Park without lights.[24] War eventually intervened and instead of baseball, Lansdowne Park was needed as a drill grounds for Canadian soldiers as World War II interrupted baseball in the nation's capital.

In 1947, local sports promoter Tommy Gorman decided it was time for a return to professional baseball in Ottawa, this time a franchise in the Border League, a short run marked by success on the field and huge popularity in the city. The first-year Nationals were led by manager Paul Dean, the former St. Louis "fireball flinger" who even made a return to the mound for the Senators on June 4, 1947 against the Ogdensburg Maples.[25] His debut drew plenty of advance skepticism, but he threw six innings and gave up four runs (only one earned) on four hits, but left trailing 4-0 before the Nationals rallied twice, in the bottom of the ninth and 10th, to pull out a 7-5 victory in "probably the most dramatic finish ever witnessed in local baseball."[26] Some 4,000 fans attended the game at Lansdowne Park. Dean had burst on to the major-league scene with back-to-back 19-win seasons before he was 23. At the age of 21, he threw a no-hitter and won two World Series games. He would, however, manage only 12 more wins and be out of baseball by the age of 30. In their prime, Dean, known as "Daffy," a moniker he detested, teamed with renowned brother "Dizzy" to create one of the most famous brother acts of the day. They took their act to vaudeville and starred in a movie (playing themselves) with Shemp Howard, who would go on to fame with The Three Stooges.[27]

Thirteen years before his arrival in Ottawa, Paul Dean reminded reporters of 1934 when he won 20 games for the St. Louis Cardinals (he exaggerated his total by one) and his brother won 30. Dean's squad won its opener 6-3 over the Ogdensburg Maples,[28] and never really looked back, but Dean decided he had to return to Little Rock, Arkansas, in September (with the Nationals in a tense playoff tussle with the Maples) because of business concerns - according to the team, at least. As Gorman put it, Dean was "anxious to return to his home where he had trouble over his business interests that had been turned over to another individual for management."[29]

Second baseman Bill Metzig, the on-field leader of the team, deemed Dean "a swell guy," who might return the following season. But Metzig was now leading the team on and off the field and he was speaking after the Nationals won the Border League championship in Dean's absence – and before signing a ball for the reporter.[30] According to Dean's SABR biography, however, his departure was more likely tied to editorial carping in the Ottawa newspaper about whether Lansdowne Park should be used for professional baseball. "You-all can't run a ballclub with opposition like that from the editorial page," he told The Sporting News.[31] Indeed, debate over the use of Lansdowne Park as a venue for a pro team of U.S. players, as opposed to its use as a recreation center for amateur athletes, had played out on the editorial pages and at city council all season long. Days before Dean departed to tend to his Arkansas "business ventures," the Ottawa Citizen had weighed in, saying professional baseball should not be played at Lansdowne. "Baseball is a popular game and there is every reason why professional baseball should be played here," its editorialists said. "But professional ball should not be allowed to monopolize the one, big city-owned park to the virtual exclusion of the thousands of amateurs – Ottawa's younger citizens – who could make far beneficial use of it. 'Pro' ball is fine – in its place. But its place is some stadium other than Lansdowne."[32] The editorial might have seemed at odds with the popularity of the team that played out of Lansdowne, but the use of that park, its condition, and its use on Sunday was an issue through consecutive iterations of professional baseball in Ottawa.

Dean's return to Little Rock ushered in the managerial era of Metzig, another Little Rock refugee. He was no returning major-league star, but his performance in Ottawa as player-manager was astonishing. As a major leaguer, Metzig, a late-season call-up to a woeful Chicago White Sox squad that finished seventh in the eight-team American League, managed two hits and a single run batted in over five games and 17 plate appearances in 1944. His debut on September 19 of that year resulted in an 0-4 with two strikeouts against Philadelphia A's pitchers Jesse Flores and Carl Scheib. But as manager of the Nationals, who became known as "the Metzigmen," from 1948-50 he won 228 games and lost only 156, finishing first twice and second once, although a league championship eluded him. In four years with the Nationals, including three as player-manager, he never hit below .317 and twice drove in more than 100 runs. He also became a man about town, hobnobbing with a young Frank Sinatra, discussing the prospects for the New York Giants and receiving regrets from "The Voice" that he couldn't stay in town to watch Metzig's boys on the diamond.[33]

His squad was boosted by Doug Harvey, the hockey hall-of-famer, who in 1949 led the Border League in batting average, runs, and RBIs and ultimately chose the rink over the diamond, turning down a professional offer from the Boston Braves.[34] The 1950 team had to play through the tragedy of the death in a car crash of 23-year-old Bob Larkin in July of that year. Larkin was traveling back to Ottawa from Watertown, New York, with four teammates when an army vehicle driving on the wrong side of the road hit their car.[35] It injured four other Nats, the team had to endure the usual 15-game road trip while the Central Canada Exhibition took over their Lansdowne Park home, and Metzig still steered them to the pennant on the final day of the season. "It is a remarkable team achievement and Metzig, the bespectacled chap who doubles as manager and second baseman, is entitled to orchards for a job well done," enthused Jack Koffman of the Citizen.[36] The team drew more than 100,000 fans that year, but it was to be the Border League swan song in the capital. Better days were ahead, though. Baseball at the Triple-A level was coming back to Ottawa for the first time since 1898.

The Border League Nationals moved to Cornwall, Ontario (quickly leading to the demise of the league), and the Jersey City Giants were headed to the capital to become the Ottawa Giants of the International League. Poor attendance in Jersey City was blamed on TV. Too many major-league games being beamed in from New York kept fans out of the park, something that was not expected to be a problem in Ottawa. Distractions were fewer in the capital and TV was not yet "underway" in Canada, as the Citizen explained, and when it arrives, Ottawa will be out of range of any American stations.[37]

Ottawa typically showed its love for its Triple-A orphans, with 7,469 pouring through the Lansdowne Park turnstiles on opening day. It had been set back a day by rain, of course, but the faithful were there to marvel at the new electric scoreboard and watch External Affairs Minister (and future Prime Minister) Lester Pearson bloop a foul down the right-field line on a pitch by Ottawa Mayor Grenville Goodwin in an unorthodox opening ceremony as the Giants beat the Springfield Cubs 5-3.[38] But the love was not fully returned by the parent New York Giants who provided Ottawa with a light-hitting, lackluster squad that escaped the basement that year by a scant half-game. The Giants lavished much more attention on their other Triple-A affiliate, the Minneapolis Millers, where they sent a 19-year-old Willie Mays in 1951.[39] Mere weeks after opening day, rumors began circulating that the Giants would pull out of Ottawa and consolidate their top farm team in Minnesota, part of a trend of such contraction at the minor-league level already underway. When the Giants finally cut ties, they complained about the facilities at Lansdowne (inferior lighting) and a ban on Sunday baseball that had hampered Ottawa baseball entrants for years.[40]

With the Ottawa franchise rumored to be headed to Newark, New Jersey, capital baseball fans were thrown a lifeline when the Giants team was purchased by the American League Philadelphia Athletics. The A's vowed stability, a competitive team in 1952 and even promised fans that, unlike the Giants, they would leave top performers on the Ottawa squad for the enjoyment of fans all season long. "We're not here on a fly-by-night proposition," promised Philadelphia general manager Arthur Ehlers.[41] The best the "Little A's" could do was to clinch seventh place in the eight-team league on the final day of the season, but not before police charged the team with illegally running a lottery in a "pot of gold" promotion in which an unsuspecting 18-year-old girl carted away an estimated $350 in nickels, a fitting capper on a disappointing season.[42] At year's end, the Athletics also let it be known they hoped Ottawans voted to allow Sunday sports in an upcoming vote, so the home team would not have to travel to play on Sundays for another season. But Ottawa voters had other ideas, decisively backing a Sunday sports ban in a December plebiscite, an ongoing obstacle and portent of things to come for professional baseball in the nation's capital.[43]

The following year was no better for the A's and by 1954 attendance plummeted as the team staggered to a record of 58-96. In 1952 the A's had drawn 153,152 fans.[44] In 1954 they drew 93,982.[45] The club's future was indeed clouded from early in the season. "Toronto sports writers have expressed the opinion that Ottawa fans must be the keenest in America to total approximately 120,000 for the season with a trailing team," wrote the columnist Tommy Shields.[46] (Shields inflated the attendance in his column). But there were larger issues out of Ottawa's control. The parent A's packed up and moved to Kansas City, Missouri,[47] and after persistent rumors that the "Little A's" were headed to Miami, the new Kansas City operation, citing the lack of Sunday baseball and poor conditions at Lansdowne Park, announced the Ottawa Athletics were headed to Columbus, Ohio. Ottawa Mayor Charlotte Whitton dismissed complaints about lack of Sunday baseball and its role in the demise of professional baseball in her city, saying the Athletics had second-rate players who couldn't play any better on a Sunday than a weekday.[48]

It would take 39 long years, and a much more supportive mayor, Jim Durrell[49], but Triple-A baseball finally returned in the name of the Lynx on April 17, 1993, and, of course, once more the Ottawa reception was rapturous. A capacity crowd of 10,332 packed newly-built (and not totally finished) JetForm Stadium, this time a park with good lighting that would open its gates on a Sunday.[50] Some things never changed. It rained. Ottawa loved their team and set an eye-popping International League attendance record of 674,258.[51] And, like every other Triple-A franchise, the Lynx eventually departed, on September 3, 2007, when 7,468 bid the team adieu. It had survived much longer than any other baseball franchise in the nation's capital. It was a beautiful Labor Day afternoon. For once, no one shivered at a September Ottawa baseball game. As the headline read, "Another one bites the dust."[52]

Soon to follow were teams with names like Voyageurs (nee Rapidz), Fat Cats, Champions, and Titans, but the spirit of baseball in Ottawa did not ebb and flow with its visiting pros. It never wavered on its ball diamonds and sandlots, or wherever some white chalk could mark the batter's box and the foul lines.

Amateur baseball in Ottawa featured everything from excellence to "scandals." One squad in the nation's capital which began in 1882 before disbanding in 1887 never suffered the agony of defeat, holding the Central Canada title and vanquishing all challengers from northern New York state over the five years, at least based on the memories shared by fans years later. All players were Ottawans, except one Toronto interloper – the catcher Sam Reid – and included third baseman Billy Kehoe, who was known nationally for his football skills. Second baseman Dick Wheatley was an acrobat of some skill who thrilled his fans with a handspring as he took the field before each game (an early-day Ozzie Smith, it would seem) and road trips and equipment were financed by a passing of the hat to spectators at games. It was an era, a letter writer told the *Citizen*, "when good fellows got together and played games in a clean and manly way for the fun that was in it and the athletic fame of the home town."[53]

In 1920, the city's "baseball scandal," more properly classified as a misunderstanding, erupted over the true recipient of the Lyall Cup, presented by William Lyall of the athletic association which bore his name. His team won the 1919 cup and held onto it as the league disbanded. But a rival league had not disbanded and the cup had been played for and won by the Strathcona Club. The league demanded the cup be presented to Strathcona and the dispute had led to county court while a wise Judge Gunn ruled in favor of the rival league, calling for cool heads on both sides and giving thanks that no money was found under the pillows of any of the disputants.[54]

And what about that bitter rivalry in the Senior League of 1925 between Montagnard and the Rideau Aquatic Club who met for the best-of-five final at Lansdowne Park in August of that year? It featured a match-up of star center fielders, the Montagnards' Clyde Moran, who hit a lusty .571 on the season and was deemed "one of the finest judges of fly balls in the city," and his counterpart Bert McInenly of the Rideaus, who similarly played errorless ball on the season and showcased his burning speed. But despite the hype for this heavyweight battle, the newspaper account of the day somewhat grudgingly conceded the series would end a "hard struggle" for a league that dealt with diminishing attendance – but always managed to complete their games.[55] Rosters in this era were perpetually in flux when life intruded. A star pitcher might choose pro hockey, a slugger might move to the gridiron, and love for a woman might move a shortstop to another town. But some teams lost stalwarts to the pro wrestling circuit, or to the railway.[56]

But the constant thread to Ottawa's baseball history are the sandlots. These leagues were populated by illustrious team names like Kerwin Realty, a number of local pizzerias, even the Slide Rulers (yes, the Slide Rulers) and the bitter rivalry between teams sponsored by two competing Westboro pubs, Whispers and Puzzles, would usually come to a dramatic climax in a late September showdown. This was the league where the home-run hitter had to retrieve the ball after his home-run trot, sometimes competing with an off-leash dog, where the definition of sheer terror occasionally awaited hitter, catcher, and umpire, all of whom would have to dive for cover as the automatic Hampton Park lights went off at 11 P.M. with a fastball in mid-route.

These were the leagues where after three consecutive home runs pinged off the roof of the change hut in the playground far beyond the left-field fence at Hampton, the little lefty hurler in the subsequent mound visit barked that the outfielders had to play deeper. There was the autumn night at Brewer Park when the veteran pitcher took a comebacker off the face on a poorly-lit diamond, spit out a couple of teeth and suggested infielders tending to his well-being get their asses back to their position and mind their own business. It was the league where a second baseman could be a national television correspondent, preparing a piece on time management, who brought a film and sound crew out to film him and the shortstop working on double plays one evening, and when that keystone duo glanced at their wide-eyed opponents watching the film crew at its work, they knew they had them, at least that night. Those Whispers-Puzzles games were never immortalized in the public prints like the Montagnard-Rideau tilts, but they took no back seat in intensity.

Ottawa, a lacrosse town, you say? Today, it is to laugh. Ottawa, a northern outpost where hockey rules? The evidence strongly suggests otherwise. Urban Shocker could have told you that.

SOURCES

In addition to the sources cited in the Notes, the author relied on Baseball-Reference.com.

NOTES

1　City of Ottawa press release https://ottawa.ca/en/recreation-and-parks/facilities/outdoor-recreation.

2　The Montreal Expos were in the National League from 1969 to 2004 and the Toronto Blue Jays have been in the American League since 1977. Ottawa has been home to Triple-A (or equivalent) franchises three times: 1898, 1951-1954, and 1993-2007. The 1898 team was Class A, but that was the highest minor-league level at the time.

3　Baseball Reference, William Metzig page https://www.baseball-reference.com/players/m/metziwi01.shtml. Accessed February 26, 2024.

4　"Who's Who on Ottawa team of 1914, Senators Strong in Every Department," *Ottawa Citizen*, May 13, 1914: 9.

5　Wayne Scanlan, "Lynx Pay Homage to Saint," *Ottawa Citizen*, June 9, 1998: 26.

6　Associated Press, "Hollandsworth Adds To Dodgers' Top Rookie Roll," *Ottawa Citizen*, November 7, 1996: 30.

7　*Daily Journal*, Ogdensburg, New York, August 31, 1867: 3.

8　"Lost the First," *Ottawa Journal*, July 16, 1898: 6.

9　Baseball Reference "Bullpen," Ottawa Wanderers page, https://www.baseball-reference.com/bullpen/Ottawa_Wanderers accessed March 4, 2024.

10　"Baseball Club Is Disbanded," *Ottawa Citizen*, August 21, 1906: 8.

11　Gary Belleville, "July 12, 1906: Frank Shaughnessy Leads Ottawa to Victory in outlaw Northern Independent League," *Society for American Baseball Research*, https://sabr.org/gamesproj/game/july-12-1906-frank-shaughnessy-leads-ottawa-to-victory-in-outlaw-northern-independent-league/ accessed February 26, 2024

12　Hugh S. Fullerton, "Baseball Fans Usually Crazy," *Ottawa Citizen*, May 19, 1906: 17.

13　"Ottawa Has Never Fallen Down as a Good Baseball 'Town'," *Ottawa Citizen*, May 4, 1912: 9.

14　"Ottawa Has Never Fallen Down as a Good Baseball 'Town'."

15　"Rousing Reception Now Assured for Members of Ottawa Ball Club," *Ottawa Citizen*, May 9, 1912: 8.

16　"Rousing Reception Now Assured for Members of Ottawa Ball Club."

17　"Duke of Connaught Will Likely Attend Opening of Canadian League Season," *Ottawa Citizen*, May 1, 1914: 8.

18　Gary Belleville, "May 24, 1922: Ottawa Senators' Fred Frankhouse tosses 14-inning complete-game win over Trois-Rivières," Society for American Baseball Games Project, https://sabr.org/gamesproj/game/may-24-1922-ottawa-senators-fred-frankhouse-tosses-14-inning-complete-game-win-over-trois-rivieres/ accessed July 9, 2024.

19　"Manager Forster Replies to Larry Gardner's Letter," Letter to the Editor, *Ottawa Citizen*, June 17, 1937: 11.

20　"Fifteen Ball Players Attend Ottawa Braves' First Workout," *Ottawa Citizen*, May 4, 1937: 11.

21　Statscrew.com https://www.statscrew.com/minorbaseball/leaders/t-ob13563 accessed April 11, 2024

22　Tommy Shields, "Something Wrong," *Ottawa Citizen*, May 30, 1938, 10.

23　"Ottawa Club Retains Identity in Canadian-American League," *Ottawa Citizen*, December 13, 1939, 10.

24　"Senators Move to Amsterdam After Monday Game Postponed," *Ottawa Journal*, September 10, 1940, 17.

25　"Here Comes Paul!" *Ottawa Citizen*, June 7, 1947: 22.

26　Tommy Shields, "Homers By Metzig and Riley Win Thriller," *Ottawa Citizen*, June 9, 1947, 18.

27　Paul Geisler Jr., "Paul Dean," Society for American Baseball Research Biography Project, https://sabr.org/bioproj/person/paul-dean/ accessed April 13, 2024.

28　Tommy Shields, "Nationals Open With 6-3 Victory," *Ottawa Citizen*, May 15, 1947: 23.

29　"Dean Leaves, Metzig Boss," *Ottawa Citizen*, September 24, 1947: 18.

30 Don Mackintosh, "Nationals Win Border Baseball Championship," *Ottawa Citizen,* September 25, 1947: 22.

31 Austin F. Cross, "Dean's Run-Out During Playoffs at Ottawa Laid to Editorial Rap," *The Sporting News,* October 22, 1947: 25.

32 "Baseball – In Its Place," *Ottawa Citizen,* September 10, 1947: 30.

33 Jack Koffman, "Joining the Sinatra Club," *Ottawa Citizen,* July 9, 1949: 14.

34 Harvey's NHL career spanned three decades. He was seven times voted the league's top defenseman and he won six Stanley Cups with the Montreal Canadiens. He was elected to the Hockey Hall of Fame in 1973.

35 "Bob Larkin's Tragic Death Big Shock to Baseball Fans," *Ottawa Citizen,* July 31, 1950: 1.

36 Jack Koffman, "A Thrilling Baseball Jamboree," *Ottawa Citizen,* September 9, 1950: 20.

37 Canadian Press, "Ottawa Gets Jersey Baseball Rights," *Ottawa Citizen,* December 6, 1950: 1.

38 Gordon Ryan, "Giants 'At Home' on Lansdowne Diamond," *Ottawa Journal,* April 27, 1951: 26.

39 Mays did not stay in Minneapolis for long, getting the call to the parent Giants after only 35 games in Minnesota, during which time he hit .477.

40 "New York Giants Cut Ottawa Link," *Ottawa Citizen,* November 9, 1951: 1.

41 Jack Koffman, "A's General Manager Says 'We'll Treat You Right,'" *Ottawa Citizen,* February 6, 1952: 9.

42 "A's Face Lottery Charge," *Ottawa Citizen,* September 3, 1952: 1.

43 "Mayor Whitton Returned in Sensational Finish, Sunday Sports Plebiscite Decisively Rejected," *Ottawa Citizen,* December 2, 1952: 17.

44 statscrew.com, https://www.statscrew.com/minorbaseball/roster/t-oa13562/y-1952, accessed May 14, 2024.

45 Baseball Reference, 1954 Ottawa Athletics page, https://www.baseball-reference.com/register/team.cgi?id=1d4d98ab, accessed May 14, 2024.

46 Tommy Shields, "'Round and About," *Ottawa Citizen,* September 14, 1954: 23.

47 The Athletics had been in Philadelphia since 1901. The Kansas City Athletics later moved to Oakland, California in 1967.

48 Canadian Press, "Triple-A Ball Club Gone," *Ottawa Citizen,* January 8, 1955: 22. Charlotte Whitton was appointed mayor in 1951 upon the death of Grenville Goodwin, then won the election in 1952 and served until 1964. She was the first female mayor of a major Canadian city, a woman known for her flamboyant and bombastic style and one who faced charges of racism and anti-Semitism.

49 Jim Durrell was mayor of Ottawa from 1985-1991 and was a huge booster of Ottawa sports, playing a leading role in landing the International League Ottawa Lynx and the NHL Ottawa Senators for the city.

50 Ken Warren, "Here's the Pitch . . . And Baseball's Return is a Hit," *Ottawa Citizen,* April 18, 1993: 13.

51 Ken Warren, "Backtracking the Lynx," *Ottawa Citizen,* September 14, 1993: 23.

52 Wayne Scanlan, "Another One Bites the Dust," *Ottawa Citizen,* September 4, 2007: 13.

53 Anonymous letters to the editor, "A Real Ball Team," *Ottawa Citizen,* October 12, 1921: 16 and "1883 Game Recalled," *Ottawa Citizen,* October 15, 1921: 20.

54 "No Money Was Found Under the Pillows," *Ottawa Citizen,* November 12, 1920: 1.

55 "Montagnards and Rideaus Start Championship Series Wednesday," *Ottawa Citizen,* August 4, 1925: 7.

56 "District Baseball Delegates to Meet at Windsor Hotel for Annual Meeting," *Ottawa Citizen,* April 28, 1928: 10.

OTTAWA'S EARLY BASEBALL HISTORY

BY STEVE RENNIE

Back in the early seventies, Ottawa had a baseball club (amateur) which was a real credit to the city. This club was Ottawa's first real effort to play the game. … that pioneer team played real classy ball, which would compare favorably with any of the amateur baseball played today.

- *Ottawa Citizen*, December 12, 1936: 2.

IMAGINE THE SCENE: ANTICIPATION HANGS in the air as a clear and pleasant summer afternoon unfolds in 1872. A large crowd has gathered on this civic holiday in the newly-constructed stands of a ballpark at the southern foot of Elgin Street. They've come to witness the best baseball team in the world take on a group of local amateurs. As the Boston players step off their horse-drawn bus and take the field in their light brown flannel uniforms and bright red stockings, the crowd is struck by their obvious athleticism and skill. The Ottawa players never stood a chance. "The few minutes previous to the commencement of the match convinced all who were present that the Ottawa club would have no show against the professionals," one reporter noted, adding "there were very few even of the most sanguine of the Ottawa men who would bet one to ten that our club would obtain a single run." For the next two hours and 13 minutes, the crowd watched in amazement as the Boston Red Stockings scored run after run to win the ballgame by a lopsided score of 64–0.[1]

This was arguably one of the most important games—if not *the* most important game—ever played in this city. The visit of the Boston Red Stockings on August 27, 1872, and the rematch a year later, helped to popularize America's pastime in Canada's new capital.

* * *

No one really knows how baseball started in Ottawa. People have been playing the game in and around the city since at least the middle of the 1860s. The earliest documented game dates back to September 13, 1865, at a Sons of Temperance picnic in the village of Metcalfe. Founded in the 1840s, the Sons of Temperance was a men's organization that strongly discouraged alcohol consumption. Over 600 people gathered in a grove for a communal meal, followed by an afternoon of entertainment featuring music—including a bagpiper—and, notably, games that included "cricket and base ball."[2] (The sport was spelled "base ball" back then). The festivities also featured "a game of ball played by the ladies—alone." It's possible that the latter is

also a reference to baseball, or perhaps another bat-and-ball game, but it seems more likely that the newspaper is describing some other activity altogether.

The brief mention of a baseball game at the picnic suggests two things. First, the lack of detailed explanation implies that the local readers were already at least somewhat familiar with the game's rules. Second, including baseball in the afternoon activities indicates that people in the area knew how to play it, further suggesting that baseball was already an established pastime.

An August 1867 game report from Ogdensburg, New York, offers us another clue that baseball was still in its early stages in Ottawa during the mid-1860s. The score—Ottawa's New Dominion Club suffered a crushing 141–20 defeat—suggests the two teams weren't evenly matched. Maybe Ottawa simply had an off day. The local newspaper chalked up the loss to the visitors' inexperience.

"In explanation it is proper to say that the Ottawa boys were not well posted on the rules of the game, and consequently missed making several tallies, and also got out several times when they should have avoided it," wrote the *Ogdensburg Daily Journal*. "They have, however, good material to make base ball players, and will do better next time. Their pitcher and catcher are as good as average, and all will do well when they understand the game better. They did not come boasting, but requested the privilege of coming to learn the game. Another year we shall expect to see them a match for the best."[3]

By 1868, baseball was gaining popularity in Ottawa, with the New Dominion Club emerging as the city's leading team. The club had over 60 members, making it the largest in the city.[4]

At least early on, there did not seem to be many other teams to challenge the New Dominion Club. The New Dominion Club planned to play a Victoria Day game against Metcalfe.[5] When that fell through, they ended up playing a game among themselves. The New Dominion first nine triumphed over the second nine with a resounding 94-25 victory. "The spectators were very numerous, including a large number of the fair sex, which gave the ground quite a lively appearance, and added to the spirits of the players," reported the *Ottawa Times*. "Further

Base Ball.

The match game of base ball played here, yesterday, between the Ottawa Club and the first nine of the Ogdensburgh Club, resulted in favor of Ogdensburgh, by a score of 141 to 20.

In explanation it is proper to say that the Ottawa boys were not well posted on the rules of the game, and consequently missed making several tallies, and also got out several times when they should have avoided it.

They have, however, good material to make base ball players, and will do better next time. Their pitcher and catcher are as good as the average, and all will do well when they understand the game better. They did not come boasting, but requested the privilege of coming to learn the game. Another year we shall expect to see them a match for the best.

In August 1867, the New Dominion Club of Ottawa lost by a score of 141–20 to their more experienced opponents in Ogdensburg, New York. That city's newspaper chalked up the lopsided loss to Ottawa's inexperience. Credit: "Base Ball," *Daily Journal* (Ogdensburg, New York), August 31, 1867: 3.

interest was thrown into the game by two prizes being offered, namely, a beautifully finished bat for the highest scorer, and a regulation ball for the best general player." Shortstop R. Wood led the New Dominion first nine with 14 runs scored and won the bat, while his teammate Walsh caught six fly balls in left field and earned the prize ball.[6]

The New Dominion Club held regular monthly meetings in a room at the Ottawa Skating and Curling Club,[7] which opened a rink on Albert Street in 1867.[8] They played their games on a field right behind the rink—which today is in the heart of the city's downtown core.

Not content with playing games against themselves, the New Dominion Club would soon face a tougher test. During the 1868 Dominion Day festivities in Ottawa, the New Dominion Club held its own against a visiting team from Ogdensburg. By the third inning, Ottawa had built an impressive 24-run lead over their opponents. But Ogdensburg somehow rallied to win the game by a score of 57–49.[9] It seems like there were no hard feelings, as the players dined together after the game, which was customary at the time. "The reception our boys met from Ottawa was princely and the supper provided most magnificent," the *Ogdensburg Journal* wrote. "They all come home with the greatest admiration for the people of the Capital of the Dominion, and unable to find words to express their good feeling."[10]

Back in Ottawa, the New Dominion Club dominated local baseball. A team of local mechanics fell to the New Dominion

Club by a score of 109-15.[11] In late July, they defeated the Ottawa Cricket Club in a game of baseball by a much-closer score of 36-27. However, the tables turned in the return cricket match, with the New Dominion Club suffering a heavy loss of 173-54. "However well the New Dominion Club may play baseball," wrote the *Ottawa Times*, "they will have to practice cricket a while before playing matches."[12] They ended up playing two more times that summer, although the newspapers offered no details about the final matches.[13]

The score of these games was typical for the time. In the 1800s, baseball scores were often high due to primitive fielding equipment, inconsistent pitching rules that favored batters, and less sophisticated defensive strategies compared to modern baseball.

Ottawa returned to Ogdensburg for a return match in late August. This time, they lost by a score of 53-19.[14] The team was disappointed to suffer such a loss to Ogdensburg after their narrow defeat earlier in the summer. But their spirits were no doubt lifted by the lavish postgame reception, where drinks flowed freely as toasts and songs filled the air well into the early hours of the morning.[15]

The next and final mention of Ottawa's baseball team appears the following year in an *Ogdensburg Journal* article, previewing a July 4, 1869, game against the St. Lawrence Club in Ogdensburg.[16] After that, the club, for all intents and purposes, disappeared.

Two years later, the fate of the New Dominion Club was revealed in a letter to the editor of the *Ottawa Times*, written by a member of the newly formed Ottawa Base Ball Club.

"Sir: In your issue this morning your reporter incorrectly states that the Maple Leaf Club of Ogdensburg is a newly organized one, and not the old Maple City Club. As this statement would materially lessen the credit accorded us for having beaten them, I beg leave to give you the following facts," he wrote.

"Four years ago we played against this same club under the name of the Ogdensburg Club, for the purpose of learning the rudiments of the game, and we were beaten by some one hundred and twenty runs. The Ogdensburg Club was then organized about six years. We played against them during the following season in Ottawa, and were again beaten, but by a majority of only eight runs. Unfortunately for our old New Dominion Base Ball Club we were unable to continue practice on account of the grounds on which we played being subdivided and sold, and our club became defunct. This season a new organization was formed, with four or five of the old players as members, under the name of the Ottawa Base Ball Club, and on the 30th June we plated at Prescott against our old opponents from Ogdensburg, who had in the interval changed their club name to the more euphonious one of 'The Maple City.' The result of this match was that we were beaten by only one run. Our next meeting took place yesterday, when with a fair field and no favor, we had the extreme felicity of beating one of the best clubs in Northern New York."[17]

* * *

Two members of the New Dominion Club who went on to play for the Ottawa Base Ball Club were Harry Cluff and his brother, Tom.[18] Tom Cluff has been credited with being of the most important early figures in Ottawa's baseball history. He was born in Ottawa in 1843 (although some records list a later birth year) to Irish immigrants. His father, Isaac, worked as a carpenter at shop on Sparks Street[19] and laid the city's first wooden sidewalks.[20]

Tom Cluff followed his father into the trades. In the early 1860s, as a teenager, he found work at a streetcar company in Cleveland, Ohio. While living in Ohio, he also trained as a

blacksmith. Before they burned down in 1916, one could see his ironwork on the original Parliament Buildings.[21]

The American Civil War broke out while Cluff was in Ohio. He joined the fight on the Union side, enlisting as a private, according to both his obituary[22] and a booklet detailing the lives of Loyalists and their descendants buried at Ottawa's Beechwood Cemetery.[23] Military pension records from July 1903 show a Thomas Cluff—who used the alias George Stephens—served with the 10th Regiment Ohio Volunteer Cavalry, Company A.[24] Since there are no other records of his military service, however, it's not certain that this is actually the same Tom Cluff from Ottawa or someone else with the same name.

We don't know much about Cluff's early years in Ohio. But we do know that he was back in Ottawa by 1868 at the latest,

The Maple Leaf Base Ball Club of 1881, one of the rare youth teams to don uniforms. Note the inverted maple leaf on their crest. Credit: Bytown Museum, P179

A young Tommy Gorman poses with his House of Commons Pages team in 1900. Credit: Gorman, Thomas Patrick / Library and Archives Canada / C-079945

working as a blacksmith. He and his brothers were active in many sports, and Tom Cluff's name appears in newspaper reports about various sports, such as lacrosse and snowshoe racing.[25]

He married Diantha Adelaide Clark in September 1869.[26] In the summer of 1870, Cluff was once again in Ohio, where his older brother, Edward (who also went by Ned), lived. The story goes that Tom Cluff fell in love with baseball after watching three Cincinnati Red Stockings players put on a show for picnic-goers at a rural Ohio farm. The dazzling display apparently left Cluff spellbound. He sought them out afterward, eager to learn more and bring that knowledge back to Ottawa.[27] The problem with this story is that we know Tom Cluff was already playing baseball in 1868 for the New Dominion Club[28]—two years before he purportedly saw the Red Stockings' exhibition in Ohio. He may not have been baseball's pioneer in Ottawa, but he was undoubtedly one of its earliest players.

Cluff was back in Ottawa by 1871, alternating between shortstop and first base for the newly formed Ottawa Base Ball Club, playing alongside another one of his brothers, Harry, who was the catcher.

The Ottawa Base Ball Club was one of several amateur teams in the city at the time, and probably the most ambitious. They built new baseball grounds on a 10-acre plot of land at the southern foot of Elgin Street near the Rideau Canal,[29] the city limits at the time, which featured a grandstand as well as concession booths that did not serve alcohol.[30] This is where Ottawa played their August 1872 game against the Boston Red Stockings (which they lost by that score of 64–0).[31] Tom Cluff managed to hit a single off future Hall of Fame pitcher Albert Spalding, while his brother Harry hit a double. Ottawa lost a rematch against Boston a year later by a score of 44–4.[32]

* * *

By the early 1870s, baseball fever had gripped the nation's capital. Newspapers of the day are filled with a kaleidoscope of colorful names like the Clippers, Unions, Nationals, Hurons, Pastimes, Capitals, Victorias, Olympics, Merchants, Electrics, and Diamonds. Like many other cities in this era, Ottawa had a team called the Mutuals—a moniker commonly associated with volunteer fire companies. This may have been a nod to the city's own volunteer firefighters, which had a hand engine called the Mutual in 1848.[33]

Other clubs, like Brittania and Billings Bridge, drew inspiration from their local neighborhoods. Workplaces, fraternal associations, and Ottawa College (now the University of Ottawa) all fielded teams. So did several government departments. It seemed like *everyone* was playing baseball in Ottawa.

Even the young messengers of Parliament, the House of Commons pages, fielded their own baseball team. Fast-forward to 1900 and the most notable player on the Pages was a 14-year-old named Thomas Patrick "T.P." Gorman—who went on to become an Olympic gold medalist[34], a sports journalist, and a hockey general manager who hoisted multiple Stanley Cups, ultimately earning his place in the Hockey Hall of Fame.

Teams from the surrounding towns and villages came to Ottawa to compete against the city's amateur teams. Baseball was one of the city's most popular pastimes.

However, this passion wasn't universally embraced. Grumbling letters to the editor documented residents' discontent. Some lamented the boisterous youth who turned their streets into makeshift diamonds. Sunday games, seen as a disruption of the traditional day of rest, faced particular scorn.

Local leagues—which only ever lasted a season or two—offered a platform for competition, but issuing open challenges in newspapers was another popular way for these clubs to prepare to face off. Typically, a team would declare themselves unbeatable, and inevitably, a rival would rise to the challenge, with local journalists covering these exchanges in great detail.

The teams played all around the growing city. Venues like the Metropolitan Grounds on Jane Street (later Pretoria Avenue) between O'Connor and Metcalfe streets, the grounds of Rideau Hall, and the parade ground by the military drill hall at Cartier Square (where Ottawa City Hall now stands) were all popular places to play.

Ballclubs that wanted to play at Cartier Square faced the bureaucratic hurdle of first having to seek written permission from the Department of Militia and Defence to use the grounds, which were used mainly for drilling and training by two infantry regiments, the Governor General's Foot Guards and the Cameron Highlanders of Ottawa. This practice is documented as early as 1872. Senator Robert William Weir Carrall petitioned the Department on behalf of the Victoria Base Ball Club, requesting permission to play at the parade grounds. A week later, written permission was granted, provided the Victorias "will not interfere with the privilege already granted to other similar clubs."[35] Library and Archives Canada has many similar requests on file, spanning nearly three decades.

One thing about living in a city like Ottawa in the late nineteenth century that made it fertile ground for baseball was that it featured a growing middle class of politicians, government officials, business owners, and other professionals who had the disposable income and ample free time to devote to leisure activities.[36]

The Ottawa Amateur Athletic Association provided a platform for mostly young men (women could join for $2 a year as "lady associate members" with far fewer privileges[37]) to engage in a variety of athletic and recreational pursuits, promoting physical activity and social interaction. The association catered to the city's elites; you could become a life member by paying $100 (a lot of money at the time) or by being a member for 15 years. Otherwise, privileged members paid $10 a year, or $2 a month, for the use of its clubhouse at the corner of Elgin and Maria (now Laurier Avenue West) and to join its sports teams.

To manage the building, the association created a new entity in 1889 known as the Ottawa Amateur Athletic Club. Funded

The Ottawa Amateur Athletic Club baseball players gather for a team photo in 1892. Credit: City of Ottawa Archives, S1978-101, CA-15266

through memberships and fundraising initiatives, the club served as an umbrella organization for the city's major sports teams.[38]

In 1894, the athletic club also became affiliated with the Ottawa Base Ball Club. However, the historical record remains unclear as to whether this was a continuation of the team that played the Boston Red Stockings in the 1870s or an entirely new organization.[39]

One aspect of the athletic club's legacy endures to this day. Notably, it embraced the red, black, and white color scheme—first worn by the Ottawa Hockey Club in 1884[40]—that has become synonymous with Ottawa sports.[41] This iconic palette was adopted by the forerunner of the original Ottawa Senators hockey team, which was affiliated with the club, and continues to be worn today by, among others, the modern Senators franchise, the Ottawa RedBlacks of the Canadian Football League, the Ottawa 67s junior hockey club, and the city's Frontier League baseball team, the Titans.

Despite a thriving amateur baseball scene in the latter half of the 1800s, the professional game wouldn't arrive in Ottawa until nearly the turn of the century. The Eastern League's struggling Rochester franchise relocated to Ottawa midway through the 1898 season. That team—which local sportswriters referred to as the Senators, and not the Wanderers as they are now often called—finished with a record of 53-70 and disbanded after the season ended. The most notable thing about this team might just be the tartan uniforms they wore. In fact, if you go to the National Baseball Hall of Fame in Cooperstown, New York, you can see a photo of the players in these outfits. This photo is also readily available online.

Baseball continued to thrive in Ottawa after the city's first professional team folded. Ottawa competed in the outlaw Northern League during the early 1900s, while another team called the Senators found success in the Canadian League. Just six days after clinching the 1928 World Series with the New York Yankees, baseball legends Babe Ruth and Lou Gehrig brought their talents to Ottawa for a barnstorming exhibition at Dupuis Park in nearby Hull.[42] For a brief stint in the 1950s, Ottawa served as a Triple-A affiliate, first for the New York Giants and then for the Philadelphia Athletics. The 1990s and 2000s saw Triple-A baseball return to Ottawa with the Lynx. Since then, the city has witnessed a revolving door of teams from independent leagues.

But what lies ahead? With so many entertainment options vying for attention, the future of professional baseball in Ottawa remains an open question. Will the independent leagues continue to provide a platform for the city's love of the game? Only time will tell.

However, one thing is clear: those formative years of the nineteenth century laid the groundwork for generations of baseball fans in this city. Ottawa's baseball story is far from over.

NOTES

1 "The Civic Holiday, The Great Cricket Match, The Boston Red Stockings," *Ottawa Daily Citizen*, August 28, 1872: 4.

2 "Sons Of Temperance Pic-Nic," *Ottawa Daily Citizen*, September 21, 1865: 2.

3 "Base Ball," *Daily Journal* (Ogdensburg, New York), August 31, 1867: 3.

4 "Local News," *Ottawa Times*, August 7, 1868: 2.

5 "Base Ball," *Ottawa Times*, May 23, 1868: 3.

6 "Base Ball," *Ottawa Times*, May 27, 1868: 2.

7 "Base Ball," *Ottawa Times*, June 4, 1868: 2.

8 "Club History," Ottawa Curling Club, Accessed October 21, 2024. https://ottawacurlingclub.ca/index.php/about-the-club/28-club-info/151-club-history

9 "Base Ball Match," *Ottawa Times*, July 3, 1868: 2.

10 "Base Ball at Ottawa," *Ogdensburg Journal*, July 3, 1868: 3.

11 "Base Ball," *Ottawa Times*, August 5, 1868: 2.

12 "Base Ball vs. Cricket," *Ottawa Times*, August 7, 1868: 2.

13 "Cricketers at Base Ball," *Ottawa Times*, August 18, 1868: 2.

14 "Base Ball Match," *Ogdensburg Journal*, August 22, 1868: 3.

15 "Base Call Club," *Ogdensburg Journal*, August 24, 1868: 3.

16 "Local and Miscellaneous," *Ogdensburg Journal*, June 4, 1869: 3.

17 "Base Ball," *Ottawa Times*, July 28, 1871: 2.

18 "Base Ball," *Ottawa Times*, August 5, 1868: 2.

19 Cluff & Campbell advertisement, *Ottawa Daily Citizen*, June 25, 1853: 3.

20 "Pioneer Of Bytown Is Fatally Injured," *Ottawa Citizen*, May 11, 1925: 16.

21 United Empire Loyalists' Association of Canada, Sir Guy Carleton Branch. "Descendants of Loyalists in Beechwood Cemetery: Celebrating the 100th Anniversary of the Dominion Association." September 14, 2014, 21.

22 "Pioneer Of Bytown Is Fatally Injured."

23 "Descendants of Loyalists in Beechwood Cemetery: Celebrating the 100th Anniversary of the Dominion Association."

24 "United States Civil War and Later Pension Index, 1861-1917," FamilySearch (https://familysearch.org/ark:/61903/1:1:NHNF-TYZ: March 24, 2016), Thomas Cluff, 1903.

25 "The Lacrosse Match At Prescott," *Ottawa Daily Citizen*, October 2, 1868: 3; "Lacrosse March," *Ottawa Daily Citizen*, May 26, 1869: 2; "The Ottawa Cup," *Ottawa Daily Citizen*, February 22, 1870: 3.

26 Thomas Cluff and Diantha Clark. "Marriage Record," Ottawa, September 8, 1869.

27 David McDonald. "Aug. 27, 1872: The Day the Tide Turned in Ottawa," *Ottawa Citizen*, August 27, 2005.

28 "Base Ball," *Ottawa Times*, August 5, 1868: 2.

29 "International Base Ball Match," *Ottawa Daily Citizen*, August 21, 1872: 4.

30 "Manly Sports," *Ottawa Daily Citizen*, August 12, 1872: 1.

31 "The Civic Holiday, The Great Cricket Match, The Boston Red Stockings," *Ottawa Daily Citizen*, August 28, 1872: 4.

32 "The Base Ball Match," *Ottawa Daily Citizen*, August 27, 1873: 4.

33   City of Ottawa, Centenary of Ottawa, 1854-1954: "The Capital Chosen by a Queen" (Ottawa: City of Ottawa, 1954), 25.

34   The medal he won was as a member of the lacrosse team. Olympic. ca. "1908 London - Canadian Olympic Team." https://olympic.ca/games/1908-london/. Accessed June 13, 2024.

35   Canada. Library and Archives Canada. Hon. R.W.W. Carrall Senator - Ottawa - Requests the use of "Cartier Square" for the Victoria Base Ball Club. RG9-II-A-1, Volume 42, File 6733, 11 June 1872.

36   Paul Kitchen, *Win, Tie, or Wrangle: The Inside Story of the Old Ottawa Senators, 1883–1935* (Manotick, Ontario: Penumbra Press, 2008), 41.

37   Ottawa Amateur Athletic Club, Constitution and By-Laws of the Ottawa Amateur Athletic Club (Ottawa: J.D. Taylor, printer, 1890), 5.

38   Kitchen, 41–42.

39   "Affiliated With The O.A.A.C.," *Ottawa Citizen*, May 18, 1894: 8.

40   Kitchen, 44.

41   Ottawa Amateur Athletic Club, Constitution and By-Laws of the Ottawa Amateur Athletic Club (Ottawa: J.D. Taylor, printer, 1890), 3.

42   Kelly Egan, "Capital Facts: That time Babe Ruth and Lou Gehrig came to Ottawa," *Ottawa Citizen*, May 1, 2017. Accessed May 14, 2024. https://ottawacitizen.com/news/local-news/capital-facts-that-time-babe-ruth-and-lou-gehrig-came-to-ottawa

BIG-TIME BASEBALL IN A "SUB-ARCTIC LUMBER VILLAGE": THE RED STOCKINGS COME TO TOWN

BY DAVID MCDONALD

> On their arrival at the grounds, the Club at once proceeded to practice with their ball, pitching and catching with an expertness that opened the eyes of the spectators. The sinewy arms of the players sent the ball almost with the velocity of a musket shot, without describing a curve, but straight and true to the hands of the catcher. . . . The "Red Stockings" are all heavy men, very strong and active, in fact, picked men. They are paid regular salaries of from $1,800 to $2,500 per annum each, by the Boston club, to do nothing else but to play base ball, and they go from one city to another through the United States and Canada, playing matches for the gate money and for large stakes.
>
> — *Ottawa Citizen*, August 28, 1872.[1]

IT WAS AS IF THE Red Sox or the Braves had come to town to play your office softball team. It was a total mismatch from beginning to end. But nobody seemed to mind.

On Tuesday, August 27, 1872, the Boston Red Stockings, of the National Association of Professional Base Ball Players, got off the train in Ottawa. The rough-hewn city of 21,545, recently dismissed as a "sub-arctic lumber village" by a visiting Oxford historian[2], was about to play host to arguably the best baseball team on the planet[3], here for an exhibition match against the fledgling Ottawa Base Ball Club, est. 1870. The match was to take place at the club's brand-new 10-acre grounds near the southern foot of Elgin Street, just beyond the then city limits. The facility featured a seven-foot-high wooden fence and seating for spectators. "Ample refreshments"[4] would be available, but no "spirituous liquors."[5]

In those early days of organized baseball, barnstorming was often a more lucrative proposition than playing erratically scheduled league games. And so the Boston team spent a chunk of each season traversing baseball's hinterlands, to smaller centers—even "sub-arctic lumber villages"—where curious fans might be willing to part with 50 cents for a glimpse of baseball played at its highest level.

For the Red Stockings the Ottawa appearance marked the seventh stop on a nine-game rail journey that began in Ypsilanti, Michigan, on August 20 and finished up in Montreal 10 days later. Apparently, the unwritten rule that a clearly superior team shouldn't go out of its way to run up the score on a hapless opponent had not been written yet: Six games into their trip the Red Stockings had outscored their amateur opponents in Michigan and Southern Ontario by a 276–19 margin. Not surprisingly, nobody expected much of a showing from the

Ottawa lads, a spirited group of amateurs in just their second year of play. But that was hardly the point.

A SPORTING HOLIDAY

As it happened Tuesday, August 27, 1872, in the capital might have been the greatest confluence of bat-and-ball talent in Canadian history, and the city declared a civic holiday to mark the day. If the Red Stockings weren't enough of a late-summer sporting diversion, the best cricket team in the world, the touring English Gentlemen, featuring a bearded bear of a man, the legendary family doctor and all-rounder William Gilbert Grace, the Babe Ruth of the wickets, was also in town.[6] In 1872 the leisurely, class-bound, British sport was still more widely played in Canada than the fast, brash, cash-driven American upstart. That would quickly change.

The big cricket match was a two-day affair, with play getting under way at Rideau Hall, the residence of Canada's Governor General, slightly before noon. The days leading up to the holiday had been hot and humid. But late Monday night, as if on cue, it had rained enough to clear the air and settle the dust, but not enough to turn the city's unpaved streets into rivers of mud. The day was fresh and breezy, with a scattering of white clouds. Three thousand spectators, including, for a few overs at least, several curious Red Stockings, packed the grounds at Rideau Hall to watch the Gentlemen XI go up against a team of 22 local players, as was their custom on these colonial visits. The final score when the match ended the following day: England 201, Ottawa 42.

AWE AT FIRST SIGHT

Ironically, the captain of the Red Stockings, a man later anointed "The Father of Professional Base Ball Playing"[7], was himself a member of a prominent English cricketing family. He was Sheffield-born Harry Wright, whose father Sam had been lured to the United States to work as a cricket professional in 1837. The younger Wright, too, had begun his athletic career as a 15-year-old cricket pro in Hoboken, New Jersey. But around 1858 he discovered baseball. And over the next decade, although continuing to earn a living at cricket, Wright became convinced that baseball was destined to become America's game, and that people would willingly pay to watch it played at an elite level.

On the day of "the great international baseball match"[8], the Red Stockings arrived at the field by horse-drawn bus for a 3 P.M. start. They stepped out in their light-brown flannel uniforms with their trademark red hose and red belts, and wowed the crowd with their rapid-fire, Globetrotteresque pregame routine. It was awe at first sight.

"The few minutes play previous to the commencement of the match convinced all who were present that the Ottawa club would have no show against the professionals," said the Eeyores at the *Ottawa Free Press*, "and there were very few even of the most sanguine of the Ottawa men who would bet one to ten that our club would obtain a single run."[9] Again—hardly the point. The event was more Chautauqua—equal parts entertainment and education—than serious sporting competition.

The Red Stockings lineup boasted three future Hall of Famers—both of baseball's Wright Brothers, Harry and George, and pitcher Albert Goodwill Spalding, the future sporting goods magnate—as well as second baseman Ross Barnes, who, four years later, would become the National League's first-ever batting champion, with an average of .429. The squad featured no fewer than four future big-league managers—both Wrights, first baseman Charlie Gould, and catcher Cal McVey.

Their opponents that day were 23-year-old refrigeration dealer Harry Cluff at second base; hotel barkeep Freeman Daniels, 23, in right field; John Cutler, likely a lumber salesman, at third; blacksmith and team founder Tom Cluff, 29, at first; 23-year-old painter Tommy Blythe (often written "Blyth") behind the plate; Bob Lang, a 28-year-old land surveyor, in the pitcher's box; Alastair Larwill (sometimes written "Larwell") in center; clerk Will (or "Billy") McMahon, in left; and another clerk, Tommy Spencer, 25, at short.

There were as yet no gloves, no catchers masks, no pitching mound. Spalding and Lang threw underhand from a distance of 45 feet, batters could call for a pitch high or low, and it took nine balls to earn a walk.

The festivities got underway at 3, before about 1,000 spectators (some estimates said up to 3,000), who had arrived on foot, by horse-drawn carriage and by boat on the Rideau Canal. The Garrison Artillery band played throughout the two-and-a-half-hour game.

SLAUGHTER OF THE INNOCENTS

Ottawa won the toss, and elected to bat second. It was downhill from there. Although the Red Stockings reportedly found Lang's pitching a little baffling early on, they adjusted quickly,

blowing the game open with 17 runs in the third. All told Barnes knocked a pair of two-run homers and tallied eight runs, as did both Wright brothers. McVey scored nine runs.

Ottawa managed about seven base hits off Spalding, including a single and a double by Harry Cluff and a single by his brother Tom. But they failed to push across a single run. Final score: Boston 64, Ottawa 0.

"The 'slaughter of the innocents was wholesale'," reported the *Ottawa Times*, "and they left the field, realizing how much they had yet to learn to obtain a degree of proficiency in the game. We do not mean to insinuate that the Ottawas are inapt players; on the contrary, we believe them to be an excellent amateur club, but totally unfit to hold a candle to the Red Stockings. . . ."[10]

Perhaps the biggest skill gap between the clubs—more of a chasm, really—was in their defensive play. The Ottawas allowed 24 men to reach base on errors, leading to 46 unearned runs.

Juice Latham, Utica, New York. January 1875.
Credit: The Miriam and Ira D. Wallach Division of Art, Prints and Photographs: Photography Collection, The New York Public Library

Boston made just two errors. "The extraordinary fielding of 'the short stop,' Mr. G. Wright, who, in this position, is excelled by none, was watched with eagerness," said the *Free Press*. "The wonderful velocity with which he delivers a ball to the first baseman is marvellous."[11]

Despite the massacre, the day was considered a great success. The new ball grounds' "close proximity to the heart of the city, and accessibility both by land and water had, no doubt, much to do with attracting such a large crowd to witness the games. . . ," the *Citizen* reported. "It is a pleasant place of resort at any time during the summer season, but it was made doubly so yesterday by good music, an exciting game, and exhilerating [sic] weather."[12]

If August 27, 1872, was a landmark day in Ottawa sports history, it was a watershed one as well: Ottawa fans had seen the future, and it was the Red Stockings.

THE RED STOCKINGS RETURN

A year later just before a return visit by the peripatetic Boston club, the *Ottawa Citizen* ran its first-ever story exposing the dangers of boys playing ball—baseball, not cricket—on downtown streets. "The police will bear this in mind," tut-tutted the anonymous reporter.[13] The game was putting down some roots in the capital.

The Red Stockings paid a return visit on August 26, 1873, with an even stronger lineup than they'd mustered the previous year. In the offseason, Harry Wright bolstered his squad with two more future Hall of Famers—future National Association and National League batting champ, catcher Deacon White, and first baseman and Yale-educated attorney "Orator Jim" O'Rourke. He also added the first Canadian-born major leaguer, Bob "The Magnet" Addy, an ex-cricketer from Port Hope, Canada West (now Ontario), the man often credited with inventing the baseball slide.

But the Ottawas had also strengthened their lineup, adding five new players. The recruits included two buddies from Utica, New York—20-year-old second baseman George "Juice" Latham and teenage hurler-third baseman William "Dink" Davis, who also served as team captain in 1873. They came to Ottawa along with catcher Mike "Bucky" Ledwith, from Brooklyn, New York. Improbably, two of these men would see big-league action within two years.

Ledwith (whose name usually appeared in the Ottawa press as "Leadworth" or even "Latchworth") played one game with the National Association Brooklyn Atlantics, on August 19, 1874, making him the first ex-Ottawa player to make it to the big time. The second, Latham, eventually played for four major-league teams and managed two. Davis, meanwhile, made headlines across the U.S. in the 1880s and 1890s, not for his baseball prowess but for his wizardry with a deck of cards. In the early 1880s he was rumored to have pocketed $100,000 during a 48-hour binge of the gambling card game faro in New York City.

How the Ottawas enticed these ringers north is unclear. It's extremely unlikely the club would have been in a position to pay them much, if anything. Perhaps it provided them opportunities for employment. Indeed, during Latham's time in Canada, he reportedly worked in a factory and as a baggage man on a train.

WEAK AND PUNY

But even with Juice, Dink, and Bucky in the lineup, the Ottawas, in their blue-and-white uniforms, were no match for the Red Stockings. "The Ottawa players are all slim, lithe young men, but they look weak and puny beside the fine brawny fellows against whom they are pitted," said the *Ottawa Times*.[14]

Fifty-five years later an elderly former Ottawa resident offered this glimpse of the kind of showmanship the brawny Bostonians brought to the game. "One peculiar incident . . . recurs to my mind," he said of the Red Stockings' 1873 appearance. "A short but very high fly was knocked towards Harry Wright. He took off his cap and held it as if to catch the falling ball, but dropped it when the sphere seemed about a foot or two away and caught the ball in his efficient hands."[15]

This time around the locals knocked 20 runs off Boston's total from the year before. They even managed to score a few runs off Al Spalding. The final score, under dark and drizzly skies, was 44-4 in favor of Boston. For the Ottawa boys it must have felt as good as a win.

The next morning, with a day to fill before heading off to Ogdensburg, New York, the restless Wright arranged for a cricket match against a patchwork 11 "hurriedly got up"[16] by the Ottawa Cricket Club. Boston, with the Wright brothers sharing the bowling, came out on top 110-62, "the large score run up by them, undoubtedly due to the wretched fielding of the Ottawa men."[17]

That was the morning. After lunch the Red Stockings returned to the Base Ball Grounds, where, in front of a small weekday crowd of mostly boys, the visitors and their hosts formed two nines, with Harry Wright's picks taking on Spalding's. The Wrights scored two in the ninth to win 19-18. It was the first remotely competitive match the Bostons played on Canadian turf.

The "got up" cricket-baseball doubleheader in Ottawa towards the end of a long road trip is indicative of how much the boys from Boston lived to play. They were keen to work up a sweat even when they didn't have to. The next morning, having further stoked baseball passions in the Canadian capital, the Red Stockings grabbed the 7:15 train for their next stop, Ogdensburg, New York. It was the last time they would visit Ottawa.

AN OTTAWA RED STOCKING

Among the Ottawa boys the two future big leaguers, Ledwith and Latham, earned especially positive reviews in the local papers for their play against (and with) the Red Stockings. The *Ottawa Times* said Ledwith "did good service, and, as a catcher, has few, if any, equals in the city."[18] Latham earned praise from the *Times* as "a quick catcher and a steady batter."[19] The *Ottawa Citizen* meanwhile called his play "equal to anything on the side of the Bostons."[20]

And Latham impressed more than just the press. Two years later George Wright, based on what he had seen in Ottawa, signed the 22-year-old to a three-year contract to play first base for the Red Stockings. The deal was worth $560 in its first year and $800 in subsequent years. But Latham, his weight increasingly becoming an issue, appeared in just 16 games with Boston, batting .269. The big-boned Latham eventually carried 250 pounds on his 5'8" frame and earned the nickname "Jumbo." Wright released him, ostensibly so he could become player-manager of National Association rival New Haven Elm Citys.

In 1876 Latham returned to Canada as second baseman-manager—and the first openly professional hire—of the London Tecumsehs of the Canadian Association of Base Ball. His old Ottawa buddy Mike Ledwith soon joined him, and the Tecumsehs won the inaugural league pennant. In 1877 Latham played for the Louisville Grays of the fledgling National League.

NOTES

1 "The Civic Holiday. The Great Cricket Match. The Boston Red Stockings, Picnic on Major's Hill," *Ottawa Citizen*, August 28, 1872: 4.

2 Goldwin Smith, quoted by Anthony Wilson-Smith. "Thomas Mackay, Ottawa's Master Builder," https://www.historicacanada.ca/news-media/president-notes/thomas-mackay-ottawas-master-builder, April 26, 2022.

3 The National Association lasted five seasons before being supplanted by the National League. The Red Stockings finished first four times.

Altogether, they won 225 games and lost only 60, for a .790 winning percentage. At the time of their 1872 tour, they had a 30-3 record in league contests.

4 "Base Ball," *Ottawa Free Press*, August 23, 1872: 2.

5 "Base Ball," *Ottawa Free Press*, August 23, 1872: 2.

6 Grace was considered the third most recognizable individual in Victorian England, after the Royal couple. Although quite ill on the day, he insisted on playing. Despite tallying 73 runs his play was considered lackluster.

7 Henry Chadwick, *Spalding's Base Ball Guide, and Official League Book for 1895-1896* (New York: A.G. Spalding & Bros., 1896), 162.

8 "International Match," *Ottawa Free Press*, August 28, 1878: 1.

9 "The Civic Holiday," *Ottawa Citizen*, August 28, 1872: 4.

10 "Base Ball," *Ottawa Times*, August 29, 1872: 3.

11 "The Civic Holiday," *Ottawa Citizen*, August 28, 1872: 4.

12 "The Civic Holiday," *Ottawa Citizen*, August 28, 1872: 4.

13 "Improper," *Ottawa Citizen*, August 8, 1873: 4.

14 "Base Ball Match," *Ottawa Times*, August 27, 1873: 2.

15 «Another Version of Famous Red Stockings-Ottawa Match," *Ottawa Citizen*, August 11, 1928: 1.

16 "Cricket," *Ottawa Times*, August 28, 1873: 2.

17 "Cricket," *Ottawa Times*, August 28, 1873: 2.

18 "Base Ball Match," *Ottawa Times*, August 27, 1873: 1.

19 "Base Ball Match," *Ottawa Times*, August 27, 1873: 1.

20 "The Base Ball Match," *Ottawa Citizen*, August 27, 1873: 4.

A FLASH IN THE PLAID: MEET THE OTTAWA SENATORS, THE CITY'S FIRST (AND SHORT-LIVED) PRO BASEBALL TEAM

BY STEVE RENNIE

THE SUMMER OF 1898 WAS a turbulent time for professional baseball. Ballpark attendance figures plummeted across the United States as the Spanish-American War raged, and the Eastern League was not immune to this downturn. Rochester, back in the league after losing its franchise to Montreal a year earlier, was once again in bad shape. Something had to be done.

So on July 10, 1898, the Eastern League's power brokers gathered in Syracuse, New York, to discuss the future of the organization. The league faced potential dissolution as its president, Pat Powers, considered drastic measures. Rather than fold the league, the owners agreed to slash player salaries by 20 percent. They also decided that Rochester needed a new home. Two cities— Ottawa and Worcester, Massachusetts—quickly emerged as potential landing spots, with Newark, New Jersey, and Hartford, Connecticut also in the mix.[1]

The owners preferred Ottawa over Worcester. It certainly helped Ottawa's case that in the weeks leading up to the Syracuse meeting, a local newspaper had been waging a public campaign to bring an Eastern League franchise to the city.

"Baseball has never been really given a first-class trial in this city," the *Ottawa Citizen* wrote in its June 23, 1898 edition.

"True, we can boast of several good amateur teams; in fact, they are second to none in the district, but baseball is a game requiring great training and the devoted attention of the men, and, therefore it has to be professional to be played scientifically. It is a game of science and a fame requiring study. To play it a man can do nothing else."[2]

In a series of editorials in the days that followed, the *Citizen* championed the idea of a professional baseball team for Ottawa. The paper argued that competing against teams from larger markets like Toronto, Montreal, and Buffalo would elevate the city's profile. The argument struck a chord with Ottawa mayor Samuel Bingham.

"I'm not very conversant with baseball as a game," Bingham said, "but I think the proposal to bring Ottawa into the Eastern League circuit a very good one. You may rest assured that I will do everything in my power to promote the enterprise, if it is found, after a careful canvass, to be at all feasible. I never yet went back on anything that was calculated to benefit Ottawa locally or make her more widely known in the outside world."[3]

The public pressure paid off. Two days after Eastern League owners met in Syracuse, a group of Ottawa investors—led by local brickmaker Alex Graham[4]—bought the struggling Rochester franchise for $2,500.[5] The *Citizen* proudly patted itself on the back, claiming it had "single-handed, took up the cause of the game in Ottawa and was instrumental in bringing the matter before the attention of the league."[6]

Finding a place to play was the next hurdle facing Ottawa's new owners. Lansdowne Park was their first choice, but the baseball schedule conflicted with that of the city's lacrosse club, the Capitals, who held a lease to the grounds.[7] Even if the ballclub could somehow coordinate its schedule with the lacrosse team, Sunday games posed a problem. Strict observance laws forced Sunday games to be played across the river in Hull.[8] Ottawa's owners decided the team would play its first two games at Lansdowne Park, on July 15 and 16, before relocating to the nearby Metropolitan Grounds on Jane Street (later Pretoria Avenue) between O'Connor and Metcalfe streets, with the exception of Sunday games played in Hull.

Meanwhile, the former Rochester players had to scramble to make it to Ottawa for their first home game on July 15. Hastily throwing together whatever belongings they could carry, they found themselves on a steamship with their Syracuse rivals, departing Ogdensburg, New York, for Prescott, Ontario. What should have been a short journey turned into an odyssey. The connecting train to Ottawa, plagued by frequent stops, stretched what should have been a relatively brisk 45-mile trip into an ordeal lasting hours. When the train finally pulled into the Ottawa station, the players were met by a large crowd of excited fans.[9]

On the afternoon of Ottawa's first home game, 2,500 people converged on Lansdowne Park from every corner of the city and its neighboring towns, paying a quarter (or 50 cents for a seat in the grandstand) for the chance to be a part of history. Samuel Bingham, the mayor, threw out the game's first pitch. After a chaotic few days, the Ottawa team took the field in their Rochester uniforms. The jerseys, victims of travel's wear and tear (or perhaps a botched attempt to erase their past city), sported a bewildering array of misspellings across the players' chests. The *Ottawa Citizen* poked fun at this alphabet soup of mismatched letters, saying "It might be gathered from the smatterings of literature on the bosoms of the Ottawa team that they belonged to the 'Roche,' 'R Este,' 'OT,' 'Chester' and various other clubs." Taking the field for their home opener with a quirky assortment of lettering on their jerseys, the Ottawa team appeared understandably nervous facing their hometown crowd for the first time. Just days removed from a nasty illness that confined him to bed for over a week, pitcher George Harper lacked control on the mound. Ottawa dropped their debut game to Syracuse by a score of 8–1.[10] The next day offered a brighter spot. Though still a loss, Ottawa pushed Syracuse to a much closer 10-7 defeat.[11]

While the Ottawa team continued to jell on the field, their mismatched uniforms remained a source of amusement. "The Ottawa boys must have played hot ball somewhere to melt all those letters off their shirts," the *Citizen* cracked after the

club's opening weekend.[12] Thankfully, a fresh set of uniforms was already in production, and they would be unlike anything Eastern League fans had ever seen. Sparks Street tailor J.R. McNeil presented the team with a bold design: tartan uniforms.

"The Ottawa baseball team will appear in the new suits presented to them by Mr. J.R. McNeil for the first time on Monday morning," the *Ottawa Citizen* wrote on July 29.

"The club's colors are red, white and tartan. The shirts and knickerbockers are made out of the McNeil tartan, the former having red collars and cuffs, with smoked pearl buttons. The players will wear a white peaked cap with red band, and red stockings. The costume is said to be unique, striking and attractive. Mr. McNeil is to be congratulated upon his generous gift."[13]

The unique uniforms got mixed reviews outside Ottawa. "It was the general impression in the Eastern League circuit that the late Rochester uniform was the most hideous the ingenuity

The Ottawa Senators sport their unique tartan uniforms, custom-made by local tailor J.R. McNeil in 1898. While these outfits were a source of pride in Ottawa, they received mixed reactions elsewhere. Though the photo is dated 1897, it was actually captured in 1898 during the team's first and only season in the city. Credit: Library of the National Baseball Hall of Fame and Museum (BL-3270.71)

of man could devise," the *Montreal Gazette* wrote. "The new Ottawa outfit, however, knocks it into a cocked hat."[14] Added another Montreal newspaper, the *Daily Star*: "Long dissertations were published on the appearance of the Ottawas, when they were known as the Rochesters, but if anybody wants to see a sight, it is worthwhile going to the ball grounds to see the awful uniforms the men are now rigged out with. It is a wonder that they don't refuse to wear them."[15] *The Sporting Life* called them "the most ridiculous that were ever seen on ball players,"[16] while the *Buffalo Commercial* published this commentary from the *Providence Journal*: "Nothing can be funnier than the coaching of Wheels Clymer, unless it is the ludicrous appearance of the Scotch plaid of the Ottawa team in a baseball uniform."[17] Ouch.

The vibrant pattern of the team's new uniforms was sure to turn heads on and off the field. Unfortunately, their on-field performance wasn't quite as captivating, leaving some fans wanting more. Financial woes began to plague the Ottawa team by early August. The initial excitement around the team failed to translate into consistent ticket sales. The situation was becoming dire. Alex Graham, the club's main financial backer, sounded the alarm. Without an additional $1,000, he warned, the team might be forced to fold before the end of the season.[18] Despite financial uncertainty, the team maintained a respectable record, hovering around .500 until late August. However, a brutal losing streak sent them tumbling down the standings, further exacerbating their financial woes as attendance plummeted. Even their biggest supporter, the *Ottawa Citizen*, couldn't resist a jab at the struggling club. In a humorous quip, the newspaper declared, "Messrs. the Ottawa baseball team: Dear Boys – All is forgiven. (Signed) Everybody."[19]

The team is often referred to as the Wanderers. But there is ample evidence they were actually called the Senators. The city's daily newspapers published at least five articles over the summer of 1898 in which the team is called the Senators. A Toronto sportswriter first suggested the moniker days after the team relocated from Rochester.

"In a signed article in the *Toronto News* J. Hay has the following: 'When a new team comes into the baseball world there is always a big hustle among the various sporting writers on the circuit to give the new team an appropriate name. For a short time the club is provided with names to cremate, but one appellation finally meets with the approbation of all concerned, and the team is put to the necessity of carrying this title while they stay with the league. What name can be inflicted on the Ottawa club? The Washingtons in the National are known as the Senators, and wouldn't it be appropriate to call the Capital City's team by the same name?'"[20]

It seems Ottawa sportswriters liked the suggestion. On August 13, the *Ottawa Citizen* refers to the team as the Senators when describing their game against Montreal ("Two more [runs] were made in the fifth by the Senators").[21]

The *Citizen* calls the team the Senators three times in an August 17 article: "The Senators played good ball this afternoon and won a splendid ten innings game from the Habitants [Montreal] … An error by Butler, who did such good work yesterday, gave the Senators the game. … Ottawa is playing gilt-edged ball these days, and the home public here have the assurance of some excellent sport when the Senators meet the Toronto club on Thursday."[22]

The *Ottawa Journal* referred to the team by this name days later when talking about their victory over Toronto: "But joking aside—aren't the Senators playing nice ball—real pennant winning ball. The score yesterday by the way was Ottawa 3: Toronto 2. Looks close, but the game wasn't quite as narrow as that. Toronto never looked as good a team as Ottawa in yesterday's contest. They aren't either and Willie Clymer has just about the warmest outfit in the league."[23]

Two days later, the *Citizen* once again used the Senators moniker. "The man that presented that Black Watch tartan uniform to the Senators ought to have added a bagpipes. Perhaps Harper would march up and down the coach line and supply the music to cheer them on to victory."[24]

The fact that two of the city's daily newspapers use the name multiple times strongly suggests that the team was called the Senators, at least unofficially. But maybe not by everyone. It seems that Toronto sportswriters had not quite settled on a nickname. Two days after the *Toronto News* suggested the Senators moniker, the Toronto *Evening Star* made its own bold proclamation: "The Ottawas are called the Lumbermen."[25] There are no other references to Ottawa being called the Lumbermen, so it appears that the Senators name won out in the end. As for the "Wanderers," it's likely that the moniker was applied later by historians, reflecting the team's midseason relocation.

The club finished last in the Eastern League with a 53-70 record. Despite only playing for two months in the Eastern League, the *Ottawa Journal* (citing a Toronto newspaper's report) revealed the team owners had already lost $4,000.[26] The club disbanded in November 1898, ending Ottawa's brief stint in professional baseball.

NOTES

1   "A Ball Team," *Ottawa Citizen*, July 11, 1898: 1.

2   "Is Sport Here On The Decline?" *Ottawa Citizen*, June 23, 1898: 8.

3   "Will Ottawa Get Into Line?" *Ottawa Citizen*, June 24, 1898: 8.

4   "The Ottawa Ball Team," *Ottawa Citizen*, July 14, 1898: 1.

5   "Left 'Em All," *Ottawa Citizen*, July 12, 1898: 8.

6   "Left 'Em All."

7   "Sporting," *Ottawa Journal*, July 13, 1898: 7.

8   "Fever Raging," *Ottawa Citizen*, July 13, 1898: 8.

9   "Clymer Was Reminiscent," *Ottawa Journal*, December 8, 1898: 6.

10   "Ottawa Lost," *Ottawa Citizen*, July 16, 1898: 6.

11   "Beaten Again," *Ottawa Citizen*, July 18, 1898: 6.

12   "Beaten Again."

13   "New Baseball Uniform," *Ottawa Citizen*, July 29, 1898: 1.

14   "Base Hits," *Montreal Gazette*, August 15, 1898: 5.

15 "Downed By Ottawa," *Montreal Daily Star*, August 13, 1898: 15.

16 "News And Comment," *Sporting Life*, September 17, 1898: 5.

17 "Baseball Brevities," *Buffalo Commercial*, September 3, 1898: 4.

18 "More Money Is Necessary," *Ottawa Journal*, August 5, 1898: 7.

19 "Comment," *Ottawa Citizen*, August 19, 1898: 4.

20 "To Call Us 'Senators,'" *Ottawa Journal*, July 19, 1898: 6.

21 "Eastern League Games," *Ottawa Citizen*, August 13, 1898: 6.

22 "The Sporting World," *Ottawa Citizen*, August 17, 1898: 6.

23 "Ottawa Did The Trick Again," *Ottawa Journal*, August 20, 1898: 6.

24 "The Sporting World," *Ottawa Citizen*, August 22, 1898: 6.

25 "Baseball Notes," (Toronto) *Evening Star*, July 21, 1898: 7.

26 "Looking For Sympathy," *Ottawa Journal*, September 10, 1898: 6.

JIMMY "GUSSIE" GANNON LEADS OTTAWA TO ITS FIRST HOME VICTORY IN PROFESSIONAL BASEBALL

JULY 19, 1898: OTTAWA SENATORS 7, BUFFALO BISONS 1, AT METROPOLITAN GROUNDS, OTTAWA, ONTARIO

BY GARY BELLEVILLE

AFTER RUNNING INTO FINANCIAL AND legal difficulties in the summer of 1898, the owners of Rochester's entry in the Eastern League were desperate to quickly unload their team.[1] The eight-team circuit – renamed the International League in 1912 – agreed to relocate the franchise at a league meeting on July 10.[2] In short order, the team was sold to an Ottawa syndicate that was eager to introduce professional baseball to Canada's capital. Suddenly, Ottawa had joined Montreal and Toronto at the highest level of the minor leagues.[3]

The ownership group was led by Alex Graham, a brick manufacturer in Ottawa East.[4] Graham was also active in the city's sporting circles and he was an officer of the Ottawa Amateur Athletic Club.[5] His determined efforts to land the professional baseball team – over competing bids from Worcester, Newark, and Hartford – drew much praise in the city's newspapers.[6] "Alex Graham is the king for the moment," wrote the *Ottawa Citizen*. "Nothing could … swerve him for an instant from the fixed purpose in his mind … the city should ever remember his gallant fight."[7]

The local syndicate must have been heartened to see a large crowd greet the players upon their arrival at the Ottawa train station on July 15.[8] That afternoon upward of 2,500 fans were at Lansdowne Park to witness the team's second home opener of the season.[9]

Ottawa's initial entry into what was known as Organized Baseball got off to a rough start. The cast of colorful characters – still wearing Rochester uniforms – lost their first two home games by a combined score of 18-8.[10]

Since Sunday baseball wasn't allowed in Ottawa,[11] the July 17 home game was played on the Hull Ball Grounds,[12] which were on the Quebec side of the Ottawa River. Ottawa trailed Syracuse by a 6-2 score when the skies opened up after four innings and the game was called because of rain.[13] The team – citing a league rule – refused to issue refunds or rain checks because at least three innings had been played, angering many of the 1,000 fans in attendance.[14]

Because of potential conflicts at Lansdowne Park with the Ottawa Capitals lacrosse club,[15] the baseball team played its remaining (non-Sunday) home games at the Metropolitan Grounds on Jane Street (later Pretoria Avenue).[16]

The Ottawas[17] hosted their first game at the Metropolitan Grounds on July 19 against the Buffalo Bisons.[18] Although Ottawa was in sixth place, its 34-37 record left it only 5½ games behind the first-place Montreal Royals in the tightly-bunched standings. Fourth-place Buffalo trailed Montreal by four games.

Ottawa was without its hard-hitting third baseman, Bill "Wagon Tongue" Keister, who had been recently recalled by the defending National League champions in Boston.[19] Despite the absence of Keister, Ottawa fielded a starting lineup that included seven former or future major leaguers.[20] None of them made a significant impact in the big leagues, although first baseman and cleanup hitter Mike Kelley went on to become a respected minor-league manager for 30 years.[21]

Jimmy "Gussie" Gannon got the start for Ottawa. The 24-year-old southpaw had pitched one game in the majors, a five-inning relief outing for Connie Mack's Pittsburgh Pirates in June 1895.[22] Gannon made headlines in the summer of 1897 when he was convicted for violating the law against playing baseball on a Sunday in Rochester.[23] He was sentenced to a $10 fine or 10 days in jail.[24]

Buffalo's batting order featured six former or future big leaguers, including 40-year-old second baseman Sam Wise, Boston's top hitter in 1887.[25] James "Farmer" Brown, a 19-game winner with the Bisons in 1897, took to the hill for Buffalo.

Ottawa put two men on base in the bottom of the first, only to have Brown wiggle out of the jam.

Brown wasn't as fortunate in the second inning. Ottawa had runners on first and second with one out when Gannon came to the plate. He slapped a single past the first baseman and Joe Bean scampered home with the game's first run. According to the *Ottawa Citizen*, the enthusiastic fans roared so loudly that "the roof of the grandstand was in danger."[26]

The next batter was Bob "Rabbit" McHale, who had an 11-game stint with the Washington Senators earlier in the season.[27] McHale singled, knocking in catcher Joe Gunson, and Ottawa led, 2-0.

Gannon cruised through the first four innings, allowing only one Buffalo baserunner to get into scoring position.

After a brief rain delay in the bottom of the fourth, Ottawa put runners on first and second with one out for its 28-year-old second baseman, Frank Bonner. Four years earlier, Bonner had hit .322 in 33 games as a utility player on the NL's pennant-winning Baltimore Orioles. Bonner singled to center field and Gunson trotted home, giving Ottawa a three-run cushion.

The Bisons scored a run off Gannon in the fifth. With one out, Ed Gremminger reached on an extra-base hit, and he was driven in by William Diggins.[28]

Kelley led off in the bottom of the fifth. The 22-year-old showed why he was considered one of the league's top prospects when he reached on a single and later scored on a "beautiful steal to home."[29] Gunson, one of several players credited with inventing the padded catcher's mitt,[30] added an RBI single to extend Ottawa's lead to 5-1.[31]

The Ottawas tacked on a run in the sixth on an RBI triple by Bonner and another in the seventh on Bean's solo home run.[32]

Gannon shut out the Bisons the rest of the way, icing a 7-1 victory and giving the team its first professional win at home since relocating from Rochester. The fans were delighted by the "best all-around baseball ever witnessed in the Capital,"[33] and the *Buffalo News* observed that Ottawa "is now red-hot for baseball."[34]

Depending on the source, Gannon threw either a six- or seven-hitter.[35] He walked two and struck out a pair of batters. Ottawa slugged 14 hits against Brown, including two extra-base hits and two singles by Bonner, who finished the season with a .298 batting average.[36]

At some point that day, J.R. McNeil, a Sparks Street tailor and local baseball booster, gave the Ottawa players a sneak preview of the new uniforms he was making for them.[37] The collared "suits" – made from material matching the McNeil family tartan - were worn for the first time on the August 1 Civic Holiday.[38] They were perhaps the boldest uniforms ever worn in professional baseball.

Not surprisingly, McNeil's audacious fashion statement drew mixed reviews. The *Ottawa Citizen* generously labeled the team the "most stylish looking aggregation in the league."[39] On the other hand, the *Providence Journal* thought the uniforms were "ridiculous," and the *Buffalo Commercial* felt they gave the Ottawas a "ludicrous appearance."[40] The *Montreal Herald* went as far as to write a poem mocking the tartan attire.[41]

While the garish uniforms may not have sparked the team, the addition of two booming bats to its lineup did give it a boost. The Bostons demoted Keister on July 24 and he returned to action with Ottawa a couple of days later.[42] The 5-foot-5, 168-pound slugger finished the EL season with a .322 batting average and 14 steals.[43] One year later, Keister was the Orioles' starting shortstop, playing to the left of a combative third baseman named John McGraw.[44]

Perhaps the best player to wear an Ottawa uniform that summer was Quiet Joe Knight, a 38-year-old left fielder from

Port Stanley, Ontario.[45] Knight had started the season with the Wilkes-Barre Coal Barons, but the two-time batting champion[46] refused to accept the 20 percent pay cut the EL imposed on all players in July.[47] Knight caught on for a short time with the St. Thomas Saints in the Canadian League[48] before joining Ottawa in mid-August.[49] He finished second in the EL batting race with a .338 average.[50]

Ottawa hovered near the .500 mark until late August, when the bottom fell out of its season. The team lost 14 of its last 15 games to finish in the basement with a 53-70 mark, 18½ games behind the pennant-winning Royals.[51]

With the Spanish-American War raging, attendance was down across professional baseball in 1898.[52] Although the EL survived a difficult summer, Montreal, Toronto, and Wilkes-Barre may have been the only teams to turn a profit.[53] Lower-than-expected attendance in Ottawa resulted in hefty losses for Graham's syndicate,[54] and in November he notified the league that "it would be useless to continue as a member of the circuit."[55]

A short time later, Ottawa's player-manager Bill Clymer looked back fondly on his time in the city, especially when the team was winning and local merchants proudly displayed signs in their windows reading 'This store belongs to the Ottawa Baseball Club.'[56] "We owned the town and did as we liked

BUFFALO.	A.B.	R.	1B.	P.O.	A.	E.
Shannon, s.s.........	4	0	0	1	2	1
White, l.f............	3	0	0	2	0	0
Griffin, c.f...........	3	0	1	3	0	0
Wise, 2b.............	4	0	1	5	2	0
Housholder, .rf......	4	0	1	3	0	0
Urquhart, 1b ...	4	0	1	6	0	0
Greminger, 3b.......	4	1	1	1	4	0
Diggins, c............	3	0	1	3	1	0
Brown, p....	2	0	0	0	2	0
Totals............	31	1	6	24	11	1

OTTAWA.	A.B.	R.	1B.	P.O.	A.	E.
McHale, l.f.........	5	1	2	1	1	0
Bonner, 2b.........	5	0	4	4	3	0
Walters, r.f.........	4	0	2	1	0	0
Kelly, 1b...........	3	1	1	9	1	0
Clymer, c.f.........	4	0	0	1	0	0
Doherty, 3b.........	2	0	1	1	2	0
Bean, s.s...........	4	3	1	5	1	3
Gunson, c.........	4	2	2	4	2	0
Gannon, p.........	4	0	1	1	1	0
Totals............	35	7	14	27	11	3

Score by innings—
Buffalo.....................0 0 0 0 1 0 0 0 0—1
Ottawa.....................0 2 0 1 2 1 1 0 x—7

SUMMARY—Two base hits, Bonner and Greminger ; three base hit, Bonner ; home run, Bean ; double play, McHale and Bonner ; bases on balls, off Gannon 2, off Brown 3; struck out, by Gannon 2, by Brown 1 ; hit batsman, Gannon 1. Time of game, 2 hours.
Umpire—Doscher.

Senators pitcher Jimmy "Gussie" Gannon gave up only one run in a 7-1 victory over the Buffalo Bisons to give the Ottawa its first professional win at home since relocating from Rochester. Credit: *Ottawa Citizen*, July 20, 1898: 6.

from start to finish … we were ace high until we had that awful slump," Clymer recalled. "Don't let anybody tell you that Ottawa isn't a good baseball town."[57]

SOURCES

In addition to the sources cited in the Notes, the author consulted Baseball-Reference.com, Retrosheet.org, *The Encyclopedia of Minor League Baseball*, and the 1901 Ottawa City Directory. Eastern League batting statistics were taken from *Spalding's Official Base Ball Guide for 1899*, which was available on the Internet Archive as of February 2024. The daily EL standings were taken from the *Boston Globe*. Unless otherwise noted, play-by-play information was taken from the article "Bisons Easy" on page 6 of the July 20, 1898, edition of the *Ottawa Citizen*.

NOTES

1 The root cause of Rochester's troubles had more to do with significant cost overruns on the construction of its new ballpark than poor attendance. Construction costs for Culver Field soared and when the 1898 season began, several local tradesmen still had not been paid for their work. In early July, those tradesmen filed liens totaling more than $14,000. "Gray in Charge of Culver Field," *Rochester Democrat and Chronicle*, July 17, 1898: 19; "Will Play Ball Just the Same," *Rochester Democrat and Chronicle*, July 3, 1898: 18.

2 "Rochester Team Will Not Come Back," *Rochester Democrat and Chronicle*, July 11, 1898: 11.

3 The highest level of the minor leagues in 1898 was classified as Class A. Two circuits earned that designation, the Eastern League and Ban Johnson's Western League.

4 "Ottawa In It Now," *Montreal Gazette*, July 12, 1898: 5; "Small City Items," *Ottawa Journal*, April 26, 1899: 7; "Snowshoers Entertained," *Ottawa Journal*, February 10, 1898: 6.

5 "Snowshoers Entertained"; "O.A.A.C. Directors," *Ottawa Citizen*, October 21, 1897: 7.

6 "Left 'Em All," *Ottawa Citizen*, July 12, 1898: 8.

7 "Ball To-Day," *Ottawa Citizen*, July 15, 1898: 6.

8 "Clymer Was Reminiscent," *Ottawa Journal*, December 8, 1898: 6.

9 General admission tickets were 25 cents, while seats in the grandstand went for 50 cents. The *Ottawa Citizen* estimated the crowd, which included many women, at "about 2,500." The *Ottawa Journal* reported attendance of "almost 2,000." The only two Eastern League games played at Lansdowne Park were on Friday, July 15, and Saturday, July 16. "Ottawa Lost," *Ottawa Citizen*, July 16, 1898: 6; "Lost the First," *Ottawa Journal*, July 16, 1898: 6; "Ball To-Day."

10 "Ottawa Lost."

11 Neither Ottawa nor Toronto – the two Eastern League teams based in the province of Ontario – could play baseball at home on Sundays in 1898. It was permitted in Québec, so Ottawa shifted Sunday games to nearby Hull; Montreal also played at home on Sundays. Toronto's first Sunday home game wasn't played until May 7, 1950. When the International League's Ottawa Athletics were moved to Columbus, Ohio, for the 1955 season, Sunday baseball was still not allowed in Ottawa. "Jersey City Beats Toronto," *Kingston* (Ontario) *Whig-Standard*, May 8, 1950: 10; Jack Koffman, "Ottawa Fans Plan

Petition to End Sabbath Blue Law," *The Sporting News*, September 1, 1954: 28.

12 "We Can't Win All the Time," *Ottawa Journal*, July 13, 1898: 6; "Championship Baseball Sunday," *Ottawa Journal*, July 30, 1898: 7; "The Sunday Game," *Ottawa Journal*, July 18, 1898: 6.

13 "Rain Saved Ottawa," *Montreal Gazette*, July 18, 1898: 2.

14 Monday's game against the Buffalo Bisons was rained out. "The Hull Game," *Ottawa Citizen*, July 18, 1898: 6; "The Sunday Game."

15 "Fever Raging," *Ottawa Citizen*, July 13, 1898: 8; "Sporting," *Ottawa Journal*, July 13, 1898: 7.

16 The Metropolitan Grounds were located on Jane Street (later Pretoria Avenue) between O'Connor Street and Metcalfe Street. The grounds were subdivided into lots in 1900. Tommy Shields, "Ottawa Teams Had Glorious Accomplishments in Lacrosse," *Ottawa Citizen*, April 28, 1953: E-6. "Somerset St. Pavement," *Ottawa Citizen*, September 5, 1900: 1.

17 Baseball-Reference.com lists the team name as the Ottawa Wanderers, although the author found no mentions of the nickname "Wanderers" in the contemporary press. The *Rochester Democrat and Chronicle* did refer to the team as "[manager] Mickey Finn's wandering band" during the period of transition from Rochester to Ottawa. "Gannon Was Not a Mystery Yesterday," *Rochester Democrat and Chronicle*, July 13, 1898: 11.

18 The *Ottawa Citizen* reported that the Metropolitan Grounds was a decent venue despite not having any seating behind home plate. "Bisons Easy," *Ottawa Citizen*, July 20, 1898: 6.

19 Keister began the season with Boston and was loaned to Rochester in late May. His most recent appearance for Rochester/Ottawa was in a road game on July 12. "Morton Resigned, Clymer Managing," *Rochester Democrat and Chronicle*, May 25, 1898: 12; "Gannon Was Not a Mystery Yesterday," *Rochester Democrat and Chronicle*, July 13, 1898: 11.

20 The seven former or future major leaguers in Ottawa's starting lineup were left fielder Bob "Rabbit" McHale, second baseman Frank Bonner (later known as the Human Flea), first baseman Mike Kelley, center fielder Bill Clymer, shortstop Joe Bean, catcher Joe Gunson, and pitcher Jimmy "Gussie" Gannon.

21 Kelley played 76 games for the National League's Louisville Colonels in 1899, his only season in the majors.

22 "Down to Third Place," *Pittsburgh Post*, June 16, 1895: 6.

23 "Gannon Was Convicted," *Rochester Democrat and Chronicle*, July 3, 1897: 11.

24 "Gannon Sentenced," *Rochester Democrat and Chronicle*, July 23, 1897: 13.

25 The other five former or future major leaguers in Buffalo's lineup on July 19 were: shortstop Frank Shannon, left fielder Jack White, center fielder Sandy Griffin, right fielder Ed Householder, and third baseman Ed "Battleship" Gremminger.

26 "Bisons Easy."

27 "Won Like Warriors," *Washington Evening Star*, May 12, 1898: 8.

28 The *Ottawa Citizen* reported Gremminger's hit as a double. The *Buffalo News* and *Buffalo Express* said he tripled. It's unclear how Diggins drove in Gremminger. According to the *Buffalo News*, Gremminger scored on an out by Diggins. The *Ottawa Citizen* said Gremminger scored on a "hit" by Diggins, although the writer appears to have used the term "hit" whenever a ball was struck by a bat.

29   The author was unable to find a game story that explained how Kelley reached third base. "Condensed Dispatches," *Sporting Life*, February 4, 1899: 4; "Bisons Easy."

30   Chuck Rosciam, "The Evolution of Catcher's Equipment," *Baseball Research Journal* (Summer 2010), https://sabr.org/journal/article/the-evolution-of-catchers-equipment/, accessed February 27, 2024.

31   The *Ottawa Citizen* credits the RBI single to Bonner, but this is not possible based on the batting order. The run must have been driven in by Gunson.

32   Bean started the 1898 season with the Brooklyn Bridegrooms, although he never got into a game. His only appearance in the big leagues came in a 50-game stint with the New York Giants in 1902. Bill Lamb, "Joe Bean," SABR BioProject, https://sabr.org/bioproj/person/Joe-Bean/, accessed February 27, 2024.

33   "Bisons Easy."

34   "Ottawans Did Us Up," *Buffalo News*, July 20, 1898: 6.

35   The *Ottawa Citizen*, *Ottawa Journal*, and *Montreal Star* reported that Gannon gave up six hits. According to several Buffalo papers and the *Rochester Democrat and Chronicle*, it was seven hits. The discrepancy appears to be a single credited to Farmer Brown.

36   Bonner's .298 batting average was third best on the team. Among players appearing in 80 or more games, his batting average ranked 18th in the league.

37   McNeil was elected an officer of the Ottawa Baseball Club in March 1898. The team participated in the Ottawa City League. "Ottawas Organized"; "Bisons Easy."

38   "The World of Sport," *Ottawa Citizen*, August 2, 1898: 6; Tom Shieber, "Bagpipes and Baseball, or Clash of the Tartans," Baseball Researcher Blog, http://baseballresearcher.blogspot.com/2012/11/bagpipes-and-baseball-or-clash-of.html, accessed February 27, 2024.

39   "The World of Sport."

40   "Base Ball News and Comment," *Sporting Life*, September 17, 1898: 5; "Baseball Brevities," *Buffalo Commercial*, September 3, 1898: 4.

41   The poem read, "A splurge of solferino, A dash of blue and cream, Some blue, some green, some yellow, The whole a fairy dream, You think perhaps I'm singing, Of a rainbow that's a beaut, But there you are mistaken, For it's Ottawa's new suit." Solferino is a moderate purplish-red color. "The Sporting World," *Ottawa Citizen*, August 19, 1898: 6.

42   "Long, Bergen and Collins," *Boston Globe*, July 26, 1898: 7; "Sports of the Season," *Ottawa Citizen*, July 27, 1898: 6.

43   Keister's .322 batting average was second best on the team. Among players appearing in 80 or more games, his batting average ranked eighth in the league.

44   Keister was a regular in the major leagues from 1899 to 1903 with the Baltimore Orioles, St. Louis Cardinals, Washington Senators, and Philadelphia Phillies. He compiled a career .312 batting average in 621 major-league games, but poor fielding cut short his big-league career. He continued to play in the minors from 1904 to 1910.

45   "Both Are Good Men," *Ottawa Journal*, August 16, 1898: 6.

46   Knight won back-to-back batting titles in the Eastern League in 1893 and 1894.

47   "Rochester's Club Goes to Ottawa!" *Wilkes-Barre Record*, July 12, 1898: 3.

48   The Canadian League was a professional circuit that was quickly organized after the collapse of the International League in mid-July. The International League had teams in Hamilton (Ontario), St. Thomas (Ontario), London (Ontario), Port Huron (Michigan), Bay City (Michigan), and Saginaw (Michigan). The four-team Canadian League comprised Hamilton, St. Thomas, London, and Chatham (Ontario). "A New League," *Montreal Star*, July 12, 1898: 2.

49   Knight's first appearance with Ottawa was on August 13. "Won Two; Lost One," *Montreal Gazette*, August 15, 1898: 5.

50   Knight's .338 batting average was second in the league among players appearing in at least 80 games. Toronto's Buck Freeman won the batting title with a .347 average. Freeman went on to become one of the top sluggers in the American League. Eric Enders, "Buck Freeman," SABR BioProject, https://sabr.org/bioproj/person/Buck-Freeman/, accessed February 27, 2024.

51   Ottawa lost 14 consecutive games from August 29 to September 10. The team snapped its losing streak in its final game by beating the Toronto Maple Leafs in the second game of the September 10 twin bill. "Ottawas Won a Game," *Ottawa Citizen*, September 12, 1898: 6.

52   "Base Ball Gossip," *Seymour* (Indiana) *Daily Democrat*, August 20, 1898: 6.

53   "Eastern League Is Doubtless Relieved at the Close of the Battle," *Sporting Life*, September 17, 1898: 12.

54   The *Ottawa Journal* reported that the team owners lost $4,000 during their two months in the Eastern League. "Looking For Sympathy," *Ottawa Journal*, September 10, 1898: 6.

55   "A Trifle Mixed," *Sporting Life*, November 19, 1898: 4.

56   Clymer took over Ottawa's managerial duties from Mickey Finn in late July. Clymer played center field, hitting .264 with 29 stolen bases. "Notes," *Ottawa Journal*, July 25, 1898: 6.

57   "Clymer Was Reminiscent."

DOC HILLEBRAND'S SHUTOUT HAS OTTAWA ON VERGE OF FIRST PLACE IN OUTLAW NORTHERN INDEPENDENT LEAGUE

AUGUST 8, 1906: OTTAWA 1, BURLINGTON 0, AT ATHLETIC PARK, BURLINGTON, VERMONT

BY GARY BELLEVILLE

ALTHOUGH THE NORTHERN INDEPENDENT LEAGUE had instituted a salary cap of $400 per week at the start of the 1906 season, the rule was largely ignored by the spendthrift owners.[1] The two prominent businessmen funding Ottawa's new entry in the circuit, Henry Sims and John Cain, were no exception.[2] Before the season began, Ottawa made a big splash by signing one of America's most famous athletes, Art "Doc" Hillebrand, for the princely sum of $150 per week.[3] With a 12-man roster to fill, that made it nearly impossible to field a winning team without exceeding the salary cap.

Hillebrand more than lived up to expectations, anchoring Ottawa's mound staff and playing a solid right field when he wasn't pitching. But his massive contract was one of several questionable financial decisions that led to the team's demise.[4]

The 29-year-old Hillebrand had been a two-sport star at Princeton University, captaining both the football and baseball teams.[5] After earning a Bachelor of Arts degree in geology, Hillebrand played two seasons in the minor leagues.[6] In the fall of 1903, he signed a lucrative contract with the Washington Senators that would have made him the highest-paid pitcher on the team.[7] To the Senators' chagrin, Art didn't report to the team in the spring, possibly because his father – a medical doctor – didn't approve of him pursuing a career as a big-league ballplayer.[8] In 1904 he played amateur baseball and helped manage the family ranch in South Dakota.[9]

Art's younger brother, Homer Hillebrand, made his major-league debut with the Pittsburgh Pirates in the spring of 1905. Although Art wanted to join his sibling on the Pirates, Washington still retained his rights, and so he was unable to play for another team in Organized Baseball.[10] His only other option was to turn to a league that operated outside of the purview of the National Association of Professional Baseball Leagues. In 1905 Art suited up for Plattsburgh in the outlaw Northern New York League, which was later renamed the Northern Independent League.[11]

The Northern Independent League was a safe haven for contract jumpers or those who had otherwise run afoul of the recently-formed National Commission.[12] The league relied heavily on players with college baseball experience, including many current collegians who played under assumed names to avoid losing their amateur status.[13] The league was a magnet for top talent, and the caliber of play was comparable to the highest level of the minor leagues.[14]

At least one former and three future big leaguers played for Ottawa in 1906.[15] Left fielder Frank "Shag" Shaughnessy, who went on to become a key figure in Ottawa's professional baseball history, had played one game for the Washington Nationals in 1905.[16] Shaughnessy was Ottawa's best hitter, and his slugging prowess led the *Ottawa Citizen* to dub him the "home run king of the Northern League."[17] Center fielder Ray Demmitt, a University of Illinois player who went on to enjoy a seven-year career in the American League, played for Ottawa under the name "C.R. Ray."[18] Leon "Doc" Martell and Jim Ball – both catchers – also went on to have brief stints in the majors.[19]

The Northern Independent League season opened in late June as a five-team circuit. In addition to Ottawa, there were three teams in Vermont (Burlington, Rutland, and Montpelier-Barre) and one in New York (Plattsburgh). But the Plattsburgh team folded on July 19 because of financial difficulties, and the league was reduced to four teams.[20]

Ottawa had been drawing good crowds to its home games at the Varsity Oval, and the team was perched in second place in early August.[21] A five-game winning streak from August 4-8 raised Ottawa's record to 17-9, moving them to within 1½ games of first place heading into a showdown with the league leaders in Burlington on August 9.[22]

During the 1906 season, Burlington's stacked roster featured eight former or future major leaguers.[23] Larry Gardner went on to have the most success in the big leagues, winning three World Series with the Boston Red Sox between 1912 and 1916 and another with the Cleveland Indians in 1920. Gardner did not face Ottawa on August 9, likely because of a sore back.[24]

Hillebrand got the start for Ottawa. The tall right-hander came into the game with a 9-3 record and an estimated ERA

35

of 1.40.[25] Hillebrand had been red-hot of late, recording three shutouts in his four previous starts. (His shutout streak was broken when he gave up an unearned run two days earlier in a 2-1, 10-inning win over Montpelier-Barre.[26])

Hillebrand was opposed by righty Jimmy Wiggs, who had made four appearances with the Detroit Tigers earlier in the season. After getting demoted to the American Association, Wiggs jumped his contract with Toledo and joined Burlington in late July.[27]

In the bottom of the first, Hillebrand gave up a two-out single to a skilled batsman with a pseudonym of "Bill Burde." The Burlington hitter was actually Penn State's Birdie Cree; he went on to play eight seasons with the New York Highlanders/Yankees.[28] After the next batter reached on an infield single, Hillebrand escaped the inning by getting Will "Doc" Hazelton to ground into a force out.

Ottawa nearly got on the scoreboard in the third. Another University of Illinois player using a nom de guerre, first baseman Jim Snyder ("Clayton"), reached on a Texas Leaguer with one out.[29] After an error by the shortstop Cree, Frank O'Brien moved both baserunners into scoring position with a sacrifice.[30] It all went for naught when Ottawa's captain, second baseman Johnny Dorman, grounded out to end the inning.

Ottawa put another runner in scoring position with two out in the sixth. The threat ended when Burlington first baseman Hazelton robbed Shaughnessy of a hit by snagging a sharply-hit ball close to the bag.

Wiggs finally blinked in the eighth. After O'Brien drew a two-out walk, he boldly stole second and third on the next two pitches.[31] He scored easily when Dorman laced a single to right-center field.

Hillebrand, meanwhile, had been cruising. Only one Burlington batter, Wiggs leading off the third with a single, reached base in innings two through eight. Hillebrand seemed to get stronger as the game progressed. After Ottawa took a 1-0 lead, he responded by striking out the side in the bottom of the eighth, giving him four consecutive strikeouts.[32]

Hillebrand retired the first two batters in the ninth, giving him 20 consecutive outs. The streak was snapped when he hit Cree with a pitch. Cree, who stole 48 bases for the Highlanders in 1911, took off for second; Ottawa's outstanding catcher, Martell, threw him out and the game was over.

Hillebrand finished with a three-hitter, walking none and striking out six. He picked up his 10th win and fifth shutout of the season. "Hillebrand is the king of them all," wrote the *Ottawa Journal*. "He pitches with lots of steam and some pretty curves, and keeps any of them guessing."[33]

The thrilling win moved Ottawa to within a half-game of first place, but it was as close as the team would get. After tossing a whopping 63 innings in the previous 18 days, Hillebrand came crashing down to earth.[34] Ottawa lost its next seven games, culminating with Hillebrand's frustrating 4-3, 11-inning loss to Montpelier-Barre at the Varsity Oval on August 18.[35]

Ottawa's Art "Doc" Hillebrand was a force to be reckoned with in what would be his final season before an arm injury cut short his career. Appearing in all 34 games, he posted an estimated 1.74 ERA and a 10-6 record, tying for the league lead in wins. His contributions extended beyond the mound, as he also hit .283 and stole 7 bases.
Credit: Historical Photograph Collection Alumni Photographs series, AC058, Princeton University Archives, Department of Special Collections, Princeton University Library.

That same afternoon, Rutland forfeited its game in Burlington.[36] The Rutland players were owed back wages, and they refused to play until they were paid. Rutland's ownership responded by fining them for insubordination and disbanding the team.[37] The next domino to fall was in Ottawa, where the team had accumulated a deficit of nearly $6,000.[38] It officially threw in the towel on August 20,[39] finishing with an 18-16 record.

The two remaining teams, Montpelier-Barre and Burlington, continued to play each other until August 25, and Burlington easily held onto first place with a 27-13 record.[40] The outlaw league collapsed, never to return.[41]

The dynamic Hillebrand appeared in all 34 of Ottawa's games. He posted an estimated 1.74 ERA and a 10-6 record, tying him for the league lead in wins.[42] He also hit .283 in 106 at-bats and stole 7 bases. Hillebrand's brief stint in Canada's capital marked his final season of professional baseball, and his August 9 shutout against Burlington turned out to be his last professional win.

Homer's promising baseball career was cut short in the spring of 1908 because of an arm injury. Around that time, Washington sold Art's rights to the New York Highlanders for $1,000.[43] The elder Hillebrand refused to report to that team too.[44]

The Hillebrand brothers ran the family ranch in South Dakota for many years, and at some point during the Depression, Homer relocated to Corvallis, Oregon. Tragedy struck when Art came for a visit in December 1941. A fire broke out at Homer's farmhouse, killing his wife and one of his children, along with his brother Art.

Art "Doc" Hillebrand was enshrined in the College Football Hall of Fame in 1970.

SOURCES

In addition to the sources cited in the Notes, the author consulted Baseball-Reference.com, the SABR biography of Homer Hillebrand, and the 1906 Ottawa City Directory. Unless otherwise noted, all play-by-play information for this game was taken from the article "Great Pitching; Battle Royal Between Hildebrand and Wiggs and Ottawa Won, 1 to 0," on page 3 of the August 10, 1906, edition of the *Burlington Free Press*. The Northern Independent League standings were also taken from the *Burlington Free Press*.

NOTES

1   "Inter-Baseball," *Ottawa Citizen*, March 12, 1906: 1; "Plattsburgh Will Stick," *Ottawa Citizen*, July 19, 1906: 8.

2   Sims was the owner of Henry J. Sims & Co., which sold hats and fur products in its Sparks Street shop. Cain was president of the Cain Brick Co. in Ottawa East. "Ball Players Hold Meeting; Locals to Make Big Effort for Northern League Honors," *Ottawa Citizen*, March 2, 1906: 8.

3   By contrast, the Detroit Tigers paid 19-year-old Ty Cobb a salary of $1,500 in 1906, his first full season in the big leagues. With 25 weeks in the season, Cobb's pay would have come to just $60 per week – less than half of Hillebrand's weekly pay. "Twelve Heart Disease Innings," *Montpelier* (Vermont) *Evening Argus*, June 28, 1906: 1.

4   Another example of excessive spending occurred during Ottawa's bid to acquire an expansion team. The owners hastily agreed to pay the traveling expenses to and from Ottawa for the league's four other teams – three in Vermont (Burlington, Rutland, and Montpelier-Barre) and one in New York (Plattsburgh). It was a commitment they would soon regret. Plattsburgh, the nearest of the four other Northern Independent League cities, was an easy 140-mile drive from Ottawa in 2024. The journey was significantly more arduous – and expensive - in 1906. Rutland was the farthest from Ottawa at approximately 280 miles. "A 5-Team League; Ottawa Admitted and Montreal Rejected – One Meant Business, Other Didn't," *Burlington Free Press*, March 10, 1906: 3.

5   Terry Bohn, "Homer Hillebrand," SABR BioProject, https://sabr.org/bioproj/person/homer-hillebrand/, accessed February 14, 2024; "Art 'Doc' Hillebrand," National Football Foundation, https://footballfoundation.org/hof_search.aspx?hof=2095, accessed February 14, 2024.

6   David L. Porter, ed., *Biographical Dictionary of American Sports: 1992-1995 Supplement* (Westport, Connecticut: Greenwood Press, 1995), 443.

7   Paul W. Eaton, "From the Capital," *Sporting Life*, August 19, 1905: 25.

8   Art Hillebrand got the nickname "Doc" because his father, Christian M. Hillebrand, was a doctor. "Art 'Doc' Hillebrand," National Football Foundation.

9   Art played for an amateur team in Webster, South Dakota. The family ranch was in nearby Waubay. "It Was a Shut-Out," *Webster* (South Dakota) *Reporter and Farmer*, July 7, 1904: 7.

10   "Court's Decrees; Handed Down by the National Commission," *Sporting Life*, September 2, 1905: 2; "Another Phase of Hillebrand Case," *Sporting Life*, September 16, 1905: 8.

11   The league was known as the Northern New York League between 1900 and 1905. In 1906 only one of the five teams (Plattsburgh) was based in New York. The league is not to be confused with the Northern League that operated from 1902 to 1905 with teams in North Dakota, Minnesota, Wisconsin, and Manitoba. "Montreal to Go in the Northern," *Ottawa Citizen*, February 26, 1906: 8.

12   A three-man National Commission was formed to oversee the sport as part of the 1903 peace agreement between the National and American Leagues. John T. Pregler and Tom Loftus: "The American League's Forgotten Founding Father," *Baseball Research Journal*, Spring 2020. https://sabr.org/journal/article/tom-loftus-the-american-leagues-forgotten-founding-father/, accessed February 14, 2024; Joe Santry and Cindy Thomson, "Ban Johnson," SABR BioProject, https://sabr.org/bioproj/person/ban-johnson/, accessed February 14, 2024; Dan Busby, "Kenesaw Mountain Landis," SABR BioProject, https://sabr.org/bioproj/person/kenesaw-landis/, accessed February 14, 2024.

13   "The Northern League," *Sporting Life*, June 23, 1906: 18.

14   A significant number of former and future big leaguers could be found on every Northern Independent League team. The league was heavily scouted, and many players made their major-league debut shortly after appearing in the circuit. For instance, Ed Reulbach played for Montpelier-Barre in 1904 under the assumed name of "Sheldon." He became a star pitcher with the Chicago Cubs the next season. Eddie Collins is another example - he made his big-league debut in 1906 just a couple of months after playing for Plattsburgh and Rutland. Rick Huhn, *Eddie Collins: A Baseball Biography* (Jefferson, North Carolina: McFarland & Company, 2008), 30; Cappy Gagnon, "Ed Reulbach," SABR BioProject, https://sabr.org/bioproj/person/ed-reulbach/, accessed February 14, 2024; "Northern League Notes," *Burlington Free Press*, August 6, 1904: 3; Paul Mittermeyer, "Eddie Collins," SABR BioProject, https://sabr.org/bioproj/person/eddie-collins/, accessed February 14, 2024.

15   There may have been more future big leaguers on Ottawa's roster, but as of February 2024 it was unclear if all players using assumed names had been identified. Two other future big leaguers were signed by Ottawa, although they did not appear in any regular-season games. Catcher Red Murray (aka "J.J. Murray") was under contract with Ottawa until mid-June when he jumped directly to the St. Louis Cardinals to begin a successful 11-year run in the National League. Spitballer Vedder Sitton (aka "C.V. Sitton," aka "Sid Sitton," aka "Sid Smith") pitched in exhibition games for Ottawa. A newspaper article on July 7, 1906, reported that he had been released, "as his arm would not get into shape." The writer lamented that it "looks like another spit ball artist gone wrong." "Baseball," *Ottawa Citizen*,

June 14, 1906: 8; "Northern League Notes," *Burlington Free Press*, July 7, 1906: 2.

16 Shaughnessy appeared in another eight games with the Philadelphia Athletics in 1908. He married an Ottawa woman and settled in the city before spearheading the effort to bring professional baseball back to Ottawa in 1912. The expansion Ottawa Senators played in the Canadian League from 1912 to 1915, winning the league championship in all four seasons. During the last three of those seasons, the ever-popular Shaughnessy served as the team's player-manager. He went on to become president of the International League from 1936 to 1960. As league president, Shaughnessy helped Ottawa land the Ottawa Giants in 1951 and the Ottawa Athletics in 1952. Gary Belleville, "July 12, 1906: Frank Shaughnessy Leads Ottawa to Victory in Outlaw Northern Independent League," SABR Games Project, https://sabr.org/gamesproj/game/july-12-1906-frank-shaughnessy-leads-ottawa-to-victory-in-outlaw-northern-independent-league/, accessed February 19, 2024; "Hubbell Inspects Ottawa," *The Sporting News*, November 29, 1950: 12; Lloyd McGowan, "'Woods Are Full of Good Players,' Shag Maintains," *The Sporting News*, February 6, 1952: 22.

17 The author compiled a game log for Ottawa's 1906 season using the box scores published in various newspapers. According to this game log, Shaughnessy hit .297 with 5 homers and an impressive .484 slugging percentage in 128 at-bats. "Frank Shaughnessy Home from Scouting Trip through South," *Ottawa Citizen*, January 23, 1912: 8; "Game Log Ottawa 1906 (Northern Independent League)," https://docs.google.com/spreadsheets/d/1dPJUHQEZun5IrHmFIsNE-2R8cTsNst-T2kVflU9Bt-0I, accessed February 14, 2024.

18 Demmitt's legal name was Charles Raymond (i.e. "C.R.") Demmitt. "Baseball"; David McDonald, "Baseball in Ottawa," *Ottawa Citizen*, April 15, 2005: B-1; "Charles Raymond 'Ray' Demmitt," Find A Grave, https://www.findagrave.com/memorial/28833873/charles-raymond-demmitt, accessed February 14, 2024.

19 Martell had been invited to attend spring training with the Boston Americans in 1906. "American League Notes," *Sporting Life*, March 24, 1906: 5.

20 "Plattsburgh Quits and Ottawa Comes," *Burlington Free Press*, July 20, 1906: 3.

21 Ottawa may have had the highest attendance in the league, although there were rumors that Ottawa was padding its figures. According to available box scores, five of Ottawa's first seven home games had at least 2,000 fans in attendance. A season-high 3,200 fans were reported to be in attendance on July 2. "Northern League Notes," *Burlington Free Press*, July 26, 1906: 3.

22 According to various Vermont newspapers, including the *Burlington Free Press*, Burlington came into the August 9 game against Ottawa with a record of 19-8. The Ottawa papers had them at 18-8, which appears to be incorrect.

23 The eight former or future big leaguers to play for Burlington in 1906 were Larry Gardner, Birdie Cree, Wilbur Good, Harry Pattee, Will "Doc" Hazelton, Ray Tift, Leon "Doc" Martell, and Jimmy Wiggs. Martell signed with Ottawa in late July after his stint with Burlington. "League Meeting Decision," *Ottawa Citizen*, July 25, 1906: 8.

24 "Notes on the Game," *Burlington Free Press*, August 8, 1906: 3.

25 The author compiled a game log for Ottawa's 1906 season using the box scores published in various newspapers. The game log includes pitching and hitting statistics for Art Hillebrand. "Game Log Ottawa 1906 (Northern Independent League)," https://docs.google.com/spreadsheets/d/1dPJUHQEZun5IrHmFIsNE-2R8cTsNst-T2kVflU9Bt-0I, accessed February 14, 2024.

26 "Ottawa Won in the Tenth," *Ottawa Citizen*, August 8, 1906: 6.

27 Terry Bohn, "Jimmy Wiggs," SABR BioProject, https://sabr.org/bioproj/person/Jimmy-Wiggs/, accessed February 14, 2024; "Wiggs in the Box There for First Time This Season; His Support Gilt Edged," *Rutland* (Vermont) *Daily Herald*, July 23, 1906: 3.

28 Birdie Cree led Burlington in hitting in 1906. He finished the season with a .333 batting average and 70 total bases in 147 at-bats. "Burlington's Batting," *Burlington Free Press*, August 28, 1906: 3; Paul Sallee, "Birdie Cree," SABR BioProject, https://sabr.org/bioproj/person/birdie-cree/, accessed February 14, 2024.

29 Newspapers referred to Ottawa's primary first baseman as "Clayton" during the 1906 season. A newspaper article on September 7 disclosed that Clayton was actually a University of Illinois player with the surname of "Sniter [sic]." This appears to be a misspelling of Snyder, since the University of Illinois roster from 1906 includes a first baseman by the name of J. B. Snyder. According to the *Fighting Illini Baseball 2023 Record Book*, his first name was James. His *Sporting News* contract card lists a full name of James Blaine Snyder and a birth year of 1884. "Ottawa Baseball Players Want Their Money," *Montpelier* (Vermont) *Evening Argus*, September 7, 1906: 3; "Illinois Baseball All-Time Rosters," Fighting Illini Baseball, https://fightingillini.com/sports/2015/7/18/baseball_alltimerosters_1900_1924.aspx?#1906, accessed February 14, 2024; "Fighting Illini Baseball 2023 Record Book," Fighting Illini Baseball, https://fightingillini.com/documents/2023/2/16/2023_Record_Book__WEB_.pdf, accessed February 14, 2024.

30 As of February 2024, Baseball-Reference.com had no record of an O'Brien playing for Ottawa in 1906. The *Burlington Free Press* refers to him as "Frank O'Brien" in an August 14 article. "Batting Rally," *Burlington Free Press*, August 14, 1906: 2.

31 "Ottawa and Burlington Tied," *Ottawa Free Press*, August 10, 1906: 9.

32 "Notes on the Game," *Burlington Free Press*, August 10, 1906: 3.

33 "Playing Great Ball," *Ottawa Journal*, August 10, 1906: 3.

34 "Game Log Ottawa 1906 (Northern Independent League)."

35 "Monte-Barre in Eleventh; Visitors Pulled Down a Lead," *Ottawa Citizen*, August 20, 1906: 8.

36 "Rutland Forfeited," *Ottawa Journal*, August 20, 1906: 2.

37 "Base Ball Peters Out," *Barre Daily Times*, August 20, 1906: 1; J.B. Taylor, "Premature Close," *Sporting Life*, September 15, 1906: 11.

38 Taylor, "Premature Close."

39 "Baseball Club Is Disbanded," *Ottawa Citizen*, August 21, 1906: 8.

40 "Season's Wind Up," *Burlington Free Press*, August 27, 1906: 3.

41 Taylor, "Premature Close."

42 Two other pitchers in the league recorded 10 wins: Burlington's Ray Tift and a Montpelier-Barre player with the pseudonym of "Eddie Burns." Burns's real name was Edward "Teddy" Opfergelt. "Final Pitching Records," *Burlington Free Press*, August 28, 1906: 3; "Base Ball Tips," *Montpelier* (Vermont) *Evening Argus*, March 13, 1906: 4.

43 "'Doc' Hillebrand; Still Refuses to Recognize the New York American Club," *Sporting Life*, April 18, 1908: 15.

44 "American League Notes," *Sporting Life*, February 13, 1909: 5.

DIAMOND DYNASTY: THE 1912-15 OTTAWA SENATORS

BY DAVID MCDONALD

IN THE EARLY DECADES OF the twentieth century, baseball was by far the most popular sport in North America. By 1911 about 400 cities in Canada and the United States had professional baseball. But not Ottawa. Ottawa, pop. 87,000, was reportedly the only city of its size north of the Rio Grande without a pro team. That was about to change.

In December 1911 the Canadian League[1] awarded a franchise to the Ottawa Baseball Club, Frank "Shag" Shaughnessy, president (as well as part owner, manager, and center fielder). The Peterborough Whitecaps were also added for the 1912 season, making the Canadian an eight-team league and bumping it up, by virtue of the total population it represented—more than 300,000—to Class C.

Over the winter Shaughnessy busied himself laying the groundwork for his new club. The first order of business was to negotiate a deal to play home games in the stadium at Lansdowne Park, 2 1/2 miles south of Parliament Hill. (Upgrades included the removal of a pesky fire hydrant in center field.) Season-ticket prices for 54 home games were set at $25 for grandstand seating and $15 for the bleachers. Single-game prices were set at 25 cents for general admission, 50 cents in the grandstand. The team would play Monday through Saturday.

Sunday was a different story. No one played Sunday ball for money in true blue Ontario. A number of sites on the lawless Quebec side offered to host the Senators on the Sabbath, but Shaughnessy declined. "Ottawas Have Yielded To Wishes Of Better Element. . ." said the *Ottawa Citizen*[2], without specifying exactly what this better element was.

Shaughnessy's biggest challenge was to fill the Senators' spiffy new maroon, black, and white uniforms with capable bodies. To that end he tapped into his extensive network of baseball contacts and even took out a few help-wanted ads in the American sporting press. The results were encouraging. "Now that Ottawa is on the ball map, letters are coming in like answers to a patent medicine ad," said the *Ottawa Journal*.[3]

Shaughnessy, however, had previously signed a deal to play for and manage the Fort Wayne Railroaders of the 12-team, Class-C Central League, and its owner insisted he honor the deal. So Shag reluctantly packed up and left for Indiana, leaving veteran second baseman Louie Cook, a University of Illinois engineering grad, in charge.

SHIPWRECK

In April 1912 candidates for a job with the Senators assembled about as far south as the club could afford—Chatham, Ontario.

The training regimen called for five hours of practice a day, no booze; smoking was OK.

Dampening the considerable excitement surrounding the upcoming baseball season was the news of an unfolding maritime disaster in the North Atlantic. In one of the great Dewey-Defeats-Truman headlines of all time, the *Ottawa Journal* reported: "White Star Liner 'Titanic,' Largest Vessel Afloat, Crashes into Iceberg; 1300 Passengers Are Safe."[4]

For weeks after the papers were filled with dramatic tales of the disaster. By early May people were looking for distraction, were longing for spring and baseball. The Senators broke camp on May 13 and battled a blinding spring snowstorm to get to St. Thomas for their opener. Their first-ever starting pitcher was a big farm kid from Palmyra, Illinois, named Joe McManus. He dropped a 6-4 decision to the hometown Saints.

Ottawa's opening-day lineup was made up mostly of career minor leaguers, and entirely of American imports, except for right fielder Billy Blake, a Toronto native. There were four youngsters on the team—McManus being one of them—who would eventually play, if ever so briefly, in the major leagues.[5] For the rest Class C was about as good as baseball was ever going to get. Which in Ottawa wasn't bad at all.

The Senators arrived in the capital by train on May 16. The city welcomed their young Americans with a civic luncheon, free tickets to the 1,500-seat Russell Theatre, a visit to the big horse show, and guest privileges at the YMCA. A flag in team colors flew over downtown Sparks Street. "Everyone is talking baseball," said the *Citizen*.[6]

OPENING DAY

Weeks earlier Shaughnessy had chosen Thursday, May 16, which was Ascension Day and therefore a civil service holiday, for the Senators' home debut. The Ottawa Electric Railway Co. laid on specially decorated street cars. There was a parade of automobiles, a number of Members of Parliament put in an appearance, Mayor Charles Hopewell threw out the first pitch, the band of the Governor General's Foot Guards played, and the *Citizen* posted out-of-town scores on big boards in front of the grandstand. Six thousand "fans" (the word still being written in quotation marks) were expected to attend.

But on Ascension Day the rain descended. And kept descending into the weekend. Finally on Saturday the weather cleared enough for the Senators to take the field against the defending champion Berlin Busy Bees.[7] Almost 7,000 fans, the biggest crowd in Lansdowne history save for the annual

The 1912 Ottawa Senators Baseball Team. Credit: City of Ottawa Archives, MG946-3

Central Canada Exhibition, jammed the park to watch the locals trounce the Berliners 7-1. In a bold marketing move, the Senators allowed 30 or 40 automobiles to park right on the field.

When it came to cars, the Senators were miles ahead of the pack. Before the advent of drive-in restaurants, movies, and even drive-in gas stations, the club, with an eye on the city's ballooning automobile population—400 and counting in the spring of 1912—offered drive-in baseball. Fans could chug right into the stadium, park along the right-field line, and take in a ball game without leaving the comfort of their own flivvers. Shaughnessy, stuck in Fort Wayne, witnessed none of this.

BASEBALL FEVER

By mid-July thanks mainly to their strong pitching, the Senators were solidly in first place. After his Opening Day loss in St. Thomas, Joe McManus won 14 straight, before finally dropping a 6-5 decision to Hamilton on July 16. After the game he confessed he'd been feeling poorly for a couple of days. A week later it was revealed that he had suffered "a light attack"[8] of typhus, a common summer occurrence in Canadian cities of the day.

McManus dropped 35 pounds from his 180-pound frame and was done for the season.[9]

Even without him the Senators kept winning. And on August 17, 1912, 4,500 fans — including the occupants of about 60 motor cars — packed Lansdowne to see the Senators clinch their first Canadian League championship. "There was such an outpouring of buzz-wagons," reported the *Citizen*, "that it was necessary to agree on some ground rules and to make many line up on the east end of the field, which had hitherto not been used for that purpose...."[10] "Ottawa has gone baseball mad as the result of the team's success," the story added.

The Canadian League schedule wrapped up on Labor Day with Ottawa nine games ahead of the second-place Brantford Red Sox. A couple of days later the *Journal*'s baseball writer penned this classic expression of postseason letdown: "Louis Cook's Senators have nearly all left town, the pennant will be purchased by the league, labelled 'Ottawa' and sent up by parcel post, and the season is ended so far as the city is concerned."[11]

Despite a sputtering Canadian economy, a soggy spring, a typhus outbreak, and a pennant race devoid of suspense, the Senators made about $1,000 on the season. Shaughnessy declared the Canadian the most successful minor league on the continent. Although at least 18 circuits across North America had lost teams or folded outright that summer, most observers expressed optimism about the future of the game in the capital. "This is sure a great ball town," said right-hander Fred Herbert (16-9).[12] "It is quite evident," said the *Citizen,* "that baseball has come to stay."[13]

Some of the players, too. Switch-hitting infielder Artie Schwind, a Fort Wayne boy, said he liked the city so much he was going to make it his permanent home. To that end he landed an offseason job as an electrician with the Ottawa Electric Railway Co. But before he could cinch up his tool belt, Schwind found himself in Boston, playing shortstop for the National League Braves in a game against the Philadelphia Phillies. The only player in Class C to be drafted by a major-league club in 1912, Schwind had one hit in two tries and acquitted himself well in the field. That was the only shot he ever got in the big time. A week later he was back in Ottawa, pinching wires for the Electric Railway and probably pinching himself.[14]

GLITTERING STARS AND A BRAND-NEW SUIT

For spring training in 1913 Shaughnessy, having shelled out a reported $750 to secure his release from the Railroaders, assembled more than 30 returning and prospective Senators in balmy Fort Wayne, where, should he have a position or two to fill, he had ready access to any reject Railroaders. "It is the hardest thing in the world to rebuild a ball team shot to pieces in the… draft. But fortunately we will have a small army of players to choose from," said Shaughnessy, adding, "There are thousands of glittering stars in the bushes and we may be fortunate to pick up maybe one or two of them."[15]

In the summer of 1913 baseball was the hottest sporting ticket in the country. A record 24 Canadian cities fielded professional teams, and even in Ottawa, which had long been a lacrosse town, baseball was king. On Saturdays and holidays most clubs played morning and afternoon contests (no lights, no night ball) and charged separate admissions for each. On Saturday, May 24, for instance, the Senators drew several thousand fans for a morning game against Brantford and another 6,000 in the afternoon. This included the trendy occupants of 52 on-field automobiles—about 10 percent of the cars in the entire city.[16] "Some of the most fashionable people in the city are regular patrons of the Ottawa ball club," noted the *Citizen.*[17]

But the Senators closed out May by dropping seven straight, and a frustrated Shaughnessy blew up his club. He suspended one player, made some trades, and re-signed some of the previous season's Senators who had failed to stick at higher levels. Despite Shag's best efforts—after 33 games he was batting .427—the revamped Senators were still mired in fifth place by mid-July.

Some fans blamed Shaughnessy's often abrasive management style, but one player who thrived under it was Edgar "Lefty" Rogers, an Arkansas native acquired from Fort Wayne for $300.

In Ottawa, Rogers created a buzz by virtue of being chauffeured to Lansdowne on game days by an attractive redhead in a white roadster—and even more of a buzz for what he did when he got there. Rogers had started as a pitcher but had been converted into an outfielder because of his lively bat. Shaughnessy insisted on using him in both capacities. Behind Shag's hitting, the pitching of returning right-hander Erwin Renfer, and a double-duty performance by Rogers, the fifth-place Senators took off.

On an early July homestand they won nine of nine to move into second place. On July 30 the Senators beat the Busy Bees 9-5 in Berlin to kick off another winning streak, this one of 13 games. On the August 4 Civic Holiday they took two from Brantford to move into first place. Renfer's win three days later was his 17th straight and 20th of the season.[18]

The Senators continued to play winning ball over the final month, but they were unable to shake off the London Tecumsehs. But whenever the Senators absolutely needed a win—as they did going into the final game of the 1913 season—Shag brought Rogers in from left field. And so on Labor Day afternoon with the Canadian League pennant on the line, Lefty took the mound before 7,000 fans at Lansdowne Park and tamed the Whitecaps, 14-2.

The win enabled the Senators to snatch their second straight flag, this time by a single game over London. On the season Rogers, the Senators' big-game player, won 13 of 17 decisions and recorded a .336 batting average. Senators first baseman and longtime Shag sidekick Frank "Cozy" Dolan also had a big year, batting .358, third best in the league. Center fielder Shaughnessy finished at .340—eighth best—along with two home runs and 37 stolen bases.

THE INTERNATIONAL PASTIME

By 1914, as historian Alan Metcalfe argues, baseball was Canada's de facto national pastime.[19] No other sport was growing as quickly—or as widely. That summer there were 19 Canadian-based professional teams spread across five minor-league circuits. The Canadian League was proving to be one of the more solid baseball ventures on the continent. But baseball, along with everything else, was about to be severely tested by events in Europe.

For the new season two of the Canadian League's smaller centers, Berlin and Guelph, were replaced by Toronto and Erie, Pennsylvania. With its larger population base the Canadian moved up to Class B, which in those days was three rungs below the major leagues.

Shaughnessy meanwhile faced the annual challenge of piecing together a club mostly of rejects and leftovers from higher classifications. While the Senators trained in Chatham, the skipper made his annual cross-border spring shopping trip. One of the players he came back with was a youngster previously with the Windsor team of the Class D Border League. He was a catcher-turned-pitcher with just 16 mound appearances at any level under his belt and a tabloid headline for a name: Urban Shocker.[20] In Ottawa everyone called him

Herbie. Herbie Shocker would be the best player the Canadian League ever produced.

For their May 14 home opener, the Senators hosted Canadian baseball legend Knotty Lee's fledgling Toronto Beavers in front of 4,500 fans. "Clergymen, politicians, rail road magnates, civil servants, office boys, school children and people of every description were amongst the excited assembly that sat through two hours of rapid fire baseball," reported the *Citizen*.[21] Royalty, too. The Governor General, Prince Arthur, Duke of Connaught, and his 28-year-old daughter, Princess Patricia, of Light Infantry fame,[22] watched the game from the royal limo.

Three days later the Senators, tired of sacrificing lucrative weekend dates to the wishes of the capital's "better element," played their first-ever Sunday game, across the Ottawa River, in Hull, Quebec. Leading up to the 3 P.M. first pitch, special streetcars departed the Château Laurier every two minutes, and more than 5,000 fans eventually squeezed into Dupuis Park, capacity 4,500. The overflow sat on the grass in front of the grandstand, and cars parked two deep down the left-field line. Toronto won 6-5.

On Saturday, June 27, 1914, the Senators celebrated the raising of the 1913 pennant with a 3-2 win over Hamilton at Lansdowne Park, Shaughnessy, as he had done the previous year, belting the Senators' first home-field homer of the season to win the game in the bottom of the ninth. Shag's heroics were reported on page 8 of the *Citizen*. Buried on page 12 was a dispatch from Sarajevo: "Austrian Heir Apparent and Wife Meet Death at Hands of Young Serb Student May Seriously Affect European Peace."[23]

GATHERING CLOUDS

In July, unrelated to the death of the archduke, the Senators went into a tailspin. By mid-month they had fallen far behind arch-rival London, managed by former major-league pitcher and offseason dentist Carl "Doc" Reisling.[24] But Shag, being Shag, was not about to roll over. "London's lead is big,"—it had, in fact, grown to 8 1/2 games, with seven weeks left in the season—"but there's plenty of time, and I'm confident I can overtake them," he declared.[25] He told the press he was willing to spend $5,000, if that's what it took to turn his club around.

Skipping a series in Hamilton, Shaughnessy set off, checkbook in hand, on a scouting expedition to Michigan. In Adrian he caught up with Jack Mitchell[26], a hotshot 19-year-old shortstop whom the Senators had faced in a spring-training game. Shag went all in. The $1,000 he coughed up for Mitchell was reportedly the most ever paid for an infielder by a Class-B club. But Mitchell more than justified the hefty price tag, solidifying Ottawa's infield defence and running up a gaudy .344 batting average. As one writer later noted, "This change put reverse English on the playing of the champions, and they inaugurated a winning streak seldom seen in organized baseball."[27]

Shaughnessy made another key midseason adjustment. Novice pitcher Herbie Shocker had struggled to find a reliable breaking pitch. Shag suggested he experiment with a spitball. The

ONCE AND FUTURE OTTAWA SENATORS MAJOR LEAGUERS

Joe McManus, 1912; Cincinnati Reds, 1913.

Fred Herbert, 1912; New York Giants, 1915.

Artie Schwind, 1912; Boston Braves, 1912.

Erwin Renfer, 1912-13; Detroit Tigers, 1913.

Frank Shaughnessy, 1913-15; Washington Senators, 1905; Philadelphia Athletics, 1908.

Frank Smykal, 1913-15; Pittsburgh Pirates, 1916.

Jack (Johnny) Mitchell, 1914; New York Yankees, 1921-22; Boston Red Sox, 1922-23; Brooklyn Dodgers, 1924-25.

Rabbit Nill, 1914; Washington Senators, 1904-07; Cleveland Indians, 1907-08.

Herbie Shocker, 1914-15; New York Yankees 1916-17, 1925-28; St. Louis Browns, 1918-24.

Al Bashang, 1915; Detroit Tigers, 1912; Brooklyn Dodgers, 1918.

Fred Payne, 1915; Detroit Tigers, 1906-08; Chicago White Sox, 1909-11.

Frank Rooney, 1915; Indianapolis Hoosiers, 1914.

day after Mitchell's July 18 debut, Shocker unveiled his spitter in a Sunday game in Hull. He won, and pretty soon scouts from higher leagues were salivating over him. Thanks to the miracle of slippery elm, Shocker was on course to becoming the pitcher who won 187 games for the Yankees and the St. Louis Browns.[28]

With Mitchell and Shocker leading the way, the Senators went on a tear. On the August civic holiday they took two one-run, extra-inning games from Hamilton. The gap with London now stood at 4½. But excitement over the improved play of the Senators was run over the following day by the real-world news that Canada had joined Britain in declaring war on Germany. Despite the darkening skies in Europe the schedule proceeded without a hiccup, and the Senators kept on winning. Mitchell continued his hot hitting down the stretch, and Shocker dominated, winning four games in a single week in August.

On August 18 Ottawa beat Brantford 8-3 at Lansdowne to close within half a game of the Tecumsehs. For this game the players had a new obstacle to contend with—soldiers camped on the edges of the outfield. "Hits into volunteers went for two bases only," said one game report.[29] The war had become a ground rule.

With a week and a half to go, Ottawa traveled to London for a crucial series. After chasing the Tecumsehs for 57 days, the Senators took three of four games to finally overtake them. But it wasn't over yet.

LET'S PLAY THREE!

The battle again came down to the final day of the season. Following a remarkable 40-13 run the Senators, with a record of 75-45 (.625), claimed a precarious hold on first place. London, plagued by an inordinate number of rainouts, ties, and the absence of Sunday ball in Ontario, sat at 69-43 (.616), two games but only .009 percentage points behind. What happened next was one of the most bizarre pennant finishes ever, and it was decided as much by long division, meteorology, and subterfuge as baseball.

Both clubs were scheduled to play a pair at home on Labor Day, the Senators against sixth-place Peterborough, the Tecumsehs against fifth-place St. Thomas. A sweep would give Ottawa the pennant no matter what London did. But beyond that, especially with a cold, low-pressure system blanketing the province from Western Ontario to the national capital, things got very cloudy.

An Ottawa split and a London sweep, to consider one possibility, would hand the flag to Ottawa by the slimmest margin in baseball history, .6229 to .6228. On the other hand, a pair of Ottawa losses, coupled with a pair of London wins, would create a virtual tie atop the standings, but hand the pennant to the Tecumsehs on the basis of superior winning percentage, .623 to .615.

The picture got even hazier if the dodgy weather were to wipe out one or both games in either city. And even more so when London manager Doc Reisling hatched a plan to play *three* games against the Saints on Labor Day, the extra contest ostensibly a makeup for an earlier rainout.[30] A third game would provide Reisling with an extra piece in this most intricate of pennant endgames. If the Tecumsehs won three (.626) and the Senators were completely rained out (.625) or lost at least once (.624), London would squeak by.

In London the weather cleared in the morning, and the Tecumsehs beat the Saints 4-1 to move to within a game and a half of the leaders. In Ottawa the showers eased long enough for the Senators to take the field against the Whitecaps. But in the second inning the skies opened up and the tarps were rolled out again. Finally in the early afternoon the rain in the capital subsided. Shaughnessy, knowing he had to win at least one game to guarantee the pennant, sent his groundskeeper out for a 20-gallon can of gasoline. It was sloshed over the soggy infield, and someone tossed a match in to burn off some of the damp. When the smoke cleared the umpire gave the go-ahead, and Shaughnessy's prize discovery, Herbie Shocker, took the mound on one day's rest in search of his 20th win of the season. Shocker delivered, and the Senators won 6-2.

Now, with Ottawa's victory in Game One, three things would have to happen for London to prevail. The rain would have to hold off in both cities, the Tecumsehs would have to beat the Saints for a second and a third time, and Peterborough's ace, the ex-Phillie Louis Schettler (20-12), would have to shut down the Senators in Game Two in Ottawa. In the end all three conditions were met: no rain, London victories in Games Two and Three,

and Schettler's continued mastery of the Senators – and yet Doc Reisling's gambit failed.

What happened was this: After a couple of chilly and scoreless innings in Ottawa, Shaughnessy and Whitecaps manager Curley Blount persuaded the umpire to call the game on account of the cold. That snuffed any hopes of London catching the Senators.

"In view … of the fact that Frank Shaughnessy and his Senators have come from behind within four weeks and have overhauled London's ten game lead, no one will dispute them the honours," said the *Citizen*.[31] Well, not exactly no one. "Probably the Cold Was in Shaughnessy's Feet," said the *London Advertiser*. "Maybe it was too cold to play ball and maybe it wasn't, but, at any rate, it is a peculiar fact that the cold was not noticed until after the second game had been started."[32]

The *London Free Press* concurred, complaining about the appearance of "fix up baseball" in Ottawa. The cancellation of Game Two, they surmised, came only "upon the discovery of what a loss to Peterboro [sic] in the second game meant."[33] The *Advertiser* nonetheless paid Shaughnessy some grudging respect. "Shag is a foxy boy and if you want to win any pennants from him you have to sit up nights and dope out a fancy line of stunts to get ahead of him."[34]

Whether the cancellation of the second game was due to Shag's cunning or simply to a confluence of nasty weather and dumb luck is not known, although it is hard to imagine that the skipper wasn't fully aware of all the permutations and combinations on that day, and catching a telegraphic whiff of a third game in London, decided to quit while he was ahead.[35] Regardless, Shaughnessy and the jubilant Senators adjourned to a hotel to get warm and celebrate. The Shagmen, as the papers called them, had won 42 of their final 55 games to grab a third straight flag for Ottawa.

Shaughnessy himself had another strong season in 1914. In 119 games he batted .289 with 37 stolen bases and a team-leading six homers. But perhaps his most significant contribution to Ottawa's success was his indomitable personality. "The continued success of this shrewd Irishman smashes all idea of luck," said one baseball writer. "That commodity might land him a winner once, but when success is spoiled on success there is something in the man himself above ordinary."[36]

Baseball, on the other hand, did not have a good season. The editor of *Sporting Life* designated it "the universal wreck of the minor leagues."[37] Forty-three minor leagues started the year; 36 finished in some form or other. Organized Baseball, involved in a territorial war with the upstart Federal League, had spread itself perilously thin. Too many clubs made too little economic sense, especially in the second year of a North American economic recession.

Despite a nail-biter of a pennant race and a Canadian League monopoly on Sunday ball, attendance at Senators games reportedly took a 40 percent attendance hit over the final month of the season. The club reported a $2,700 loss. Shag's gamble on baseball in the capital was beginning to look a little less secure.

TO SHREDS

In 1910 there were 52 minor leagues in operation, the most in any year until after the Second World War. By the spring of 1915, the number was down to 32, only 23 of which staggered through the season. A no-frills, bargain-basement, six-team, Class-C Canadian League was one of them. So stripped down were the teams that star pitcher Herbie Shocker was assigned to prepare the diamond for the Senators' abbreviated spring training in Chatham.

Few, however, paid much attention to the petty compromises of baseball. In the spring of 1915 Canadians of ball playing age were being gassed at Ypres, and the government was contemplating conscription. On May 7, a German U-boat torpedoed the Cunard liner *Lusitania* off the coast of Ireland; 1,193 passengers and crew were killed, including 128 Americans.

The Senators, hobbled by injuries, got off to their usual sluggish start. By the King's Birthday holiday, June 4, they were mired in fifth place, and for the rest of the month they hovered around .500. But in July they took off. They played at a .705 clip for the rest of the way, leaving 1915 pretenders Hamilton and Guelph in the dust. The season played itself out without much excitement, the Senators eventually stretching their lead to 12½ games over the Maple Leafs of Guelph. "…Ottawa had the championship clinched so early this year that the enthusiasm fell to shreds," said the *Citizen*.[38] Attendance dropped by half.

A $750 draft fee from the New York Yankees for Herbie Shocker, who had tossed 303 innings and won 19 games, helped the club's bottom line. But the future of baseball in the capital—and the future of minor-league baseball itself—remained uncertain. Rumors and speculation swirled all fall and winter: Shag would manage Toronto in the International League. Or maybe a team in the upstart Federal League. The Senators would replace Richmond in the International. Or they would join the New York State League. Or maybe there would be another iteration of the Canadian League, which might or might not include Ottawa.

But even professional athletes were not above the European fray. A couple of Ottawa hockey players, including scoring star Harry "Punch" Broadbent, announced they were enlisting. Guelph Maple Leafs pitching ace Bobby Auld, a Toronto boy, announced he, too, would sign up.

FROZEN IN TIME

On Valentine's Day 1916, the Parliament Buildings burned down. It would serve as an apt metaphor for Ottawa baseball that season. In March, St. Thomas resigned from the Canadian League. The remaining clubs debated the wisdom of carrying on, but the discussion ended when a new battalion, the 207th, moved into Lansdowne Park in April. There was now no place for the perennial champion Senators to play. And with that, the team and the league suspended operations for 1916. It never resumed. The Senators' peerless record—four pennants in four seasons—remains frozen in time.

NOTES

1   The presumptuously named Canadian League operated only in Ontario.

2   "No Sunday Ball to Be Played Here in Canadian League," *Ottawa Citizen*, April 23, 1912: 8.

3   "Ottawa Ball Club Sign Up a Star Catcher," *Ottawa Journal*, March 2, 1912: 5.

4   *Ottawa Journal*, April 15, 1912: 1.

5   They were pitchers McManus (Cincinnati Reds, 1913); Fred Herbert (New York Giants, 1915); Erwin Renfer (Detroit Tigers, 1913); and shortstop Artie Schwind (Boston Braves, 1912).

6   "Rousing Reception Now Assured for Members of Ottawa Ball Club," *Ottawa Citizen*, May 9, 1912: 8.

7   Formerly the Berlin Green Sox. The city itself was rebranded Kitchener in the midst of World War I.

8   "Expect McManus to Recover Quickly," *Ottawa Journal*, July 26, 1912: 5.

9   The following spring, still feeling the lingering effects of his illness, McManus failed in his only big-league audition, with the Cincinnati Reds.

10 "Canadian League Pennant Comes To Ottawa," *Ottawa Citizen*. Aug. 19, 1912: 8.

11 "Watch the Race," *Ottawa Journal*, September 4, 1912: 4.

12 "Ottawa Baseball Team Disbands, Kind Words for Local Friends," *Ottawa Citizen*, September 4, 1912: 8.

13 "Ottawa Didn't Play Yesterday, All Games Off Because of Rain," *Ottawa Citizen*, August 20, 1912: 9.

14 Schwind's residency in Ottawa was short-lived. In 1913 he landed with San Antonio of the Texas League. He played the next four seasons in Texas.

15 "Ottawa and Brantford Teams Open Local Season Month from Today," *Ottawa Citizen*, April 15, 1913: 8. The Senators had lost three key players to higher classifications in the 1912 draft: Schwind (Boston Braves) and pitchers Fred Herbert and Frank Kubat (Toronto Maple Leafs).

16 Later that year Shaughnessy, as he had done when he played and managed in Roanoke, bought into an Ottawa automobile dealership.

17 "Great Pitching Duel Expected at Lansdowne Park Today," *Ottawa Citizen*, May 17, 1913: 8.

18 Renfer finished with 21 wins. He was drafted by the Detroit Tigers and joined them in the fall of 1913. After a four-week layoff, he started – and lost – a game against the Washington Senators. That was the extent of his major-league career.

19 Alan Metcalfe, *Canada Learns to Play: The Emergence of Organized Sport in Canada, 1807-1914* (Toronto: McClelland and Stewart, 1987).

20 Shocker was born Urbain Jacques Shockcor, in Cleveland, Ohio, in 1890.

21 "Toronto Broke Ottawa's Winning Streak in First Game of Canadian League Season, Bullock's Error Paved Way for Defeat," *Ottawa Citizen*, May 15, 1914: 8.

22 A Canadian Army regiment formed in 1914 and named for Princess Patricia, a granddaughter of Queen Victoria. It was the first Canadian infantry unit to serve in France in the First World War.

23 *Ottawa Citizen,* June 29, 1914: 12.

24 Reisling and Shaughnessy both played with Coatesville/Shamokin in the Tri-State League in 1905.

25 "Ottawas Have Chance to Make Fresh Start Against St. Thomas Team This Afternoon," *Ottawa Citizen,* July 16, 1914: 8.

26 Mitchell (born Kmieciak) went by the name Johnny Mitchell during a five-year major-league career, 1921-25.

27 "Champs. Caught London after Stern Chase of 57 Days," unattributed newspaper clipping, 1914. Courtesy Honora Shaughnessy.

28 Shocker would be the last legal spitballer on the Yankees after the pitch was outlawed in 1920.

29 "Ottawas Scored 8 Runs in Two Innings and Easily Disposed of Brantford," *Ottawa Citizen,* August 19, 1914: 8.

30 A triple header was not unprecedented. There had already been two at the major-league level. On September 1, 1890, the Brooklyn Bridegrooms beat the Pittsburgh Alleghenies three times on their way to the NL title. On September 7, 1896, the pennant-bound Baltimore Orioles swept a Labor Day triple header from the Louisville Colonels.

31 "Canadian Ball League Pennant Comes to Ottawa; Champions Downed Peterboro and Won Flag Again," *Ottawa Citizen,* September 8, 1914: 8.

32 "Probably the Cold Was in Shaughnessy's Feet," *London Advertiser,* September 8, 1914: 7.

33 "London Trounces Saints Three Times but Loses Pennant by Two-Point Margin to Ottawa," *London Free Press,* September 8, 1914: 6.

34 "Probably the Cold Was in Shaughnessy's Feet."

35 In any event Canadian League president J.P. Fitzgerald, citing an obscure Organized Baseball prohibition against playing more than two games on one day, subsequently ruled that the third game of Doc Reisling's tripleheader would not count in the standings. Thus the official final standings had Ottawa at 76-45 and London 1 1/2 games back, at 71-43. Despite the alleged prohibition, the Reds and Pirates played a tripleheader on October 2, 1920, that counted in the standings.

36 Unattributed clipping from summer 1915. Courtesy Honora Shaughnessy.

37 M.H. Sexton, "By the Editor of 'Sporting Life'," *Sporting Life,* December 12, 1914: 13.

38 "Hard to Prove Ottawa Broke Limits," *Ottawa Citizen,* September 22, 1915: 9.

"BIG, BOW-LEGGED AND DOMINEERING": FRANK SHAUGHNESSY IN OTTAWA

BY DAVID MCDONALD

IN A MULTISPORT CAREER THAT spanned more than half a century, he was a player, a coach, a manager, an owner, and an executive. And with four pennants in four years at the helm of the Canadian League Senators, "the big, bowlegged and domineering pilot of the Ottawas"[1] was almost certainly the preeminent character in local baseball history, and perhaps even, as long-time Montreal sportswriter Tim Burke asserted, "one of the most extraordinary figures in the history of sport."[2]

NOTRE DAME

Francis Joseph Shaughnessy was born in 1883 in Amboy, Illinois, the seventh child of parents from Limerick, Ireland. His father, Patrick, emigrated to Canada as a boy. But after an unsuccessful attempt at farming near Montreal, Patrick, now 25, moved to the United States and spent the next 35 years with the Illinois Central Railroad. Two of his sons, William and John, also worked for the Illinois Central. Youngest son Frank was determined not to.

Smart, ambitious, and perpetually in motion, Shaughnessy worked in a pharmacy while attending high school. "I got up at six to open the drug store at seven, then ran three or four miles to school," he recalled. "At noon I hurried back to the store to give the boss time for lunch, got my lunch at home about two blocks away, and dashed back to school. When school let out, I ran again to be at the store by 4 P.M. I got a half-hour off for supper, and, at 10 P.M., I could walk home. It's no wonder I always could run fast—I had to!"[3]

Young Frank could also hit a baseball, and it earned him a partial scholarship to study pharmacy at Indiana's Notre Dame College, then little more than "a farm, and the nuns made our meals and washed our clothes."[4] "Shag," as he was called, also excelled at track, and especially at football.[5] In 1904, his final season at Notre Dame, he captained the Fighting Irish.[6]

"It seems like I can't remember a time when I wasn't working hard," he said in later years. "While at Notre Dame, I also ran the campus newspaper, a confectionery concession and was the correspondent for several Chicago newspapers."[7]

Using the *nom de guerre* "Shannon" to protect his collegiate athletic eligibility, Shag spent his summers playing professional baseball in outposts like Sioux City, Iowa, and Cairo, Illinois. In the spring of 1904 he finished his pharmacy degree and immediately began working toward another in law. But neither potions nor motions held much appeal for the restless Shaughnessy—"Indoors irks this man," as *Maclean's* magazine once said.[8] So in the fall of 1904, right after football season, he signed with the Washington Senators of the American League.

NO FIXED ADDRESS

Shaughnessy's 1905 season was a crash course in the vicissitudes of Deadball-Era baseball. On April 17, a week and a half past his 22nd birthday, the lanky, copper-haired outfielder had his first sip of big-league coffee, playing right field for the Senators in a game against the Highlanders of New York. He went 0-for-3, with a hit-by-pitch.

"It wasn't easy in those days, believe me," Shaughnessy said. "Regulars would actually chase a rookie with a bat if he attempted to take a turn hitting. A regular held his job until somebody drove him out, and every youngster was regarded as a menace."[9]

Shag got into another game four days later and hit a bases-loaded triple off future Hall of Famer Jack Chesbro. But the game—and Shag's first major-league hit—were washed out before becoming official. The very next day Washington shipped him out, to the Montgomery Senators of the Southern Association.

Shaughnessy hated Alabama—the heat, the mosquitoes, the very real prospect of contracting yellow fever. He dropped 20 pounds, played poorly, and after seven games he was released, whereupon he packed his glove and spikes and headed north to Pennsylvania to play for Coatesville of the "outlaw"[10] Tri-State League. After a few games there he ventured even further north, to join the Montpelier-Barre Intercities, a.k.a. Hyphens, of the even more outlaw Northern League,[11] a colorful but financially shaky circuit operating in Vermont and northern New York.

It was already Shag's fourth club of the year, and it was only June. Life had become a blur of steam trains, cheap hotels, and precarious employment. His halcyon days as big man on campus were long behind him. Now the only constant was the nagging worry that the next paycheck might not clear, that one's current club—or even the whole league it was part of—might not survive the season, that the opportunities to forge a career in the snakes-and-ladders, musical-chairs world of Deadball Era baseball might simply dry up.

HELLO KITTY

The Northern turned out to be the most eventful stop on Shaughnessy's baseball odyssey. It was during this time he attended some sort of Roman Catholic function in Ogdensburg, New York, where he was introduced to a young woman named Katherine Quinn, called Kitty, the convent-educated daughter of an Ottawa hotelier, Michael Quinn.[12]

That brief encounter might go a long way to explaining Shaughnessy's decision to sign a $140-a-month contract to play for Ottawa, an expansion franchise in the re-jigged Northern League,[13] in 1906. Once again the quality of play was surprisingly fast.[14] Shag acquitted himself well, finishing with a .297 batting average and a league-leading five homers. He also proved a fan favorite. "Shaughnessy is the idol of the small boy and incidentally the ladies also," said the *Ottawa Journal.* "His appearance at bat is always the signal for an outburst of applause and kindly advice to slam it over the fence again or to murder the umpire when he calls a strike."[15]

Despite its blaze of talent the cross-border Northern League proved no more durable than its 1905 iteration. The Ottawa club folded on August 20, and Shaughnessy and several others had to sue to try to collect their final pay.

While the league withered around him, Frank's romance with Kitty blossomed. But with several weeks of summer left and a few more dollars to be had, he reluctantly hopped a train back to Indiana, where he joined the South Bend Greens of the Class-B Central League. There he was said to have hit "the ball like a fiend,"[16] batting .333 in 18 games.

That fall—it was still an era of distinct sporting seasons—Shaughnessy launched a second career, coaching football at Clemson Agricultural College in South Carolina. The following summer he played left field for the San Francisco Seals of the Pacific Coast League. Frank and Kitty exchanged a lot of letters in those years.

In 1908 Shag returned to Washington to join the D.C. entry in a wannabe third major circuit, the Union League. Sportswriters soon branded it the Onion League, "because it was cheap and smelled bad."[17] The loop lasted two months before landing on baseball's compost heap. Shaughnessy though landed on his feet—Connie Mack immediately signed him to play for his Philadelphia Athletics in the American League.

This time Shag's big-league dream lasted all of two weeks. "I thought I had a good chance with the A's," he recalled years later. "I was hitting .321[18] after eight games and feeling pretty proud of myself. Then one cold day in Chicago, I had to make a hard throw to the plate and something snapped in my arm. I couldn't throw overhanded for a year...."[19]

Mack promptly shipped Shag and his wounded wing off to Reading, Pennsylvania, of the Class-B Tri-State League, in exchange for a player to be named later. The player turned out to be a young third baseman named Frank "Home Run" Baker, who went on to a Hall of Fame career. "That was a pretty good deal for the Athletics, I would say," said Shag, adding, in faux self-deprecating style, "I guess I wasn't much of a player."[20]

That fall 25-year-old Frank Shaughnessy, vagabond baseball player and football coach, married 20-year-old Kitty Quinn at St. Brigid's, the English-language Roman Catholic church serving Ottawa's Lower Town.

KLAN COUNTRY

In 1909 Shaughnessy bought his release from Reading so that he could take a job playing for—and, for the first time in his baseball career, managing—the Roanoke Tigers, a.k.a. Highlanders, of the Class-C Virginia League. At 26 he was reportedly the youngest manager in Organized Baseball. It was an auspicious debut. Shag batted .285 with a league-leading five home runs and guided his team to the pennant. In a cliff-hanger of a finish—which would become something of a Shaughnessy managerial trademark—the Tigers nipped the Norfolk Tars by half a game and .003 percentage points.

Roanoke was also an opportunity for the indefatigable Shaughnessy to try his hand at a number of business sidelines. He bought into a couple of cigar stores, a garage, and one of the first automobile dealerships in the country.[21] He also found time to pass the Virginia bar exam and hang out a shingle, although, according to legendary Montreal sportswriter Dink Carroll, Shag lacked the patience to build up a practice.

On the surface Roanoke appeared a good fit for the Shaughnessys, and the prospect of putting down roots must have seemed appealing, especially with the arrival of their first two boys. (The brood would eventually number nine—eight boys and one girl.) But Kitty missed her family in Ottawa, and, equally, as a devout Roman Catholic, never felt entirely comfortable in the Protestant South. The anti-Catholic KKK was between waves of terror at this time, but Virginia was still the heart of Klan country.

A CAPITAL IDEA

So Shag began to formulate a plan, one that would accommodate both his wife's desire to raise a family in a more hospitable environment and his own to assert some measure of control over a chronically precarious baseball career. After the 1911 season the Shaughnessys packed their bags, bundled up their babies, and boarded a northbound train, destination Ottawa.

Despite the failure of the Northern League, Shaughnessy had long felt the city was ripe for baseball. "Well, this always

A true Ottawa baseball legend, Frank Shaughnessy's impact on the Senators is undeniable. Credit: Courtesy Honora Shaughnessy.

looked like one good ball town to me, and I am surprised you haven't entered some league before this," he said during a 1910 visit.[22] He decided he would be the one to remedy that.

Shag had been keeping an eye on the fortunes of the Canadian League, a Class-D loop operating in Western Ontario, with teams in London, Hamilton, Brantford, St. Thomas, Guelph, and Berlin.[23] The Canadian had just completed a moderately successful first season, and Shag was confident an Ottawa team could make a go of it in such company. He sought out a couple of prospective partners—Tommy Gorman, the 25-year-old Olympic lacrosse gold medalist turned "sporting editor" of the *Ottawa Citizen,* and Malcolm Brice, 36, sporting editor of the *Ottawa Free Press*—to put together a franchise bid. Publicity for the venture was not going to be a problem.

Nor was money. A good chunk of the financial backing for the team came from Frank Ahearn,[24] son of wealthy inventor and entrepreneur Thomas "Electricity" Ahearn, known as "the Edison of Canada." The senior Ahearn was the principal owner of the Ottawa Electric Railway Company—game-day transportation would not be an issue either.

RAILROADED

In December 1911 the Canadian League awarded a franchise to the Ottawa Baseball Club, dubbed the Senators, and Shaughnessy spent the winter preparing for his club's inaugural season. But then came the revelation that Shag was something of a baseball bigamist, having previously signed a contract to play for and manage the Fort Wayne Railroaders of the Class-B Central League. He might have gambled on Fort Wayne owner Claude H. Varnell not standing in the way of his new Ottawa venture, but Varnell made it abundantly clear he had no intention of divorcing his two-timing manager. "Shaughnessey [sic] will manage the Fort Wayne team unless he dies or gives up baseball," he announced.[25] Shag reluctantly said goodbye to his family in Ottawa and left for Indiana.

Shaughnessy was determined to make the best of his exile in Indiana by adroitly managing both sides of his divided loyalties. Without kiboshing Fort Wayne's chances in the Central, he funneled a handful of surplus Railroaders north to round out the Ottawa roster. Without this injection of talent, it's safe to say the Senators would not have challenged for the Canadian League pennant in their first year.

Shag's juggling act worked out pretty well for both teams. The Senators cruised to the Canadian League title, nine games ahead of second-place Brantford Red Sox. The Railroaders, a last-place club as late as July 1, eventually clipped the Youngstown Steelmen by 2½ games for the Central League flag. Shag batted .304 and stole 34 bases.

When it was all over, Kitty back in Ottawa received this terse telegram from Indiana: "Ft Wayne won the pennant. Had a hard battle we play Cleveland Wednesday at Ft Wayne expect to get home Friday phone Brice about pennant. Frank."[26] The two-timing Shaughnessy had somehow parlayed his divided loyalties into two pennants in two countries in a single season.

After the season he touched down in Ottawa just long enough to pack his whistle and report to McGill University in Montreal, where he became the first professional coach at a Canadian school. "I worked hard because I liked it," he said, "and if I needed a better reason, I had a big family and had something of a grocery bill every week."[27] It was a move that led to his third sporting championship of the year – a Yates Cup[28] win for his Redmen over the University of Toronto. Shag went on to coach McGill football for 19 seasons, during which time he helped define and refine the Canadian game.[29]

ICEMAN

Now Shaughnessy needed something to bridge the icy gap between football and baseball seasons. He accepted a job to coach and manage Frank Ahearn's Ottawa Stewartons senior amateur hockey club in the Interprovincial Union. "I told them I didn't know anything about the game and, in fact, hadn't even seen hockey, aside from kids playing in the neighborhood rinks," said Shaughnessy. "They insisted I knew how to handle men and organize sports, and that's what they were interested in...."[30] It was here, unsurprisingly, that Shag's string of sporting championships came to an abrupt end.

The experience, however, launched a third career for Shaughnessy. The following winter he debuted as "business manager"[31] of the other Ottawa Senators, those of the National Hockey Association (NHA), the forerunner of the NHL.[32] That spring Shag came close to adding the Stanley Cup to his rapidly expanding championship résumé, but the NHA-champion Senators dropped the final to the Pacific Coast Hockey League Vancouver Millionaires.

A BRAND NEW SUIT

Shaughnessy might have continued his cross-border juggling act in 1913. He actually liked Fort Wayne, and he really liked the idea of owning a club in one league while pulling in a salary in another. But Kitty wanted him home, and this time owner Varnell agreed to his release.[33]

On Thursday, May 16, much of the federal government shut down at 1 P.M. so civil servants could get out to the ballpark in time to witness Frank Shaughnessy's long-awaited playing debut as a Senator. A Sparks Street tailor, A.J. Curry, announced he would present a new $30 suit to the first Senator to hit a home run at Lansdowne Park. It seemed like a pretty generous offer, until you consider the Ottawas had failed to hit a single homer at home during their first season. Said one writer: "Any man to get credit for a four play wallop at the local ball yard (has) to sock the ball a quarter of a mile, more or less, and complete the circuit at a Ty Cobb clip"[34]—which is exactly what Shaughnessy did in his first game back in his adopted city since the demise of the old Northern League in 1906.

As Shag stepped to the plate in the fourth inning, the game was halted as a local MP presented him with a floral horseshoe wishing the team "Good Luck 1913." After the interruption the pumped-up skipper drove the first pitch he saw over the head of the Brantford right fielder. The ball bounded up a slope and skipped toward the cattle barns near the Rideau Canal. Shag scored standing up. He finished the day with the Senators' first-ever home-field homer, a single, a double, and a brand-new suit.

Shaughnessy's debut was a harbinger of what was to come in his three seasons as the star center fielder and fiery field boss of the perennial champion Senators. Wherever he went, whatever he did, whatever he said, the spotlight was always on Shag, with his out-sized physical presence[35] and his perceived Simon Legree management style—"more like McGraw's than Mack's," as one baseball writer put it.[36] He was said to hand his men a raise one minute and a "blue envelope" (i.e., a pink slip) the next.[37]

"Shaughnessy's methods are unpopular at times with the fans and with his players," the London Advertiser conceded in the aftermath of Ottawa's third straight pennant in 1914, "but he gets results...."[38] The respect was sometimes grudging but it was always genuine. "All credit must be given to Shag," said the rival London Free Press, "for he not only drives his players, never overlooks an opening, but he makes mediocre performers live wires." [39]

"The continued success of this shrewd Irishman smashes all idea of luck," said another baseball writer, as the Senators captured a fourth-straight flag, in 1915. "That commodity might land him a winner once, but when success is spoiled on success there is something in the man himself above ordinary."[40]

The Senators' victory in 1915 gave Shaughnessy a hand in six pennants in three leagues in only seven years of managing.

Now, after finally experiencing some years of stability, Shag's baseball future—and the future of the Senators—remained uncertain. The War in Europe had upended everything. Rumors swirled all fall and winter. When the Canadian League failed to take the field for the 1916 season, for Shaughnessy it was back to the uncertainties of life as a minor-league gun-for-hire. He was forced to accept a last-minute offer to manage the Warren (Pennsylvania) Warriors of the Class-D Interstate League.

With a population distracted by preparations for the war in Europe and by an actual war with Mexico, attendance in the Interstate was down by half. On August 3 Warren, some $800 in debt and owing players two weeks' salary, became the second of three Interstate clubs to fold in less than a month. The Wellsville Reporter speculated that Shaughnessy would return to Canada to raise a company of athletes to fight in the war. Instead Shag signed with the first-place Bradford Drillers, but as a player only. A few weeks later he moved over to the also-ran Wellsville Rainmakers, as player and manager. In an unsettled, no-fixed-address sort of season, Shag recorded a .301 batting average and stole 19 bases in 76 games. But for the first time since 1912, he failed to win a pennant.

SIBERIA

For Shaughnessy fall meant football. But with collegiate ball on hold for the year due to the War, the autumn of 1916 found him coaching the 207th Battalion team to the championship of the military's Overseas Football League. He also continued as business manager of the hockey Senators, even swinging a deal to pry future Hockey Hall of Famer Cy Denneny away from Toronto. But in November Shaughnessy, now 33 and the father of four boys, decided to enlist. It was what most of the Ottawa athletic community had already done. "Before the current call is exhausted ... the Capital will be without ninety per cent of its leading athletes, and unless the war ends shortly, it will be difficult for the various local clubs to carry on successfully," said the Citizen."[41]

On his Officer's Declaration form Shaughnessy gave his profession as "attorney and athletic director."[42] His medical sheet lists him at 6-feet-1½ inches and 195 pounds, with "excellent physical development."[43] Said the Citizen: "Frank has worn baseball and football togs for so many years that he had no difficulty in adapting himself to the King's uniform."[44]

At first, Shaughnessy's military career wasn't much different from his civilian one. He coached and played baseball, coached football and even coached hockey. ("... Frank's advice is invariably brief, but to the point, viz: 'Get the goals and then lay back on the defense.'"[45]) But Shaughnessy's real value to the military was his wide web of contacts in the sporting world. After all, who better to beat the Hun than an army of elite athletes?

Shag was placed in charge of Ottawa recruiting for the 207th Battalion, and in typical Shag style soon out-recruited his fellow recruiters. "In his short-term as re-inforcing officer, Lieut. Shaughnessy established a record for recruiting as he secured over a hundred men."[46]

Shag spent the early summer of 1918 in familiar surroundings. His battery was quartered at Lansdowne Park, a fairly short walk from his home on Powell Ave. in Ottawa's Glebe neighborhood. Summer evenings his men played baseball.

In September Shaughnessy transferred to the Ammunition Column, 35th Battery, Canadian Expeditionary Force (Siberia). The big show in Europe had only a few weeks left to run, but Canada was still involved in—and in command of—a confused and half-hearted Allied campaign to support the White Russian Army against the Bolsheviks in Russia's Far East. Shag had experienced any number of baseball Siberias, but never before the real thing. And now, at the peak of the Spanish flu pandemic, he found himself in New Westminster, British Columbia, preparing to embark on a slow boat to Vladivostok.

On November 28, 17 days after the war ended on the Western Front, Shag and his mates sailed from Vancouver on the "remount ship" S.S. War Charger. They carried a load of 16- and 18-pound artillery shells and some 500-600 horses. "I think they picked me because I was as big as a horse," Shag said.[47] The Charger wallowed 500 miles in 23 days until, in danger of running out of coal, it was ordered to turn back. "The funniest thing that happened to me was that I was sentenced to Siberia—and never got there," said Shag.[48] On January 21, 1919, Lieut. Frank Shaughnessy left the army by "reason of General Demobilization"[49] and returned home to Ottawa.

A BRISK NORTH WIND

Shaughnessy resumed his McGill position, which had expanded to include responsibility for all outdoor sports. But, as always, he needed a baseball gig to see him through the summer. Shag pursued a number of leads, including the possible formation of a new all-Canadian circuit, featuring Ottawa and Montreal, along with the Canadian entries from the Michigan-Ontario League. "If the new league is formed, I will take either the Montreal or Ottawa franchises, or at least will take a financial interest in them. . . ," he said. "There is no doubt in my mind that an all-Canadian league would be a howling success."[50] But there were serious doubts in other minds, and the league Shag envisioned failed to get off the ground.

Reluctantly Shag accepted an offer to play for and manage the Hamilton Tigers of the Class-B Michigan-Ontario League. Now 36 and returning after a two-season layoff, he nonetheless put up one of the best offensive seasons, batting .313 with a .412 on-base percentage in 109 games. His Tigers, featuring several former Senators, finished a close second, behind the Saginaw Aces.

Shaughnessy appeared to be wearying of his baseball life. "Managing a baseball team is far from being what it may seem to the average fan in the bleachers," he told the *Citizen*. "The player who has nothing to do but play his position each game, and whose worries end with the game each day, has an easy time; but the manager has just as many worries off the field as on. I will make a desperate effort to win the pennant this year, but win or lose I am not going to attempt to fill the role of manager any more."[51]

And yet in 1920 he returned to Hamilton. His team again finished second, this time 14½ games behind the runaway London Tecumsehs. But it was the same old fiery Frank. In late May he was arrested for getting into a fight in game in Flint. His offensive production, however, declined dramatically—a .262 batting average with 16 stolen bases in 93 games. It was his swan song as a regular or semi-regular player.[52]

BYE-BYE BYTOWN

During the 1920-21 offseason Shaughnessy teamed with Canadian baseball legend Knotty Lee in another attempt to bring high-level baseball back to either Ottawa or Montreal. But in the end the Shaughnessy-Lee duo failed to make a business case for either city. In 1921, after a decade in Ottawa, the Shaughnessys decamped with their seven boys to Montreal, with the half-baked idea of Frank selling insurance to supplement his McGill income. The Shaughnessy era in Ottawa was over.

But, as *The Sporting News* noted, "every time Shag decided to 'settle down,' baseball sounded a recall."[53] And so at midseason in 1921 Shaughnessy took over as manager of the chronically second-division Syracuse Stars of the International League. The Syracuse gig marked the beginning of a 40-year relationship with the International. By 1936 he was president of the league, and for the next 24 years he served as a passionate defender of the interests of minor-league baseball. Said the *New York Times*: "He's as big as all outdoors and as hearty as a brisk north wind."[54]

His "Shaughnessy playoff system"[55] is often credited with saving minor-league ball during the Depression. In 1946 he presided over the re-integration of the International League. Said Shag of Jackie Robinson: "He's the best player in minor league ball. He's also the smartest."[56]

Kitty Shaughnessy, whose homesickness led to the creation of the Ottawa Senators, died in 1958 in Montreal, a week after the Shaughnessy's 50th wedding anniversary. Shag finally retired at the age of 77, in 1960. He died on May 15, 1969, at the age of 86. He was among the first inductees to the Canadian Baseball Hall of Fame, in 1983.

"I remember him as kind and big and gruff," his granddaughter Honora Shaughnessy recounted. "He would always have a TV and one or two portable radios going at the same time, listening to various games. I remember my father always called him 'Sir.'"[57]

EDITOR'S NOTE

This profile is based on a similar version by the same author that appeared in the 2022 SABR book *Our Game, Too: Influential Figures and Milestones in Canadian Baseball*. https://sabr.org/latest/sabr-digital-library-our-game-too-influential-figures-and-milestones-in-canadian-baseball/

For a deeper dive into Frank Shaughnessy's career, please refer to Charlie Bevis' profile on the SABR website: https://sabr.org/bioproj/person/frank-shag-shaughnessy/

NOTES

1   "Shag" Deserves Credit," *Hamilton Herald*, August 29, 1914: 9.

2   Tim Burke, "Shaughnessy Clan Full of Rich History," *Montreal Gazette*, June 15, 1982: B-5.

3   Joe King and Cy Kritzer, "Diamond Ace, Gridiron Star and Executive," *The Sporting News*, December 14, 1960: 10.

4   "The Man Has Better Things to Do Than Talk About Himself," unattributed 1968 newspaper clipping. Courtesy Honora Shaughnessy.

5   After two previous Shaughnessys who attended Notre Dame, both nicknamed "Shag."

6   Shaughnessy was the starting right end on the undefeated 1903 team that outscored its opponents 291-0 over nine games.

7   David Pietrusza, *Minor Miracles: The Legend and Lure of Minor League Baseball* (Lanham, Maryland: Taylor Trade Publishing, 1995), 119.

8   Frederick Edwards, "Old-Fashioned Father," *Maclean's*, October 1, 1934: 15.

9   King and Kritzer, 16.

10   An "outlaw," or independent, league is one that is not part of the National Agreement and therefore beyond the jurisdiction of Organized Baseball.

11 Officially, the Northern New York League. Not to be confused with the Northern League operating in the same period in Manitoba, Minnesota, and North Dakota.

12 Quinn was the proprietor of Revere House, 475-479 Sussex Drive, Ottawa, until selling out in 1912.

13 Officially the Northern Independent League in 1906.

14 Rival Rutland, for example, boasted future Hall of Fame second baseman Eddie Collins and right-hander Dick Rudolph, a 26-game winner for the Boston Braves in 1914.

15 "Notes of Sport," *Ottawa Journal,* July 13, 1906: 2.

16 "Greens Take One of the Doubleheader," *Wheeling News Register,* September 2, 1906: 6.

17 Jerry Kuntz, *Baseball Fiends and Flying Machines: The Many Lives and Outrageous Times of George and Alfred Lawson* (Jefferson, North Carolina: McFarland Publishing, 2009), 126.

18 It was actually .310 — on a team with a .223 batting average.

19 Pietrusza, 120.

20 Pietrusza, 120.

21 The dealership sold – or at least attempted to sell – the Virginian, a short-lived make built in Richmond.

22 "'Home Run' Shaughnessy Pays Ottawa a Visit," unattributed 1910 newspaper clipping. Courtesy Honora Shaughnessy.

23 Re-named Kitchener in the midst of World War I.

24 Ahearn became part-owner of the hockey Senators, 1920-1934. He was selected to the Hockey Hall of Fame as a builder in 1962.

25 "News Notes," *Sporting Life,* February 24, 1912: 15.

26 Telegram from Frank to Kitty Shaughnessy, September 2, 1912. Courtesy Honora Shaughnessy.

27 Joe King and Cy Kritzer, "Shag, as a Farm Manager, Polished Rickey's Kid Stars," *The Sporting News,* December 14, 1960: 26.

28 The oldest active football trophy in North America, first awarded in 1898.

29 "It was largely through his campaigning that the Canadian game adopted the forward pass, 12-man teams and the direct snap from center. …" (Marven Moss, "Frank 'Shag' Shaughnessy Is Still Rolling in High Gear Despite His Age, Leading Battle for Minor Clubs," *Sherbrooke Daily Record,* January 11, 1958: 8.) "He is credited with having more to do with changing Canadian football, by introduction of American football tactics, than any other man." (King and Kritzer, "Diamond Ace, Gridiron Star and Executive.")

30 King and Kritzer, "Diamond Ace, Gridiron Star and Executive."

31 Equivalent to today's general manager position in hockey.

32 The Senators joined the NHL when it began play in 1917-18.

33 Hardly an act of charity, it cost Shaughnessy $750.

34 "Ottawa and Brantford Teams Open Local Season Month from Today," *Ottawa Citizen,* April 24, 1913: 8.

35 Shaughnessy is usually listed at 6-1 1/2, 185 lbs.

36 "Shaughnessy May Become Big League Manager," *Ottawa Citizen,* August 12, 1915: 8.

37 "Shag" Deserves Credit," *Hamilton Herald,* August 29, 1914: 9.

38 Bert Perry, "Looks Like Fourth Straight Pennant for Ottawa Club," *London Advertiser,* August 4, 1915: 8.

39 Bill Rhodes, *London Free Press,* undated 1915 clipping. Courtesy Honora Shaughnessy.

40 Unattributed clipping from summer 1915. Courtesy Honora Shaughnessy.

41 "Many More Ottawa Athletes Called in First Draft under New Military Service Law," *Ottawa Citizen,* May 6, 1918: 8.

42 Officers' Declaration Paper, Canadian Over-Seas Expeditionary Force, December 22, 1916.

43 Medical History Sheet, February 17, 1917.

44 "Shag in New Role," *Ottawa Citizen,* December 21, 1916: 8.

45 "Shag in New Role."

46 "Ottawa Athletes to Kingston School," *Ottawa Citizen,* January 15, 1917: 8.

47 John Kieran, "Under Two Flags," *New York Times,* January 23, 1941: 27.

48 Kieran, "Under Two Flags."

49 Canadian Expeditionary Force Certificate of Service, March 4, 1920.

50 "Shaughnessy Is Planning for New Baseball League," *Ottawa Citizen,* August 4, 1919: 8.

51 "Shaughnessy Is Planning for New Baseball League."

52 Shag's last professional at bat came at age 41, with an unsuccessful pinch-hit appearance for the Shaughnessy-managed Syracuse Stars, of the International League.

53 King and Kritzer, "Shag, as a Farm Manager, Polished Rickey's Kid Stars," *The Sporting News,* December 14, 1960: 26.

54 Kieran, "Under Two Flags."

55 A format for determining the champion of a one-division sports league, in which the top four teams in the standings battle it out in post-season competition.

56 Sam Blackman, Tim Bourret, and Dabo Swinney, *If These Walls Could Talk: Stories from the Clemson Tigers Sideline, Locker Room, and Press Box* (Chicago: Triumph Books, 2016), 56.

57 Honora Shaughnessy, telephone interview with author, August 6, 2002.

OTTAWA IN THE 1922-23 EASTERN CANADA LEAGUE AND THE 1924 QUEBEC-ONTARIO-VERMONT LEAGUE

BY CHRISTIAN TRUDEAU

FOLLOWING THE DEMISE OF THE Canadian League after the 1915 season and departure of the Montreal Royals of the International League in 1917, baseball promoter Joe Page dreamt of a baseball league that would cover Quebec, Ontario and even further west.[1] That the Canadian Pacific company, his employer, would provide transportation for these teams probably played a part in his plans.[2]

After many failed attempts, the Eastern Canada League was created in 1922. While it did include teams in the two provinces, the initial league was modest in scope: to the Quebec teams in Montreal, Valleyfield, and Trois-Rivières was added a single team in Ontario - Ottawa. Still, the addition of the federal capital was seen as a stepping stone to the future addition of teams further west.

The Ottawa Senators played their first season at Lansdowne Park, initially managed by Dick Dawson. After a slow start, the team had a successful season on the field, battling until the end and finishing 2 1/2 games behind first-place Trois-Rivières. Key to the turnaround was a gutsy 14-inning complete game by young pitcher Fred Frankhouse on May 24 against Trois-Rivières.[3] Frankhouse, who on his way to 106 wins in a 13-year career in the majors, won 18 games for Senators, and even hit .284 in part-time duty in the outfield. The change of fortune was also due to a string of acquisitions, including semipro slugger Paddy Hogan (.326 average in 36 games) and George Underhill from Trois-Rivières (.300 with 10 home runs in 107 games between the two teams). Hogan took up the manager role from Dawson in June, before leaving the team to report for duty in the US army.[4] Catcher George Army finished the season as the manager.[5] Another highlight of the season was the no-hitter thrown by Red Parkes on July 25.[6] Parkes would win 40 games over his three seasons with the team.

After a relatively successful first season, Joe Page offered to merge his league with the Michigan-Ontario League.[7] But not only was his offer rejected, he was in for a surprise when Ottawa officials granted exclusive use of Lansdowne Park to amateurs. Page was said to have jumped in a train to Ottawa and stormed city hall, where a tumultuous meeting took place. He was unable to change their minds.[8] With no time to secure a field on such short notice, it was decided that the Ottawa club would play its games in Montreal.[9] While still listed as Ottawa in the Spalding Guide and other official documentation (including Baseball-Reference to this day in 2024), the team, now known as the Canadians, would only play one regular-season game in Ottawa (another was rained out).[10]

The Canadians joined the Royals in Montreal, with Trois-Rivières returning, and Quebec City replacing Valleyfield. The Canadians won the first-half pennant, and when a best-of-15 championship series was organized against the second-half champions Royals, the first two games were scheduled for Ottawa. The two teams split the games played on September 5 and 6. The first game attracted 1,000 spectators, with a smaller audience witnessing the second.[11]

Having failed to expand west, Page went south in 1924, adding two teams in Vermont: Rutland and Montpelier. He also did manage to get some time in Lansdowne Park for the Ottawa team, who also played on Sundays across the river in Dupuis Park in Hull (now Gatineau), Québec. Adding to the confusion, this was the same franchise as the 1922 Ottawa Senators and 1923 Canadians (who played in Montreal), while a new franchise, the Montreal Canadiens, replaced Trois-Rivières. The newly minted Canadiens were owned by Léo Dandurand, also the owner of the NHL team of the same name.[12] The league, now expanded to six teams, was rebranded as the Quebec-Ontario-Vermont League.

Former major leaguer Jean Dubuc, who had been a part owner of the team in 1923 while pitching for Syracuse in the International League, moved as player-manager of the newly named Ottawa-Hull Senators for 1924.[13]

Expectations were high, with the core of the 1923 finalist team almost intact, but as the team played around .500 ball, the wheels fell off as Dubuc suspended star slugger Frank Delisle in late June. Delisle, who hit a combined 40 home runs in 1922-23, was hitting well but was accused of indifferent play in the outfield and breaking team training rules.[14] The team finished the first half in third place with a 26-25 record, a distant seven games behind Quebec City.

With the expanded travel, most teams were struggling financially, and the two Vermont teams dropped out after the first half. Ottawa-Hull, cutting its losses, sold many of its best players during the second half, notably Delisle, back after 15 games of suspension, to the Canadians. Frank Jacobs (.338 average) and NHL player Jess Spring were also sold to the same team. The Senators finished in last place in the second half with a 20-30 record.

The lackluster play of the Senators gave ammunition to those who were opposed to the decision to bring back the professionals to Ottawa. For the second season in a row, their use of Lansdowne Park was contested, as with the upcoming annual fair, the team was warned that it would lose Lansdowne Park after September 1. This led the league to cut short its season, with Quebec City the runaway winner anyway.[15] The *Ottawa Citizen* had already cut bait with the team, ending its coverage after an August 10 ugly incident on the field, in which players yelled obscenities at the home-plate umpire.[16]

At the end of the season, all teams except Quebec City were in the red.[17] The next spring, the project was still in limbo in April, but when Ottawa did not even send a representative to a meeting in Montreal, it was evident that the league was dead.[18] Given its tumultuous experience in the league, it is no surprise that Ottawa was without professional baseball until 1936, when it joined the Canadian-American League.

SOURCES

Baseball-Reference.com was the main reference for standings and list of players, as well as the list of players constructed by the author from newspapers accounts. Many Quebec newspapers (as well as *Le Droit*, from Ottawa) were consulted (available on the website of the *Bibliothèque et Archives Nationales du Québec*).

NOTES

1   "Canadian Nat'l Baseball League," *Quebec Chronicle*, January 27, 1922: 6.

2   Patrick Carpentier, "Joe Page," SABR BioProject, accessed July 20, 2024.

3   Gary Belleville, "May 24, 1922: Ottawa Senators' Fred Frankhouse tosses 14-inning complete-game win over Trois-Rivières," SABR Games Project, accessed July 20, 2024.

4   "Senators by 7-5 Beat Three Rivers," *Ottawa Citizen*, June 20, 1922: 11

5   "Senator Pilot Will Be Out for Few Days," *Ottawa Citizen*, August 29, 1922: 11.

6   "Parkes Credited With No-Hit Game," *Montreal Gazette*, July 26, 1922: 12.

7   "M.-O. League Magnates In Session Today To Discuss Plans for 1923," *Hamilton Spectator*, January 4, 1923: 16.

8   "Joe Page Bangs Bombs at Council," *Ottawa Journal*, March 1, 1923: 17.

9   "Continuous Ball for Montreal," *Quebec Chronicle*, March 26, 1923: 3.

10   "Canucks Beat Trios Pro Baseball Game," *Ottawa Citizen*, August 18, 1923: 10.

11   "Canadians Even Count In Eastern Canada Playoff," *Ottawa Citizen*, September 7, 1923: 13.

12   Patrick Carpentier and Christian Trudeau, "Léo Dandurand, nationalisme canadien-français et baseball: Quand la sainte flanelle transpose sa formule aux autres sports," *Revue du baseball canadien*, Vol. 1, 2022 : 26-37.

13   This is the name found in the Spalding Guide and other official documents. The team was more often called Aces or Dubucmen in the press.

14   "Pepper Box Army Back in Action Again to Help Aces in the Weekend Fixtures," *Ottawa Citizen*, June 28, 1924: 22.

15   "Sport Gossips," *The Labor World/Le Monde Ouvrier*, August 23, 1924: 4.

16   "Underhill's Three Bagger Wins Final From Canadiens," *Ottawa Citizen*, August 11, 1924: 9.

17   "Fin de la saison du baseball professionnel," *Le Devoir*, September 2, 1924 : 7.

18   "La ligue Québec-Ont. ne sera pas réorganisée cette année," *Le Soleil*, April 13, 1925 : 9.

A SWING AND A MISS: OTTAWA'S TEAMS IN THE CAN-AM LEAGUE (1936-1940)

BY STEVE RENNIE

OTTAWA ENJOYED A FIVE-YEAR FLING with professional baseball between 1936 and 1940, fielding teams in the Class-C Canadian-American (Can-Am) League, which stretched across New York, Vermont, Quebec, and Ontario. While their tenures were brief and met with mixed success, these teams left their mark on baseball in the nation's capital.

1936 OTTAWA SENATORS: A PROMISING START

The first Ottawa Senators of the Can-Am League took the field in 1936 under the ownership of Don Stapleton[1] and the leadership of Walter "Wally" Masters, a 29-year-old Pennsylvania native who juggled the roles of president, business manager, and field manager. A jack-of-all-trades, he also played for the team. As he recalled in David Pietrusza's definitive Can-Am League history, "I pitched that year, and played other positions too, even the outfield."[2] The team played their home games at Lansdowne Park, a football stadium alongside the Rideau Canal that could seat 10,000 spectators. While the stadium provided a scenic backdrop, it lacked a fundamental baseball feature: an outfield fence—at least, not to start the season.[3]

The Senators clinched the second-place finish in the league with a solid 53-37 record (.589). Despite making the playoffs, their season ended with a 3–1 series loss to the Brockville Pirates.[4] Ultimately, the Perth Royals—who had gone by the moniker "Blue Cats" until they changed their name in July 1936[5] emerged victorious as league champions. Offensively, Billy Caldwell led the team with 80 runs scored, while Jimmy Nolan recorded 111 hits.[6] "Nolan's worth to his club is also reflected by his batting average of .335," observed the *Ottawa Journal*.[7] Masters left Ottawa at the end of the season for Philadelphia.[8]

1937-1938 OTTAWA BRAVES: STRUGGLES ON THE DIAMOND

In 1937, the Ottawa team rebranded as the Braves, reportedly as a way "to line up a pennant contender."[9] Unfortunately, the name change failed to translate into on-field success. Managed by player-coach Clair Forster in 1937 and George

Army in 1938, the Braves struggled to find their footing, finishing eighth in the league both seasons with records of 32-75 (.299) and 38-83 (.314), respectively.[10]

One of the few bright spots of an otherwise dismal 1937 season was the play of first baseman Ed Mohler, a 22-year-old University of Pennsylvania graduate who joined the Braves midseason. Mohler finished the season with a .305 batting average, 47 runs scored, 100 hits, 17 doubles, two triples, and five home runs. Ottawa sold him to the Boston Bees of the National League at the end of the season.[11]

The Braves' 1938 campaign might have unfolded differently had they secured several key players. If the team managed to sign talented pitchers Joe Dickinson and John "Whitey" Tulacz, or trade for talented shortstop Al Tarlecki, the local press speculated the outcome of the season might have been dramatically different.[12]

1939 OTTAWA SENATORS: ANOTHER DISAPPOINTING SEASON

The team began 1939 as the Braves but reverted to its former Senators name when Utica joined the league and adopted the Braves moniker. This once again resulted in Ottawa's hockey and baseball teams sharing the Senators name—a fact not lost on the local press. "There was a suggestion last night at the hockey dinner to discard calling the football team Rough Riders and hang 'Senators' on them, too," quipped the *Ottawa Journal*. "What with the hockey and ball clubs and the Upper House [the Senate], the town has about all the senators it can well stand."[13]

The name change didn't improve their fortunes. The 1939 season proved challenging for the Senators, even under the guidance of former big-league catcher Wally Schang.[14] Hired as player-manager, Schang's contract offered a unique incentive: a weekly bonus for keeping the team in the top three, along with additional rewards tied to attendance figures.[15] Despite Schang's efforts and the financial incentives in his contract, the team finished in sixth place with a disappointing record of 55 wins and 69 losses, placing them 27 games back from the league-leading Amsterdam Rugmakers. Ottawa once again missed out on the playoffs.[16]

1940 OTTAWA-OGDENSBURG SENATORS: PENNANT WINNERS

The 1940 season marked a high point for Ottawa baseball in the Can-Am League. The irony was that for all its pennant-winning success, the city had to share half the glory with Ogdensburg, New York. This arrangement was necessitated by two wartime challenges. First, the Canadian army required Lansdowne Park for military training, which took precedence over baseball and would make scheduling games at the stadium next to impossible. Second, exchange rate issues stemming from the war created financial difficulties.[17] As a result, owner Don Stapleton secured permission to play approximately half the team's games across the U.S. border in Ogdensburg.[18]

Despite this unusual circumstance, the Ottawa-Ogdensburg club, under the leadership of 25-year-old manager Cy Morgan, finished the season in first place.[19] They lost in the semi-finals in five games to the Amsterdam Rugmakers, who went on the win the league title.[20] Following the loss, the owners declared the team would not be returning for the 1941 season.[21]

The roster featured several players who went on to play in the majors: pitchers Bill Peterman, Paul Masterson, and John "Specs" Podgajny, catcher Homer "Dixie" Howell, and infielder George Jumonville.[22] "It wasn't so much that they were a strong team, although they were," wrote David Pietrusza. "It was that their parent club, the [Philadelphia] Phillies, was so putrid and their farm system so small, that they were willing to grab any player, anywhere, that looked halfway decent for a tryout."[23]

NOTES

1 David Pietrusza, *Baseball's Canadian-American League: A History of Its Inception, Franchises, Participants, Locales, Statistics, Demise, and Legacy, 1936-1951* (Jefferson, North Carolina: McFarland & Co., 2006), 42.

2 Pietrusza, 66.

3 Pietrusza, 115.

4 "Brockville Eliminates Senators From Can-Am Playoffs," *Ottawa Journal*, September 15, 1936: 16.

5 Pietrusza, 12.

6 "Can-Am League," Baseball-Reference.com. Accessed August 2, 2024, https://www.baseball-reference.com/bullpen/Can-Am_League.

7 "Can-American Leaders," *Ottawa Journal*, September 23, 1926: 19.

8 "Wally Masters to Leave for Home in U.S. Shortly," *Ottawa Journal*, September 30, 1936: 20.

9 "Local Baseball Club Now Known as Braves," *Ottawa Citizen*, February 24, 1937: 13.

10 "Can-Am League."

11 "Ed Mohler, Sold to Boston Bees, Ranked With Best in Can-Am Loop," *Ottawa Evening Citizen*, September 11, 1937: 13.

12 "Lost Opportunities," *Ottawa Evening Citizen*, September 2, 1938: 10.

13 "Senators Building for Baseball Season," *Ottawa Journal*, February 14, 1939: 18.

14 "Wally Schang to Pilot Ottawa Baseball Team," *Ottawa Journal*, February 7, 1939: 15.

15 "Senators Building for Baseball Season."

16 "Can-Am League."

17 Gary Belleville. "August 7, 1939: Ottawa Senators' Wally Schang homers two weeks before his 50th birthday," SABR Baseball Games Project. Accessed August 2, 2024. https://sabr.org/gamesproj/game/august-7-1939-ottawa-senators-wally-schang-homers-two-weeks-before-his-50th-birthday/.

18 "Can-Am Directors Okay Splitting Ottawa Games with Ogdensburg in '40," *Ogdensburg Journal*, February 19, 1940: 4.

19 "Can-Am League."

20 "Amsterdam Eliminates Senators in Fifth Game by 6–4," *Ottawa Journal*, September 12, 1940: 23.

21 Jack Maunder, "Another Angle," *Ottawa Journal*, September 12, 1940: 22.

22 Pietrusza, 204.

23 Pietrusza, 84.

URBAN SHOCKER, THE OTTAWA-TRAINED SPITBALLER WHO BESTED BABE RUTH

BY SHARON HAMILTON

ON A HOT AFTERNOON IN mid-July 1920, Ottawa-trained spitball pitcher Urban Shocker of the St. Louis Browns found himself at New York City's Polo Grounds in a showdown with Babe Ruth. At the time, most major-league pitchers had taken to just walking Ruth, who was busy breaking major-league home run records. But not Shocker. Having already struck Ruth out once, when Ruth approached the plate for a second time, Shocker turned around and motioned to the outfielders to come in closer.

In evident disbelief, they followed their pitcher's directions and moved forward. This astounding move rattled the great batter. He swung at one of Shocker's slow balls and missed. Shocker turned around again, motioning the outfielders in a bit closer. For a second time, a swing and a miss. A last time, Shocker turned around and motioned the outfielders to move in closer yet, guiding them almost into the infield. Once again, the terror of opposing pitchers took a swing, and missed. Ruth was out. Commentators who observed this stunt suggested perhaps Shocker had risked this delightful piece of baseball theatre—which had precisely its desired psychological effect on the batter—because he knew if Ruth hit the ball, none of the outfielders would have been able to catch it anyway.[1] Like everyone else in the park, they would have watched it sail over their heads and past the stadium's back wall.

After the game, reporters praised Shocker for his virtuoso "spitball, curve, and change of pace" with which he had tormented the Yankees, including Ruth. The media noted in particular the success of the "headwork" Shocker had used to outwit opposing batters.[2] During the game Shocker struck out 14 New York batters, including Ruth (three times), in the 6 to 4 victory.[3] As the *New York Herald* declared in its headline the next day: "38,823 Paid Fans See Shocker Tame the Babe."[4] As a spitball pitcher in the major leagues, Shocker won 187 games and lost only 117, with a 3.17 ERA and 983 strikeouts to 657 walks. This remarkable baseball player—who was once one of Babe Ruth's most successful antagonists, before later becoming his teammate, learned how to throw his spitball in Ottawa.

THE ROAD TO OTTAWA

Urban Shocker was born in Cleveland, Ohio, on September 22, 1890; his siblings retained the family name of "Shockcor." In his biography on Urban Shocker, baseball historian Steve Steinberg speculates Urban may have adopted the simplified spelling of "Shocker" because newspaper reporters were not able to get the more complicated spelling of his name right.[5] He also speculates journalists may have heard him being called "Urb" and thought it was "Herb," a name often used for him during his minor-league career, including by journalists based in Ottawa.[6]

Growing up in the baseball-loving city of Cleveland appears to have infected Shocker, who enjoyed playing sandlot games. Sometime around 1909 he moved to Detroit to live with his older sister, and in 1911, he joined the nearby Windsor Canucks, primarily as a catcher.[7] At this time the Windsor Canucks were not yet a professional team, as they would become in 1912 with the formation of the Border League;[8] however, the local papers were already taking note of Shocker's play. On May 1 an article in the Windsor *Evening Record* noted that "Shocker performed in a very satisfactory manner behind the bat."[9] By June 14 a large headline in the Windsor *Evening Record* proclaimed, "CATCHER SHOCKER LEADS LIST OF WINDSOR'S HEAVY SLUGGERS."[10] The article noted that "the blond fellow" had been "hitting at a terrific clip all season," achieving a .400 batting average. They opined that Shocker had shown his value in other ways as well, especially in his "coaching of the pitchers" and in his general "pepper" and "enthusiasm."[11]

One day while playing with the Windsor team, Shocker broke the tip of the third finger on his right hand. In the Windsor *Evening Record* for June 9, 1913, reporters noted that Shocker had started to make a catch but "received a bump on the finger in the fourth inning."[12] When his finger healed, it had a hook at the last joint. In important ways, this accident would change the trajectory of Shocker's baseball career. As Shocker would explain later, "That broken finger may not be pretty to look at but it has been very useful to me. It hooks over a baseball just right so that I can get a break on my slow ball and that's one of the best balls I throw."[13]

On an early outing as a pitcher (Shocker volunteered for the position when the team was short of pitching staff) he deeply impressed the game's onlookers. The Windsor *Evening Record* reported in May 1913 that "with the form that Shocker displayed in the box on Sunday afternoon, the stock of the Windsor Border league team was given a big boost."[14] In that game, Shocker struck out 13 of the opposing batters.[15] Canadian reporters watched him continue to serve as a pitcher throughout the season and were impressed by how the whole team appeared to rally naturally behind him in this role. An article appearing in the Windsor *Evening Record* on August 12, 1913, remarked that "If the players have confidence in a pitcher they will give him better support every time."[16] With respect to Shocker they noted: "The boys know Shocker's capable of pitching a good game and they play behind him different than to other heavers."[17]

Shocker had a 4.54 ERA with Windsor that year. The hook in the third finger of his pitching hand made a difference, giving him remarkable control. He began to develop his slow ball and worked on his curve balls. Already, at this early stage, his strike-outs to walks ratio was an impressive nearly 3 to 1. By the fall, Windsor media were making unabashed pronouncements about his promise as a pitcher. In an article published on September 19, 1913, they wrote: "'Shock' has a better assortment of curves, more experience, and many other little points that go to make a successful pitcher."[18]

In 1914 Shocker joined the Class-B Ottawa Senators of the Canadian League, where he had the good fortune of playing under the management of Frank "Shag" Shaughnessy, who would teach him "the spitter." Shaughnessy was a player-manager for the Senators, himself an outfielder of considerable talent. Like Shocker, he was an American; it was falling in love with a woman — Katherine Quinn from Ottawa — that brought him to the city, first to court her and then, later, when they moved there as a young family, with the first of their children, owing to her love for the place.[19] Shaughnessy built baseball up into a popular sport in Ottawa observing, "All the visiting clubs were happy to come to Ottawa," noting that they received 20 cents on admission from huge crowds and that he had solved the problem of baseball games being banned on Sundays in Ontario by booking a field across the river in Quebec.[20]

Observers were immediately impressed with Shocker as he began to come into his own as a pitcher under Shaughnessy's expert mentorship. In April, a story in the *Ottawa Citizen* observed that "Pitcher Shocker, of the Ottawas, has a lot of electricity up his sleeve."[21] By June the *Ottawa Citizen* was expressing raptures about Shocker's pitching, noting that he had been "invincible" in a game's tightest moments.[22] Shocker still lacked some basic pitching skills, however. In an interview for *The Sporting News*, Shaughnessy later recalled that when he first started to work with Shocker, the pitcher's curve ball still needed work. But he also saw promise; Shag's impression of Shocker was that he was "'as smart as they come.'"[23]

One day while Shocker was sitting on the bench waiting to warm up, Shaughnessy came up to him.

"Ever tried the spitter?" Shaughnessy asked.

"No," Shocker replied. "But I'm sure I could throw anything."[24]

Shaughnessy encouraged him to try. Shocker got up and asked a teammate if he could borrow a piece of slippery elm, then he approached an older pitcher on the team and asked if he could instruct him how to throw a spitball.[25] As Shaughnessy remembered, Shocker was "so clever he learned the spitter the first time he threw it."[26]

Shocker tried out his new pitch for the first time in a July 19 Senators game against the St. Thomas Saints. A blazing headline in the next day's *Ottawa Journal* proclaimed: "Champs Slaughtered Saints on Sunday winning 19 to 1."[27] A subheading summed up in block capitals the performance of the Senator's pitcher: "SHOCKER TWIRLED WELL."[28] The *Ottawa Citizen* similarly praised Shocker for pitching "clever ball from start to finish."[29] Shag's mentorship was already paying off. The same *Citizen* article noted that Shocker had "used his 'spitter' for the first time" in this game and "had things all his own way."[30] Shocker continued to improve his new pitch throughout the summer and by August the *Citizen* had begun referring to Shocker as the "Senators' spitball artist," noting that batters swung without effect at Shocker's "moist ball."[31]

In 1914 Shocker won 20 games with the Ottawa Senators. Throughout, he continued to hone his impressive control with, now, in addition to his slow ball developed in Windsor, his spitball learned in Ottawa. This growing arsenal of specialized pitches enabled him to strike out 158 batters that year. In September, Shocker helped lead the Senators to their third straight Canadian League title. The Senators sealed their championship on September 7 (see sidebar) and within a matter of days Shocker was called up to try out for the majors.

The *Ottawa Citizen* reported, "Pitcher Shocker goes to Detroit Tigers and will get a trial immediately," referring to him in the article's subtitle as the "Canadian League 'Iron Man.'"[32] The *Citizen* also commented on Shocker's character and general contributions to the team describing him as the "most willing pitcher who has ever worn the Ottawa spangles," and a "thorough gentleman on and off the field."[33] The *Citizen* pointed out that Shocker's rapid movement up the ranks that season had taken place mainly owing to his improvement as a pitcher, beginning in "the middle of the season, when he began working on his spitball."[34]

The *Ottawa Journal* similarly trumpeted the news. In their article they included a dramatic photograph of Shocker mid-pitch while wearing his Senator's uniform with its prominent white "O." A caption above the photo read: "PITCHER URBAN

PITCHER URBAN SHOCKER, who will receive a try out with the Detroit Tigers —Shocker was easily the class of the Senator's twirling staff.

Urban Shocker, the legendary pitcher who perfected his signature spitball while playing for the Ottawa Senators. Credit: *Ottawa Journal*, September 10, 1914: 4.

SHOCKER, who will receive a tryout with the Detroit Tigers;" to which they added, "Shocker was easily the class of the Senator's twirling staff."[35] Shocker did not make it into the majors on that occasion and ended up returning to Ottawa. With his expert support, the Senators won the Canadian League pennant again in 1915.

Meanwhile, scouts for the major leagues had continued to watch what was happening with Shocker. An article in the *Detroit Free Press* in August 1915 proclaimed, "Shocker Fairly Burned Up the Canadian Circuit During Month of July."[36] The same article said the next time the team was on the road a National League scout intended to check out "the young spitballer."[37] Shocker was recruited at the conclusion of the 1915 season by the New York Yankees and never returned to the Senators. However, he did make a return trip to Ottawa in October 1916 as a participant in an exhibition game between Tris Speaker's All-Star American Leaguers and a team of "Internationals" (for whom Shocker played) in Lansdowne Park. An article in the *Ottawa Citizen* noted that Shocker—had enjoyed a "flashy season" with the Toronto Maple Leafs and the New York Yankees. The article said Shocker was held up before his first trip to the plate to be presented with a gold locket from "local admirers," for which he bowed his thanks.[38]

SHOCKER'S SPITBALL IN THE MAJORS

After his major-league debut on April 24, 1916 with the New York Yankees, Shocker spent some time optioned by the Yankees, who had a pitching surplus, to the International League. In this way Shocker ended up playing again in Canada, this time in Toronto.[39] After spectacular play for the Maple Leafs that summer he was recalled by the Yankees, and in the spring of 1917 *Baseball Magazine* included Shocker in its list of the most promising major-league recruits.[40] In January 1918 Shocker found himself traded by the Yankees to the St. Louis Browns as part of a multi-player deal. It was for the Browns from 1918-24 and then with the New York Yankees from 1925-28 that Urban Shocker served out his career in the majors.[41]

When the Browns acquired Shocker from the Yankees in 1918, a St. Louis sports reporter raved about the hurler's "wicked spitball."[42] The Ottawa press had not forgotten Shocker's connections to the city, and local coverage of this trade noted that the deal had almost been scuttled by the Yankees' unwillingness to let Shocker go. Ottawa sports writers proudly claimed Shocker as part of Ottawa's baseball history by referring to him in their coverage of the trade as an "Ex-Ottawa Heaver"[43] and "the former Ottawa spit baller."[44]

In 1920, for a variety of reasons – including wishing to recalibrate the relationship between batters and pitchers for a higher scoring game – major-league baseball's club owners agreed to ban "trick" pitches, a list in which, with some debate, they considered including the spitball.[45] The league's spitball pitchers protested this anticipated change noting that they had acquired this specialization when the throw was legal. An example of the arguments made appears in the November 25,

1920 edition of *The Sporting News* in which Burleigh Grimes—the "Brooklyn Moist Ball Artist"—argued that it was unfair to suddenly remove from a pitcher's repertoire something that had been a legal throw, and a skill, that for most spitballers good enough to throw in the majors, had taken 10-15 years to perfect.[46]

For his part, Shocker reacted to the proposed spitball ban by saying that he felt he would be fine since he used the spitball sparingly, and mainly "only in the pinches" although he also added that he bluffed it frequently.[47] Although major-league baseball's owners ultimately decided that the spitball should be included in the list of banned trick pitches, in a concession to the arguments made by the spitball pitchers, they decided that those hurlers for whom the spitball was an important pitch would be grandfathered, and therefore able to continue to use this pitch. Shocker was among the 17 spitballers to whom this exemption applied.[48]

Throughout his time in the major leagues—which included playing for the World Series-winning 1927 Yankees—Shocker persistently impressed onlookers with his pitching smarts and range of pitching styles, including his Ottawa-derived spitter. An article in a September 13, 1924 St. Louis newspaper was typical of sports coverage of the 1920s in its praise of Shocker's ability to learn the batters' individual styles and getting them to "hit at pitches tossed to their weaknesses."[49] This intellectual form of pitching was something they described as the key to his "puzzling effectiveness."[50] Similarly in 1922, in its coverage of a Browns/Yankees match (with Shocker playing for the Browns) the *New York Times* reported that Shocker had risen to "magnificent heights in the pinches" and that his control was perfect as his "spitball broke across the corners, and a puzzling slow ball floated past Yankees' bats."[51]

In 1926, in assessing Shocker's value as a pitcher, reporters for *The Sporting News* suggested Shocker was "worth his weight in diamonds," noting the "big spitball expert" had become a Yankee mainstay.[52] And when Burleigh Grimes, who was the last legal spitballer in the majors, was elected to the Hall of Fame in 1964, he was asked who, in his opinion, had been the best spitball pitcher. Grimes responded that it had been Urban Shocker, "because he had everything else to go with it."[53]

In 1928 the Yankees were forced to release Shocker owing to his by then obvious health issues. Shortly before his unconditional release from the team, in an interview with *The Sporting News* Shocker revealed that for the previous two years he'd had to sleep sitting up because lying down, even a little, choked him.[54] He'd been suffering from—and playing through–heart failure. He died in Denver, Colorado on September 9, 1928 at the age of 37.

The next day, the *Ottawa Journal* ran a story about Shocker's death under the headline "Heilmann Grieves at Death of Friend: Pays Tribute to Urban Shocker as one of the greatest right-handers."[55] Harry Heilmann, a champion batter with Detroit of the American League, described Shocker in this article as "the greatest right-handed pitcher of the last decade."[56] The article also mentioned Shocker's Canadian apprenticeship, as someone who had played in both Toronto and Ottawa.

Ultimately, it was that initial training in Ottawa, under Shaughnessy, when Shocker had played for the Senators that had helped shape him into the kind of major-league pitcher he became at his best—as he was that day in July 1920 in front of a record crowd of 38,823 fans at the Polo Grounds when he bested the Babe. An unbeatable force, he tossed the ball with such controlled mastery observers said it "jumped away from the Yankee bats like a grasshopper."[57] At that moment, Shocker was at the top of his game, using the skills he'd fine-tuned during his formative years in Ottawa, to tame some of the game's greatest batters, including Ruth. Commenting especially on the potency of his Ottawa-originating spitball, awed New York scribes remarked, "the slippery ball never cut such capers at Shocker's command before."[58]

NOTES

1 "How's this for a Star Battery?" *The Sporting News*, July 22, 1920: 3.

2 "38,823 Paid Fans See Shocker Tame the Babe," *New York Herald*, July 14, 1920: 11.

3 "Shocker's Hurling in First Game Gives Browns Split with Yankees," *St. Louis Globe-Democrat*, July 14, 1920: 7.

4 "38,823 Paid Fans See Shocker Tame the Babe," *New York Herald*, July 14, 1920: 11.

5 Steve Steinberg, *Urban Shocker: Silent Hero of Baseball's Golden Age* (Lincoln: University of Nebraska Press, 2017), ebook.

6 Steinburg, *Urban Shocker.*

7 Steinburg, *Urban Shocker.* Steinberg notes that Shocker also played for some Southern Michigan League teams during this period as well.

8 "1912 Border League," https://www.baseball-reference.com/register/league.cgi?id=e19fecf2, Accessed September 4, 2023.

9 "Windsor Takes a Game of Detroit," *Evening Record* (Windsor), May 1, 1911: 1.

10 "Catcher Shocker Leads List of Windsor's Heavy Sluggers," *Evening Record* (Windsor), June 14, 1911: 2.

11 "Catcher Shocker Leads List of Windsor's Heavy Sluggers."

12 "Windsor Loses to Both Ypsi. and Port Huron" *Evening Record* (Windsor), June 9, 1913: 3.

13 *Baseball Magazine*, January 1921, 381 qtd. in Joseph Wancho, "Urban Shocker," Society for American Baseball Research, https://sabr.org/bioproj/person/urban-shocker/#sdendnote2sym, Accessed April 9, 2023.

14 "Shocker Made Good in Box," *Evening Record* (Windsor), May 20, 1913: 3.

15 "Shocker Made Good in Box."

16 M. R. Winters, "Team Plays Behind Shocker," *Evening Record* (Windsor), August 12, 1913: 3.

17 "Team Plays Behind Shocker."

18 "Windsor Plays First Rugby Game Sept. 17," *Evening Record* (Windsor), September 19, 1913: 5.

19 See, David McDonald, "Frank Shaughnessy: The Ottawa Years" *Our Game, Too: Influential Figures and Milestones in Canadian Baseball*, Andrew North, editor (Phoenix, Arizona: Society for American Baseball Research, 2022), ebook.

20 "The Frank Shaughnessy Story," *The Sporting News*, December 14, 1960: 18.

21 "Canadian Ball League Race Will be in Full Swing Two Weeks from Today," *Ottawa Citizen*, April 24, 1914: 8.

22 "Ottawas Began Important Home Series with Shutout Victory over Hamilton 'Doc' Yeats and his Tigers Beaten 6-0," *Ottawa Citizen*, June 26, 1914: 8.

23 The Frank Shaughnessy Story," *The Sporting News*, December 14, 1960: 18.

24 This dialogue is recreated based on Shaughnessy's description of this exchange in "The Frank Shaughnessy Story."

25 "The Frank Shaughnessy Story."

26 "The Frank Shaughnessy Story."

27 "Champs Slaughtered Saints on Sunday winning 19 to 1," *Ottawa Journal*, July 20, 1914: 5.

28 "Champs Slaughtered Saints on Sunday winning 19 to 1."

29 "Senators Avenged Saturday's Waterloo by Burying St. Thomas Pitchers Under Avalanche of Hard Hits in Final Clash," *Ottawa Citizen*, July 20, 1914: 8.

30 "Senators Avenged Saturday's Waterloo by Burying St. Thomas Pitchers Under Avalanche of Hard Hits in Final Clash."

31 "Heavy Hitting and Good Pitching in Pinches Resulted in Double Win on Saturday," *Ottawa Citizen*, August 24, 1914, 8.

32 "Pitcher Shocker goes to Detroit Tigers and will get a trial immediately," *Ottawa Citizen*, September 10, 1914: 8.

33 "Pitcher Shocker goes to Detroit Tigers and will get a trial immediately."

34 "Pitcher Shocker goes to Detroit Tigers and will get a trial immediately."

35 "Shocker to get tryout by Detroit Tigers," *Ottawa Journal*, September 10, 1914: 4.

36 "Former Local Mound Artist Making Good," *Detroit Free Press*, August 15, 1915: 19.

37 "Former Local Mound Artist Making Good."

38 "With Urban Shocker in box Royals Turned Tables on Americans in Final Game," *Ottawa Citizen*, October 10, 1916: 9.

39 For more on Shocker's time in Toronto see Steve Steinberg, "A Shocker on the Island," *Dominionball: Baseball Over the 49th* (Cleveland, Ohio: SABR, 2005), and Sharon Hamilton, "The Canadian Apprenticeship of Jazz Age Baseball Superstar Urban Shocker," *Journal of Canadian Baseball* vol 2: no. 1 (2023) https://ojs.uwindsor.ca/index.php/jcb/article/view/8348/5632

40 J. C. Kofoed, "The Youngsters of 1917," *Baseball Magazine*, August 1917: 434.

41 In the midst of his major-league play, Shocker was also called up for the draft. He served in France with the 340th Regiment of the 85th Infantry Division from the summer of 1918 until the spring of 1919. Biographer Steve Steinberg believes he likely did not experience combat.

42 Sid C. Keener, "Browns Trade Pratt and Plank to Yankees," *St. Louis Times*, January 22, 1918, qtd. in Steinberg.

43   "Urban Shocker Goes to St. Louis Browns," *Ottawa Journal*, January 23, 1918: 10.

44   "Yanks didn't want to give up Shocker," *Ottawa Journal*, January 24, 1918: 8.

45   For a detailed overview on the banning of trick pitches, including the spitball, in 1920 see Steve Steinberg, "The Spitball and the End of the Deadball Era," https://sabr.org/research/article/the-spitball-and-the-end-of-the-deadball-era/. Accessed April 9, 2023. This article was originally published in SABR's *The National Pastime, Vol. 23 (2003)*. For an examination of how this rule change affected Shocker while he played for the Browns see Rick Huhn, *The Sizzler: George Sisler, Baseball's Forgotten Great* (Columbia: University of Missouri Press, 2004), 81-86.

46   "Burleigh Grimes as Pleader for Spitters," *The Sporting News*, November 25, 1920: 3.

47   Sid C. Keener Browns, "Spitball Hurlers use more Speed and Wider Curve with Ban on Freak Shoots," *St. Louis Times* (St. Louis, Missouri), March 4, 1920. Qtd. in Steinberg.

48   Although Shocker threw a variety of pitches, and said he used the spitter only sparingly and mainly in a game's tightest moments, he clearly viewed this pitch as a key tool in his arsenal and was among the 17 pitchers who asked in 1920 when the new rules against trick pitches were introduced that they be exempted from the prohibition on the spitball. This exemption was granted to Shocker and the others who applied for it in 1920, and this exemption was later made permanent, lasting for each one of these spitters until the end of their careers (see Steinberg "the seventeen veterans who had registered for the 1920 one-year exemption.").

49   "Shocker is in Form and Browns Shut Out Indians, 5 to 0," *St. Louis Globe-Democrat* (St. Louis, Missouri), September 13, 1924: 9.

50   "Shocker is in Form and Browns Shut Out Indians, 5 to 0."

51   "Yankees Outluck Browns in Opener," *New York Times*, July 12, 1922: S16.

52   Joe Vila, "Yank Boss makes a few 'Mind Bets'" *The Sporting News*, July 29, 1926: 3.

53   Ed Rumill, "Shocker Threw Best Spitball," *Christian Science Monitor*, July 30, 1964 qtd. in Steinberg.

54   Arthur Mann, "Gamest of the Game," *The Sporting News*, August 11, 1938: 3.

55   "Heilman Grieves at Death of Friend: Pays Tribute to Urban Shocker as one of the greatest right-handers," *Ottawa Journal*, Sept. 10, 1928: 16.

56   "Heilman Grieves at Death of Friend: Pays Tribute to Urban Shocker as one of the greatest right-handers."

57   "38,823 Fans See Yanks Break Even," *New York Times*, July 14, 1920: 11.

58   "38,823 Fans See Yanks Break Even."

URBAN SHOCKER SEALS OTTAWA SENATORS' THIRD STRAIGHT CANADIAN LEAGUE TITLE

SEPTEMBER 7, 1914: OTTAWA SENATORS 6, PETERBOROUGH PETES 2, AT LANSDOWNE PARK, OTTAWA

BY GARY BELLEVILLE

AS THE FIRST WORLD WAR approached, baseball—not hockey—was Canada's national sport.[1] Inconsistent winter weather in many parts of the country, coupled with a lack of indoor ice, hampered hockey's early development.[2] Baseball, on the other hand, was flourishing. In the summer of 1914, there were 19 Canadian-based teams in five minor-league circuits.[3] Two of those leagues, the Canadian League and the Western Canada League, were made up almost entirely of Canadian-based teams.[4]

The Canadian League was established as a six-team Class-D circuit in 1911. The league expanded to eight teams with the addition of Ottawa and Peterborough in 1912, and by 1914 it had progressed to Class B, the third-highest minor-league classification at the time.[5] The Ottawa Senators baseball club quickly established itself as the most successful franchise in the Canadian League, winning the pennant in each of its first two years and attracting up to 7,000 fans to its games.

The team's pursuit of a third consecutive title hit a snag in the middle of July 1914 when a slumping Ottawa team fell 10 games out of first place. Frank "Shag" Shaughnessy, the Senators' president and player-manager, refused to throw in the towel. He addressed the team's biggest weakness by acquiring 19-year-old shortstop Jack (Johnny) Mitchell from the Class-C Southern Michigan Association for the princely sum of $1,000.[6] The purchase price for Mitchell, dubbed "the thousand dollar beauty" by the *Ottawa Citizen*, was thought to be the largest amount ever paid for a Class-B infielder.[7]

Shaughnessy made another midseason move that drastically improved the Senators' fortunes. One of his young hurlers had a mediocre curveball and needed another pitch in his arsenal, and so Shaughnessy suggested that he start throwing a spitball.[8] That pitcher was 23-year-old right-hander Urban Shocker, who was in his third year of professional baseball after playing for Windsor, Ontario

in the Class-D Border League in 1912-13.[9] Shocker took Shaughnessy's advice and added the spitter to his repertoire. The results were better than anyone could have hoped for.

On July 18 Mitchell made his debut with the Senators. The very next day, with Ottawa 8½ games behind the first-place London Tecumsehs, Shocker unleashed his spitball.[10] The Senators romped to a 19-1 blowout win that day, their first in a long string of victories. Shocker went on to win four games in a single week in August, and he completely dominated the opposition down the stretch.[11] Mitchell justified his hefty price tag, solidifying Ottawa's infield defense and batting a spectacular .343 for the season. After a stunning 40-13 run, the Senators found themselves in first place heading into the final day of the season with a 75-45 (.625) record, nine percentage points ahead of London at 69-43 (.616).

Despite the electrifying pennant race, the mood in Ottawa had darkened over the summer of 1914. The governor general had declared war on Germany on August 4, and the nation focused on far more important matters than sport. Civil servants were no longer allowed to leave work early to attend weekday afternoon games at Lansdowne Park. The team took a 40 percent attendance hit over the final month of the season.[12]

Ottawa and London were each scheduled to wrap up the season with Labor Day doubleheaders at home against relatively weak opponents.[13] Since teams could finish the season with a significantly different number of games completed, the title was awarded to the team with the best winning percentage.[14] That meant either a single Ottawa win or a London loss would give the Senators their third consecutive championship.

London kept its pennant hopes alive by defeating the St. Thomas Saints 4-1 in their morning affair, while rain forced the cancellation of the morning contest between Ottawa and the Peterborough Petes. The Ottawa twin bill was rescheduled for the afternoon, with the rain finally letting up around 1 P.M. After 20 gallons of gasoline were spread around the diamond and set on fire, the field was deemed playable.[15]

Shocker, pitching on one day's rest, got the start for Ottawa. He had earned his 19th win of the season by pitching seven scoreless innings against Erie on the 5th.[16] Shaughnessy, looking ahead to the final day of the season, had wisely yanked Shocker once the outcome was decided. Peterborough countered Shocker with Ken Tracey (10-13).

Mitchell led off the bottom of the first inning with a single. After a one-out single by Rabbit Nill, Shaughnessy flied out to left fielder Oliver Welsh. Mitchell tagged up and advanced to third on the fly ball, and when Welsh uncorked a wild throw, the Ottawa speedster came home with the game's first run. Carl "Dad" Stewart followed with a two-out hit to drive home Nill and put Ottawa up 2-0.[17]

Another poor defensive play by Welsh cost the Petes in the bottom of the second. After a walk to Frank Smykal, Mitchell singled into left field. Welsh booted the ball all around the outfield, allowing Smykal to score and extend Ottawa's lead to 3-0.[18]

Peterborough right fielder Frank Rooney, who had a brief stint in the majors with the Federal League's Indianapolis Hoosiers earlier in the season, was unimpressed with Welsh's fielding miscues.[19] The pair exchanged words at the end of the inning and nearly came to blows before order was restored by first baseman Biddy Dolan, a teammate of Rooney's on the Hoosiers.[20]

Shocker faced the minimum number of batters through five innings but ran into some trouble in the top of the sixth. Weak-hitting Frank Fox led off with an infield single. Shocker retired the next two hitters before Curley Blount, Welsh, and Dolan came through with consecutive two-out hits to score a pair of runs and cut Ottawa's lead to 3-2.

The "Shagmen" padded their lead in the bottom of the sixth with four consecutive hits. Shocker got things rolling with a one-out single. After Mitchell singled, Edgar "Lefty" Rogers doubled to deep center field to score Shocker.[21] Nill singled Mitchell home and Shaughnessy capped the inning with a sacrifice fly that brought Rogers home to make the score 6-2.[22]

Shocker faced only nine batters over the final three innings to easily nail down the victory and give the Senators their third consecutive Canadian League title—or so they thought. The Tecumsehs had defeated the Saints 8-5 in the second game in London, but they refused to concede defeat. Their 40-year-old player-manager, Doc Reisling, had a trick up his sleeve. Without seeking permission from league

president James Fitzgerald, Reisling had made an agreement with the Saints to play a third game later that afternoon.[23] Another London win coupled with an Ottawa loss in the second game of the doubleheader would theoretically hand the championship to the Tecumsehs by three percentage points. There was a distinct possibility of that happening, since Peterborough had tabbed the league's best pitcher, 20-game winner Lou Schettler, to start the second game against the Senators.

At some point in the afternoon, Ottawa caught on to Reisling's ruse.[24] With the Senators and Petes locked in a scoreless tie after two innings in the second game, Shaughnessy conferred with Peterborough player-manager Blount, and the game was called because of "cold weather" by umpire Buck Freeman.[25] Regardless of the outcome of the third game in London, the cancellation ensured that Ottawa would prevail. The Tecumsehs won the third game by a score of 9-2, but the shenanigans were moot; Fitzgerald ruled the following day that the third game would not count. The decision was based on a little-known rule preventing teams in Organized Baseball from playing more than two games in one day.[26]

Shocker's breakout 1914 season made him a bona fide big-league prospect. He posted a 20-8 record and a 2.17 ERA, leading to rumors that he might join the Detroit Tigers the next season. However, Tigers manager Hughie Jennings disliked spitball pitchers, and Shocker returned to Ottawa in 1915.[27] He put up even gaudier numbers: 19 wins, a 1.99 ERA, and an incredible 0.772 WHIP.[28] He also set Canadian League records with 186 strikeouts and 303 innings pitched. Shocker was drafted by the New York Yankees after the 1915 season, and went on to become one of the best American League pitchers of his era.[29]

A scaled-back Canadian League operated for the 1915 season with the war raging in Europe. Salaries and roster size were reduced, and the league cut back to six teams. The Senators waltzed to their fourth consecutive championship, finishing 12½ games ahead of the Guelph Maple Leafs, although the Ottawa fans understandably lacked their normal passion that summer.[30]

In the spring of 1916, the league debated whether to continue operating. When the 207th (Ottawa-Carleton) Battalion moved into Lansdowne Park in April, the Senators found themselves without a ballpark, and the circuit suspended operations for the 1916 season.[31] The league never resumed after the war. The Ottawa Senators, led by the masterful Shaughnessy, ended their existence with a perfect record of four Canadian League championships in four seasons.[32]

SOURCES

In addition to the sources cited in the Notes, the author consulted Baseball-Reference.com, Retrosheet.org, *The Encyclopedia of Minor League Baseball*, and the SABR biography of Urban Shocker. Unless otherwise noted, all play-by-play information was taken from the article "Third Consecutive Pennant Came to Ottawa When Shag's Senators Trimmed Peterboro 6-2 in Only Game Yesterday," in the September 8, 1914, edition of the *Ottawa Journal*. League standings were taken from the *Ottawa Citizen*.

NOTES

1 William Humber, *Diamonds of the North: A Concise History of Baseball in Canada* (Don Mills, Ontario: Oxford University Press, 1995), 8, 202.

2 The National Hockey League didn't even exist until late in 1917.

3 The 19 Canadian-based teams in the minor leagues in 1914 were Toronto and Montreal in the Double-A International League; Brantford, Hamilton, London, Ottawa, Peterborough, St. Thomas, and Toronto in the Class-B Canadian League; Vancouver and Victoria in the Class-B Northwestern League; Winnipeg and Ft. William-Pt. Arthur (now Thunder Bay, Ontario) in the Class-C Northern League; and Calgary, Edmonton, Medicine Hat, Moose Jaw, Regina, and Saskatoon in the Class-D Western Canada League. As of 2024, the most minor-league teams ever based in Canada was 24 in 1913.

4 The Erie Yankees were the only American-based squad in the eight-team Canadian League. All six teams in the Western Canada League were based in Canada.

5 The Canadian League was classified as Class C in 1912 and 1913.

6 "Thousand Dollar Shortstop to Play in Tomorrow's Doubleheader Here; Mitchell Now on Way from Adrian," *Ottawa Citizen*, July 17, 1914: 8.

7 David McDonald, "The First Diamond Dynasty," *Ottawa Citizen*, May 4, 2003: C-3.

8 Steve Steinberg, *Urban Shocker: Silent Hero of Baseball's Golden Age* (Lincoln: University of Nebraska Press, 2017), 14.

9 Shocker appeared as both a pitcher and catcher for Windsor. In 1913 he posted a 6-7 record and a 4.54 ERA. Shocker went 13-for-93 (.140) at the plate for Windsor in 1912-13, which might explain why he became a full-time pitcher.

10 "Senators Avenged Saturday's Waterloo by Burying St. Thomas Pitchers Under Avalanche of Hard Hits in Final Clash," *Ottawa Citizen*, July 20, 1914: 8.

11 Steinberg, 14.

12 Steinberg, 14-15.

13 Doubleheaders in the Canadian League usually comprised separate-admission morning and afternoon games.

14 Since there weren't any lights in ballparks of this era, it was common for tie games to be called on account of darkness. These games were not resumed later, and they did not count in the standings. In addition, games canceled because of inclement weather were not always made up.

15 "Canadian Ball League Pennant Comes to Ottawa; Champions Downed Peterboro and Won Flag Again," *Ottawa Citizen*, September 8, 1914: 8.

16 "Erie Yankees Were Snowed Under in Final Game of Their Series Here," *Ottawa Citizen*, September 7, 1914: 8.

17 "Canadian Ball League Pennant Comes to Ottawa; Champions Downed Peterboro and Won Flag Again."

18 "Canadian Ball League Pennant Comes to Ottawa; Champions Downed Peterboro and Won Flag Again."

19 Rooney was born in 1884 in Poděbrady, about 25 miles east of Prague in what was then part of the Austro-Hungarian Empire. As of 2024, the area was part of the Czech Republic. His birth surname was Rovný, although he played baseball in North America as Rooney, which sounded more American. Rooney became the first Czech player to hit a home run in the major leagues when he homered against the Chicago Chi-Feds at Weeghman Park on May 30, 1914. Gary Belleville, "May 30, 1914: Frank Rooney Becomes First Czech Player to Homer in the Major Leagues," SABR Games Project, https://sabr.org/gamesproj/game/may-30-1914-frank-rooney-becomes-first-czech-player-to-homer-in-the-major-leagues/, accessed March 4, 2024.

20 "Canadian Ball League Pennant Comes to Ottawa; Champions Downed Peterboro and Won Flag Again."

21 "Canadian Ball League Pennant Comes to Ottawa; Champions Downed Peterboro and Won Flag Again."

22 "Canadian Ball League Pennant Comes to Ottawa; Champions Downed Peterboro and Won Flag Again."

23 David McDonald, "Let's Play Three!" *The National Pastime*, no. 23 (2003): 40-43. The Canadian League was part of Organized Baseball.

24 "Third Consecutive Pennant Came to Ottawa When Shag's Senators Trimmed Peterboro 6-2 in Only Game Yesterday," *Ottawa Journal*, September 8, 1914: 4.

25 There were no reports of a significant temperature change during the day. Freeman was a former star first baseman and outfielder with the Boston Americans. He was Boston's top slugger from 1901 to '04 and a big reason why the team won the 1903 World Series.

26 McDonald.

27 Steinberg, 17-18.

28 By comparison, the lowest single-season WHIP in the American or National League (through 2023) was 0.7373 by Pedro Martínez in 2000.

29 Shocker compiled a record of 187-117 with a 3.17 ERA over a 13-year major-league career. He won 20 or more games in four consecutive seasons (1920-23) for the St. Louis Browns, tying Carl Mays for the most wins in the American League in 1921. He also went 18-6 for the 1927 New York Yankees.

30 McDonald.

31 McDonald.

32 Frank Shaughnessy went on to serve as president of the International League from 1936 until 1960.

ACROSS THE RIVER:
EARLY BASEBALL IN THE OUTAOUAIS

BY CHRISTOPHER SAILUS

THE OUTAOUAIS—A UNIQUE REGION OF southwestern Quebec situated along the Ottawa River—lives a double life. Though most of its communities began as administrative centers for the Quebec-based timber industry and the *draveurs* who worked the Gatineau River, the twenty-first century economy of the region is quite different. As anyone who has walked the halls of the brutalist architecture-clad buildings on the Quebec side of the Ottawa River can tell you, the region today is dependent on the federal government and its workers.

At the same time, Gatineau and its environs (Hull, Gatineau, and several other Quebec-side towns were amalgamated into the city of Gatineau in 2002) in the Outaouais are still very much part of Quebec. Despite its proximity to the nation's capital, many of the Outaouais' Francophone residents are Quebeckers first, Canadians second.

That dual influence in the region extends to most walks of life, and baseball is no different. Indeed, baseball has a long and well-documented history on both sides of the Ottawa River. In Quebec, the game is perhaps most principally known for its early games and clubs in Montreal. Beginning with the city's first organized ballclub in the early 1870s, the Montreal Baseball Club, the game grew quickly there. Students in the city were soon playing games between colleges. Interest in baseball continued to grow, and in 1873 members of the typographers' union formed the first Francophone-based team, Club Jacques-Cartier.[1]

At the same time, though to less fanfare and organization, the game was being played in and around Ottawa. The *Ottawa Daily Citizen*, for instance, noted in its "Miscellaneous" section on August 3, 1872, that "It is considered a curious fact, that whilst sunstroke has occurred almost everywhere else this summer, no case has yet been reported from a base-ball field."[2] The matter-of-fact reporting suggests the game was played regularly across the national capital region even at this early date.

In fact, avid players of the game were soon starting clubs and challenging one another. Throughout the later 1870s, accounts of matches between clubs from settlements like Fitzroy, Metcalfe, Manotick, and others were treated as curious stories in local papers. Newspaper write-ups often included the match's circumstances, notable players and plays, as well as the activities of the teams before and after matches. Accounts of local baseball games became regular features of the news rundown in Ottawa papers throughout the 1880s and 1890s.

Though stories of baseball played on the Quebec side of the Ottawa River in this period are harder to find, the few we have suggest the game was equally popular in the Outaouais. In August 1882, for example, a rather acrimonious exchange played out between baseball clubs from Aylmer (now part of Gatineau) and "Quio" (likely in reference to the village of Quyon, which today lies roughly a half-hour's drive from Aylmer). The account comes from the captain of the Aylmer club, a Mr. W.H. Klock, who explained in the *Citizen* that his club was refusing to play a rematch with the Quio club "who feels its defeat very keenly" from an earlier match between the two clubs. The refusal to replay the Quio club stemmed from a disagreement as to the terms on which the rematch would be played, including the grounds, the players (presumably to avoid Quio from picking up too many hard-hitting, fast-pitching ringers), the umpire, and the stakes for the match (teams in this period routinely played other clubs for sums ranging from $50-$200; sums roughly equal to $1,000-$6,000 today).[3]

One wonders if the clubs ever managed to arrange another game again, relations between them being what they were: Klock was not content in his letter to the *Citizen* just to detail the dispute, but also wanted it known that "we consequently stigmatize [Quio's baseball club] as 'cowards' and deem their challenge a 'canard.'"[4] Despite the slander, it's likely the Quio club would have had some sympathetic readers, as Klock and his 1880s Aylmer outfit appear to have been a finicky lot—earlier in the month the Citizen reported that Aylmer refused to reply to multiple challenges from the Olympiques ballclub of Ottawa.[5]

While the game was clearly popular for those with the time, energy, and funds to play it, not all were as keen, especially when it was played on the traditional day of rest. This was particularly true in Ottawa, where pious Ottawans complained in letters to the *Citizen* as early as 1877 about "a large crowd of boys and young men" who "play baseball and carry on other sports" on Sundays, something the writer complained was "anything but becoming a Sabbath day in a Christian land."[6] This sentiment was not new, though it was perhaps the first time it had been publicly associated with baseball in the region. Prohibitions against certain practices on Sundays were a part of English common law, upon which much of the English-speaking Canadian legal tradition was based. These protections did, however, see an increased zeal in Canada during this period. The Lord's Day Alliance of Canada, founded in 1888, was supported and founded in part by a group of Presbyterian churches who fought what they considered as the loss of the Sabbath's sanctity in Canadian society. Their lobbying efforts over the decades that followed led to the 1906 passing of the *Lord's Day Act* by the government of Prime Minister Sir Wilfrid Laurier. Becoming law in March 1907, it aimed to restrict all forms of commercial and recreational activity on Sunday, though it had varying degrees of success.[7]

The institution of the Act reinforced a pious sensibility that by the 1890s was already common practice on the Ottawa side of the river. In fact, when Ottawa acquired its first professional ballclub, a troubled Eastern League club from Rochester, New York, midway through the 1898 season, it set up "the best field for baseball in America" at Lansdowne Park, according to one observer. Despite its suitability for games, Ottawa society would not condone play on its surface on Sunday, and the organizers of the team arranged for Sunday games to be played in Hull—just across the river to be sure, but most importantly further from the reach of English Canadian Protestantism.

Though the Sunday games in Hull and the Ottawa ballclub in general were a success, the team did not continue play beyond the 1898 season. Its demise was more a result of circumstances surrounding the team and the Eastern League; it was certainly not a sign of baseball's declining popularity in the region. The game remained a popular pastime in the villages on the Quebec side of the Ottawa River and accounts from local clubs and those further afield in the nascent major leagues in the United States were popular features in papers across Ottawa and the Outaouais.

A baseball field was even built as part of a Coney Island-style amusement park, Belle Isle Park, which opened in 1912. Built on the Quebec-controlled Belle Isle (today called Kettle Island), its operating company at times provided hourly steamer ferry service to and from Queen's Wharf in Ottawa. The ballfield, situated alongside a boxing ring, featured seating for hundreds of spectators.[8] The first game at the field took place between the home team, Belle Isle (an irregular exhibition team pulled from local players), and a club from Brushton, New York, then part of the Northern New York League. The game was scheduled for Sunday, August 4,[9] no doubt positioned to try to draw spectators from Ottawa whose team at that point led the 1912 Canadian League standings, but importantly still couldn't play home games at Lansdowne Park on the Sabbath. The advertisement for the game earlier in the week in the *Ottawa Citizen* served not only to draw attention to the game, but also to notify the players Belle Isle had selected as to when they should show up to play. A little surprisingly, the home side won their inaugural contest against the American semipro outfit, 8-7.[10]

Baseball at the amusement park (Belle Isle Park was renamed Capital Park the following year) remained an exhibition affair during its short existence, which ended at some point during the first World War.

Baseball remained a mainstay pastime in western Quebec in the years that followed. Regardless of the on-again, off-again status of Ottawa's minor league clubs and semi-regular Sunday games in Hull, baseball was regularly played throughout the Outaouais. Most towns and villages had amateur clubs that played one another in leagues of varying formality. These amateur games generally took place on Saturdays and were also a social affair, with the home club often hosting a dinner and a dance afterward. More genial affairs aside, they played competitively as well: the Cascades Club, for instance, still proudly claims itself as 1922-23 Lower Gatineau Valley hardball champions.[11]

Baseball's popularity in the Outaouais grew to the point where it was a viable location for profitable barnstorming efforts. Organized by Montreal businessman Len Forteous, the world champion New York Yankees came to Hull in 1928, with Babe Ruth and Lou Gehrig, among others, playing in front of more than 3,000 people in Dupuis Park,[12] as covered elsewhere in this volume.

Suffice it to say, though baseball's popularity never rivaled hockey, it was arguably the sport of the summer in the Outaouais in the first half of the twentieth century. The Hull Volant, an athletic club which still exists but no longer fields a baseball team, won local championships for three years running in the early 1940s. Their successful streak culminated in a 1944 Quebec provincial championship, according to the club's own history books, though corroborating records elsewhere of wartime baseball at the provincial level are scant.[13]

Baseball's popularity in the Outaouais may have peaked during this period (several clubs who fielded baseball teams in the period before World War II no longer do), though it is hard to say enthusiasm for the sport has fallen in the past half-century. Gatineau has continued to live the double life of the Outaouais region—heavily influenced by its larger, mainly English-speaking neighbor across the Ottawa River while retaining its proudly independent, Québécois attitude. The remaining competitive ballclubs across the region, for example, play in the Ligue Baseball Outaouais, a part of Quebec baseball. These same clubs still commonly have partnerships and ticket nights with whatever minor-league team happens to be inhabiting Ottawa's minor league baseball stadium off Coventry Road (the Frontier League's Ottawa Titans, at the time of this writing).

Baseball, like the rest of life in the Outaouais, has a unique history all its own, with one foot in two equally Canadian worlds.

NOTES

1   Mario Robert, "A Brief History of Baseball in Montreal from 1860 to 1960," *Archives de Montreal*, April 2, 2015. Accessed June 13, 2024, https://archivesdemontreal.com/2015/04/02/a-brief-history-of-baseball-in-montreal-from-1860-to-1960/.

2   "Miscellaneous," *Ottawa Daily Citizen*, August 3, 1872: 2.

3   Statistics Canada only keeps currency inflationary records from 1914. The figures have been broadened to account for the missing 32-year period, based on the Statistics Canada numbers that do exist ($50-$200 in 1914 being equal to $1,368-$5,474 in 2024).

4   "Correspondence," *Ottawa Daily Citizen*, August 29, 1882: 2.

5   "Local and other notes," *Ottawa Dailys Citizen*, August 25, 1882: 2.

6   "Sabbath Breakers," *Ottawa Daily Citizen*, May 11, 1877: 3.

7   Paul Laverdure, *Sunday in Canada: The Rise and Fall of the Lord's Day* (Yorkton, Saskatchewan: Gravelbooks, 2004).

8   Randy Boswell, "A bridge to Ottawa's past: Kettle Island saga isn't just a debate – it's a journey into history," *Ottawa Citizen*, October 8, 2020. Accessed June 16, 2024, https://ottawacitizen.com/news/a-bridge-to-ottawas-past-kettle-island-saga-isnt-just-a-debate-its-a-journey-into-history.

9   "Baseball at Belle Isle," *Ottawa Journal*, July 31, 1912: 5.

10 "Baseball at Belle Isle," *Ottawa journal*, August 6, 1912: 8.

11 Carol Martin, "The Cascades Club," *Up the Gatineau!* Gatineau Valley Historical Society, 2001. Accessed July 21, 2024, https://www.gvhs.ca/publications/utga-cascades-club.html

12 "Capital Facts: That time Babe Ruth and Lou Gehrig came to Ottawa," *Ottawa Citizen*, May 1, 2017. Accessed June 14, 2024, https://ottawacitizen.com/news/local-news/capital-facts-that-time-babe-ruth-and-lou-gehrig-came-to-ottawa.

13 "Historique: Hull-Volant 1932-2017; 85 ans de présence en Outaouais," *Association Hull Volant*. Accessed June 13, 2024, https://www.hullvolant.ca/index.php?page=pages&entity=page&action=show&id=20.

THE BABE COMES TO TOWN

BY DAVID MCDONALD

"Don't tell me about Ruth; I've seen what he did to people…. I've seen them: kids, men, women, worshipers all, hoping to get his famous name on a torn, dirty piece of paper, or hoping to get a grunt of recognition when they said, 'H'ya, Babe.' He never let them down; not once! He was the greatest crowd pleaser of them all." — Waite Hoyt[1]

JUST SIX DAYS AFTER WINNING the 1928 World Series, Babe Ruth and Lou Gehrig got off a train at Union Station in Ottawa. It was a Monday noontime in mid-October, and some 500 fans, many of them boys conspicuously absent from school, milled expectantly in the concourse. Suddenly the two greatest players on the greatest team in baseball came through the gate. For all the attention he attracted, the younger one, a handsome, Columbia University-educated 25-year-old, who would one day screen-test for the role of Tarzan, might have been a railway clerk on his way to lunch. Every eye in the place was locked on his companion, a beaming, pug-faced 33-year-old in a brown suit, brown overcoat, and a brown felt hat. The crowd engulfed him, slapping him on the back, yelling "Hurrah for the Babe."[2]

Despite his 6 feet 2 inches and 217 pounds, Ruth moved with a surprising nimbleness, hailing knots of kids with a scattershot "Howdy, bud," as he made his way through the hall.[3] Breaking stride for an instant he centered out one small boy on the fringes of the mob for a cheery "Hello." The boy went popeyed and almost fell over.[4] The biggest kid on the continent had spoken to him.

One reporter found Ruth "far from the phlegmatic type many imagine… He had a cheery word for everybody and, while he is perhaps one of the most pestered people in the world, he stands the often trying adulation of the sport mob with great patience and takes zest in everything and everybody, particularly the youngsters."[5] In fact one of the first things Ruth had done when he arrived was to dash off a wire to the superintendent of the Ottawa Boys' Club, with his best wishes for the organization.

The Murderers' Row Yankees, hit by illness and injury, had won nine fewer games in 1928 than they had the previous season. Ruth's average had dipped from .356 to .323, and his home runs from an iconic 60 to a mere league-leading 54. Gehrig's average had held steady, but his home run total had plummeted, from 47 to 27.

It was just enough to carry the Yankees to their third straight American League pennant, by 2 ½ games over the Philadelphia Athletics. In the Series they would be up against the St. Louis Cardinals, a team featuring six future Hall of Fame players and a Hall of Fame manager.

It was no contest. Ruth batted .625 (10 for 16), with three home runs, all coming in the fourth and final game. "The able Ruth, heralded as a cripple, pounded the crack St. Louis hurlers as if they were but Class 'C' pitchers in a bad slump," the *Ottawa Journal* reported.[6] Gehrig, for his part, batted .545 with four

Parc Dupuis, Hull, Quebec. October 15, 1928. L. to. r., unidentified in striped tie; Peter St. Pierre, umpire; Lou Gehrig; Hull mayor Théo Lambert (wearing Lou's cap); Babe Ruth (wearing Lambert's bowler); Gene Coderre, umpire. Credit: Estate of Théo Lambert. In collection of Centre régional d'archives de l'Outaouais. Fonds de l'Association athlétique et sociale Hull-Volant.

home runs and nine runs batted in. Sweep, Yankees. Babe and Lou each pocketed a winner's share of $5,531.97. Now it was time to make some real dough.

Star players could make as much or more with a postseason barnstorming tour as they could in an entire major-league season. Ruth, for one, had barnstormed practically every fall since 1916, when he was still a member of the Boston Red Sox. Given his prodigious appetite for flivvers, floozies, stogies, hooch, and weenies, the postseason appearances had become something of a financial necessity.

In 1927, Ruth recruited rising superstar Gehrig and embarked on a 21-game "Bustin' Babes and Larrupin' Lous" odyssey, from Providence, Rhode Island, to San Diego, California. Playing with and against mostly amateur and semiprofessional squads, the pair drew some 220,000 fans. Ruth netted about $70,000 from the tour, the equivalent of his annual Yankees' salary. Gehrig received a flat $10,000, which was $2,000 more than he'd earned during a regular season in which he had batted .373 and driven in 173 runs.

The 1928 World Series wrapped up on October 9. Five days later Ruth and Gehrig kicked off their second Bustin' Babes and Larrupin' Lous tour in Montreal, where they lined up with Ahuntsic, champions of the racially-integrated, semipro Ligue de la Cité (City League), against Chappie Johnson's All-Stars[7], an all-Black team from the same circuit. Before the game they staged a home run derby, swatting pitch after pitch out of the park to the delight of 14,000 fans. Ruth, who had last pitched in the majors in 1920, tossed three innings for the winners. At the plate, he managed just a pair of singles. The game itself ended—as these games frequently did—with the fans flooding onto the field to celebrate a late-inning Gehrig home run.

Arriving in Ottawa the next day, Babe and Lou repaired to a first-floor suite at the landmark Château Laurier hotel, just across the Rideau Canal from the Parliament Buildings. Ruth invited local newsmen to hang out as he and Gehrig prepared for their game later that afternoon in Hull, Quebec, just across the Ottawa River from the capital.

Inevitably, having landed in a political town, Babe was pressed for his thoughts on the upcoming U.S. presidential election. He was an Al Smith supporter, he said, referring to the anti-Prohibitionist Democratic governor of New York, but conceded Smith had "a tough fight ahead of him."[8] Gehrig's political opinions, if any, went unrecorded.

"I know that as long as I was following Ruth to the plate I could have stood on my head and no one would have known the difference." — Lou Gehrig[9]

While the reticent Gehrig did his best to blend in with the wallpaper, the Babe held court. "Tell the boys we are both glad to be here, even for such a short visit," he said, "and at Dupuis Park this afternoon we will try and provide our share of the entertainment."[10] Asked how he was feeling, Ruth said, "I bet I can't even throw a ball today, that arm of mine is so sore."[11] Was he going to pitch in Hull? "You bet your life I'm not," he guffawed, adding that he had also signed 18 dozen baseballs as part of the Montreal appearance.[12]

"Babe Ready for Hull Swatfest,"[13] announced the *Ottawa Citizen*, while the *Ottawa Journal* colorfully stated the obvious: "The thousands who are likely to crowd the park will want to see Lou and Babe whang the apple over the car tracks."[14]

For a 3 o'clock game on a Monday afternoon in the middle of October, more than 3,000 spectators paid a dollar apiece—50 cents for kids—to see Ruth, in his black Bustin' Babes uniform (which, one reporter quipped, "showed his figure to advantage"[15]) and Gehrig, in his Larrupin' Lous whites, do some heavy whanging. Ahuntsic and the Montreal All-Stars again made up the supporting cast. The promoters had brought five dozen baseballs so there would be a ready supply for the pre-game home run exhibition and autograph session.

On this day Ruth and Gehrig swapped their usual positions. Babe shifted to first base to give his sore wing a rest, a move that would also give him opportunity to engage in non-stop banter with the fans. Lou started in left field, then came in to pitch the last two innings.

A swatfest it wasn't. Neither slugger was able to make solid contact against the All-Stars' pitcher, from the Guybourg club of the Montreal City League. He was identified in the box scores as Guillaume, but his real name was Ralph Williams, nicknamed "Bill." Guillaume was the gallicized *nom de guerre* he assumed when he played for francophone teams.[16]

After the match there were grumblings from fans about Guillaume's perceived failure, whether dictated by nervousness or competitive pride, to groove some of his offerings to the Yankee sluggers. For eight innings he held Babe and Lou not just homer-less but hitless. One reporter would liken the disappointing spectacle to "a performance of Hamlet without the Dane."[17]

The All-Stars, bolstered by some local athletic royalty—future Hockey Hall of Famers Frankie Boucher, star center of the Stanley Cup champion New York Rangers, and his brother George, an Ottawa Senators defenseman—led, 1- o. George belted a double off Gehrig and also robbed

Ruth with a one-handed stab up against the center-field scoreboard.

Ahuntsic tied the game in the seventh, when Gehrig reached base on an infield error and later scored. Then in the eighth Ruth finally got hold of one, doubling to drive in two and break the 1-1 tie. Gehrig followed with a fly out, stranding Babe at second. With that the kids in the stands, unable to restrain themselves any longer, poured onto the field, bringing the game to an early end.

Over the fence they came in hundreds," the *Citizen* reported, and the Babe was engulfed by "a milling, shouting, worshipping mob of youngsters who clamored for handshakes, autographs and what have you in general."[18] The what-have-yous included Ruth's Bustin' Babes cap and both sluggers' bats, which were borne off like religious relics.

Babe and Lou eventually managed to jostle their way to the parking lot. They drove away, a swarm of kids pursuing their car through the streets of Hull. Back in Ottawa they boarded an 11 P.M. train at Union Station. Next stop: Buffalo.

NOTES

1   John Tullius, *I'd Rather Be a Yankee: An Oral History of America's Most Loved and Most Hated Baseball Team* (New York: Macmillan, 1986), 40.

2   ""Babe Is For Al; Home Run King Talks Politics," *Ottawa Journal*, October 15, 1928: 1.

3   "Babe Ready for Hull Swatfest," *Ottawa Citizen*, October 15, 1928: 2.

4   "Babe Is For Al; Home Run King Talks Politics," *Ottawa Journal*, October 15, 1928: 14.

5   "Home Run Twins Perform Here Monday; Great Babe Ruth and Gehrig, Heroes of 1928 World Series," *Ottawa Citizen*, October 12, 1928: 15.

6   "Sultan of Swat," *Salt Lake City Tribune*, October 10, 1928: 1. Courtesy John Delahanty.

7   A.k.a. the Chappies, a team owned and operated by former Negro Leagues star George "Chappie" Johnson Jr., a native of Bellaire, Ohio. The Chappies played in the Montreal City League in the late 1920s and early 1930s.

8   "Babe Is For Al,; Home Run King Talks Politics." Rarely shy about expressing his political opinions, Ruth nevertheless failed to cast a ballot in 1928 or in any presidential election until 1944.

9   Tom Meany, *Baseball's Greatest Players* (New York: Grosset & Dunlop, 1953), 99.

10   "Babe Ready For Hull Swatfest."

11   "Babe Ready For Hull Swatfest."

12   "Babe Ready For Hull Swatfest."

13   "Babe Ready For Hull Swatfest."

14   Baz O'Meara, "Sport Facts and Fancies," *Ottawa Journal*, October 15, 1928: 34.

15   "Ruth and Gehrig Failed to Hammer Out Keenly Awaited Circuit Wallops, Disappoint Three Thousand Fans," *Ottawa Journal*, October 16, 1928: 14

16   Bert Williams, 92-year-old son of Ralph Williams, telephone interview with author., December 17, 2009. The elder Williams, a.k.a Guillaume, was 35 years old when he faced Ruth and Gehrig. "He said that was the best thing he ever did," recounted Bert Williams.

17   "Ruth and Gehrig Failed to Hammer Out Keenly Awaited Circuit Wallops, Disappoint Three Thousand Fans."

18   "Ruth And Gehrig Thrill Crowd in Exhibition Game at Dupuis; Home Run Kings Play Before Huge Throng on Hull Diamond," *Ottawa Citizen*, October 16, 1928: 10.

OTTAWA NATIONALS / SENATORS (1947-1950), BORDER LEAGUE

BY WARREN CAMPBELL

THE SECOND WORLD WAR ENDED, sparking a boom in affiliated minor-league baseball across Canada and the United States. In 1945, there were 12 leagues with 86 teams. The 1946 season began with 43 leagues and 316 teams.

On December 9, 1945, a meeting chaired by Father Harold Martin took place at St. Raphael's Catholic Church in Heuvelton, New York. Father Martin played baseball at Fordham University and pitched minor-league ball for teams in Albany and Toronto.[1] His goal was to bring minor-league baseball back to northern New York State. Six teams were represented: Ogdensburg Maples, Watertown Athletics, Auburn Cayugas, Geneva Redbirds, Granby (Quebec) Red Sox, and the Kingston (Ontario) Ponies. The league was known as the Border League and played at Class-C level, the fifth of six levels of minor-league baseball.

1946

The first year of the Border League began with the six teams, but the Sherbrooke (Quebec) Canadians replaced Geneva, creating a balance of Canadian and American teams. The Kingston Ponies were the only team to have an affiliate relationship with a major-league team, as the Philadelphia Athletics supplied Kingston with players. The Auburn Cayugas were the regular-season champions but were eliminated in the first round of the playoffs by Kingston. Watertown defeated Kingston in the final to become the first champions of the Border League.

1947

Two teams changed cities for the second season. Granby moved to Geneva, and sports promoter Tommy Gorman relocated the Sherbrooke team to Ottawa, renaming them the Ottawa Nationals. This move established a Nationals baseball franchise in both the capital cities of Canada and the United States. Gorman announced that home games would be played at Lansdowne Park in Ottawa. State-of-the-art lighting, consisting of six 100-foot-high poles in the outfield and lights on top of the grandstand for the infield, were installed.

Weeknight games were scheduled to start at 9:00 P.M. Ticket prices were set at $1 for most seats, 50 cents for bleachers, and 25 cents for youth. Sunday baseball was prohibited under Ontario provincial law, so the Nationals played home games at a baseball diamond built at Connaught Park racetrack across the river in Aylmer, Quebec.

Tommy Gorman was no stranger to the sports world. He co-founded the National Hockey League and managed race tracks across North America. In 1947, preparations began to assemble a competitive team for what became the first professional baseball team in the nation's capital since the shared Ottawa-Ogdensburg franchise of the 1940 Can-Am League.

Gorman wasted no time announcing that two hockey stars from Montreal would join the Nationals, and negotiations were underway with a high-profile baseball figure to manage the team. On March 11, Gorman revealed that the Nationals had added Montreal Canadiens star forward Maurice Richard to their negotiation list, intending for him to play center field. In April, it was announced that Paul "Daffy" Dean had signed on as manager.[2] On April 23, Dean, accompanied by his wife and three children, arrived in Ottawa after a 1,600-mile drive from Little Rock, Arkansas. This marked his first visit to Canada and his first managerial position.[3]

The roster began to take shape as players arrived from across the United States and Eastern Canada. Only two players–pitchers Leon St. Dennis and George Smith–remained from the last-place Sherbrooke team. In early May, they departed for a training camp in Saratoga Springs, New York, playing exhibition games against teams in Bristol, Connecticut, and Malone, New York. The team was promoted to fans in Ottawa and the Hull region, with particular emphasis on manager Dean and the new recruits, including "the $50,000 infield."[4]

On May 14, Opening Day arrived in Ottawa amid much excitement. Mayor Stanley Lewis threw out the first pitch to Hull mayor Ray Brunet, though it sailed behind him, preventing a swing.[5] Reports varied, but between 3,500 and 4,000 spectators attended the game on a sunny but chilly afternoon.[6] The home fans left happy as the Nationals defeated the Ogdensburg Maples, 6–3, thanks to a stellar pitching performance by Nick Butcher, who scattered seven hits over nine innings and contributed a triple that drove in the final Nationals run.

There was considerable buzz surrounding the new team. Local newspapers reported that within minutes of the final out of the home opener, police received four calls requesting the dispersal of boys playing baseball on Ottawa's streets.[7] While all was well in Ottawa, some issues persisted at Lansdowne Park; fences were absent, and children interfered with players. An Ogdensburg player even had his glove stolen.[8] By the Nationals' return after the opening homestand, fences were in place, and measures had been implemented to prevent fan interference.

Early in the season, the Nationals emerged as one of the stronger teams in the league, prompting speculation about whether manager Dean would pitch in a game. His major-league career had been cut short by bursitis, with his most recent outings comprising a few games at the AA level in 1946. Finally, on June 7, before a crowd of 4,000 people, Paul Dean made his debut as the starting pitcher. He departed after six innings, trailing 4-0, though three runs were unearned. Dean also contributed a hit in two at-bats. When asked about his pitching style, he remarked, "I was throwing easy all day. I was always a sidearm pitcher, just like Diz. I was an under-and-up pitcher, sometimes going higher when using my curve."[9]

Approaching the season's midpoint, the Nationals began to pull ahead of Watertown and Auburn, their closest challengers. Strong pitching and defensive play characterized their performance. On July 16, 21-year-old pitcher Len Seamon pitched a masterful no-hitter against the Geneva Redbirds, marking the fourth no-hitter in Border League history and Seamon's second, having achieved one as a rookie with Granby in 1946. By month's end, five Nationals players had been selected to participate in the all-star game in Kingston, representing the North team against players from the league's three Southern teams.

The second half of the season proved even more successful for the Ottawa team, winning 35 of their final 46 games after the all-star break, comfortably securing the league title by 12 games over Watertown. On and off the field, the team's success drew interest from other Canadian promoters. Peter Campbell, president of the International League's Toronto Maple Leafs, sought teams for Peterborough and Belleville, Ontario, with plans for a working relationship with the IL Maple Leafs for the Peterborough franchise.

At the conclusion of the 1947 regular season, the Nationals clearly stood out as the league's top team. The Border League implemented a playoff system to determine its champion, and the Nationals, finishing in first place, swept third-place Auburn 4-0 in a best-of-seven series. In the championship series, they faced their Opening Day opponents and second-place finishers, the Ogdensburg Maples. The Nationals were missing one of their ace pitchers, 40-year-old Walt Masters, who, alongside his baseball duties, also coached the Ottawa football team. Masters had some major-league experience, having pitched three games for the 1931 Washington Nationals, one game for the 1937 Philadelphia Phillies, and four games for the 1939 Philadelphia Athletics. Despite his 11-4 record for the Nationals, Masters opted to focus on football coaching rather than pitching during the playoff run.

Game One of the finals saw 31-year-old Charles Schupp deliver a masterful one-hitter in front of 4,000 chilly hometown fans. Ogdensburg responded by winning Game Two, but Ottawa ultimately prevailed in six games. After Game Four of the series, manager Dean abruptly departed the team and drove back home to Arkansas.

A playoff souvenir from the Ottawa Nationals. Credit: City of Ottawa Archives, MG-946-1-1

The Sporting News conducted an interview with Paul Dean, who discussed his challenges with the local media's lack of support for Lansdowne Park as a professional baseball venue. He acknowledged that the sports pages were supportive of the team but Dean was never the same after reading those editorials about the quality of the home field. He didn't feel that it was healthy for a professional baseball team to play in a city with that level of criticism. In response, the Gorman family—Tommy and his sons—assured Dean that they would handle those concerns and he should concentrate on winning the playoffs. They had provided him with a comfortable life in Ottawa including a residence on Clemow Ave., a car for transportation, and ensured the local community welcomed his family.[10]

To make up for the loss of their manager, owner Gorman responded swiftly by appointing 28-year-old Bill Metzig as the new player-manager and he managed the team to the championship. Metzig had appeared in five games for the 1944 Chicago White Sox.

1948

In January 1948, the Border League held its owners' meetings in Watertown, New York, deciding to maintain six teams. Player-manager Metzig confirmed his return, and most of the Ottawa lineup from the championship '47 season would remain intact.

One notable addition generating considerable interest was young hockey star Doug Harvey, who also excelled in Canadian football. In 1944, Harvey played for the combined Marine St-Hyacinthe-Donnacona team, winning the Grey Cup, Canada's football championship, although he did not participate in the final due to being on active duty for the Canadian military.

Alongside the young Montreal Canadiens defenseman, rumors again circulated about Tommy Gorman potentially bringing star forward Maurice Richard to Ottawa. However, Richard never played for the Nationals due to an injury sustained while playing third base for the Drummondville team in the outlaw Provincial League of Quebec.[11]

The Nationals held their preseason in Chambersburg, Pennsylvania, playing exhibition games at historic Henninger Field. Once again, they asserted their dominance in the league, rebounding from two initial losses in Ogdensburg to secure an Opening Day victory in front of 4,000 fans at Lansdowne Park. As in 1947, the mayors of Ottawa and nearby Hull participated in the festivities. This time, Ottawa mayor Lewis threw a pitch over the plate to Hull's mayor Brunet, who swung and missed. The Nationals enjoyed a successful outing with a 15-3 victory. Sunday games were relocated from the Aylmer, Quebec racetrack to Décosse Field, a more baseball-friendly stadium built by longtime Hull athlete and sports personality Gene Décosse.[12]

Kingston franchise owner Nelles Megaffin accused the Nationals of exceeding the salary cap by allegedly paying some players more than the league limit of $750 per season. Megaffin

The 1948 Ottawa Nationals dominated the regular season but faced an unexpected upset in the playoffs. Despite finishing 11 games ahead of Ogdensburg, the Nationals fell 4-1 in the best-of-seven series to the eventual champions. Credit: City of Ottawa Archives, MG-946-2

lodged a complaint with league president John Ward, though no public statement was made on the matter.[13]

By the mid-season all-star game, the Nationals held a seven-game lead over Geneva, with several players drawing interest from major-league scouts. Pitchers Len Seamon and Harry Baker, Doug Harvey, and shortstop Pete Karpuk were all closely monitored by scouts from the Chicago White Sox and New York Yankees. The Montreal Royals also extended an offer to Harvey.

The Nationals traveled to Montreal for an exhibition game against the Atwater All-Stars at Delorimier Park, a benefit for Father Ryan's Boys Town Club of Montreal. Seamon impressed the crowd with 11 strikeouts over six innings, while local favorite Doug Harvey went 1-for-4 in the game.

Left-hander Seamon finished the season with a remarkable 21-4 record. Harvey emerged as a breakout star after adjusting his batting stance early in the season—his hands noticeably apart and resting his bat on his shoulder "as if he was in the box for a short rest"[14]— resulting in a .340 batting average. Metzig also distinguished himself as one of the league's top hitters. The team boasted the best fielding percentage, batting average, and pitching records, clinching the season championship by 6 ½ games ahead of Geneva.

Despite their regular-season success, the Nationals faced disappointment in the playoffs, matched against third-place Ogdensburg, who finished 11 games behind. The Nationals struggled both offensively and defensively, losing the best-of-seven series 4-1 to the eventual champions.

Following the playoff setback, tragedy struck the Nationals in October when Len "Lefty" Seamon passed away suddenly at the age of 22. A standout pitcher in the Border League with multiple opportunities to advance in professional baseball, Seamon had received offers from the New York Yankees, Cleveland Indians, Pittsburgh Pirates, Brooklyn Dodgers, and Chicago Cubs. Initially suspected to have appendicitis after complaining of abdominal pain at season's end, doctors discovered a large tumor that proved fatal.[15]

1949

In early 1949, baseball interest in Ottawa grew as the city emerged as a potential location for a higher-level minor league team. The New York Yankees' top farm team, the Newark Bears, considered relocating, with discussions including the possibility of moving to Ottawa or establishing a second team in Montreal. Tommy Gorman proposed a plan to play weeknight games in Ottawa and Sunday games in Montreal.[16]

Once again, the Nationals began their season with two games in Ogdensburg, splitting the series unlike their 1948 opening games. Returning home, they secured a 4-3 victory in the home opener, where Mayor E.A. "Eddy" Bourque threw the first pitch to team president Theo Lanctot. Throughout the season, the Geneva Robins led the league standings, with the Nationals fluctuating between second and third place. For the first time, fan voting determined the all-star teams, resulting in

five Nationals players being selected. Ottawa players featured prominently, with catcher Bill Kivett hitting a two-run homer and shortstop Michael Pontarelli driving in the winning run. The game drew an overflow crowd of 2,800 at Geneva.

Following the all-star game, manager Metzig hoped for an improved second half of the season. The team lagged behind Geneva in batting and ranked third in fielding across the league. Inconsistent pitching left them 5½ games behind the league-leading Geneva Robins.

Despite efforts, the Nationals couldn't close the gap beyond 2½ games behind Geneva. Strong performances from hitters Doug Harvey, Bill Kivett, and player-manager Bill Metzig buoyed the team, but pitching inconsistencies persisted. In mid-August, they faced Geneva in a crucial three-game series, their final opportunity to challenge the Robins directly. After losing the opener and splitting a doubleheader, their hopes of winning the regular-season pennant faded.

Earlier in the season, the league introduced the Len Seamon Award, honoring the top pitcher. During a break in the doubleheader, Walt Balash of the Nationals received the award, voted by Border League managers.[17] Interestingly, this followed Balash's challenging outing, allowing 11 runs in his worst start of the year, resulting in a loss to Geneva.

As in 1948, the playoffs proved disappointing for the Nationals. In the Border League's playoff format, second-place Ottawa faced fourth-place Auburn in the semi-finals. After a seven-game series, Auburn emerged victorious, highlighting the Nationals' struggles with key hitting and consistent pitching.

1950

The 1950 season saw the Nationals retain many regulars from '49 while integrating rookie replacements from leagues in Ontario and Quebec, necessitated by a new league rule limiting rosters to eight veterans. To aid adjustment, teams were allowed to retain all players, up to 24, for the first 30 days of the season.

Even with the need for rookies, the Nationals were still on the hunt for quality veteran players. Manager Metzig made a strong effort to sign former St. Louis Browns outfielder, one-armed Pete Gray.[18]

Opening the season with a two-game sweep in Ogdensburg, the Nationals returned to Ottawa for the home opener festivities. League president John Ward threw the first pitch to Hull mayor Brunet, who reportedly hit a "clean single."[19] However, a sluggish start left the Nationals in last place after seven games with a 2-5 record, marking the first time they had trailed all other teams in the standings. It wasn't until the end of May that Ottawa's offense ignited, sparking an 11-game winning streak and propelling them into first place.

By Canada Day, the Nationals held a commanding 6½ game lead over second-place Watertown, prompting the decision to host the all-star game at Lansdowne Park on July 12. League founder Rev. Harold J. Martin delivered the first pitch to Nationals Club President Theo Lanctot. Tragically, President Lanctot suffered a stroke in the fourth inning and had to be escorted from the stadium. Facing the league all-stars, the Nationals prevailed 4-3 in 12 innings, winning the game when right fielder Frank Schwartz stole home on a missed squeeze play.

Despite holding a nine-game lead over Ogdensburg just before the all-star break, the Nationals encountered difficulties, allowing their lead to dwindle to four games. Throughout July, the pennant race evolved into a three-team battle with Ottawa maintaining first place, closely pursued by Ogdensburg and Kingston. To bolster their lineup, Ottawa signed 22-year-old catcher Jim Wallace, formerly of the Newark Eagles in the Negro National League. Metzig expressed optimism about Wallace's potential, stating "For my money Wallace is a good bet to be another Jackie Robinson."[20]

On July 31, tragedy struck as pitcher Robert Larkin was killed in a car accident involving a US Army truck near Watertown, New York, while returning from a game. Four teammates were injured in the crash. Nationals executives personally delivered the heartbreaking news to Larkin's wife and infant daughter, who lived at 393 MacLaren Street in downtown Ottawa.

On August 3, Ogdensburg swept a doubleheader, resulting in a tie atop the standings. They extended their lead by sweeping Ottawa in a subsequent series. In need of reinforcements, Ottawa signed Willard Brown, fresh from winning two batting Triple Crowns in the Puerto Rican league and becoming the first African American to hit a home run in the American League.[21] Brown would later earn induction into the National Baseball Hall of Fame and the Salón de la Fama del Béisbol Profesional de Puerto Rico.[22]

Throughout August, the lead changed hands between Ottawa and Ogdensburg, culminating in Ottawa securing the pennant with a season-ending five-game winning streak highlighted by Don Bryant's no-hitter. Strong performances from Bryant, Ed Flanagan, and newcomers Brown (.352 average) and Wallace (.278) bolstered Ottawa's confidence heading into the playoffs.

In the postseason, Ottawa and Ogdensburg advanced by defeating Kingston and Watertown, respectively, in five games. The championship series saw Ottawa struggle with inconsistent hitting against Ogdensburg, resulting in a six-game series loss.

By mid-October, discussions arose about a new team potentially coming to Lansdowne Park, prompting speculation about the Nationals relocating to Cornwall. On December 6, 1950, it was confirmed that Horace Stoneham, owner of the New York Giants, had acquired the minor-league rights in Ottawa, intending to relocate his AAA affiliate, the Jersey City Giants, to the Canadian capital. Consequently, the Nationals moved to Cornwall, becoming the Cornwall (Ontario) Canadians. However, the franchise's tenure was short-lived, ceasing operations on June 26, 1951, preceding the Border League's dissolution on July 16 by a few weeks.

NOTES

1   Jack Smith, "Baseball's Bloodstream," *(New York) Daily News*, July 22, 1942: 491.

2   Paul Geisler Jr, "Paul Dean," https://sabr.org/bioproj/person/paul-dean/

3   Tommy Shields, "Sports Roundup," *Ottawa Citizen*, April 23, 1947: 18.

4   Advertisement, *Ottawa Citizen*, May 10, 1947: 2.

5   Tommy Shields, "Sports Roundup," *Ottawa Citizen*, May 15, 1947: 23.

6   Shields, "Sports Roundup." *Ottawa Citizen*, May 15, 1947: 23.

7   "Nats Start Wave Sandlot Baseball," *Ottawa Journal*, May 15, 1947: 24.

8   Tommy Shields, "Sports Roundup," *Ottawa Citizen*, May 19, 1947: 20.

9   Tommy Shields, "Sports Roundup," *Ottawa Citizen*, June 9, 1947: 18.

10 Austin F. Cross, "Dean's Run-Out During Playoffs at Ottawa Laid to Editorial Rap," *The Sporting News*, October 22, 1947: 25.

11 André Rivest, "Histoire du Baseball à Montréal," *La Presse,* October 22, 2023. https://plus.lapresse.ca/screens/4187-64ec-5335da14-b13d-1 38aac1c6068%7CXAMK27~RIxCq.html. Accessed on May 13, 2024

12 "Gene Decosse – In the System – 1924," HabsGoalies.blogspot.com, May 24, 2007. https://habsgoalies.blogspot.com/2007/05/gene-decosse-1924.html. Accessed on May 20, 2024.

13 Ken Cuthbertson, *When the Ponies Ran* (Kingston, Ontario: Cataraqui Press, 2021), 31.

14 Bill Westwick, "Sports Roundup," *Ottawa Journal*, May 29, 1948: 24.

15 "Lefty Seamon, 23, Star Ottawa Pitcher Dies of Cancer," *Ottawa Journal*, October 14, 1948: 1.

16 "Suggest Ottawa as Home of International League Team," *Ottawa Journal*, January 17, 1949: 29.

17 "Walt Balash Star Hurler Border Loop," *Expositor* (Brantford, Ontario, Canada), August 24, 1949: 19.

18 "Metzig Will Continue Efforts to Land One-Armed Pete Gray," *Ottawa Journal*, April 15, 1950: 19.

19 "Battery for Opening Ceremonies," *Ottawa Journal*, May 13, 1950: 20.

20 "Colored Slugger and Catcher Signed by Nats," *Ottawa Journal*, July 18, 1950: 1.

21 Jake Bell, "August 13, 1947: Willard Brown hits first American League home run by a Black player," https://sabr.org/gamesproj/game/august-13-1947-willard-brown-hits-first-american-league-home-run-by-a-black-player/

22 Rory Costello, "Willard Brown," https://sabr.org/bioproj/person/willard-brown/

OTTAWA NATIONALS CLINCH THIRD BORDER LEAGUE PENNANT IN FOUR SEASONS

SEPTEMBER 8, 1950: OTTAWA NATIONALS 2, GENEVA ROBINS 1, AT LANSDOWNE PARK, OTTAWA

BY GARY BELLEVILLE

THE OTTAWA NATIONALS WERE THE most successful team in the Border League during their brief four-year existence.[1] After running away with the pennant in 1947 and 1948, Ottawa took a small step backward the next season and finished second to the Geneva Robins, a Brooklyn Dodgers affiliate. In 1950 the Nationals were determined to reclaim the top spot in the Class-C circuit.[2]

Despite not being as strong as the 1947-48 teams, the Nationals treated their fans to a spine-tingling 1950 pennant race that was one of the most dramatic in Ottawa's storied baseball history. Pivotal events that summer included the tragic midseason death of a key pitcher, the recruitment of the first two Black players to play professionally in Ottawa, and a back-and-forth battle for first place with the Ogdensburg Maples that wasn't decided until the final day of the season. Few were surprised when Ottawa led the league in attendance for the third consecutive season.[3]

The Nationals looked as though they might run away with the pennant in the early going, and at the end of June they had a 6½-game cushion. But the Nationals took their foot off the gas in July, and Ogdensburg got back into the race by winning 22 games that month.[4]

Ottawa's lead was just 2½ games over Ogdensburg after it swept a doubleheader in Watertown, New York on Sunday, July 30. The season took a sudden, shocking twist on the drive back to Ottawa. Around 12:30 A.M., a United States Army truck veered onto the wrong side of the highway just outside of Watertown and collided with an oncoming car carrying five Ottawa players.[5] Pitcher Bob Larkin, a 24-year-old native of Toronto, Ohio, was killed in the crash.[6] The four other Nationals in the vehicle were badly injured.[7]

The stunned and depleted Nationals lost their next six games, dropping them two games out of first place. Ottawa snapped the losing skid in Ogdensburg on August 6 when player-manager Bill Metzig slammed a game-winning homer in the ninth inning.[8]

The Nationals got an even bigger lift on August 12 when Negro Leagues legend Willard Brown joined the team from the Kansas City Monarchs.[9] The 35-year-old outfielder, nicknamed "Home Run" Brown by renowned slugger Josh Gibson, had been the Negro American League's RBI leader for eight seasons and its home-run leader six times.[10] Buck O'Neil, Brown's teammate on the Monarchs for nine seasons, called him "the most natural ballplayer I ever saw."[11]

In July 1947—just two weeks after Larry Doby had integrated the American League—Brown and Hank Thompson briefly integrated the St. Louis Browns.[12] Brown became the first Black player to hit a home run in the AL when he tagged Hal Newhouser for a pinch-hit homer on August 13.[13]

But Brown was not the first Black player to play professionally for Ottawa. Less than a month earlier, 21-year-old outfielder Jim "Bo" Wallace, who had an eight-game stint with the Newark Eagles of the Negro National League in 1948, debuted with the Nationals. News of Wallace's signing was splashed across the front page of both Ottawa dailies on July 18, with a local scribe classifying the team's move as a "dramatic change in policy."[14] Wallace soon settled into a role as a backup outfielder, hitting .278 in 90 at-bats for the season.

Ottawa and Ogdensburg remained locked in a tight struggle as the calendar flipped to September. On the season's penultimate day, Ottawa clinched a tie for first place by sweeping a doubleheader from Geneva, raising its record to 74-53. Don Bryant tossed a seven-inning no-hitter in the opener.[15] In the second game, Brown paced the attack with three hits, four RBIs, and a stolen base in a 15-3 blowout victory.[16]

Ogdensburg's last hope was to sweep a twin bill in Watertown on September 8 and have fifth-place Geneva upset Ottawa in the finale of their four-game series. Both Ottawa and Ogdensburg entered the last day of the season on a four-game winning streak. Metzig took no chances against Geneva, starting the league's top pitcher, Ed Flanagan (15-10, 2.00 ERA), on two days' rest.[17]

The Robins countered with another 26-year-old righty, Norman Gosselin. He had lasted just five innings in his start the previous evening, giving up 10 runs (3 earned) in the nightcap.[18] Gosselin had a 19-11 record a 3.20 ERA.

Ottawa got off to a fast start with six singles and three walks in the first two innings, although Gosselin minimized the damage by escaping with the bases loaded both times.

The Nationals opened the scoring in the first on a two-out RBI single by first baseman Vernon "Moose" Shetler.[19] After third baseman Johnny Russian walked to load the bases, left fielder Carl Hodson drew another walk to force in a run and give Ottawa a 2-0 lead. Gosselin recorded the third out before Ottawa could extend its lead any further.

Flanagan started the second by loading the bases on a pair of walks sandwiched around a single by Geneva backstop Tony Mlynarek.[20] Don Newman grounded the ball over second base, only to have shortstop Mike Pontarelli range to his left and make a diving stop; the runner from third scored as Pontarelli threw Newman out at first, cutting Ottawa's lead to 2-1.[21]

Ottawa loaded the bases in the bottom of the inning on singles by Pete Karpuk and Brown and an intentional walk to the dangerous Shetler.[22] The free pass worked like a charm, as Gosselin wiggled out of the jam.

The game turned into a pitchers' duel over in the final seven frames. Gosselin moved away from his fastball and began relying on his knuckleball and slow curve, limiting Ottawa to one single and one walk the rest of the way.[23]

Geneva threatened to tie the game in the fourth on singles by Mlynarek and Newman before "neat Ottawa fielding spoiled the uprising."[24] Hodson made the best defensive play of the night when he made a long running catch to retire the side in the eighth with the potential tying run on base.

The tense atmosphere at Lansdowne Park ratcheted up further when it was announced that Ogdensburg had won in extra innings in the first game of its twin bill.[25]

After getting the first out of the ninth on a long fly ball, Flanagan surrendered a single to Bob Toole, and Bryant began to quickly warm up in the bullpen. But Newman hit a slow roller to the right side; the second baseman Metzig came charging in, tagged Toole, and threw to first to com-

plete the game-ending double play. "The crowd of more than 4,000 raised the roof with a terrific roar of applause and relief," wrote Jack Kinsella in the *Ottawa Citizen*.[26]

Flanagan finished with a five-hitter, picking up his 16th win of the season. His victory proved critical to clinching the pennant, as Ogdensburg also won the second game of its doubleheader.

Brown played in the final 30 games of the season, hitting .352 and saving several games with his electrifying defense.[27] The Nationals went 21-9 (.700) with Brown in the lineup. "The acquisition of Moose Shetler and Willard Brown has been like money from home," wrote the *Citizen*'s Jack Koffman.[28] "Willard has been a favorite since he hit the capital."[29]

Brown returned to the Monarchs in 1951, winning the NAL batting title, and he continued to play professionally until 1958. In 2006 Brown and six other former Negro League players were elected to the National Baseball Hall of Fame in Cooperstown.[30] "I'm sorry we couldn't do this 30 or 40 years ago when some of our candidates were alive," said former commissioner Fay Vincent. "But we're here now to make this right."[31]

Two Ottawa stalwarts, Metzig and Russian, were named to the All-Star team in 1950. Both players had been regulars on the team since it joined the Border League, with Metzig named the league's All-Star second baseman in all four seasons.[32] Russian earned All-Star honors at third base three times.

In the first round of the Shaughnessy playoffs, Flanagan tossed a pair of shutouts against the Kingston Ponies, running his streak of scoreless innings to 25.[33] After defeating Kingston four games to one, the Nationals faced Ogdensburg in the final round. The Maples won the best-of-seven series in six games despite Flanagan's best efforts. He finished the playoffs with a 3-1 record and a 0.79 ERA.[34] The disappointing loss left Ottawa with only one playoff championship (1947) in four Border League seasons.

Less than three months after the playoffs ended, Nationals owner T.P "Tommy" Gorman announced that the New York Giants were relocating their International League affiliate from Jersey City to Ottawa for the 1951 season.[35] Under the deal engineered by Gorman, the Triple-A team remained under the ownership of its parent club, while the Nationals were shifted to Cornwall, Ontario. Ottawa returned to the highest level of the minor leagues for the first time since the Eastern League's Rochester Patriots were moved to Canada's capital for the last half of the 1898 season.[36]

SOURCES

In addition to the sources cited in the Notes, the author consulted Baseball-Reference.com, *The Encyclopedia of Minor League Baseball*, the SABR biography of Willard Brown, and *The Sporting News* contract cards. Unless otherwise noted, all play-by-play information for this game was taken from the article "Nats Take Pennant by Shading Robins 2-1," on page 20 of the September 9, 1950, edition of the *Ottawa Citizen*. League standings were taken from the *Ottawa Citizen*.

NOTES

1   As of June 2024, Baseball-Reference.com incorrectly listed the Ottawa team's nickname as Senators. The author conducted a thorough search of articles on newspapers.com and the team was consistently referred to as the Nationals from 1947 to 1950.

2   The minor leagues were organized into six levels in 1950: Triple A, Double A, Single A, B, C, and D.

3   The Ottawa Nationals drew 97,091 fans in 1950, almost 50 percent more than the second-best attendance mark in the league. The Watertown Athletics were second with a total attendance of 65,329.

4   Ottawa went 16-18 in July, while Ogdensburg went 22-13.

5   "Bob Larkin's Tragic Death Big Shock to Baseball Fans," *Ottawa Citizen*, July 31, 1950: 1.

6   Larkin had a record of 12-6 and a 3.51 ERA with Ottawa in 1950. The southpaw had gone 12-10 in 1949 pitching for both Watertown and Ottawa.

7   The four other players in the car were pitchers Otto Kossuth, Jim St. Clair, and Frank Schwartz, along with outfielder Pete Karpuk. Kossuth spent significant time in a Watertown hospital. According to his *Sporting News* contract card, Schwartz later played under the surname Howlan. "Ogdensburg Here Tonight; Help Promised for Nats," *Ottawa Citizen*, August 4, 1950: 22.

8   "Metzig's Homer in 9th Payoff for Flanagan," *Ottawa Citizen*, August 7, 1950: 14.

9   "Nats Using New Pitcher; Brown Due?" *Ottawa Citizen*, August 12, 1950: 14; Michael Birchwood, "Nats Defeat Auburn, 5-2, on Hot Fielding Show," *Ottawa Citizen*, August 14, 1950: 22.

10   According to Baseball-Reference.com, Brown led the Negro American League in both homers and RBIs in 1937-38, '41, '43, '46, and '48. Brown missed most of the 1944 season and all of 1945 because of his military service. He tied Turkey Stearnes for the league lead in RBIs in 1939 and led all Negro League players in RBIs in 1947.

11   "Willard Brown," Baseball Hall of Fame, https://baseballhall. org/hall-of-famers/brown-willard, accessed February 23, 2024.

12   Brown and Thompson were released by the Browns on August 23. It was almost four years before the next Black player, Satchel Paige, appeared in a game for the team.

13   During Brown's stint in the AL, the team did not supply him with suitable bats; he preferred to use 40-ounce bats and the rest of the team used lighter ones. Brown hit the home run off Newhouser using a bat with a broken knob that had been discarded by Jeff Heath, who used the heaviest bats on the team. Heath destroyed the bat in a fit of rage after Brown's home run. Jake Bell, "August 13, 1947: Willard Brown Hits First American League Home Run by a Black Player," SABR Games Project, https://sabr.org/gamesproj/game/august-13-1947-willard-brown-hits-first-american-league-home-run-by-a-black-player/, accessed February 23, 2024.

14   "Nationals Sign Negro," *Ottawa Citizen*, July 18, 1950: 1.

15   "Ottawa's Bryant Hurls No-Hitter," *Rochester Democrat and Chronicle*, September 9, 1950: 20.

16   Clare McDermott, "Two Wins Over Geneva Robins Clinches First Place Tie," *Ottawa Journal*, September 8, 1950: 21.

17   Flanagan finished the season with a 1.96 ERA, tops in the league. Ottawa's Don Bryant was next with a 2.52 ERA. Flanagan's previous appearance was on September 5 in Watertown. He gave up six hits and three runs (two earned) in a complete-game victory. "Flanagan Hurls Ottawa to Important Win," *Ottawa Citizen*, September 6, 1950: 18.

18   Gosselin was easily Geneva's best pitcher. He was likely starting his second consecutive game in an attempt to earn his 20th victory of the season more than to prevent Ottawa from winning the pennant. McDermott, "Two Wins Over Geneva Robins Clinches First Place Tie."

19   After Pete Karpuk singled to open the inning, Mike Pontarelli reached base on a bunt single. Brown followed by lining into a double play. Clare McDermott, "Nationals Win Third Border Pennant in Four Years," *Ottawa Journal*, September 9, 1950: 17.

20   McDermott, "Nationals Win Third Border Pennant in Four Years."

21   McDermott, "Nationals Win Third Border Pennant in Four Years."

22   McDermott, "Nationals Win Third Border Pennant in Four Years."

23   McDermott, "Nationals Win Third Border Pennant in Four Years."

24   McDermott, "Nationals Win Third Border Pennant in Four Years."

25   Jack Kinsella, "Nats Take Pennant by Shading Robins 2-1," *Ottawa Citizen*, September 9, 1950: 20.

26   Kinsella, "Nats Take Pennant by Shading Robins 2-1."

27   Brown had the highest batting average in the Border League, although he did not have enough plate appearances to qualify for the batting title. "Ottawa Nationals Win Border Title," *Montreal Gazette*, September 9, 1950: 8.

28   Shetler was also a late-season acquisition. He played in his first game for Ottawa on August 9. Clare McDermott, "Don Bryant Stops Ottawa Losing Streak; Hurls Nats to 5-2 Victory; Shetler Impresses in Debut," *Ottawa Journal*, August 10, 1950: 18.

29 Jack Koffman, "Along Sports Row," *Ottawa Citizen*, September 9, 1950: 20.

30 The other former Negro Leagues players elected to the Hall of Fame in 2006 were Ray Brown, Andy Cooper, Biz Mackey, Mule Suttles, Cristóbal Torriente, and Jud Wilson. Five pre–Negro Leagues players were also inducted. They were Frank Grant, Pete Hill, José Méndez, Louis Santop, and Ben Taylor.

31 Craig Muder, "Historic 2006 Election Honors Negro Leagues Legends," Baseball Hall of Fame, https://baseballhall.org/discover/inside-pitch/historic-2006-election-brings-negro-leagues-legends-to-cooperstown, accessed February 23, 2024.

32 With the exception of the 1948 season, the Border League All-Star teams are listed in *The Encyclopedia of Minor League Baseball*. "Gerken Voted Most Valuable; Three Nats on All-Star Team," *Ottawa Journal*, September 15, 1948: 18.

33 Flanagan's streak started with the final seven innings of his September 8 start. He then tossed complete-game shutouts against Kingston on September 12 and 18. His streak was snapped when he gave up an unearned run in the first inning of his September 21 start against Ogdensburg. Clare McDermott, "Flanagan Raises Ottawa's Playoff Chances," *Ottawa Journal*, September 13, 1950: 20; Clare McDermott, "Flanagan's Second Shutout Eliminates Ponies," *Ottawa Journal*, September 19, 1950: 15; Edward MacCabe, *Ottawa Journal*, "Flanagan Gets Ottawa's First Series Win," September 22, 1950: 20.

34 Flanagan's playoff statistics were calculated by the author using the box scores in the Ottawa newspapers. His final playoff appearance was on September 25 against Ogdensburg.

35 Gary Belleville, "April 26, 1951: Ottawa Giants Bring Triple-A Baseball Back to Canada's Capital," SABR Games Project, https://sabr.org/gamesproj/game/april-26-1951-ottawa-giants-bring-triple-a-baseball-back-to-canadas-capital/, accessed February 23, 2024.

36 Gary Belleville, "July 19, 1898: Jimmy 'Gussie' Gannon Leads Ottawa to Its First Home Victory in Professional Baseball," SABR Games Project, https://sabr.org/gamesproj/game/july-19-1898-jimmy-gussie-gannon-leads-ottawa-to-its-first-home-victory-in-professional-baseball/, accessed February 23, 2024.

WILLARD BROWN

BY MARTIN LACOSTE

ONLY 21 BORDER LEAGUE (1946-51) players made it to the major leagues.[1] Of these, only one made it all the way to the National Baseball Hall of Fame.

Willard Jessie Brown was born in Shreveport, Louisiana in 1915. In 1934, Brown played with the Monroe Monarchs of the Negro Southern League. He rose to the major leagues only three years later with the Kansas City Monarchs, a charter member of the Negro American League, and quickly established himself as a superior player. He led the league in home runs (10), hits (81), triples (10), and RBIs (60) in his rookie season, and led the Monarchs to the first Negro American League title. In his sophomore season, he led the league in hits, doubles, home runs, and RBIs, and in 1939 he similarly led the league in six offensive categories while batting .368.

He only played two games with the Monarchs in 1940 as he was tempted by a better salary to head south to play in the Mexican Leagues, as did many other Negro Leaguers. Returning to Kansas City in 1941, he continued to dominate by leading the league in nine offensive categories including home runs, RBIs and stolen bases, showcasing his combination of power and speed. He continued to excel over the next two seasons, batting .338 and .340 respectively, but only played three games in 1944 as he joined the U.S. Army in Europe at the height of World War II. He missed the entire 1945 season due to his service, and upon his return to Kansas City in 1946, he again led the league in hits, home runs, and RBIs. From 1937-1946, Brown led the Monarchs to six pennants in 10 years.

In July 1947, only months after the landmark signing of Jackie Robinson and only days after the signing of the first Black player by an AL team (Larry Doby with the Cleveland Indians), the last-place St. Louis Browns signed him and infielder Hank Thompson from the Monarchs for $5,000 each. It would be almost another full year before another Black player was signed in the AL (Satchel Paige with Cleveland in July 1948). With Brown's signing, "outfielder Brown was considered to be the prize package of the lot, with only his age against him."[2]

Brown never really got on track in St. Louis (despite displaying his enormous power in batting practice). His best game with the Browns was at Yankee Stadium on July 23, where he went 4-for-5 and drove in three runs. On August 13, Brown hit his only homer with St. Louis, the first in the AL by a Black player, an inside-the-parker off Detroit's Hal Newhouser.

On August 23, Browns manager Muddy Ruel released both Brown and Hank Thompson, stating that they lacked major-league talent. During his tenure with St. Louis, he played in 21 games and hit .179. Brown and Thompson both rejoined the Monarchs, where the money was better, and at season's end, Brown led the league in batting with a .377 average.

During the offseasons, Brown often went south to play in the Puerto Rican Winter League. In the winter of 1947-48, while playing for the Santurce Cangrejeros (Crabbers), Brown won the Triple Crown, hitting .432 (fourth-highest in Puerto Rican Winter League history) and 27 home runs (still a Puerto Rican Winter League record). He also drove in 86 runs, impressive for only a 60-game season. He again won the Triple Crown in the 1949-50 season.

In 1948, he continued to lead the Negro American League in several offensive categories, including home runs, RBIs and slugging, while batting .408, second only to Artie Wilson (.433). Brown continued to play with Kansas City for several more seasons, winning the Negro American League batting title again in 1951 with a .417 average.

On August 5, 1950, Brown was purchased by the Ottawa Nationals of the Border League. As he was tending to his ailing wife, he felt that Ottawa was too far for him to go and was reluctant to report. He nevertheless arrived in Ottawa on August 12 and in the 30 games he played with the Nationals he batted .352 to help lead the team to the league championship. In the playoffs, Ottawa defeated Kingston four games to one, aided by Brown's strong showing, notably in Game Three where he went 3-for-6 with four RBIs. Ottawa eventually fell four games to two to Ogdensburg in the finals. In Game Six, Brown went 2-for-5 including a "two-bagger [that bounced] off the right-center field fence"[3] in what proved to be his last game with Ottawa.

Over the next few years, Brown played in Venezuela and in the Dominican Republic, then in the Texas League and Western League from 1953-1956. He continued to play in Puerto Rico until the 1956-57 season and was named to the Puerto Rican Baseball Hall of Fame in 1991. He played in 1957 for the Minot Mallards of the Manitoba-Dakota League before closing out his career barnstorming with the Monarchs in 1958.

He is regarded by some as having the most raw power in Negro Leagues history, and possibly in all of baseball. He hit home runs more often than Josh Gibson, who gave him the nickname "Home Run" Brown. He is also considered by many as one of the fastest players in baseball in the late 1930s and 1940s. Despite this, he would not live to celebrate his election to the National Baseball Hall of Fame. After baseball, he retired to Houston and died there on August 4, 1996. Almost 10 years later, in February 2006, a special committee elected Willard Brown along with 16 other Negro League and pre-Negro League candidates to Cooperstown. Dick Clark, a member of the selection committee, said of his enshrinement: "Brown's credentials made his election an easy one… [he] was the preeminent right-handed slugger for the Negro American League throughout the '40s."[4]

SOURCES

In addition to the sources listed in the endnotes, the author consulted various newspapers, including: *The Sporting News* (at Paper of Record), *Ottawa Journal* (at Newspapers.com) and *Le Droit (Ottawa)* (at Bibliothèque et Archives Nationales du Québec)

The author also consulted:

Baseball-reference.com

"Willard Brown," Hall of Fame Explorer, https://baseballhall.org/hall-of-famers/brown-willard, accessed January 11, 2023.

NOTES

1   This includes all leagues considered major by Major League Baseball as of June 2024, including the Negro National (II) and Negro American Leagues. Along with Willard Brown, there were six other Negro Leagues players: Gideon Applegate (1949-51 Kingston Ponies), Joe Campini (1950 Watertown Athletics), Pedro Miró (1951 Geneva Robins), Maurice Peatros (1949 Geneva Robins), John Sanderson (1951 Geneva Robins), and Bo Wallace (1950 Ottawa Nationals).

2   Rory Costello, "Willard Brown," SABR Baseball Biography Project, https://sabr.org/bioproj/person/Willard-Brown/.

3   "Ogdensburg Captures Border League Title," *Evening Citizen (Ottawa)*, September 26, 1950:18.

4   Ted Lewis, "Willard Brown's Legacy Remains As Prominent Slugger." Original publication may have been in the *New Orleans Times-Picayune*, where Lewis was employed as sportswriter. Reposted on the W.E. A.L.L. B.E. blog, June 15, 2007. (http://weallbe.blogspot.com/2007/06/legend-of-willard-brown-forgotten.html)

DOUG HARVEY

BY MARTIN LACOSTE

TWO PLAYERS FROM THE BORDER League (1946-51) would become Hall of Famers. One, Willard Brown, played 30 games for the Ottawa Nationals in 1950 and narrowly missed being a teammate of another Hall of Famer. This other star athlete is not in Cooperstown, however, but rather in Toronto, home of the Hockey Hall of Fame. Regarded as one of the top defensemen in NHL history (ranked third by *Sports Illustrated*, behind only Bobby Orr and Ray Bourque), Doug Harvey excelled in virtually every sport he played, and for a time, many wondered if he was destined to find fame on the diamond rather than on the hockey rink.[1]

Douglas Norman Harvey was born on December 19, 1924, in Montreal, Quebec, and as a youth was a versatile and competitive athlete. Harvey tried badminton, track, lacrosse, and boxing during his high school years, and helped lead his school's football team to the championship game.

While at home during the summer of 1943, Doug was asked to play fast-pitch softball in the newly formed Snowdon Fastball League. In the fall of 1943, Harvey joined the Navy, and he was assigned to play for Donnacona in the Quebec Rugby Football Union. In 1944 he was sailing across the Atlantic Ocean as a gunner on a merchant ship. After the war, he resumed his hockey career with the Navy and the Junior Royals, and the following year, he starred at defense on the Senior team.

In between hockey and football seasons, Harvey continued to play softball, and in the summer of 1947, a new opportunity arose. "Thomas Gorman (one of the founders of the NHL), now back in Ottawa, having recently retired as GM of the Montreal Canadiens, approached him about playing baseball for a new franchise he had landed in the Class C Border League."[2] Gorman admired Harvey's durability and determination. So, while he had never seen Harvey play baseball, "he offered him a contract and never regretted it."[3]

Despite being very new to the sport (with second-hand equipment and holding a bat with his hands several inches apart), in his very first game with Ottawa he came off the bench and managed two hits.

That season he made it into only 10 games but made the most of it as he went 6-for-15, "an amazing performance for someone facing professional baseball pitching for the first time."[4] As the Montreal Canadiens training camp had opened, Harvey missed the playoffs.

In 1948, Harvey showed up for spring training leaner than he had been the summer before and was determined to make the team, knowing the Nationals needed an outfielder. He hit the ball hard during exhibition games, picking up where he had left off the previous fall. On the eve of the season opener, manager William Metzig announced that Harvey would be his starting right fielder.

With the opportunity to play more regularly, Harvey made the most of it, and steadily moved up in the batting order. "By August, he was the team's cleanup hitter and was contending for the Border League batting title. He was also named as a starter in the league's mid-season All-Star game."[5]

Harvey helped the Nationals win the pennant in 1948, and finished sixth in batting (.340) and second in runs scored (107). In the playoffs, he batted .357 with two HRs and five RBIs in the first four games against Ogdensburg but missed the final game because he had to report to the Montreal Canadiens training camp.

In early May 1949, as the Nationals began spring workouts, Metzig telephoned Harvey to ask him when he would be reporting to camp. Though Metzig had the impression Harvey wanted to play, a knee injury and an impending marriage were casting his return to Ottawa in doubt. He did eventually report to the team, and despite missing spring training, Harvey continued to terrorize Border League pitchers, winning the batting title with a .351 average and leading the league in runs (121) and runs batted in (109). He also demonstrated increased power with 14 home runs and continued to display impressive speed, stealing 30 bases, and hitting 10 triples. He was once again named to the All-Star team and "to Metzig's satisfaction, he also became a team leader."[6]

Now with two outstanding seasons under his belt, major-league scouts began to take notice. Harvey was offered a spot on the National League's Boston Braves' Class-B team in Pawtucket, Rhode Island, and the Boston Red Sox were interested as well. He declined all offers in favor of the opportunities available to him from the Montreal Canadiens.

In 1950, he agreed to play with Ottawa when available, as he now had to focus on his hockey career and his family. He played only 10 games for the Nationals that season. He did not leave baseball entirely at this time however, as he played semiprofessionally in Quebec until 1952.

Harvey was a natural both at the plate and on the basepaths, and we can never know if he had the skills and talent to make it to the major leagues, but baseball, he noted, "is a sport that I always loved to play. ... If I chose hockey over baseball, it was that my chances of progress within the organization with the Canadiens were better than they were with the Boston Braves. Personally, I think I made a wise decision to abandon baseball."[7]

What is known is the result of his decision to commit to hockey. As part of the great Montreal hockey dynasty in the 1950s, Harvey helped Montreal win the Stanley Cup six times including a record five in a row from 1956-1960. He also played with the New York Rangers, then briefly with Detroit and St. Louis before retiring in 1969. He was named to the NHL All-Star Game 13 times and won the Norris Trophy as the league's top defenseman a total of seven times from 1955-1962 (second only to Bobby Orr who won eight). Doug Harvey was inducted into the Hockey Hall of Fame in 1973. The Canadiens retired Harvey's number 2 in 1985, a few years before his death on December 26, 1989, in Montreal at the age of 65.

SOURCES

In addition to the sources listed in the endnotes, the author consulted various newspapers, including:

Ottawa Journal & The Gazette (Montreal) (at Newspapers.com), *Gazette de Valleyfield & Ottawa Citizen* (at Google News Archive), and the following papers online at the Bibliothèque et Archives Nationales du Québec: *Le Devoir (Montréal), Le Droit (Ottawa), La Presse (Montréal), La Tribune (Sherbrooke), Montréal-Matin, Photo Journal (Montréal), Sherbrooke Record, The Gazette (Montreal)*

The author also consulted:

Baseball-reference.com

"Douglas Harvey," The Sporting News Player Contract Cards, https://digital.la84.org/digital/collection/p17103coll3/id/69118/rec/5, accessed December 23, 2022.

"How Doug Harvey Loafed His Way To Fame," http://archive.macleans.ca/article/1958/2/15/how-doug-harvey-loafed-his-way-to-fame, accessed December 5, 2022.

NOTES

1 "Top 25 NHL Defensemen of All Time," https://www.si.com/nhl/2015/01/16/top-25-nhl-defensemen-all-time, accessed December 8, 2022.

2 William Brown, *Doug: The Doug Harvey Story.* (Montreal, QC: Véhicule Press, 2002), 29.

3 Lloyd McGowan, "Canadiens' Doug Harvey Border League Slugger," *The Sporting News*, February 23, 1949: 2:5.

4 William Brown, 31.

5 William Brown, 43.

6 William Brown, 56.

7 Bert Souliere, "Harvey aurait pu se créer une carrière au baseball," *La Patrie du Dimanche*, December 3, 1959: Section Spéciale, 4.

NO SUNDAY BALL, AND NO TELEVISION –
THE OTTAWA GIANTS & ATHLETICS, 1951-1954

BY ANDREW FORBES

1 - THE INTERNATIONAL RETURNS

In the case of Ottawa's return to the International (née Eastern) League, as has so often been the case in Organized Ball, one town's misfortune proved to be another city's gain, however briefly.

The New York Giants' Triple-A club in Jersey City, affectionately or derisively known as the Little Giants, struggled in the standings and suffered at the gate,[1] with attendance depressed by Roosevelt Stadium's proximity to New York's three resident big-league clubs, and the availability of television and radio broadcasts. By the close of the 1950 season the parent club's leadership, led by owner Horace Stoneham, were looking to relocate their affiliate.

By contrast the 1950 Ottawa Nationals of the Class-C Border League enjoyed success both on and off the field, reaching the championship series (ultimately bowing to the Ogdensburg Maples) and leading the circuit in attendance by a wide margin.

When Stoneham and company considered alternative locales for their farm club, Scranton was a possibility, but Ottawa was preferred if it could be arranged. The city, when combined with Hull, Quebec, just across the river, boasted a population of a quarter million people, an absence of available baseball broadcasts, and in Lansdowne Park a stadium capable of seating 10,000 fans, with a plan to expand to 12,000.[2] In late November, International League president Frank Shaughnessy (no stranger to the capital city) and Carl Hubbell—the old lefty screwball specialist, retired from play and serving as the Gothams' director of minor league clubs—toured the park.[3]

They apparently found the facilities to their satisfaction, as a week later it was announced that Ottawa had acquired Jersey City's International League rights, with the Giants name moving with the club. Charles A. (Charlie) Stoneham, cousin of New York owner Horace, retained his role as the club's president and general manager. The arrangement entailed a payment to the Border League for territorial rights, while the Border League Nationals were to be transferred to Cornwall, Ontario. The departing team's owner, Ottawa sports impresario Tommy Gorman, managed to insert himself into the operation of the town's new team, too, explaining that he would "look after the business administration of the Ottawa Giants while the New York National League Giants will arrange for the players under

the partnership deal."[4] Ex-Giant backstop Hugh Poland was announced as manager.[5]

To hear Austin F. Cross tell it, the whole chain of events was kicked off by a stray comment he made while covering the 1950 World Series for the *Ottawa Citizen*. Cross, a veteran journalist who also penned a column for *The Sporting News*, was extolling the capital's many advantages to fellow writers, "then paused and, like a ham actor, said with emphasis: '…And no television.'" Encouraged to include this in a new column, Cross obliged and said *Citizen* piece was read by Gorman, who quickly dashed off a note to Horace Stoneham proposing this new arrangement. Stoneham replied by inviting Tommy to New York. "So a deal was mapped out," said Gorman.[6] Horace and Charlie Stoneham, Hubbell, and Polo Grounds PR director Art Flynn traveled to Ottawa together in January to jointly inspect Lansdowne Park.[7] One expects that, surveying the bleak frozen expanse of Ottawa in midwinter, they required a little imagination to picture baseball being played there.

2 - THE OTTAWA GIANTS'
FIRST—AND ONLY—SEASON

By mid-March the Little Giants were encamped with their big-league brethren in Sanford, Florida to train for the 1951 season. Twenty-seven players earmarked for Ottawa—ex-Jersey City team members, as well as new additions—made their way to camp, to be joined by manager Poland, en route from his home in Kentucky.[8] The Giants, having finished fourth in the eight-city loop (albeit in a different city) the previous year, were expected to remain somewhere around the middle, their chances anticipated to get a boost via "considerable help from the New York Giants."[9]

To observers, and likely to many if not most members of the Giants organization, the most exciting young prospect in camp was a player destined for Triple-A for some more seasoning. Alas, Willie Mays didn't break camp and head north to Ottawa, but rather with the Minneapolis Millers of the American Association—the Giants' other Triple-A club. When New York skipper Leo Durocher drove himself from Orlando to Sanford to take in an exhibition between Ottawa and the Millers, it wasn't to see the Canadian side's George Bamberger or Stanley Jok. It was to see Mays.[10]

When the Little Giants left Florida to begin regular season play, their first stop was Springfield, Massachusetts, home of the Cubs, then entering their second year in the International League, who'd finished just behind Jersey City in 1950. The two clubs were slated to play three games at Pynchon Field. For the start Hugh Poland tabbed righty Andy Tomasic, a Pennsylvanian who'd previously played football with the Pittsburgh Steelers.[11]

Pregame festivities in Springfield included Ottawa mayor Grenville Goodwin fouling off the first pitch as delivered by Dan Brunton, mayor of Springfield. An American Legion band featuring two majorettes entertained, and a ceremony was held to raise the flag, which flapped in a frigid breeze, bedeviling the fewer than 3,000 fans who'd braved the less-than-ideal conditions, though on warmer nights Pynchon could accommodate 7,000.

The game proved to be a harbinger of things to come for the Little Giants: good pitching, scarce hitting. Tomasic took a 1-1 tie into the eighth inning before running into trouble and ceding the bump to George Heller. Ottawa managed only three hits, but two them were triples—by corner outfielders Stan Jok and Milton Joffe—and the Cubs contributed two errors and six bases on balls. It all added up to an Ottawa victory. Said Hugh Poland, "It doesn't matter how you win them, just so long as you wind up in front."[12]

The club didn't wind up in front for the remainder of their debut road trip, dropping the rest of the series in Springfield and going winless in Baltimore. They finally arrived in the Nation's Capital ahead of their scheduled opener on April 25, only to see the contest washed out.

The extra day gave Poland time to get his second baseman into the game. The big club had expected Ottawa's everyday man at the keystone to be Armando Ibanez, but the Cuban import broke his leg in camp.[13] Into the fray stepped Bill Metzig—ex-Ottawa National, who'd been tabbed to manage the now-Cornwall-based Border League club. Metzig held down second on the Little Giants' opening road trip while Poland awaited the arrival of Bobby Hoffman, most recently with Oakland of the Pacific Coast League. Hoffman joined the team in Ottawa in time for the home bow.[14]

The pregame pomp included Mayor Goodwin once more, this time delivering the pitch to External Affairs Minister, noted baseball fan, and future Prime Minister Lester B. Pearson, while Agriculture Minister James Gardiner played catcher. Pearson fouled it off.[15]

About 7,500 fans pushed through the turnstiles at Lansdowne Park that afternoon.[16] The vast majority of the seating was in the north-side grandstand, with fewer scattered around the playing surface in bleachers placed at a considerable distance from the field of play. The park was never intended as baseball facility; its primary tenants were the Ottawa Rough Riders of the Interprovincial Rugby Football Union (and later the Canadian Football League). The single-decked covered stands buffeted the field's football orientation, stretching in a straight line from end zone to end zone. With home plate situated just

out of bounds at midfield, those seated at the grandstand's outer extremes found themselves looking in on the action at a sizable remove.

The shared field was also the cause of some friction. When the Border League club was resident, the infield was nearly solid turf, broken only by "three-feet-wide strips running from base to base and from the pitchers' mound to home plate," per the team's agreement with the Central Canadian Exhibition Association (CCEA), owners of Lansdowne Park. Giants farm director Hubbell scoffed upon first viewing the field, remarking that such a layout wouldn't do for a Triple-A outfit. Said King Carl, "it wouldn't take any more than a close loss for a visiting team on a bad hop, or an injury, before Ottawa would be getting bad publicity and a lot of squawks." Poland and Charlie Stoneham apparently agreed, calling for the diamond to be "skinned." The football club protested. As there was no International League rule demanding the removal of sod, and the contract signed by the Giants with the CCEA was clear in its requirements, the grass remained in place.[17]

Andy Tomasic was again handed the ball for the Lansdowne opener, and he rose to the occasion, turning in a complete game and chipping in a triple in a 5-3 Giants win. Center fielder Paul Mauldin and left fielder Stan Jok each added a pair of hits, and the latter drove in three. Other than the presentation of a horseshoe wreath to Poland on behalf of *Les Tapaguers* ("the rowdies"), a booster group of French-Canadian supporters, those were the highlights.

The losing recommenced the next day, as the Giants committed nine errors behind lefty Frank Fanovich. In the rubber match, the Giants' Red Hardy tossed a one-hitter, shutting out Springfield 4-0.

Let it not be said that the club left their home worse than they'd found it: improvements during the homestand included new light towers to allow for night games, and a new batting cage sent all the way from New York by the parent club.[18] The latter did not appear to have been of material benefit to the Little Giants, who struggled to hit .200 in the season's early going.

But an anemic offense was not the biggest threat to the team's well-being. Rather, two factors prevented the Ottawa Giants from achieving success and longevity in their new home: the minor leagues' convulsions as baseball tried to find equilibrium after a postwar boom, and the continued embargo on Sunday baseball in the city.

In 1948, there were 263 minor-league ballclubs formally affiliated with the 16 National and American League organizations. By 1951, there were 180. The industry as a whole was experiencing a period of retrenchment; eight of 58 lower leagues had disbanded since the late-1940s peak, accounting for nine of the 83 severed connections. A bigger chunk of those cut from affiliation—21 teams—had been owned by their parent clubs (like the Ottawa Giants), their elimination reflecting decisions to reduce operating costs.[19]

Troublingly for Ottawa fans, Horace Stoneham made comments indicating the Giants would make the Minneapolis

Millers their sole entry at the Triple-A level. "Here's the truth about our minor league set-up," Stoneham told Minneapolis journalist Charles Johnson in late July, "[w]e've got too many tie-ups, especially in Triple A... Our plan is to have only one Triple-A tie-up, and that will be Minneapolis."[20]

One of the Little Giants' problems surely dovetailed with the other: the trouble and expense of scheduling around the continued ban on Sunday baseball in Ottawa might have made the Millers the more appealing option. The embargo on staging games on the seventh day put the city of Ottawa out of step, standing as the lone entry in the International League obliged to keep the Sabbath baseball-free. As a result, homestands were interrupted by the need to go elsewhere on Sunday. Efforts to overturn the local dictum were repeatedly foiled by plebiscites which indicated the public's desire to uphold the ban.[21]

Attendance remained decent, though, even when a disastrous month of June—21 losses in 30 games—dropped them from fourth place to seventh,[22] where they would eventually wind up at season's end with a record of 62-88, just a half-game up on Springfield. Though offensively challenged, and with their often-promising pitching[23] frequently stripped for parts by the parent club, the Little Giants drew a total of 132,096 paid spectators to Lansdowne Park in 1951, better than twice as many as had shown up for the club's final season in Jersey City (63,191)[24]—and all with no Sunday dates.

If the season had a high point, it came on July 9, when Leo Durocher and the big club visited Ottawa for an exhibition—a game brokered by Tommy Gorman when negotiating for his Border League side to vacate the city to make room for the Giants. The Internationals emerged triumphant over their big brothers, 4-1, and a gate-busting crowd in excess of 10,000 was on hand to witness it.[25]

But the writing was on the wall for the Ottawa Giants, with Stoneham and company looking to pull the plug on the club. By midseason the talk was that Gorman would be given the opportunity to exercise his option to purchase the Ottawa team for $125,000, allowing the Giants to pull back and Gorman to keep a team in the capital.[26]

But Gorman's contractual deadline of November 15 came and went without a handshake or a signature, and the Little Giants hit the open market. Interested buyers in Newark got deep into the process, but couldn't come to lease terms with the Yankees, who owned that town's Ruppert Stadium.[27] Scranton was briefly in the running, too, as was a return to Jersey City.[28]

A 1953 newspaper advertisement for Bob Trice Night at Lansdowne Park. Credit: *Ottawa Journal*, August 13, 1953.

3 – THE A'S SET UP SHOP

It so happened, while all this transpired, that Connie Mack's Philadelphia Athletics were in the market for a Triple-A team. The A's had last had an affiliate in the top minor tier in 1950, when they'd been tied to the International League's Buffalo Bisons for one season, and had passed the '51 campaign with farms only at Class A and below. With the New York Giants looking to sell their way out of Ottawa, the A's began to kick the tires.

Initially interested in buying the Ottawa club and transferring it to Newark or back to Jersey City, the A's indicated in late December that the players remaining on the team's roster were of "inferior quality," and so the Mack family—The Grand Old Man, Connie, and his sons Roy and Earle—and general manager Arthur Ehlers had opted not to pursue the purchase.[29] Just weeks later, though, the A's hadn't definitively shut the door on the notion, with the Macks and Ehlers meeting with civic leaders in Jersey City and saying they'd "sleep on it."[30] The sticking points appeared to be in the facilities the New Jersey options had to offer, with the Newark park's Yankees-related complications, and both cities' stadiums having installed hard surface auto racing tracks around their respective fields, presenting a risk of physical harm to ballplayers.[31] By January 23, *The Sporting News* was announcing that the Athletics decision not to buy was "final," citing the challenge of setting up a franchise in a new/old city in mere months.[32] But just days later the deal closed, with the A's brass announcing "they would continue operation of the International League club in the Canadian capital."[33]

Boosters in Ottawa were optimistic, as was Frank Shaughnessy, president of the International League. Ehlers and scout Bernie Guest were in town in early February, and they assured the public that they would operate the club differently than the Giants' revolving-door approach to roster construction. Said Ehlers, "We won't take anybody from Ottawa who is helping Ottawa. We want to promote baseball here and in the surrounding district. We don't want to lose money and to make sure of not losing money you must have a contending team. We're going to do our best to provide one." Elmer Burkart was installed as the club's business manager, and the well-traveled Frank Skaff named manager.[34] The big club also poured a reported $75,000 into refurbishing Lansdowne Park, including new seats.[35]

The team set up camp in Leesburg, Florida, with the full squad reporting March 12. On hand were some familiar faces who'd stuck around when the Giants had declined to keep them in the organization—pitcher Frank Fanovich, catcher Neal Watlington, and outfielder Stan Jok all fit that description—and many new, Philadelphia-penned additions. Among those who looked to be gearing up for a promising season was Lou Limmer, a lefty-hitting bopper who'd led the American Association with 29 homers in 1950 while with St. Paul, and spent '51 with the big A's, nabbing time at first base when Ferris Fain broke his foot kicking a bag in anger.[36]

The A's opened at Buffalo where they dropped two games, hitting well but giving up too many late runs.[37] On to Syracuse they motored, losing three contests there. Once home, the pageantry and ceremony dispensed with, they went winless in three tries against Buffalo to put them at 0-8 on the young season.[38]

A win came at last when Charlie Bishop threw a five-hitter for a 6-4 win over Buffalo on April 26, in the last of the Bisons' four-game visit to the banks of the Rideau Canal.[39] But winning was not the norm: Ottawa was 2-12 and in last place in the International League come the first of May. And of equal concern was the public reception. Just 845 fans showed up on May 1, and 703 the next day.

Rays of hope took the form of outfielder Johnny Metkovich, who had nine steals through 19 games, and second-sacker George Moskovich, who reeled off an 11-game hitting streak.[40] Starter Marion Fricano was quietly effective, keeping his ERA to 2.26, a figure that would wind up pacing the circuit and earn the righty a September call-up.

Bishop provided a highlight on Saturday, May 24 when, in the first game of a doubleheader with Syracuse, he threw a no-hitter for a 1-0 win in front of 5,676, the largest home crowd of the year. The A's also scooped the capper, 6-5.[41] By mid-August Bishop was 12-10, good enough for Philadelphia to buy him out of the International and employ him in half a dozen AL contests down the stretch.[42]

The club remained firmly in the second division, and things weren't rosy off the field, either; in September the team was charged by Ottawa police with conducting a lottery after holding "Pot of Gold Night" on August 12. The promotion promised one fan a chance to grab as much loot as they could carry, but A's administrators apparently failed to obtain the proper paperwork.[43] A nominal fine of $10 was eventually imposed upon the A's, reflecting a lack of nefarious intent.[44]

The A's wrapped up the season in seventh place, though an attendance total of 167,000 apparently pleased the Philadelphia heads enough that, when GM Ehlers was approached by representatives from Toledo interested in moving the club to Ohio, he rebuffed the advance. Ehlers did take the opportunity to campaign in favor of Sunday baseball, citing both its benefit to attendance and simplified travel plans.[45] A proposal to allow Sunday ball was once more presented to voters in December, and was resoundingly defeated, throwing some doubt into the A's future in the city.[46]

Skipper Skaff returned in 1953 though, as did the mound trouble; said *The Sporting News*, "The pitching outlook [was] not good."[47] There were some notable names on the squad

coming out of spring training: Kell and Shantz. Unfortunately they bore the wrong given names, with George Kell's younger brother, Everett ("Skeeter") set to play second, and Bill Shantz, kid sibling of Bobby, donning the tools of ignorance.[48]

Outfielder Taft "Taffy" Wright was hot early (his average stood at .405 on June 3), and the A's rode a late-May streak of six wins and 11 victories in 18 games to the cusp of the first division. Crowds swelled as the weather warmed.[49] But Lou Limmer hurt his shoulder, and Wright was dealt a fractured skull when hit by a pitch on June 24, sending the team sagging back down to seventh place.[50]

As the season wore on, against all odds, a hero emerged. Tall hurler Bob Trice began his pro career with the Homestead Grays, then spent three years in the Class-C Provincial League, going 16-3 for St. Hyacinthe in 1952. In 1953 he'd been moved up to Ottawa coming out of spring training, and quickly showed that the assignment was no mistake. He was 12-5 by mid-July, the first International League pitcher to a dozen wins.[51] When Ottawa hit another rough patch, going 4 and 10 over 10 days in July, Trice secured three of the victories.[52] He was no slouch with the bat, either, routinely helping his own cause, and occasionally being asked to pinch-hit in games he hadn't started.

The club decided to honor their best pitcher with Bob Trice Night on August 13, during a doubleheader against Springfield. With the team in the midst of a grueling stretch—six games in three nights—Skaff tabbed Trice himself to pitch the opener on short rest.[53] He responded by throwing a two-hitter, beating the Cubs 2-1 for his 16th win. Between matches he was presented with gifts, and surprised by the presence of his parents, flown in by the team for the occasion. There were 4,219 on hand to witness the celebration, and for good measure the A's took the second game, too, 4-1.[54]

Trice wound up 21-10 on the year for Ottawa, earning a call-up to Philadelphia—breaking the color barrier for the A's in the process, as Mack's club had been among the last to integrate.[55] At the end of the season, Trice's trophy shelf required expansion, after he'd been named an All-Star, the International League's Rookie of the Year, and the circuit's MVP.[56]

Their ace's accomplishments helped Ottawa squeak into sixth in the International League's final standings, and attendance at Lansdowne Park crept north of 175,000, an increase over 1952. Ownership was pleased enough with how things had gone that they recommitted to the city. "We're satisfied and happy," said Ehlers in announcing that Philadelphia would leave its Triple-A entry in place (though he did take the opportunity to rally once more for Sunday baseball in the capital).[57]

Easing the pain of another second-division finish was the farm's victory over the Philadelphia A's when the latter visited Ottawa on September 4. Catcher Ray Murray's homer proved the difference in the exhibition.[58]

The winter was marked by changes ahead of the 1954 season. Manager Skaff was out, having followed Arthur Ehlers to Baltimore, where the latter was appointed GM of the new American League Orioles (the relocated St. Louis Browns), and Skaff signed on as a big-league coach.[59] Ottawa GM Elmer Burkart was out, too.[60] Skaff's replacement was Les Bell, promoted from Savannah,[61] and filling the GM role was George MacDonald, who'd held the same post in St. Hyacinthe.[62]

Things started poorly for the 1954 team, and got worse from there. Uncertainty and rumors of financial insolvency swirled around the parent club, as well as intimations that the Macks were looking to sell.[63] Connie Mack was aging and increasingly frail, his sons steering the ship in his absence, and losing money. Down on the farm, Ottawa fell to the International League cellar and stayed there.

Cause for excitement arrived in May when big-hitting Cleveland first baseman Luke Easter, working his way back from injury, was optioned to Ottawa.[64] Initially reluctant to report—preferring instead an assignment to the Pacific Coast League—Easter did eventually land in town, where he set about sending towering home runs clear out of the stadium, including "the longest home run in the history of Lansdowne Park," estimated at 435 feet.[65]

But things turned ugly on June 24 when Easter ignored his catcher's shouts and cut a throw from the outfield, turning and gunning at the plate a runner trying to score. A spirited disagreement ensued between the slugger and his manager when Easter said he had heard Neal Watlington express his wish that the ball be allowed to travel but had chosen to cut it anyway. The result was a suspension for Easter (later changed to a $100 fine), and Bell losing the reins of his club, transitioning to a scouting job within the A's organization.[66]

Reserve outfielder and baseball lifer Taft Wright (he of the fractured skull) was named manager, but his popularity among both players and fans couldn't stir the club from their torpor. Securely in last place, the Ottawa A's saw attendance slump accordingly, and the winds of change swirl all about them. The International League, in the person of Frank Shaughnessy, began making overtures to Miami, with Shags saying of Ottawa, "we have no chance there without Sunday baseball."[67] Local fans took note, and a committee was organized to try to drum up support for another vote on the matter.[68]

It was too little, too late. The A's fate was sealed in late 1954 with the sale of the Philadelphia team from the Macks to Chicago real estate baron Arnold Johnson, who announced his intention to take the American League club to Kansas City. Johnson became owner of the Ottawa club as part of the deal, and suggested he'd move immediately to relocate them to Miami.[69]

In the end it wasn't Miami, but Columbus, Ohio that marked the next stop on the franchise's peregrinations. Pulling up stakes, the team adopted the name Jets, maintaining its relationship with the Athletics, and remained in the Ohioan capital for 15 years.

Tommy Gorman opined that the failure of the team in Ottawa was the responsibility of television, claiming the medium had "deteriorated all big-time sports,"[70] though it's clear from our vantage that lackluster on-field performance and turmoil among the club's parent organizations played significant roles.

But in all likelihood, the greatest culprit was the city's continued insistence on keeping Sundays baseball-free.

Whatever the cause, when the 1955 baseball season opened there began a span of 38 years without affiliated baseball in Canada's National Capital.

NOTES

1   "Jersey City Giants," BR Bullpen, Baseball Reference, last modified June 21, 2012, https://www.baseball-reference.com/bullpen/Jersey_City_Giants.

2   "Capacity of Ottawa Park to Be Expanded to 12,000," *The Sporting News*, January 10, 1951: 11.

3   "Hubbell Inspects Ottawa," *The Sporting News*, November 29, 1950: 12.

4   "Ottawa Gets Jersey Baseball Rights; Increase Lighting At Park," *Ottawa Citizen*, December 6, 1950: 1.

5   The Canadian Press, "Stoneham Tells Of Transfer; Ex-Big Leaguer To Manage Club," *Ottawa Citizen*, December 6, 1950: 1.

6   Austin F. Cross, "'Ham Actor' Remark Led to Club Move," *The Sporting News*, January 10, 1951: 11.

7   "Caught On the Fly," *The Sporting News*, January 17, 1951: 26.

8   "Contracts Sent to 27 Members of Ottawa International Club," *Ottawa Journal*, February 19, 1951: 17.

9   Cy Kritzer, "Royals, Red Wings Loom as Standouts; Toronto Club Rated as Most Improved; Orioles Seen as First-Division Threat," *The Sporting News*, March 14, 1951: 23.

10 Ken Smith, "Giants' Only 'If' Is Their Ability to Hit," *The Sporting News*, April 4, 1951: 11.

11 "Andy Tomasic," Pro Football Reference, retrieved June 20, 2024, https://www.pro-football-reference.com/players/T/TomaAn20.htm, and "Andy Tomasic," BR Bullpen, Baseball Reference, last modified January 26, 2011, https://www.baseball-reference.com/bullpen/Andy_Tomasic.

12 Bill Westwick, "Giants Off to Winning Start in International," *Ottawa Journal*, April 19, 1951: 17.

13 Cy Kritzer, "Powerized Orioles Pack Threat in Int," *The Sporting News*, April 18, 1951: 18.

14 "Giants Set to Raise Curtain on Ottawa Baseball Season; Club Gets Warm Greeting On Arrival for Opener Here," *Ottawa Journal*, April 25, 1951: 23.

15 Bill Westwick, "The Sport Realm," *Ottawa Journal*, April 27, 1951: 26.

16 Bill Westwick, "7,469 See Giants' Victorious Home Opening; Stan Jok Drives in Three Runs; Tomasic Hurls Well in 5-3 Win," *Ottawa Journal*, April 27, 1951: 26.

17 "Not Skinning Baseball Infield Gorman Assures Football Club," *Ottawa Journal*, December 29, 1950: 16.

18 "International League," *The Sporting News*, May 9, 1951: 24.

19 Clifford Kachline, "Majors Still Cutting Farms; Total Drops to 180 for '51," *The Sporting News*, April 25, 1951: 22.

20 "Millers No. 1 Giant Farm—Stoneham Assures New Park," *The Sporting News*, July 25, 1951: 36.

21 "International League," *The Sporting News*, May 9, 1951: 22.

22 "International League," *The Sporting News*, July 4, 1951: 26.

23   "If Ottawa's attack was as strong as its pitching has been this season," observed *The Sporting News* in August, "the club would be in the first division instead of trying to avoid the basement." "International League," *The Sporting News*, August 8, 1951: 32.

24   "International League," *The Sporting News*, September 19, 1951: 34.

25   "Many Major Clubs Busy in Exhibitions," *The Sporting News*, July 18, 1951: 15.

26   "International League," *The Sporting News*, July 18, 1951: 15.

27   Cy Kritzer, "Drum-Beater Cooke Tells Int Officials How to Chase Gloom; Leafs' Prexy Presents Brochure of Promotion Ideas; Way Being Cleared for Shift of Ottawa Club to Newark," *The Sporting News*, December 12, 1951: 9.

28   Cy Kritzer, "Ottawa May Return to Jersey City; Scranton Also Indicating Its Interest; Giants Strip Franchise of All Players," *The Sporting News*, October 24, 1951: 21.

29   Arthur Morrow, "Athletics Pass Up Chance to Acquire Ottawa Franchise," *The Sporting News*, January 2, 1952: 23.

30   "Jersey City Makes Pitch, Now Awaits Macks' Answer," *The Sporting News*, January 16, 1952: 17.

31   Arthur Morrow, "A's Take New Look at Jersey; Macks Reconsidering Site as Farm After Receiving Pledges of Co-Operation," *The Sporting News*, January 16, 1952: 17.

32   Arthur Morrow, "A's Pass Up Jersey Offer, Aim for Triple-A Club in '53," *The Sporting News*, January 23, 1952: 17.

33   Arthur Morrow, "Athletics Acquire Ottawa Franchise; Won't Move Club," *The Sporting News*, January 30, 1952: 21.

34   Bill Westwick, "A's Promise Ottawa Players Will Stay Here; Frank Skaff Named Manager In New Deal for Baseball," *Ottawa Journal*, February 6, 1952: 22.

35   "International League," *The Sporting News*, April 30, 1952: 26.

36   Arthur Morrow, "Macks Clear Decks for Florida Exit by Shipping Out Eight," *The Sporting News*, April 2, 1952: 18.

37   "Bisons Rally in 8th Inning to Beat Ottawa; Jack Conway Hits Home Run; Lou Limmer Gets Three Hits," *Ottawa Journal*, April 19, 1952: 27.

38   Robert Mellor, "Bisons Explode in 8th to Keep A's Winless; Come From Behind to Win, 6-4; Moskovich Knocks Homer," *Ottawa Journal*, April 26, 1952: 25.

39   "International League," *The Sporting News*, May 7, 1952: 32.

40   "International League," *The Sporting News*, May 14, 1952: 36; "International League," *The Sporting News*, May 21, 1952: 26.

41   Jack Koffman, "Top Ottawa Gate Treated to No-Hitter; Bishop Blanks Syracuse With 5,676 in Stadium," *The Sporting News*, June 4, 1952: 27.

42   "A's Buy Bishop From Ottawa," *The Sporting News*, August 20, 1952: 19.

43   "Pot of Gold Night Brings Lottery Charge Against A's," *The Sporting News*, September 10, 1952: 38.

44   "Ottawa Fined $10 for Lottery," *The Sporting News*, February 18, 1953: 34.

45   "Toledo Feeler for Ottawa Franchise," *The Sporting News*, October 15, 1952: 32.

46   "Ottawa Sunday Ball Beaten; A's May Look for New Site," *The Sporting News*, December 10, 1952: 19.

47   Cy Kritzer, "International Loop Faces Old Question: Who'll Halt Royals?," *The Sporting News*, April 15, 1953: 16.

48   "Int Pre-Season Items; Shantz, Kell with Ottawa," *The Sporting News*, April 22, 1953: 25.

49   "International League," *The Sporting News*, June 10, 1953: 28.

50   Cy Kritzer, "Ottawa Loses Taft Wright, Skull Fractured by Pitch," *The Sporting News*, July 1, 1953: 25.

51   Jack Koffman, "Lofty Trice Tops Int Hurlers With 7th-Spot Ottawa," *The Sporting News*, July 22, 1953: 25.

52   "International League," *The Sporting News*, July 22, 1953: 30.

53   "Trice May Pitch in Night," *Ottawa Journal*, August 13, 1953: 18.

54   "International League," *The Sporting News*, August 26, 1953: 28.

55   Arthur Morrow, "Trice, Ottawa Hill Ace, First Negro to Join Athletics," *The Sporting News*, September 16, 1953: 5.

56   "Robert Trice Breaks the Color Barrier With the Philadelphia Athletics (September 13, 1953)," Barrier Breakers; The Negro League Baseball Museum, retrieved June 27, 2024, https://barrierbreakers.nlbm.com/player/bob-trice/.

57   "A's 'Satisfied,' Will Retain Ottawa Farm Next Season," *The Sporting News*, September 16, 1953: 10.

58   "A's Lose to Int Farm," *The Sporting News*, September 16, 1953: 15.

59   Jesse A. Linthicum, "Baltimore Fears Elephant Stampede; Wants More Athletes, Not So Many A's," *The Sporting News*, December 16, 1953: 1.

60   "Burkart Out at Ottawa," *The Sporting News*, November 25, 1953: 23.

61   "Macks Revamp Farm System, Cut to Six Clubs; Three Are Dropped, One Added and Another Shifted," *The Sporting News*, January 13, 1954: 9.

62   "Crowe Returns to Riders; Athletics Name MacDonald," *Ottawa Journal*, November 20, 1953: 1.

63   "Wrigley and Veeck Deny A's Will Transfer to L.A.," "Two Philadelphia Groups Eyeing A's," *The Sporting News*, May 19, 1954: 8.

64   Carl T. Felker, "28 Extra Men on Major Lists After Cut Down; Bickford and Hal White Among Veterans Released," *The Sporting News*, May 19, 1954: 11.

65   "International League," *The Sporting News*, June 2, 1954: 38.

66   Jack Koffman, "Easter Out $100, Bell Fired After Run-In at Ottawa; Luke Draws Plaster as Result of Rhubarb on Bench; Wright Takes Over Helm of Slump-Ridden Athletics," *The Sporting News*, July 7, 1954: 17.

67   Jimmy Burns, "Miami May Be Next in the Int, Shag Predicts; City Displays New Interest in O.B., Takes Steps to Buy Park from Aleman," *The Sporting News*, September 8, 1954: 7.

68   Jack Koffman, "Ottawa Fans Plan Petition to End Sabbath Blue Law," *The Sporting News*, September 1, 1954: 28.

69   Dan Daniel, "Johnson 'Ear-Marks $1,000,000' for Three-Year Player-Buying; New Owner Realizes that Athletics Need 'Drastic Changes'," *The Sporting News*, November 17, 1954: 6.

70   "Failure of Game in Ottawa Due to TV, Gorman Charges," *The Sporting News*, February 16, 1955: 21.

TRICE HURLS TWO-HITTER FOR OTTAWA ATHLETICS ON BOB TRICE NIGHT

AUGUST 13, 1953: OTTAWA ATHLETICS 2, SPRINGFIELD CUBS 1 (GAME ONE OF DOUBLEHEADER), AT LANSDOWNE PARK, OTTAWA, ONTARIO

BY GARY BELLEVILLE

IN THE SPRING OF 1953, someone asked Bob Trice about the likelihood of him winning the International League's Rookie of the Year Award. Some might have considered it a long shot for a pitcher who had recently advanced four minor-league levels in a single jump. Trice responded to the question with confidence. "I'd like that," he said. But the 26-year-old Georgia native didn't stop there. "I'd like to win a place on the all-star team. I'm going to try to be the most valuable player in the league."[1] Remarkably, Trice went on to achieve all three of those lofty goals.[2]

Trice had spent parts of three seasons (1948-50) with the Homestead Grays, one of the Negro Leagues' most successful clubs. In 1949 he barnstormed with the ageless Satchel Paige, learning at least a dozen pitching tricks from the legendary hurler.[3] After Trice's stint with the Grays, he played three seasons in the Class-C (Québec) Provincial League, and in 1952 he helped the Saint-Hyacinthe Athlétiques, a Philadelphia Athletics farm team, win the pennant by posting a 16-3 record.[4]

Philadelphia sent Trice to spring training with Triple-A Ottawa in 1953 as a learning experience, although he was expected to start the season with Williamsport of the Class A Eastern League.[5] To the surprise of the Philadelphia front office, Trice made the Ottawa roster and returned to Canada for the fourth year in a row.

Trice got the start in Ottawa's home opener, earning the victory with a complete-game five-hitter over Syracuse.[6] Despite his strong initial showing, the rookie right-hander soon fell into a slump. He got knocked around in his next three outings, causing manager Frank Skaff to shift him to the bullpen on May 18.[7]

Trice pitched effectively in three relief appearances, and he was back in the starting rotation by the end of the month.[8] He reeled off seven consecutive victories, culminating with a four-hit shutout of the Montreal Royals on June 17.[9] The winning streak set a new professional record for Ottawa pitchers, breaking the previous mark of six straight victories by James "Gussie" Gannon, who played for the Ottawa entry in the Class A Eastern League in 1898.[10] Trice tied another Ottawa record – this one for hitting – by driving in five runs in the game.[11] He was so skilled with the bat that Skaff regularly used him as a pinch-hitter.[12]

Trice continued to pitch well, and his popularity in Ottawa soared. On August 13, the team held a Bob Trice Night to honor its ace hurler during a twin bill against the Springfield Cubs. With Ottawa playing its third doubleheader in three nights, Skaff approached Trice the evening before and asked if he could pitch on one day's rest.[13] He agreed to do it.

Trice took to the mound in the seven-inning opener of the twin bill sporting a record of 15-8. Ottawa began the day in seventh place with a 52-65 record, 10½ games out of the final playoff spot. The cellar-dwelling Cubs started 23-year-old righty Gene Tarabilda (4-6).

Trice did not disappoint the 4,219 fans in attendance.[14] He retired the first 12 men he faced,[15] and the game remained scoreless until the bottom of the fourth. Joe Taylor, formerly of the Negro American League's Chicago American Giants,[16] reached on an error by second baseman Jack Hollis. After an infield out and a failed fielder's choice, Ottawa right fielder Fred Gerken singled to bring Taylor home with the game's first run.[17]

Springfield finally got to Trice in the top of the fifth. George Freese and Ron Northey opened the inning with singles. After a sacrifice advanced the runners, Doc Daugherty tied the game, 1-1, with an RBI groundout.[18] Hal Meek drew a two-out walk before Trice got out of the inning without any further damage.

It was all the offense that the Cubs could muster in the first game, as Trice set them down in order in the sixth and seventh innings.

In the bottom of the seventh, catcher Andy Tranavitch and Trice singled off Tarabilda, putting the potential winning run on third base with only one out.[19] The count was 1-and-1 on the next batter, Skeeter Kell, when Skaff sent in a left-handed pinch-hitter, Taft Wright. The 42-year-old veteran, who had led the IL in hitting for much of the season,[20] boasted a .362 batting average.[21] Wright jumped on the first pitch from Tarabilda, hitting a long sacrifice fly that scored Tranavich and gave the Athletics a thrilling 2-1 walk-off victory. Trice finished with a two-hitter to earn his league-leading 16th win of the season.

A ceremony to honor Trice took place between games of the doubleheader. The toast of the town was presented with roughly 40 gifts from fans, teammates, members of the media, and park staff.[22] But the most meaningful tribute was still to come. Trice's parents had been flown in by the Athletics to surprise him, and they were driven onto the field in style. "I had a speech made up," Trice said. "But when I saw my mother and father, well …"[23] It was the first time his parents had seen him pitch since his rookie season with the Grays in 1948.[24]

Trice gave a short speech in which he thanked the fans. He also acknowledged his teammates "for all their cooperation that made [his season] possible."[25] Trice's mother also made brief remarks.[26]

The Athletics topped off the evening by defeating the Cubs, 4-1, in the nightcap.

Less than three weeks later, Trice won his 20th game of the season,[27] which was remarkable considering Ottawa was 10 games under .500 at the time.

Trice's magical season did not go unnoticed. On September 8, an announcement was splashed across the front page of both English-language newspapers in Ottawa: Philadelphia had purchased Trice's contract.[28] The big-league team permitted him to make one final start in Ottawa that evening, and he defeated the Buffalo Bisons to raise his record to 21-10.[29] It was the most victories in a season by an IL pitcher since Al Widmar won 22 games for the Baltimore Orioles in 1949.

The fan favorite expressed his gratitude before he departed for Philadelphia. "So many good things have happened to me this year," Trice recalled. "They've been wonderful to me in Ottawa … all the people and my teammates."[30]

Trice made his Philadelphia Athletics debut on September 13 against the St. Louis Browns.[31] In doing so, he became the first Black player on a Philadelphia team in the American or National League.[32]

Trice won two of his three starts for Philadelphia in September, and his future appeared bright. He bolted out of the gate in 1954, tossing complete-game victories in his first four regular-season starts. With a 4-0 record and a 1.75 ERA, Trice seemed poised for a run at the American League Rookie of the Year Award.

And then suddenly, it all fell apart. Between May 9 and July 11, Trice went 3-8 with a 7.27 ERA. After getting shelled by the Boston Red Sox in an 18-0 rout on the final day before the All-Star break, he stunned his teammates by requesting that he be sent back to Ottawa. Despite his struggles, he was still leading the lowly Athletics in wins.[33] Trice explained that playing in the major leagues wasn't fun for him anymore. "Maybe I am crazy, as everyone says, but to me the reasons seem logical enough," he concluded.[34]

The details behind Trice's unhappiness in the AL weren't widely known until decades later. Not surprisingly, many of the issues were race-related. For instance, on his first day in Philadelphia, none of his teammates would speak to him, except for pitcher Bobby Shantz.[35] He was also upset with the Athletics organization for not properly addressing the incidents of racial intolerance that he faced while traveling with the team in the South.[36]

Although Philadelphia had hired future Hall of Famer Judy Johnson in 1954 as a spring-training coach to help Trice, Taylor, and Vic Power manage their trailblazing roles,[37] Johnson wasn't retained for the regular season.[38] When Trice began to struggle on the mound, he was without "a willing mentor and companion."[39]

Years later, he told his son, Bob Trice Jr., that "dealing with race took precedence over the game."[40] Given that Triple-A salaries weren't significantly different from those paid to big-league rookies, requesting a return to Ottawa was perfectly "logical."

Even though Trice pitched just as well for Ottawa in the second half of 1954 as he had the previous season,[41] his record fell to 4-8 with a much weaker team behind him.[42]

The next year, he made the Kansas City Athletics out of spring training.[43] After four relief appearances in which he gave up 10 earned runs in 10 innings, Trice soon found himself back in Triple A. Since the Ottawa Athletics had moved to Columbus, Ohio, for the 1955 season,[44] his run of five consecutive summers in Canada came to an end. Trice never played in the major leagues again.

ACKNOWLEDGMENTS

The author thanks SABR member Christian Trudeau for sharing his knowledge of the (Québec) Provincial League.

SOURCES

In addition to the sources cited in the Notes, the author consulted Baseball-Reference.com, the Negro Leagues Database at Seamheads.com, *The Encyclopedia of Minor League Baseball*, Retrosheet.org, and the SABR biography of Bob Trice.

NOTES

1   Art Morrow, "A's May Call Up Trice, First Negro to Join Club," *Philadelphia Inquirer*, September 6, 1953: 25.

2   Trice won the International League's Most Valuable Pitcher Award in 1953, while Rocky Nelson of the Montreal Royals won the MVP award for position players. The league named one right-hander and one left-hander to its 1953 all-star team: Trice and Tommy Lasorda of the Montreal Royals.

3   Jack Koffman, "Along Sport Row," *Ottawa Citizen*, September 9, 1953: 18.

4   Trice played for the Farnham (Québec) Pirates in 1950 and 1951. In 1950 he had a record of 5-3 on the mound. Trice was a two-way player in both 1951 and 1952. In 1951, he went 7-12 with a 5.15 ERA, and he hit .237 with two home runs in 194 at-bats. In addition to pitching, Trice played several outfield and infield positions in 1952, hitting .297 in 300 at-bats. Tommy Shields, "'Round and About," *Ottawa Citizen*, September 10, 1953: 22.

5   Morrow, "A's May Call Up Trice, First Negro to Join Club."

6   Tommy Shields, "Trice in Little Trouble Pitching Ottawa Victory," *Ottawa Citizen*, April 30, 1953: 25.

7   Jack Kinsella, "Limmer Gets 2 Home Runs as A's and Cubs Split Bill," *Ottawa Citizen*, May 19, 1953: 22.

8   "Athletics in First Division Following Split with Birds," *Ottawa Citizen*, June 1, 1953: 22.

9   Trice earned the victory in his final two relief appearances in late May and his five starts between May 30 and June 17.

10 Jack Kinsella, "Trice Sets New Mark and Equals Another in Win," *Ottawa Citizen*, June 18, 1953: 25.

11 Trice hit a three-run home run off Ed Roebuck in the June 17 game. He also knocked in two runs with a single off reliever Earl Mossor. The *Ottawa Citizen* reported that the only other Ottawa hitters to previously knock in five runs in a professional game were Lou Limmer, Stan Jok, Charlie Bishop, and Tommy Kirk. Kinsella, "Trice Sets New Mark and Equals Another in Win."

12 "International League," *The Sporting News*, July 29, 1953: 28.

13 "Trice May Pitch in Night," *Ottawa Journal*, August 13, 1953: 18; "Honoring Trice at Games Tonight," *Ottawa Citizen*, August 13, 1953: 22.

14 The crowd was bigger for Bob Trice Night than it was for Ottawa's home opener that season (4,001). Both were weeknight crowds.

15 Bob Mellor, "Mates Help Make a Real 'Night' of It for Trice," *Ottawa Journal*, August 14, 1953: 19.

16 Joe Taylor played for the Chicago American Giants from 1949 to 1951. He was one of three Black players on the 1953 Ottawa Athletics; Trice and 35-year-old Al Pinkston were the others. Pinkston began the regular season with Ottawa, but he was optioned to Williamsport on July 9 after hitting only .198 in 101 at-bats. Taylor was promoted from Williamsport that same day. Taylor, Pinkston, and Trice were teammates on the 1951 Farnham (Québec) Pirates, who were managed by Sam Bankhead. The trio also played together on the 1952 Saint-Hyacinthe (Québec) Athlétiques. Steve Kuzmiak, "Joe Taylor," SABR Bio Project, https://sabr.org/bioproj/person/joe-taylor/, accessed March 7, 2024; "Joe Taylor Joins Athletics in Deal with Williamsport," *Ottawa Journal*, July 10, 1953: 17.

17 Doug Milton, "Bob Trice Night at Lansdowne; Hurls Two-Hitter as A's Win Two," *Ottawa Citizen*, August 14, 1953: 18.

18 Milton, "Bob Trice Night at Lansdowne; Hurls Two-Hitter as A's Win Two."

19 Mellor, "Mates Help Make a Real 'Night' of It for Trice."

20 Taft "Taffy" Wright finished the season with a .353 batting average in 331 at-bats, which were not enough to qualify for the batting title. Wright might have been the batting champion had he not been struck in the head by a pitch from Jack Faszholz on June 24. Wright suffered a fractured skull and missed four weeks of the season. He was leading the league with a .398 batting average at the time of his injury. His final batting average was slightly higher (.35347 to .35250) than the one posted by the batting champion, Sandy Amoros of the Montreal Royals.

21 "A's Batting and Hurling," *Ottawa Citizen*, August 13, 1953: 23.

22 The offerings included a gold wristwatch, clothing, gift certificates, auto accessories, rugs, and cigars. His teammates chipped in to buy him a new traveling bag. "Trice Hands Credit to Mates for 'Making It All Possible,'" *Ottawa Journal*, August 14, 1953: 19; Milton, "Bob Trice Night at Lansdowne; Hurls Two-Hitter as A's Win Two."

23 Milton, "Bob Trice Night at Lansdowne; Hurls Two-Hitter as A's Win Two."

24 Jack Koffman, "Along Sport Row," *Ottawa Citizen*, August 14, 1953: 18.

25 "Trice Hands Credit to Mates for 'Making It All Possible'."

26 Mrs. Trice received a bouquet of roses during the ceremony. She was also given a chest of silverware by Bob Simpson, mayor of Arnprior, Ontario. Milton, "Bob Trice Night at Lansdowne; Hurls Two-Hitter as A's Win Two."

27 Doug Milton, "Bob Trice Wins No. 20 as A's Edge Leafs, 3-2," *Ottawa Citizen*, September 3, 1953: 18.

28 "Ottawa's Bob Trice Sold Outright to 'Big A's,'" *Ottawa Citizen*, September 8, 1953: 1; United Press, "Trice Called Up by Philadelphia," *Ottawa Journal*, September 8, 1953: 1.

29 Trice led the International League in wins (21) and shutouts (4), and he tied Don Elston for the league lead with 20 complete games. No other International League pitcher won 20 games in 1953.

30 Bill Westwick, "The Sport Realm," *Ottawa Journal*, September 9, 1953: 16.

31 Under the new definition of what constituted major leagues that was proclaimed by Major League Baseball in the year 2020, Trice did not make his major-league debut with the Philadelphia Athletics on September 13, 1953. His major-league debut was in 1948 for the Homestead Grays of the Negro National League II.

32 The Athletics were the seventh team in the American or National League to integrate, while the Phillies were the last National League team (and 14th overall) to do so. John Kennedy became the first Black to play for the Phillies when he appeared as a pinch-runner on April 22, 1957 – more than 4½ years after Trice's Philadelphia debut.

33 Trice did not throw a single pitch for Philadelphia in the second half of the 1954 season, yet he still finished second on the team with seven wins.

34 Larry Moffi and Jonathan Kronstadt, *Crossing the Line: Black Major Leaguers, 1947-1959* (Jefferson, North Carolina: McFarland & Company, 1994), 103.

35 Ron Thomas, "A's First Black Player Is Subject of Tribute," *Marin Independent Journal* (San Rafael, California), February 7, 1997: C-1.

36 In one humiliating incident, Trice was refused entry into a restaurant in the South, and he sat on the team bus while his White teammates dined at the establishment. After finishing their meals, they brought him three hot dogs in a doggie bag. He declined to eat the hot dogs. Thomas, "A's First Black Player Is Subject of Tribute."

37 Thomas Kern, "Judy Johnson," SABR Bio Project, https://sabr.org/bioproj/person/judy-johnson/, accessed March 7, 2024.

38 Lloyd H. Barrow, *Team First: History of Baseball Integration & Civil Rights* (New York: Page Publishing, 2018).

39 Bill Madden, *1954: The Year Willie Mays and the First Generation of Black Superstars Changed Major League Baseball Forever* (Boston: Da Capo Press, 2014), 4.

40 Thomas, "A's First Black Player Is Subject of Tribute."

41 Trice's ERA with Ottawa increased slightly from 3.10 in 1953 to 3.23 in 1954, although he improved his walks plus hits per innings pitched (WHIP) from 1.271 to 1.265. His strikeout-to-walk ratio also bumped up, from 0.68 to 0.74.

42 The Ottawa Athletics were 71-83 in 1953. The next year, they finished dead last in the International League standings with a 58-96 mark. Ottawa scored the fewest runs per game and had the lowest fielding percentage in the league in 1954.

43 Arnold Johnson purchased the Philadelphia Athletics in November 1954 and moved them to Kansas City for the 1955 season. They lasted 13 seasons in Kansas City before moving to Oakland.

44 Since the last-place Ottawa Athletics lost 96 games in 1954, it was not surprising that they had the lowest attendance in the International League. Their move to Columbus cannot be blamed entirely on a lack of fan interest. While Lansdowne Park was a decent venue for professional football, it was poorly suited to baseball. Most important, Ottawa was the only city in the International League that did not allow Sunday baseball, and so the Athletics missed out on the large crowds that typically attended Sunday games. The ban on Sunday baseball also increased the team's travel because it was sometimes required to make an overnight excursion after Saturday home game(s) to play on the road Sunday and then return to Ottawa for game(s) on Monday. Bill Westwick, "The Sport Realm," *Ottawa Journal*, December 2, 1952: 18; Bill Westwick, "Schedules and Rules but TV Uppermost," *Ottawa Journal*, January 28, 1960: 11.

BRINGING TRIPLE-A BASEBALL TO OTTAWA

BY STEVE RENNIE

IN A RECEPTION HALL AT the Marriott Rancho Las Palmas resort, the mood of the five-member Ottawa delegation might be best described as cautious optimism. Local entrepreneur Howard Darwin stood alongside his son, Jack. Joining them were Ottawa's deputy mayor, Joan O'Neill, councillor George Kelly, and Don Gamble, the city's culture and recreation commissioner. Their September 1991 trip to Palm Springs marked the end of a turbulent three-year effort to bring a Triple-A franchise to Ottawa. Now, on the eve of learning their fate, they stood among the movers and shakers of minor-league baseball, awaiting a decision that could reshape the future of the sport in Canada's capital.

While some at the Friday night reception hosted by the Calgary Cannons considered the following day's announcement a formality, Darwin—who had invested heavily in bringing Triple-A baseball to Ottawa—held his breath. Nothing was certain until Commissioner Randy Mobley confirmed the news. Despite the lingering uncertainty, Darwin struck a confident note.

"Everything being equal, we're there," he told the *Ottawa Citizen* hours before the announcement. "One guy even welcomed me into the International League. I'm not sure they've even decided which league the two teams should play in. But yes, I'm optimistic. When owners from the Pacific Coast League are saying 'You're there,' that's something."[1]

The following day, at noon Ottawa time, the news became official: Professional baseball was back in Ottawa for the first time since the 1950s. But the work to bring a Triple-A franchise to the city had started with a mid-afternoon phone call to an Ottawa jewelry store in the spring of 1988.[2]

* * *

"Howard," came the unmistakable voice on the other end of the telephone. "Why don't you come down to my office for a chat?"[3]

Puzzled, Howard Darwin hung up the phone. In April 1988, calls from Mayor Jim Durrell were not everyday occurrences at Darwin's west-end jewelry store. As he drove downtown, Darwin's mind raced. Could the meeting be connected to the lease for the city-owned arena housing his junior hockey team? At City Hall, Durrell surprised Darwin. Baseball, not hockey, was on the agenda. The mayor proposed an unexpected opportunity: owning a Triple-A baseball club in Ottawa. Durrell

floated a figure of $1.2 million[4], and Darwin promised the mayor he would think about it.[5]

Darwin spent the next few months mulling the mayor's offer. Though owning a sports team was already familiar territory, having brought major junior hockey to Ottawa two decades earlier, this opportunity presented a new challenge. The city had not seen professional baseball since the 1954 departure of the International League's Ottawa Athletics, leaving Darwin to wonder if Ottawa could rally behind a new team.

Others had the same question. At Durrell's urging in September 1988, Ottawa's city council tasked officials with scouting potential locations for a Triple-A baseball stadium. The Department of Recreation and Culture came back in January 1989 with a list of eight candidate sites.[6]

Before that, in the fall of 1988, newspaper reports emerged of an unnamed businessperson—later identified as Darwin—willing to back a Triple-A franchise if the city built a new stadium. Fueling the growing public interest, the mayor's office announced in late October that a delegation would be sent to baseball's 1988 Winter Meetings in Atlanta to connect with Triple-A Alliance executives.[7]

With the Winter Meetings on the horizon, Darwin emerged as the local investor, stepping into the spotlight to express his interest in purchasing a team. He joined the city's delegation to Atlanta at his own expense. Undeterred by the rising franchise costs, which now exceeded $1.5 million USD, Darwin remained determined to bring professional baseball to Ottawa. "That's what we're going to try to do, dig deeper and see what it might cost to first get a franchise and second, get it here," he said. "That's why we're going."[8]

Little did he know that he would get unexpected help from a powerful source.

* * *

As Howard Darwin returned to his room at the Marriott Marquis Hotel in Atlanta after a late-night dinner with Durrell and Ottawa city officials Don Gamble and Jeff Polowin, the flashing red message light on the telephone grabbed his attention. Darwin had spent the day rubbing elbows with baseball's power brokers at the Winter Meetings. Over lunch in the Champlain Room of the Marriott Marquis, he and his partners made an impassioned pitch for baseball in Canada's capital to Triple-A Alliance president Harold Cooper. Now Darwin was eager to get some sleep. He picked up the phone and listened to the message. One of the richest men in Canada wanted Darwin to come up to his suite. Right now.[9]

As he entered the room, the size of Charles Bronfman's suite struck Darwin. "I was meeting one of the richest men in the world. The suite was the size of this room," he would later recount, comparing it to the Assembly Hall at the Ottawa Civic Centre. Waiting for him were the Montreal Expos' owner himself and two of his most trusted lieutenants: Claude Brochu, the Expos' president and CEO, and longtime club executive Jim Fanning. Darwin didn't know it at the time, but the Expos executives had done their homework on him. "Charles did some checking," Brochu said. "He didn't know Howard. And everybody he talked to said he was an outstanding citizen and businessman. A man of his word. Ottawa needed our support and we jumped on it." Brochu and Fanning had already laid the groundwork for Darwin's pitch before his late-night visit to Bronfman's suite. "Brochu and Fanning had already talked to Bronfman, suggesting it was a good idea to get Ottawa onside," Darwin told the *Ottawa Citizen*. "The Expos were losing a lot of fans in the market to the (Toronto Blue Jays)."[10]

The Ottawa contingent was encouraged by their reception at the Winter Meetings, which included a second sit-down with Cooper and another meeting with Expos brass that went into the early hours of Monday morning. Montreal, whose affiliation with the Indianapolis Indians was set to run out at the end of the 1990 season, was interested in having a farm team just two hours down the road. "We are so much further ahead for the three days we've spent here," Durrell said at the time. "Really, I don't think there's anything more we can do before we get home and start getting some plans laid out." The city had two options: buy another club and relocate it to Ottawa or secure an expansion franchise. At least one Triple-A owner openly mused about moving his team to Ottawa. "I'd be very interested in relocating our Triple-A team to Ottawa," said Denver Zephyrs' owner Dick Becke. But that was a non-starter for Durrell, who was only interested in having an Ottawa-based owner for the prospective team. "I don't want anything but local ownership," he said. "Local ownership is there in good times and bad, and that's what makes it so important." Those words would ring especially prophetic nearly two decades later.[11]

Ottawa's baseball dream was gaining momentum. The city was actively pursuing a Triple-A franchise, and a potential shared facility with another tenant was already on the table. Baseball Canada saw Ottawa as a prime location for a new 10,000-seat stadium and national team training center, given the city's proximity to the many clubs scattered across the eastern parts of Canada and the United States.[12]

The search for the new ballclub's home narrowed down to two options, each presenting significant challenges. The first, a 100-acre swathe of Greenbelt land near Highway 417 and Innes Road in the city's east end, boasted ample space but suffered from poor accessibility and a lack of nearby amenities. The second, the Rideau River Park site, offered a central location just east of downtown, close to both a bus station and the city's train station, but faced the daunting task and cost of remediation due to its former use as a city dump. The National Capital Commission (NCC), a federal government agency responsible for planning and development in the capital region, owned both sites. Neither option sparked much excitement.[13]

A third site instantly captured the public's imagination: LeBreton Flats. This crown jewel on the banks of the Ottawa River in the shadow of Parliament Hill boasted breathtaking views, historical significance, and ample space for development. LeBreton Flats, however, carried a complex history. Once a thriving working-class neighborhood and industrial hub, it faced significant challenges and was controversially cleared in the 1960s. The NCC-owned parcel of land had long been eyed as a potential location for transformative development. Revitalizing this prime location was a captivating prospect.[14]

But a baseball stadium was not at the top of NCC Chair Jean Pigott's list of priorities, as the commission was focused on developing a long-term plan for LeBreton Flats. They were put off by the short notice on which they were being asked to consider the stadium proposal, questioning whether it aligned with their long-term vision for the site. "This (tight timetable) would concern me," she said in early February 1989, "because we have a lot of long-term thinking to do in that area."[15]

Darwin had done a lot of thinking of his own, and in his mind, it was LeBreton or bust. Fresh off three days of talks with Triple-A executives in Oklahoma, where he also kicked the tires on a local team, Darwin eagerly scanned his Saturday newspaper. However, his optimism quickly faded upon reading Pigott's remarks about LeBreton Flats. "As far as I'm concerned the only site is LeBreton," he said. "If it's the 417 site (Hwy. 417 and Blair Road), forget me. In fact, I'm not interested if the park's not at LeBreton." Under mounting pressure from some local politicians, Pigott and the NCC left open the possibility of setting aside space for a stadium at LeBreton Flats, contingent on overwhelming public support for the idea.[16] [17] [18]

The city's quest for a professional baseball team hit a snag in March 1989 when Darwin's $5 million (approximately $4 million USD) offer to buy the Oklahoma City 89ers, a Triple-A affiliate of the Texas Rangers, and relocate them to Ottawa was rejected. Undeterred, Darwin continued his pursuit. "My approach," he said during a July 1989 visit to Columbus, Ohio, to meet with Triple-A executives, "is still to get the first team that comes available."[19]

Darwin remained optimistic about Ottawa's chances of becoming a farm club for a potential major-league baseball expansion team. This hope received an unexpected boost when Bob Rich, owner of the Triple-A Buffalo Bisons and leader of that city's own expansion bid, suggested Ottawa as a potential farm club location if he were awarded a major-league franchise.[20]

Buoyed by a flurry of reports—including market analyses, estimates of noise levels from potential stadium sites, and studies examining the impact of vehicle traffic at various locations—city officials were optimistic that baseball could thrive in Ottawa. "It is the conclusion that there is a strong potential market," noted a November 1989 report. "If a quality product was delivered, the area is quite capable of filling a 10,000-seat stadium occasionally and could realistically average at least 50 per cent attendance. In fact, the survey evidence suggests that a 10,000-seat stadium may not be capable of meeting all demand for some dates."[21]

Despite these positive findings, the report ruled out LeBreton Flats as a potential stadium location, favoring instead two alternate sites near the downtown core: Rideau River Park to the east and Bayview Yards to the west. Officials deemed Rideau River Park easier to develop due to its proximity to transit, but it required expensive remediation. Bayview Yards, while more complex, was less expensive and enjoyed greater public support. "Both sites can successfully accommodate a multi-purpose recreational complex," the report said, "however given the costs implications and public reaction to date, the Department recommends the City pursue Bayview as a primary site to be developed."[22]

Ottawa's dream of a minor-league baseball team was shattered as city council narrowly voted down the Bayview Yards stadium proposal, 9–7. The $4-million city contribution towards the $15.9-million project proved a sticking point for the opposing council members. Disappointment hung heavy in the air as the mayor slumped in his chair, absorbing the final vote. He quietly excused himself after a long moment of contemplation. News of the rejection reached Darwin in Nashville, where he was attending baseball's Winter Meetings. His reaction was one of profound disappointment. He emphasized that Ottawa, contingent on a stadium plan, was the top choice for minor league expansion. "At noon I had a franchise," Darwin lamented. "We were first on the list … either International League or American Association. We had met all the criteria. Then this. I can't believe it."[23]

Exhausted and fed up, Darwin walked away.

"It's done and I'm done – that's all there is to it," he vented. "Now I just want to get on with life and forget it ever happened. Naturally, it was all a big waste of time."[24]

Undeterred by Ottawa's rejection, regional officials in surrounding areas stepped forward to keep the dream of minor league baseball alive. In the weeks that followed, they began exploring ways to bring a team to the Ottawa area, some even contacting Darwin directly to gauge his interest. However, the recent setback had dampened his enthusiasm. "People are calling me and saying, 'We can't let this thing die,' but it is up to somebody to pick up the ball and bring up something concrete," he said in early 1990. "Right now, I am taking a sabbatical."[25]

* * *

The March wind whistled around the car as mayor Jim Durrell's driver, Lenny Cregan, who went by the nickname "Snake," expertly navigated the Vanier Parkway. Durrell, lost in thought after a meeting in the city's east end, gazed out the window, his attention drawn to a sprawling 18-acre plot across from the Royal Canadian Mounted Police complex. It was

nothing but a snow dump, a barren patch within the urban landscape. But to the mayor, it was potential, a canvas waiting to be painted. "Snake," he said, his voice breaking the silence, "There's the perfect place for a baseball stadium."[26]

Intrigued by the possibility, the mayor wasted no time in directing his staff to find out who owned the Coventry Road property. Their investigation revealed that it belonged to the Department of Public Works. In March 1990, the city quietly initiated talks with their federal counterparts to buy the land, although at the time neither level of government would say anything publicly.[27]

Darwin, too, was slowly getting back in the fold. That spring, he endorsed a ballpark on Coventry Road during a site tour. "A ball stadium here would be a lot better than that," he said, gesturing at the mounds of melting snow. But he was hesitant to fully recommit, insisting on a firm commitment from the city to build a ballpark before once again throwing his weight behind the project.[28]

While negotiations with the federal government continued through spring, city officials unveiled plans for a gleaming new 10,000-seat stadium at a public meeting in the Overbrook neighborhood, slated to be the ballpark's future home. The proposed stadium at the Coventry Road site came with an estimated price tag of $21 million. As a condition of the sale, the city agreed to take responsibility for some roads owned by the federal government, at a cost of around $10.7 million in repair costs and another $550,000 a year in maintenance.[29]

Triple-A Alliance commissioner Randy Mobley flew to Ottawa in late June of 1990 at Darwin's behest, aiming to bolster support before the pivotal stadium vote. Noting the league's "extreme interest" in the city as a potential home for an expansion franchise, Mobley struck a chord with Ottawa city councillors, who voted 13–2 a week later to spend $800,000 on a feasibility study for the Coventry Road stadium and to start raising millions of dollars from corporate backers. Energized by this victory, Darwin set off for Las Vegas in early July. The Triple-A All-Star game awaited, along with a crucial series of meetings with league executives aimed at solidifying Ottawa's position for a future expansion bid.[30]

Darwin, who had previously explored relocating an existing team to Ottawa, now shifted his focus to securing an expansion franchise. He flat out rejected the idea of buying the Denver Zephyrs, the Triple-A affiliate of the Milwaukee Brewers. Instead, he spent his summer meticulously preparing Ottawa's 70-page application for a new Triple-A franchise.[31]

Corporate sponsors like Labatt's Breweries of Canada emerged, expressing interest in the prospective team. Momentum for Ottawa's bid grew as Darwin, eager to secure the franchise, submitted his application ahead of the competition.[32] However, Darwin's confidence took a hit when he discovered how many other cities and groups had also applied, each shelling out the non-refundable $5,000 (USD) application fee. "I'm surprised. No, I'm shocked there's that many," he said. "I figured there'd be no more than half that many." With a total of 19 competitors in the running, including Ottawa, Darwin now faced an anxious wait until November to learn if the city's bid would be shortlisted for expansion.[33]

* * *

The Triple-A executives around the table in the Ramada O'Hara conference room in the Chicago suburb of Rosemont, Illinois, fell silent as the video on the screen flickered to life. On the Ottawa side, the five-person delegation held their collective breath. This was it; the culmination of nearly two years of work and more than $100,000 out of Darwin's bank account. The video opened with a familiar face. Ottawa's own Doug Frobel, the local boy whose legendary swing once terrorized major-league pitchers, stood on his front porch. For the next six minutes, he took the power brokers of Triple-A baseball on a tour of his hometown, from his childhood stomping grounds in the City View neighborhood to the iconic Museum of Civilization, and finally, the promised land: the proposed stadium site on Coventry Road. Darwin, Durrell, and city recreation commissioner Don Gamble fielded questions from the expansion committee for the next half hour. The stadium, naturally, dominated the discussion. But Ottawa's pitch had resonated with the committee. "The Ottawa bid was very impressive," committee chair Larry Schmittou said afterwards. "I think if it relied upon the mayor to build a stadium, he'd be out there tomorrow with a shovel."[34]

Darwin did not waste a second back in Ottawa. He set out to raise $5 million from private investors by April 1— about two months before a crucial visit by Triple-A executives. Darwin knew a well-funded local effort would send a powerful message. He also aimed to rally the community. He offered season tickets to Ottawa's anticipated Triple-A club, available through the purchase of $25 pledges. The response was immediate. Within three days, he had sold more than 2,000 pledges. To top it all off, all 20 of the stadium's private suites were leased within days, each for a full five years at $18,000 a year. It was a clear sign: Ottawa was hungry for Triple-A baseball, and Darwin was proving he had the city firmly behind him.[35]

The Triple-A expansion committee whittled down the hopeful cities vying for a franchise. By early April, the field had narrowed to nine: Ottawa; Annapolis, Maryland; South Bend, Indiana; Memphis, Tennessee; Jacksonville, Florida; Quad Cities, Illinois/Iowa; Birmingham, Alabama; Charlotte, North Carolina; and Tulsa, Oklahoma.[36]

Ottawa's bid for the Triple-A team hit a snag when city staff revealed the need for unforeseen infrastructure upgrades. Widening roads and improving sewers around the stadium could cost an additional $3 million. This unexpected expense sparked concern among city politicians, with some voicing strong opposition to taking on the extra financial burden.[37]

In a surprising shift, Darwin reversed course. Having recently dismissed the Toronto Blue Jays' Triple-A affiliate, the Syracuse Chiefs, he now set his sights on the Omaha Royals of the American Association. This move strayed from his initial focus on securing an expansion franchise. However, with the blessing of Triple-A Alliance commissioner Mobley, Darwin could pursue both options: Omaha and Ottawa's expansion bid.[38]

On May 31, 1991, the Triple-A expansion committee, led by chair Larry Schmittou, arrived in Ottawa. Their key concern was Ottawa's ability to finance the proposed $21.6-million stadium. Weeks later, a significant boost came from Eastern Beverages, a division of Pepsi-Cola Canada Ltd. They secured the official soft drink sponsorship for the stadium, contributing $800,000.[39]

The Triple-A expansion committee narrowed the field further, selecting Ottawa as one of its final five candidates. The other contenders included Bowie, Maryland (formerly Annapolis), Birmingham, Charlotte, and Tulsa. Darwin focused on securing financing for the stadium project. The city agreed to sell part of the Coventry Road site, generating roughly $4 million in revenue. Additionally, sales of luxury boxes and in-park advertising added over $5 million (Canadian). Darwin himself committed to repaying $4 million over 15 years. Further revenue was expected from scoreboard advertising and stadium naming rights, potentially bringing in another $2 million.[40]

The final hurdle for stadium construction remained: securing the Ontario government's $4-million contribution. With a deadline set by Triple-A for Ottawa to confirm construction by August 15, time was of the essence. However, a week before the deadline, the province announced a change in its contribution. Instead of a grant, it would be a loan, requiring Ottawa to repay the funds. This unexpected shift in financial responsibility threatened the viability of the bid. Faced with the revised terms, the city scrambled to adjust the stadium plan within a tight timeframe. Ottawa met the deadline by submitting a revised proposal for an $18-million ballpark. While this scaled-down version met the construction requirement, and won enough votes on city council to go ahead, it fell short of Triple-A's initial expectations, casting some doubt on the success of Ottawa's bid. "We sold the (expansion) committee on one stadium," Darwin said. "They were very pleased with it. And now we've gone and changed the rules. In effect, we sold them a bill of goods. I don't like it." An air of uncertainty hung over Ottawa's delegation as they boarded the long flight to Palm Springs to meet the 26 Triple-A owners who would determine the fate of professional baseball in Canada's capital. Would the scaled-down stadium proposal be the difference between Ottawa's dream becoming reality and another city dashing their hopes?[41]

In the end, the stadium issue proved not insurmountable enough to derail Ottawa's bid for a Triple-A baseball franchise. Outside the Marriott Rancho Las Palmas, a wave of relief and triumph washed over Howard Darwin. A wide grin stretched across his face as he raised a toast with fellow delegation members Jack Darwin, Don Gamble, George Kelly, and Joan O'Neil. Reflecting later, Darwin acknowledged the day had been a rollercoaster. Yet, a deeper sense of vindication settled over him. "It was emotion more than excitement," he said. "I said all along if somebody could convince me Triple-A baseball was bad for Ottawa, I'd step aside and call it quits. No one did."[42]

NOTES

1 Don Campbell, "Ottawa Bid Seems Assured," *Ottawa Citizen*, September 28, 1991: 33.

2 Don Campbell, "Baseball Is Back: Howard Darwin's Triple-A Field of Dreams Becomes Reality," *Ottawa Citizen*, September 29, 1991: 1.

3 Jeff Darwin, *The Ten Count: Howard Darwin's Remarkable Life in Ottawa* (Ottawa: Jeff Darwin, 2015), 115.

4 All amounts quoted are in Canadian dollars except where noted.

5 Darwin, 115–116; Howie Mooney, "The Lynx That We Will Go To," *Fired Up Network*, April 17, 2022. Accessed March 6, 2024. https://web.archive.org/web/20220910164140/https://firedupnetwork.ca/Features/Baseball/THE-LYNX-THAT-WE-WILL-GO-TO

6 City of Ottawa. Department of Recreation and Culture, *Triple "A" Baseball: Market Study, Detailed Site Analysis, Costs and Financial Strategy* (Ottawa: The Department, 1989), 8.

7 Don Campbell, "Ottawa Making First Pitch for Pro Baseball Franchise," *Ottawa Citizen*, September 30, 1988: 65; Don Campbell, "City to Push for Triple-A Franchise at Winter Meetings," *Ottawa Citizen*, October 29, 1988: 83.

8 Don Campbell, "Darwin's Theory has Triple-A Baseball in Ottawa," *Ottawa Citizen*, December 3, 1988: 97.

9 Wayne Scanlan, "Darwin's Dream Becoming a Reality," *Ottawa Citizen*, September 23, 1992: 39; Don Campbell, "Triple A Pitch Strikes the Right Note," *Ottawa Citizen*, December 5, 1988: 19.

10 "Darwin's Dream Becoming a Reality."

11 Don Campbell, "Two Baseball Clubs Eye Ottawa as Triple-A Site," *Ottawa Citizen*, December 6, 1988: 51; "Triple A Pitch Strikes the Right Note."

12 Don Campbell, "Interest in Proposed Baseball Stadium as National Training Base," *Ottawa Citizen*, January 19, 1989: 44.

13 Jack Aubry, "Ottawa Urged to Look at 2 Sites for Ball Stadium," *Ottawa Citizen*, January 21, 1989: 8.

14 Don Campbell, "LeBreton Flats to be Pitched as Stadium Site," *Ottawa Citizen*, February 1, 1989: 19.

15 Wendy Smith, "Pigott Tags Out Flats as Site for Triple-A Ball Stadium," *Ottawa Citizen*, February 4, 1989: 9.

16 Lynn McAuley, "Will Ottawa Strike Out?" *Ottawa Citizen*, February 7, 1989: 47.

17 Doug Yonson and Jack Aubry, "Pigott Might Reconsider LeBreton Ballpark Stand," *Ottawa Citizen*, March 1, 1989: 35.

18 Jack Aubry and Ron Eade, "2 Flats Plans Have Space for Ball Stadium," *Ottawa Citizen*, April 5, 1989: 17.

19 Don Campbell, "Darwin Offers $5M for Triple-A Club," *Ottawa Citizen*, March 8, 1989: 21; Don Campbell. "Triple-A Bid Rejected, Darwin Still Looking," *Ottawa Citizen*, April 10, 1989: 44; Don Campbell. "Head-Start Expansion Plan Buoys Ottawa Hopes," *Ottawa Citizen*, July 12, 1989: 65.

20 "Head-Start Expansion Plan Buoys Ottawa Hopes"; Don Campbell, "Ottawa Appeals to Buffalo Rich," *Ottawa Citizen*, July 14, 1989: 53.

21 City of Ottawa. Department of Recreation and Culture, *Triple "A" Baseball: Market Study, Detailed Site Analysis, Costs and Financial Strategy* (Ottawa: The Department, 1989), 8.

22 City of Ottawa. Department of Recreation and Culture, *Triple "A" Baseball: Market Study, Detailed Site Analysis, Costs and Financial Strategy* (Ottawa: The Department, 1989), 3–7.

23 Jack Aubry, "Council Split on Bayview for Ballpark," *Ottawa Citizen*, November 24, 1989: 29: Ron Eade and Don Campbell, "Struck Out: Council Rejects Ballpark Study," *Ottawa Citizen*, December 7, 1989: 1; John MacKinnon, "A Dream Dies a Painful Death," *Ottawa Citizen*, December 7, 1989: 57.

24 Don Campbell, "Darwin: 'I'm Done,' Baseball Backer Dejectedly Quits Chasing Team" *Ottawa Citizen*, December 21, 1989: 35.

25 Carrie Buchanan, "Nepean Eyes Triple-A Ball," *Ottawa Citizen*, December 23, 1989: 17; Anne Tolson, Carrie Buchanan, and Doug Yonson, "Baseball Gains at Region," *Ottawa Citizen*, January 11, 1990: 25.

26 Darwin, 117.

27 Ron Eade, "East-End Site Being Eyed for Ballpark?" *Ottawa Citizen*, March 15, 1990: 15.

28 Ron Eade, "Snow Dump Top Ball Site," *Ottawa Citizen*, April 7, 1990: 17.

29 Jack Aubry, "Stadium Could Cost $21M," *Ottawa Citizen*, June 19, 1990: 17; Doug Yonson, "Ball Site Deal Close: Officials," *Ottawa Citizen*, June 23, 1990: 20; Ron Eade, "Triple-A Plans Need Probe, Says Resident," *Ottawa Citizen*, July 11, 1990: 33.

30 Don Campbell, "Triple-A Official Checks Out Site," *Ottawa Citizen*, June 27, 1990: 27; Jack Aubry, "Stadium Approval Appears Assured," *Ottawa Citizen*, June 28, 1990: 1; Don Campbell, "Howard Darwin Happy with His Triple-A Field of Dreams," *Ottawa Citizen*, June 28, 1990: 29; Don Campbell, "Darwin's Field of Dreams," *Ottawa Citizen*, July 5, 1990: 28.

31 Don Campbell, "Zephyrs Don't Interest Darwin," *Ottawa Citizen*, July 19, 1990: 30; Don Campbell, "Ottawa's Triple-A Bid Outraces Opposition," *Ottawa Citizen*, September 13, 1990: 43.

32 Doug Kelly, "Labatt's May Back Triple-A Team," *Ottawa Citizen*, July 24, 1990: 45; "Ottawa's Triple-A Bid Outraces Opposition."

33 Don Campbell, "19 Bids for Triple-A Franchises Shock Darwin," *Ottawa Citizen*, September 18, 1990: 69.

34 Don Campbell, "Darwin Strides to the Plate," *Ottawa Citizen*, November 13, 1990: 47; Don Campbell, "Lack of Stadium Main Drawback in Triple-A Pitch," *Ottawa Citizen*, November 16, 1990: 30.

35 Wayne Scanlan, "Darwin's Still in There Swinging," *Ottawa Citizen*, February 3, 1991: 20; "Darwin's Still in There Swinging"; Ron Eade, "Darwin Will Sell Triple-A Coupons," *Ottawa Citizen*, January 29, 1991: 21; Don Campbell, "Triple-A Pledges Pour In," *Ottawa Citizen*, February 12, 1991: 33; Tom Spears, "Suites for Proposed Stadium Are Leased," *Ottawa Citizen*, March 17, 1991: 25.

36 Don Campbell, "Ottawa Bid for Triple-A Survives Cut." *Ottawa Citizen*, April 2, 1991: 44.

37 Ron Eade, "Triple-A Stadium Costs May Rise," *Ottawa Citizen*, April 9, 1991: 33; Ron Eade, "Public Costs for Stadium Anger Aldermen," *Ottawa Citizen*, April 10, 1991: 25.

38 Don Campbell, "Darwin Committed to Expansion," *Ottawa Citizen*, April 12, 1991: 19; Don Campbell, "Darwin Taking 2nd Look at Buying Omaha Royals," *Ottawa Citizen*, April 19, 1991: 60.

39 Don Campbell, "Triple-A Officials to Visit Ottawa," *Ottawa Citizen*, April 30, 1991: 50; Martin Cleary and Ron Eade, "Triple-A Bid Needs Bucks," *Ottawa Citizen*, June 1, 1991: 49.

40 Don Campbell, "Ottawa Bid One of Final 5 for Triple-A," *Ottawa Citizen*, June 25, 1991: 21; Tom Casey, "Darwin Confident Ottawa

Bid Will Result in Triple-A Franchise," *Ottawa Citizen*, July 16, 1991: 48.

41   "Darwin Confident Ottawa Bid Will Result in Triple-A Franchise"; Ron Eade, "Baseball Franchise in Jeopardy," *Ottawa Citizen*, August 9, 1991: 1; Ron Eade, "Ottawa Likely to Scale Down Ballpark Plans," *Ottawa Citizen*, August 15, 1991: 1; Wayne Scanlan,

"Committee to Reassess Ottawa Bid," *Ottawa Citizen*, August 16, 1991: 25; Don Campbell, "Darwin Tripped Up On Way Home," *Ottawa Citizen*, September 19, 1991: 32.

42   Campbell, "Baseball Is Back: Howard Darwin's Triple-A Field of Dreams Becomes Reality."

POTENTIAL SITES FOR THE NEW STADIUM

BY STEVE RENNIE

IN AN ALTERNATE BASEBALL UNIVERSE, Ottawa fans might be cheering their teams from a different ballpark. Back in the late 1980s and early 1990s, before the familiar Coventry Road stadium became a reality, the city explored eleven other locations for a potential new stadium.

Eight potential sites were ultimately rejected for various reasons. A Conroy Road location was deemed too noisy for nearby residents, lacked convenient rapid transit options, and presented parking challenges. Carlington Park faced similar issues with noise and traffic concerns from residents, along with a complete lack of parking and public transit access. A nearby quarry site served as a major regional snow dump, raising concerns about traffic congestion at Woodward Drive and Clyde Avenue if developed. The Experimental Farm offered a promising location due to its size, access, and potential for parking, but ultimately fell short in other criteria. Carleton University land offered limited parking and raised potential noise and traffic concerns. A site by Highway 417 and Innes Road was deemed a non-starter due to its remote location, making it a long and unattractive drive for fans. The RA Centre land, owned by the federal government, boasted an ideal location, but lacked essential utilities like sewer and water infrastructure, and crucially, didn't receive approval from the RA Board of Directors. Finally, the Ontario Ministry of Transportation headquarters on Tremblay Road, while a good location overall, lacked a direct connection to the nearby St. Laurent rapid transit station.[1]

Three sites made the city's shortlist: LeBreton Flats, Bayview Yards, and Rideau River Park.

LEBRETON FLATS

LeBreton Flats emerged as the frontrunner for the new ballpark, boasting a prime location and immense potential. However, securing the land from the National Capital Commission proved too challenging, ultimately derailing this promising option.

BAYVIEW YARDS

Emerging as the second most attractive option after LeBreton Flats, Bayview Yards presented a unique challenge. Though boasting excellent access to public transit, this former landfill site would necessitate significant remediation efforts. While on-site parking was limited, surrounding neighborhoods offered potential solutions.[2] The price tag to develop this site was pegged at $15.9 million.[3]

RIDEAU RIVER PARK

While boasting good public transit access and ample parking, this site presented the most significant environmental challenges. Extensive remediation work would be required at a substantial cost.[4] The city estimated it would cost $25.6 million to develop this site.[5]

None of these sites proved to be the perfect fit for Ottawa's new baseball stadium. Coventry Road ultimately emerged as the site of the city's ballpark, where baseball is still played today.

NOTES

1   City of Ottawa. Department of Recreation and Culture. *The Prospectus for a Multi-purpose Recreational Complex in Ottawa for Baseball, Other Sports and Entertainment* (Ottawa: The Department, 1989), 31–34.

2   City of Ottawa. Department of Recreation and Culture. *The Prospectus for a Multi-purpose Recreational Complex in Ottawa for Baseball, Other Sports and Entertainment* (Ottawa: The Department, 1989), 44–52.

3   City of Ottawa. Department of Recreation and Culture, *Triple "A" Baseball: Market Study, Detailed Site Analysis, Costs and Financial Strategy* (Ottawa: The Department, 1989), 18.

4   City of Ottawa. Department of Recreation and Culture, *Triple "A" Baseball: Market Study, Detailed Site Analysis, Costs and Financial Strategy* (Ottawa: The Department, 1989), 6.

5   City of Ottawa. Department of Recreation and Culture, *Triple "A" Baseball: Market Study, Detailed Site Analysis, Costs and Financial Strategy* (Ottawa: The Department, 1989), 18.

A HISTORY OF THE OTTAWA LYNX, FROM THEIR FIRST SEASON TO THEIR LAST

BY MIKE TRICKEY

THE FRESHLY-MINTED OTTAWA LYNX WERE to make their debut March 20, 1993 in a preseason game against the Albuquerque Dukes in Dodgertown. The mixture of prospects and borderline major leaguers who made up the new Triple-A International League affiliate of the Montreal Expos hopped on the bus for the 90-minute ride from Lantana, Florida to Vero Beach.

They were rained out.

They were rained out the following day as well. On the third day, the sun came out, but the field was too wet to play.

It was an omen of what was to come. Dark clouds hung over the Lynx for most of a 15-year existence that began brilliantly but was forever plagued by an ongoing battle with the weather, squabbles with the Expos over the quality of players sent to Ottawa, disputes with the City of Ottawa over parking, and the ascendance of the National Hockey League's Ottawa Senators, who stole attention and ticket-buying customers just as the new-team sheen was wearing off the Lynx.

The International League approved Ottawa businessman Harold Darwin for a franchise in September 1991, with the team scheduled to begin play in 1993. The return to Canada would put the international into the International League for the first time since former Expos affiliate the Winnipeg Whips decamped for Hampton, Virginia after the 1971 season. The timing was serendipitous. Baseball was enjoying unprecedented popularity in Canada, with the Toronto Blue Jays having won their first World Series championship in 1992 and embarking on another title run in 1993. The Expos, only a two-hour drive east of Ottawa on Highway 417, were putting the final touches on a good young team that had the best record in the major leagues in 1994 before the players' strike finished off their World Series dreams—and expedited their eventual exit out of Montreal a decade later.

Ottawa baseball fans—and, as it would turn out, non-baseball fans—were quick to jump on the bandwagon. The brand-new ballpark was *the* place to be in the spring and summer of 1993. Despite a cold and constant drizzle and a first-pitch temperature of 7 degrees (44 F), a sell-out crowd of 10,332 was on hand for Opening Night against their expansion partners, the Charlotte Knights. The Lynx had sold more than 5,000 season tickets two months before the season started and by Opening Day had sold 500,000 game tickets, breaking the all-time attendance record for any Ottawa team in any sport. By the end of the season,

the Lynx had shattered the International League regular season attendance record that had stood since 1947 with 663,926 paying fans, including 44 sell-outs for its 71 home dates. Throw in a pair of playoff-games and an exhibition game against the Expos, and the Lynx final attendance was 693,043.[1]

Despite the success in the stands, front-office squabbling led to tensions between fans and management. Promoting the team was not a priority for ownership. A public relations officer was not hired until two days before the season started. Season-ticket holders complained that their tickets had not arrived. Ticket prices were the second-highest in the 10-team league and there were no discounts for children or seniors, which meant the Lynx were charging more for kids tickets than were the Expos or Blue Jays.[2] Except for Sunday afternoons, all but four of the other remaining 55 games started at 7:30 P.M., giving rise to complaints that children wouldn't be able to attend and questions being asked about the wisdom of playing night games on frigid Ottawa spring nights when snow usually blanketed the city and daytime temperatures rarely reached 10 degrees Celsius. The club's early rain-out policy dictated there would be no rain-checks for games that were rained or snowed out after five innings, even if there was no winner and the game would be completed at a later date. The policy was changed in May in response to fan and media criticism.

Internally, disputes between Darwin and General Manager Tom Maloney, the 1991 minor-league executive of the year, over how to run a minor-league team were already percolating and resulted in Maloney's firing at the end of the season.

Darwin's disagreements with the Expos over the quality of players sent to Ottawa and how to use them drew a rebuke from Expos manager Felipe Alou. In their third game of the season, Lynx manager Mike Quade pulled pitcher Gil Heredia, who the Expos had on a 65-pitch limit, five innings into a perfect game at Richmond. "I've never before taken out a pitcher who is throwing a no-hitter, let alone a perfect game," said Quade. "But every so often you've got to do stuff down here to help out the major-league club."[3]

Six weeks later, on a frigid Victoria Day (night game) in Ottawa, Chris Nabholz threw eight innings of no-hit baseball in his first start with the Lynx after being sent down by the Expos earlier in the week. Working on three days' rest, he was on an Expos-mandated 80-pitch limit and had reached 78 after eight innings. Quade took him out and was roundly booed for his decision. "We all have somebody from above who gives orders. If I had a direct line to Duke (Expos General Manager Dan Duquette) in the dugout, I would have called him…I felt a little bad for (Nabholz), but much worse for the fans."[4]

Darwin was incensed. "I'm not happy with what happened. I've got to go to the Expos . . . They've got to clean up their act and use better judgment, give Quade more freedom." Alou dismissed the complaining, saying, "Some people don't understand the minor leagues are for development. A no-hitter doesn't come into the picture."[5]

Though Alou often touted Quade's abilities as a baseball man, Quade's relationship with Duquette was tense and he was fired at the end of the season despite leading the team to a 73-69 record and a wild card spot in the playoffs, being voted International League manager of the year, and named minor-league manager to watch by *Baseball America*. Duquette didn't offer a specific reason for the sacking, saying, "We elected to make a change. We think we can run a more efficient player development operation in '94 with a new manager."[6] Quade ended up winning over 1,000 games as a minor-league manager and managed the Chicago Cubs for the last month of the 2010 season and all of 2011.

On the field, it was a tale of two seasons marked by a disappointing first half as the Expos remained true to their philosophy of player development and keeping their most promising young prospects in Double-A Harrisburg in the Eastern League instead of moving them up too early to Triple A. By the end of June, the Lynx were fighting to stay out of the Eastern Division basement with a 33-49 record. "Two-and-a-half runs a game isn't going to win you many games, no matter how much pitching you've got," said Quade. "We don't have a ton of speed and we're not getting a lot of extra-base hits."[7]

The Expos were talented and young. Future All-Star outfielders Marquis Grissom, Moises Alou, and Larry Walker, and catcher Darrin Fletcher were all 26 years old during the 1993 season. Second baseman Delino DeShields was 24. The next generation, headlined by Cliff Floyd, 20, Rondell White, 21, and Curtis Pride, 24, spent the first half of the season marinating in Double A. The Lynx, for the most part, were spare parts and injury fills for the Expos, who took full advantage of their proximity to Ottawa to call up and send down players. By the end of the season, Quade had had to deal with 107 player transactions.

As summer arrived, the Expos decided to promote some of its Double-A talent and the Lynx season turned around. Led by Canadian pitcher Denis Boucher, who went 6-0 with a 2.72 ERA in 11 appearances and White, who hit .380 with seven homers and 32 RBIs in 37 games, the Lynx moved above .500 for the first time since April on August 19, clinched a playoff spot with a week to go in the season and narrowly missed winning the division when they lost their final game. Their playoff championship chances were dealt a blow when the Expos called up Boucher and White during the final week of the Triple-A season and then summoned Charlie Montoyo, the future Blue

Jays manager, who led the Lynx with a .411 OBA, before Game Three of the playoffs with the series tied 1-1.

The Lynx dropped the series 3-2 to the Rochester Red Wings, but not before providing one final lasting memory for the home fans when outfielder Scott Bryant cracked a three-run walk-off homer in Game Two. Bryant led the team with 12 homers and 65 RBIs but was released at the end of spring training the following February.

Over the course of the season, hometown fans developed a love affair with the gritty, get-your-uniform dirty kind of players on the roster, like Montoyo, and particularly "The Saint," F.P. Santangelo. Drafted in 1989 by the Expos, Santangelo had reached Triple A in 1992 with Montreal's team in Indianapolis and came to Ottawa for the inaugural 1993 season when the Expos switched affiliates. He was the first batter in Lynx history, scored their first run, played outfield, shortstop, and second and third base, ran hard on every play, dove into bases, and crashed into walls with little concern for his body. Santangelo is the all-time Lynx leader in runs scored (186) and runs in a season (86) and graced the cover of the 1995 media guide. That didn't save him from punishment by the Expos at the beginning of the 1995 season for his refusal to cross the players' picket line in spring training, as did Canadian catcher Joe Siddall, who began work as a Blue Jays television analyst in 2014. The Expos ordered manager Pete Mackanin to keep both players out of the opening day line-up. Siddall ended up in the starting line-up when his replacement, Clemente Alvarez, forgot his passport and was denied entry into the U.S. Santangelo was back in the starting lineup after also being held out of the first home game.[8] His number was retired by the Lynx on June 8, 1998 when he returned to Ottawa for the annual exhibition game with the Expos.

Expectations were high for the 1994 season, with new manager Jim Tracy (who later managed the Dodgers, Pirates, and Rockies for a total of 10 years) promoted from Harrisburg, where he had led the Double-A team to a 94-44 record and the Eastern League championship. Many of those prospects were expected to spend the season with the Lynx, but it didn't work out that way. The team's record fell to 16-25 by Victoria Day. After scrapping their way back above .500, they dropped a doubleheader to Columbus on August 5 and lost 10 of their last 16 to finish 70-72 and out of the playoffs. Highlights included Tim Laker rediscovering his "can't-miss prospect" status and being named International League catcher of the year while hitting .309 with 12 homers and 71 RBIs and third baseman Shane Andrews breaking team records with 16 homers and 85 RBIs.

Off the field, there were continuing signs of problems to come. Despite responding to a fan survey that showed a clear preference for earlier start times for night games and more afternoon games, attendance dropped by about 1,000 a game, although the 607,000 tickets sold again led the league by a wide margin.[9] Cold weather continued to be a culprit. The season opener was postponed by a 15-centimetre (six-inch) snowfall. The temperature was just above freezing when the game was

An Ottawa Lynx batter in action, swinging for the fences.
Credit: Copyright Seregal / Dreamstime.com

mayor, Mark Sutcliffe, and another 17 in French by CKCH in neighboring Hull, Quebec, with Paul Lajoie (grandson of Hall-of-Famer Nap Lajoie) delivering the play-by-play.[13] The players' strike at the end of the 1994 season led to the flagship stations of the Expos adopting the Lynx for the final month of the season. CFRA was one of the stations carrying the English Expos network, which resulted in the Lynx finally having all of their games available on hometown radio.[14] The arrangement didn't survive the end of the season and reached tragicomedy levels in 1995 when, after failing to reach agreement with CFRA or any other commercial station, the Lynx struck a deal with CKDG, a student-radio station run by Algonquin College, to broadcast 10 games. It might have been more but the station went off the air when the student year ended at the end of April. The other problem was that the station had an eight-watt signal with a range of about eight kilometers, meaning that Lynx Stadium itself was out of listening range.[15]

The 1995 season opened under the shadow of the major-league baseball players' strike, which wasn't resolved until April 2, leaving organizations and fans uncertain about the future. For a team entering its third year of existence, generally considered the end of the honeymoon period for a new franchise,[16] the timing couldn't have been worse. Season tickets were down by nearly 1,000 from 1994, which were down 700 from 1993. "Instead of paying their full deposits, people have come to Joe (Fagan, ticket manager) and said 'Here's $100. Hold my seat. I want to see what the team's going to look like,'" said Darwin.[17] The Lynx ended up looking pretty good, winning their only league championship, but the fans did not come back, with attendance dropping to 511,865, fourth in the league, and managing only one sell-out.[18]

On the field, former Expos second-baseman Pete Mackanin was appointed the team's third manager in three years after Tracy was promoted to bench coach for the Expos. In addition to the usual revolving door of players headed to Montreal and back (the 23-man roster switched out 10 players on a week-long road trip in late April),[19] Mackanin had to deal with potential tensions between replacement players and those who refused to cross the picket line to play with them during major-league baseball's spring training. One of those replacement players, Kevin Castleberry, had been destined to be the Expos' starting second-baseman after hitting .400 in spring training prior to the strike being settled. He was signed by the Expos and sent to the Lynx where he played 118 games and led regular starters with a .294 batting average (future Expos All-Star Mark Grudzielanek hit .298 but played only 49 games with Ottawa between call-ups to Montreal). A number of players were unhappy about replacements being on the team and Castleberry was confronted by player association representative Tom Foley.[20] When Castleberry, an International League all-star in 1995, was asked prior to spring training before the 1996 season whether he was concerned about player backlash to him being there, he responded, "Not really. They should be worried about me

played the next day. "In April, people were coming here with skidoo suits on," said Darwin. "There's no way I would have been here if I didn't have to be."[10] Darwin was also still unhappy with Expos player moves that he believed were damaging his team. As well as releasing Bryant, the Expos traded Montoyo in the final week of spring training. "It's like they've taken our heroes the hell out of town."[11]

Lynx management was also struggling to land a deal with local radio stations. When Maloney was named general manager in 1992, he described that as his first priority. "Radio is essential to any ball club," he said. "We have to maximize all revenue streams and radio and television are certainly two big areas. They are also two great marketing tools."[12] It was especially important for the Lynx, which did little in the way of game promotions and advertising. However, a full-season deal was never reached with any of the 12 radio stations in the city. By the start of the 1994 season, the Lynx had arranged for 24 games to be carried by English radio CFRA, with play-by-play done by current Ottawa because I'm here to take one of their jobs."[21] Castleberry never did make it to the majors.

Despite the chaos, and what was generally considered to be a lack of talent (they finished tied for last in team batting and fifth in pitching, and Expos general manager Kevin Malone described the roster as "serviceable major leaguers"),[22] the Lynx had clawed their way to a 53-42 record, a franchise-best 11 games over .500 by mid-July.

Things went south from there, dropping 17 of 23 games to fall out of first place and out of the playoff picture before a successful late-season road trip brought them to a season-ending homestand against the Pawtucket Red Sox needing one win to qualify for the postseason. Playing in front of a crowd of 9,885, their largest of the season, the light-hitting Lynx won the first game 10-0.

More magic awaited in the playoffs, where they came from down two games to one on the road to defeat the Rochester Red Wings, beating Baltimore ace Ben MacDonald, who was making a rehab start in Game Four, and then getting a two-run single in the ninth inning from replacement catcher Ben Heffernan, who had started the season as a coach, to win the series. After that, the 3-1 championship series win over the Norfolk Tides, who had finished 13 games ahead of the Lynx in the regular season, seemed inevitable. The Lynx won the final game 4-0, but not without the Ottawa weather making an appearance and forcing separate delays of 55 and 45 minutes.

"It's like we couldn't stop this thing," said Mackanin. "I think what makes this so satisfying is where we were in the regular season. Us winning is like the .200 hitter getting the winning hit in the World Series."[23]

Fan-favorites Santangelo and Siddall, both called up earlier in the season, got the news from the Expos' clubhouse TV monitor after their game and drove to Ottawa to celebrate with their former teammates.[24] Two weeks later, Darwin was named International League executive of the year and *The Sporting News* then selected Mackanin as minor-league manager of the year.

But then came 1996, and as the Tragically Hip, the monster Canadian band from down the road in Kingston, Ontario could have told the club, "When it starts to fall apart, Man, it really falls apart."[25]

There was no positive momentum from the 1995 Governors' Cup championship. Attendance continued to fall, dropping to a franchise-worst 347,050, seventh in the league and barely half of the 1993 love fest. The stadium was less than half-full for an Opening Night victory and the largest cheer of the night was an announcement that the NHL Ottawa Senators were leading Mario Lemieux's Pittsburgh Penguins in a sold-out game across town. The product on the field was not good, with the team finishing a franchise-worst 60-82 and last in the league. The radio situation continued unresolved as local stations chose instead to continue to carry the full schedule of Blue Jays and Expos games, as well as those of the Senators and Canadian Football League Ottawa Rough Riders.

But worse than that, and the error that many believe was the death knell for a franchise that stayed in town for another decade, came on May 30, in what should have been the highlight of the season—the near-annual exhibition game with the parent Expos. After four years of a mediocre career, Expos outfielder Henry Rodriguez had taken major-league baseball by storm early in the season with a power barrage that would end with him hitting a career-high 36 homers in 1996. Expos fans responded by celebrating his homers by throwing Oh Henry! chocolate bars on to the field. An Ottawa rock station encouraged Lynx fans to replicate the celebration at the exhibition game. However, Darwin, citing rules against bringing outside food into the stadium, ordered stadium staff to confiscate the treats, sparking public and media outrage. It also prompted Murray Wilson, the club's marketing and sales director, to resign. "(This) should have been the crown jewel of the season for this organization," he said. "The Expos were here, the stadium was nearly full, a four-year association with Montreal was announced and all you read about the next day was the Oh Henry! controversy."[26]

The episode was symptomatic of a bigger problem. The club had never done much marketing. *Ottawa Citizen* columnist Wayne Scanlan described the strategy as "open the gates and pray for sunshine." There were very few of the in-stadium giveaways common in other ballparks, or discounted tickets for children or organizations looking for an outing. Security was described as "fastidious."[27]

Little was done to address those concerns and, as bad as 1996 was, it was a high-water mark for the rest of team's years in Ottawa. Attendance never again cracked 300,000 and finished below 200,000—and last in the league—for its final six years. The team finished above .500 only three more times (2002, 2003, 2006) and made the playoffs once, in 2003.

The dismal 1997 season was marked by the Lynx fielding their worst team to that point in their history, finishing 54-86 and getting recognition in late May for its .255 winning percentage (12-35) that made it the worst team in professional baseball.[28] Another fiasco with the Expos game marred the 1997 season. Anxious to make up for the previous year's Oh Henry! debacle, the Lynx announced they would be giving away 10,000 Oh Henry! bars to fans. Game day had been bright and sunny. In fact, it hadn't rained in three weeks. But then those dark clouds that had followed the club around since its birth showed up just before first pitch and drenched the stadium, creating a one hour and 22-minute rain delay. The teams played on the soggy surface for five innings before it was called because of unsafe conditions. A mob of angry fans surrounded the ticket office demanding refunds, which Darwin granted the next day.[29]

A similar "beyond their control" event scuttled another Lynx event scheduled in 2003 with the best of intentions. Jamey Carroll, who had replaced Santangelo as Lynx fans' favorite pepper-pot during his 2000-2002 tenure in Ottawa, was to have his number retired. A big crowd was anticipated for the August 14 event and an extra 8,000 hot dogs were prepared for sale. But at 4:11 P.M., three hours before game time, Ottawa was hit by a power blackout that affected 50 million people across Ontario and the U.S. northeast. About 500 people showed up to the stadium and were invited into center field for an intimate ceremony that was missing video clips and a microphone. The lost gate and spoiled hot dogs cost the club and concessions company about $30,000.[30]

A new stadium-naming agreement was reached in February 1997 with JetForm, an Ottawa-based software multinational, which paid the municipality $1.5 million for a 10-year-deal to name the stadium JetForm Park. While welcoming the involvement of JetForm, Darwin was critical of the overall Ottawa corporate community's lack of support and warned for the first time that the team needed more or he might have to sell or move the team. In August, he sent a letter to the league and Ottawa Mayor Jacquelin Holzman, informing them of his intention to sell the team.[31]

Appropriately, the season ended with the final home game being rained out.

Darwin's warnings about selling the team and back-and-forth lawsuits with the City over monies owed were the dominant story of 1998, but on the field, the club overcame a desultory start to the season to roll off a franchise-record nine-game

An Ottawa Lynx pitcher delivers a pitch during a Triple-A game. Credit: Copyright Seregal / Dreamstime.com

winning streak to get back in the playoff race, before losing 10 of their final 11 games. After selling off their best players, who they could no longer afford, the Expos, who finished 41 games behind the National League East champion Atlanta Braves, had again stripped the Lynx of prospects, leaving them with the lowest batting average in the league and only 76 homers in 143 games—30 behind the second-last Toledo Mud Hens. Opined Ottawa Citizen columnist Bruce Deachman, "All in all, it was another year in which the Ottawa manager was handed a clubhouse full of straw and told to turn it into gold."[32]

Darwin changed his mind about selling the team before the 1999 season, saying he would keep it at least until the end of the 2000 season when the affiliation agreement with the Expos ended even though the Expos continued to decimate the Lynx roster. At one point the Lynx were so short of players they had to start pitcher Scott Mitchell in right field. The Lynx had made 147 transactions in 144 games, picking at a scab that had irritated the owner since 1993. He said the Expos had committed to giving the Lynx better players in 1999 to reverse the poor records they had had since the 1995 championship. "It's one thing having one or two bad years, but this is four straight years. I can't afford to deal with their problems," he said. "Things have to change drastically."[33]

Things did not change and despite renewed commitments from the Expos that there would be fewer disruptions to the Lynx roster in 2000, the team started slowly and went on to have its worst record (53-88). The team also endured the worst early-season weather in its history with eight of its first 11 home games being rescheduled. With the NHL Senators playing into late April in the playoffs, paid attendance dropped below 900, with the actual number of fans in the park well below that. Darwin had had enough and agreed in June to sell the team to Vermont entrepreneur Ray Pecor, owner of the Expos Single-A Vermont Expos.[34]

Unfortunately for Pecor, who had resurrected the failing Vermont franchise and hoped to do the same in Ottawa by doubling service staff, discounting tickets for seniors and children under 14, cutting parking costs, and more promotions, local fans were unmoved. Only 3,834 fans showed up for Opening Day, the best opening crowd since 1997, but only about half of what had been anticipated. The next night attracted only 814 people, the smallest crowd to that point in Lynx history. However, with warmer weather in summer, season attendance improved by 70,000, the most fans since 1998, providing some hope to new ownership. Things were better on the field, with a franchise-best 14-11 record in April. By mid-July, the Lynx had a six-game lead in the wild card race. But once again, the Expos came knocking and in short order summoned slugger Fernando Seguignol, outfielder Brad Wilkerson, starting pitchers Bobby Munoz and Britt Reames, and closer Joey Eischen. "Our offence just went to the major leagues," said manager Stan Hough.[35] They lost 15 of 18 and limped home 24 games off the lead.

The Lynx did have an all-time moment at JetForm on August 22 when future Hall of Famer Tim Raines, in Ottawa on a rehab assignment from the Expos, played against his son Tim Jr. with the Rochester Red Wings. The pair exchanged line-up cards at home plate before game one of a doubleheader, marking the first time a father and son faced each other in a regular-season professional game.[36]

Despite putting together the best team in franchise history in 2002, going 80-61 and led by International League batting champion Endy Chavez who hit .343 and Joey Vitiello who finished third at .329 and added 82 RBIs, the longstanding problems of attendance and roster raiding by the Expos continued. Pecor, who lost about $1 million in each of his first two seasons as owner,[37] said more stability was needed and opted out of continuing the relationship with the Expos. After the new affiliation with the Baltimore Orioles was announced in September, speculation immediately began that the Lynx would soon be leaving Ottawa.

The Orioles provided the Lynx with a stronger roster in 2003 than had been the norm with Montreal, although the 123 transactions over the season were familiar. Future everyday major leaguers Luis Matos, Darnell McDonald, Jack Cust, and Larry Bigbie led a strong offense that carried the team to a 79-65 record and their first playoff appearance since 1995. However, few in Ottawa seemed to care as less than 3,000 fans attended the playoff games.

The 2004-05 NHL lock-out of players provided another glimmer of hope for the Lynx as the 2005 baseball season started with no Stanley Cup playoffs to distract fans. Perhaps in the most definitive message from would-be fans, attendance dropped despite an Opening Day crowd of 7,651. But even that rare large crowd came with problems. Because development over the years around the stadium had reduced the number of parking spaces from 2,800 to 1,000, many fans didn't get into their seats until the second inning.[38] Fewer than 4,000 combined attended the next two games. As Yogi Berra may or may not have said, "Nobody goes there anymore. It's too crowded." The team launched a lawsuit against the City in 2006, charging that it had violated its own rules on the number of parking spaces required.

By mid-2006, despite denials from Pecor and the International League in June, it was clear that the Lynx were going to move. On August 28 it was made official that majority ownership was being sold to Joseph Finley and Craig Stein, who would be moving the team in the 2008 season to a new stadium being built in Allentown, Pennsylvania.[39] Lynx affiliation shifted in 2007 from Baltimore to the Philadelphia Phillies.

The Phillies populated the 2007 edition of the Lynx primarily with older players who were hoping to get back to the majors or who were minor-league lifers. After being named the Lynx MVP in 2003, Pedro Swann bounced around the minors before returning to Ottawa to finish his career. It was the kind of season where neither the players nor the fans seemed to care much. The team finished last at 55-88 and last in attendance, averaging under 2,000 fans a game. In one of those cosmic moments that are baseball, the relationship was cemented by milestone wins and losses. On July 15, the Phillies lost their 10,000th game. On August 30, their new junior partner won their 1,000th. "It's nice, especially to do it at home," said Lynx manager John Russell. "Of course, we'd like to have about 80 wins to go with that, but it's a nice thing for Ottawa."[40]

A season-high crowd of 7,468 showed up for the final game. There were standing ovations for the Lynx as they took the field for their final game and again during the final at-bat – a Dusty Wathan groundout to second.

There wasn't enough parking. The concession stands ran out of beer.

At least the sun was shining.

NOTES

1   Wayne Scanlan, "Year three beckons," *Ottawa Citizen*, April 13, 1995: C1.

2   Michael Prentice, "Baseball is Baseball, One Price for All, says Lynx Management," *Ottawa Citizen*, March 24, 1993: C1.

3   Ken Warren, "Quade Yanks Lynx 5-inning no-hit pitcher for reasons beyond his control," *Ottawa Citizen*, April 12, 1993: C3.

4   Stephanie Myles, "Nabholz pulled after eight in Lynx' first no-hitter," *Ottawa Citizen*, May 25, 1993: C1.

5   Stephanie Myles, "Darwin has reason to smile, but there are problems," *Ottawa Citizen*, May 28, 1993: D1.

6   Stephanie Myles, "Quade's first season with Lynx also turns out to be his last," *Ottawa Citizen*, September 23, 1993: E8.

7   Ken Warren, "Road woes continue as Lynx get pounded again," *Ottawa Citizen*, June 28, 1993: C3.

8   Wayne Scanlan, "Dirty pool scratches F.P. from Opening Day line-up," *Ottawa Citizen*, April 9, 1995: D2.

9   Ken Warren, "Darwin's theory breeds success," *Ottawa Citizen*, September 4, 1994: D3.

10 Wayne Scanlan, "1993 Lynx tough act to follow," *Ottawa Citizen*, May 25, 1994: C1.

11 Wayne Scanlan, "Home is where the heroes are, for a while," *Ottawa Citizen*, April 7, 1994: D1.

12 Don Campbell, "Local radio broadcasts high on GM's agenda," *Ottawa Citizen*, April 3, 1992: E7.

13 Michael Prentice, "Lynx radio: The sound of silence," *Ottawa Citizen*, June 8, 1994: D1.

14 Ken Warren, "Major-league strike shifting spotlight to Lynx," *Ottawa Citizen*, August 12, 1994: D1.

15 Wayne Scanlan, "Students signal end to Lynx radio," *Ottawa Citizen*, August 19, 1995: B1.

16 Ken Warren, "Darwin's theory breeds success," *Ottawa Citizen*, September 4, 1994: D3.

17 Wayne Scanlan, "Clouds of doubt over Lynx," *Ottawa Citizen*, February 25, 1995: G1.

18 Allen Panzeri, "1995 International League champions,' *Ottawa Citizen*, September 15, 1995: B1.

19 Allen Panzeri, "Lynx await players they can call their own," *Ottawa Citizen*, April 28, 1995: B2.

20 Allen Panzeri, "No one wants to be in the minors, no one is putting the team first," *Ottawa Citizen*, April 3, 1996: F1.

21 Mal Florence, "At $500 a game, he had it made 'til he checked," *Los Angeles Times*, February 28, 1996: 2.

22 Allen Panzeri, "Majors far, far away for Lynx." *Ottawa Citizen*, July 16, 1995: B3.

23 Wayne Scanlan, "Misfit Lynx roar to unlikely title," *Ottawa Citizen*, September 14, 1995: A1.

24 Wayne Scanlan, "Memories of magic night linger as Lynx go their separate ways," *Ottawa Citizen*, September 15, 1995: B1.

25 Lyrics to "Boots or Hearts" from Tragically Hip's *Up to Here* album

26 Wayne Scanlan, "Oh Howard! Chocolate bar ban last straw for Lynx sales director," *Ottawa Citizen*, June 1, 1996: A1.

27 Wayne Scanlan, "Where have Lynx fans gone?," *Ottawa Citizen*, June 2, 1996: B1.

28 Allan Panzeri, "Lynx last – in all of North America," *Ottawa Citizen*, May 24, 1997: F1.

29 Wayne Scanlan, "Lynx yet to reap benefits of farm visits," *Ottawa Citizen*, June 3, 1998: G1.

30 Darren Desaulniers, "Lynx defeat to PawSox on field follows promotion loss," *Ottawa Citizen*, August 16, 2003: C3.

31 Allen Panzeri, "Darwin plans to sell Lynx," *Ottawa Citizen*, August 13, 1997: A1.

32 Bruce Deachman, "Lack of offence dominates Lynx season," *Ottawa Citizen*, September 12, 1998: F3.

33 Lisa Burke, "Lynx owner set to cut Expos connection," *Ottawa Citizen*, September 8, 1999: B7.

34 Tom Casey, "It's Pecor's ballgame now," *Ottawa Citizen*, June 20, 2000: D1.

35 Tom Casey, "Short-staffed Lynx hit tough stretch," *Ottawa Citizen*, July 30, 2001, C3

36 Lisa Burke, "Family fun day for Raines," *Ottawa Citizen*, August 22, 2001: B3.

37 Wayne Scanlan, "Fickle Lynx fans get reacquainted with spurred franchise," *Ottawa Citizen*, September 3, 2002: C1.

38 Wayne Scanlan, "How good was that, for openers," *Ottawa Citizen*, April 17, 2005: B1.

39 Ken Warren, "Lynx are outta here," *Ottawa Citizen*, August 29, 2006: A1.

40 Darren Desaulniers, "1,000 wins and counting," *Ottawa Citizen*, August 31, 2007: B1.

BASEBALL'S OTTAWA-BORN
MAPLE WOOD REVOLUTION

BY CHRISTOPHER SAILUS

FOR AN EAGER BASEBALL FAN, there's nothing quite like the crack as bat meets ball. But it's that sharper crack—and maybe a few splinters flying through your field of view—that signals that a wooden bat has broken in the line of duty.

It's not an unusual sight to anyone who watches professional baseball, but in the 1990s it was becoming too common for Bill Mackenzie, at that time a scout for the Colorado Rockies organization.[1] Bill related his complaints to friend Sam Holman in 1996 over a beer at Ottawa's now-closed Mayflower Pub on Elgin Street. "Do you think you could come up with an answer to that?"

Holman thought maybe he could. An American transplant to Ottawa and long-time stagehand at Canada's National Arts Centre, he read up on the physics of baseball and its equipment before fashioning his own bat out of a leftover wooden stair banister in his home.[2]

The banister was salvaged not only because it was close at hand, but because of the type of wood: maple. Maple trees grow slower than ash trees, then the wood most used for baseball bats. Slower growth makes maple wood's grain tighter, resulting in a denser, stronger, and stiffer wood.[3] On the field that translates to wooden bats that are less prone to splintering or flaking—the method by which many ash bats break.[4]

Holman took his banister-borne bat for testing to the turnkey ballfield in the east end of Ottawa, then home to the Montreal Expos' AAA team, the Ottawa Lynx. The bat was an immediate hit.[5] Holman soon traveled to Toronto, meeting several Toronto Blue Jays players through mutual contacts. The bat was popular there as well, with Jays legend

Joe Carter becoming Holman's first major-league client. Carter famously snuck a maple bat into a game during the 1997 season, even before it was formally approved for use by major-league baseball for the 1998 season.[6]

The year 1998 also saw Carter's departure from the Jays, with the five-time All-Star playing parts of the season in Baltimore and San Francisco before retiring. His Canadian exodus proved to be fortuitous for the maple bat, as Carter extolled the virtues of the heavier, denser maple bat to other players, most importantly Giants teammate Barry Bonds. Ever skeptical, Bonds was not sold until he met Holman and tried the bat during batting practice at spring training in 1999. After a home run–filled session, the outfielder was soon chatting with Holman about sourcing bats directly from the former stagehand turned hobbyist carpenter.[7]

However you might view Bonds's 2001 record-setting season of 73 home runs, one thing is certain—he did it with Holman's maple bats. And while he may have been the most prolific hitter, he wasn't the only one—by 2001 more than 300 major leaguers were using maple bats.[8] Though many sported the recognizable Sam Bat logo and the nickname "Rideau Crusher" (an allusion to the river that bisects Holman's adopted hometown), most major manufacturers followed Holman's success and soon produced and sold maple bats.

Though Bonds's home run hitting may have helped popularize the maple bat with big leaguers, it was not performance-enhancing. Maple bats' higher density made them harder to splinter, but it also made them heavier. Heavier bats require more muscle to get the same swing velocity, making them ideal for power hitters like Bonds, but they provide no added advantage based on the material alone. "Wood is wood when it comes to hitting performance," materials engineering Professor Lloyd V. Smith of Washington State University told the *Washington Post* in 2014.[9]

While maple bats might not provide extra pop to the ball, they do have an extra pop when they eventually break, leading to a backlash in the mid-2000s. Despite the initial success, maple bats were breaking more often and doing so in violent and dangerous ways. Players and coaches were injured on multiple occasions when hit by sharp or heavy maple splinters. MLB tried to raise this issue during the 2006 collective bargaining negotiations, but the MLBPA was unwilling to seriously discuss any impositions on players' bat preferences.[10]

Not satisfied, the MLB Safety and Health Advisory Committee consulted the U.S. Forest Service in 2008 to learn how and why maple bats were breaking. After analyzing more than 2,200 broken bats and video footage over the course of that season, experts determined that the problem stemmed from two issues: the slope of grain in a shattered maple bat not being straight (a common issue in maple wood), and the use by some manufacturers of lighter, low-density maple.[11]

MLB promptly instituted new regulations that required the straightness of a bat's grain to be measured during the manufacturing process, and outlawed bats made with low-density maple. From 2009-2013 instances of bats breaking across the league were down more than 50% and have continued to fall since.

The problem was always less of an issue for Sam Bat, who used and continue to use high-density rock maple wood, now the only species of maple approved for use in professional leagues. It wasn't long before the demand for Holman's bats exceeded the capacity of his quite literally homegrown business. Sam Bat opened a factory in the early 2000s in Carleton Place, a half-hour's drive from central Ottawa. Holman sold most of the business to partners in 2008, though he remained involved in the company until a 2021 heart surgery caused him to lessen his public activity.[12]

Today, Sam Bat estimates that more than 80% of major-league players now use a maple bat, and Sam Bat sells to roughly 100 major leaguers every season. Their reach is global as well; they are the #1 North American brand in Japan's Nippon Professional League, and the bats are also used in major leagues in Korea, Taiwan, and Mexico.[13]

From an Ottawa garage to the major leagues and around the world, Sam Holman and Sam Bat changed the bat—and baseball—forever.

NOTES

1 "Bill Mackenzie," *Baseball Reference*. Accessed May 17, 2024, https://www.baseball-reference.com/bullpen/Bill_MacKenzie.

2 "Sam Bat Was the First Professionally Approved Maple Bat – Accept No Imitations!" *Sam Bat – The Original Maple Bat Corporation*. Accessed May 15, 2024, https://canada.sambat.com/pages/about-sam-bat.

3 Isabelle Khurshudyan, "Nats have their wood bat preferences, but science suggests there is no difference," *Washington Post*, July 25, 2014.

4 Dave Mance III, "Batter Up: Ash or Maple?" *The Outside Story*, June 18, 2012.

5 "Bonds' bats Canadian-made," *CBC Sports*. Accessed May 16, 2024, https://www.cbc.ca/sports/baseball/bonds-bats-canadian-made-1.296895.

6 Jack Curry, "Why Bonds Will Never Have to Borrow a Bat," *New York Times*, July 28, 2007.

7 "Bonds' bats Canadian-made," *CBC Sports*. Accessed May 16, 2024, https://www.cbc.ca/sports/baseball/bonds-bats-canadian-made-1.296895.

8 "Bonds' bats Canadian-made."

9 Isabelle Khurshudyan.

10 Jeff Passan, "Baseball at breaking point over maple bats," *Yahoo Sports*, May 9, 2008. https://sports.yahoo.com/jp-maple-bats050808.html.

11 "Rate of Shattered Baseball Bats 50 Percent Less, thanks to Major League Baseball and the U.S. Forest Service," U.S. Department of Agriculture, July 12, 2013.

12 Denis Armstrong, "Sam Holman reinvented baseball with his new bat," *City News Everywhere*, October 19, 2022. https://ottawa.citynews.ca/2022/10/19/sam-holman-reinvented-baseball-with-his-new-bat-5970768/.

13 Kevin Rothwell, interview via email, May 16-23, 2024.

THE PECOR ERA (2000-2006)

BY STEVE RENNIE

IN THE SPRING OF 2000, Ray Pecor, a prosperous Vermont businessman, emerged as a promising candidate to purchase the team. Lynx owner Howard Darwin said that Pecor, who built his fortune as the owner of a successful ferry company, first approached him in August 1999 to explore a potential sale. He claimed Pecor, who also owned the Montreal Expos Single-A affiliate in Vermont, was "one of the nine people who have shown interest" in purchasing the Lynx. Darwin set the asking price for the ballclub at CAD 10 million, according to the *Ottawa Citizen*.[1]

Pecor soon emerged as the frontrunner to buy the team. Two major obstacles stood in the way of a sale. The first one, which was relatively easy to overcome, involved getting the approval of the International League, minor-league baseball owners, and the baseball Commissioner's office. The second and more challenging one was to work out new financial arrangements with the city. Darwin said he had paid the city half a million dollars in 1999 to use the ballpark—now called JetForm Park—and he and Pecor wanted to lower that to a base rent plus a share of the attendance revenue.[2]

City council agreed to review the lease terms, and Darwin and Pecor reached a tentative deal. They agreed that Darwin would retain a 25 percent stake in the Lynx, while Pecor would become the majority owner by acquiring the rest. Pecor also pledged to keep the team in the city for at least five years, and to cover the outstanding CAD 2.8 million debt on the stadium if he relocated the team before the lease expired in 2009. The city agreed to lower the rent to CAD 108,000 a season, along with taking a cut of the club's ticket sales.[3][4]

Pecor's purchase of the team was approved by the International League during a half-hour conference call on the morning of May 26, 2000. "I'm proud to have brought baseball to Ottawa, but it's time to move and get new blood," Darwin told the *Ottawa Citizen*. "I'm very pleased that the club is staying in Ottawa and I want it to be successful."[5][6]

On June 19, 2000, Pecor acquired majority ownership of the Lynx for approximately USD 7 million. This investment also granted Pecor the rights to operate and manage JetForm Park through a renegotiated lease agreement with the city. As part of the agreement, Darwin would maintain his 25 percent stake in the team until January 1, 2001. At the start of the new year, Darwin sold his remaining shares to Pecor for an undisclosed amount.

NOTES

1   Bruce Deachman, "Lynx find tentative buyer," *Ottawa Citizen*, April 12, 2000: 21.

2   Tom Casey, "Two hurdles to Lynx sale," *Ottawa Citizen*, April 26, 2000: 62.

3   Tom Casey, "Darwin a step closer to selling Lynx," *Ottawa Citizen*, May 12, 2000: 25.

4   Tom Casey, "Council OK's new lease for Lynx," *Ottawa Citizen*, May 18, 2000: 44.

5   Tom Casey, "Red Wings pick on Powell for eight runs against Lynx," *Ottawa Citizen*, May 24, 2000: 68.

6   Tom Casey, "IL approves sale of Lynx," *Ottawa Citizen*, May 27, 2000: 62.

JOSEPH FINLEY AND CRAIG STEIN (2006 – 2008)

BY STEVE RENNIE

IN JUNE 2006, NEWS OUTLETS in Pennsylvania reported that American sports entrepreneurs Joseph Finley and Craig Stein had acquired the Lynx as part of a complex farm club exchange between the Philadelphia Phillies and Baltimore Orioles.[1][2][3] The news coincided with city officials in Allentown, Pennsylvania giving their approval for the construction of a USD 34-million ballpark, which was scheduled to be completed in time for the 2008 season.[4] Both the Lynx and the International League denied the reports of a sale.[5]

Throughout the 2006 season, the Lynx consistently struggled with the lowest attendance in the league.[6] Uncertainty loomed over the team's future as owner Ray Pecor stated that the Lynx would continue playing in Ottawa for the 2007 season, but he offered no guarantees beyond that. Tensions heightened after a meeting between Pecor and Ottawa mayor Bob Chiarelli on August 24, 2006, to discuss the parking situation at the stadium.[7] Pecor vehemently denied reports suggesting that he had informed the city about the Lynx's impending departure.

He sold the team four days later.[8]

Under the terms of the deal, Finley and Stein would become majority owners of the team, with Pecor retaining an undisclosed minority stake.[9] Although the move to Pennsylvania wasn't made official until nearly a year later, the ballclub would remain in Ottawa for the 2007 season before moving to the newly built, 7,000-seat stadium in Allentown in 2008 to become the Lehigh Valley IronPigs. The team also signed a two-year deal to become the Phillies farm club after the Orioles ended their affiliation with the Lynx in favor of the Norfolk Tides.[10]

NOTES

1   "Phillies make it official, leaving Scranton," *Press Enterprise* (Bloomsburg, Pennsylvania), June 11, 2006: 14.

2   Romy Varghese, "Planning unit gives thumbs up to Allentown stadium," *Morning Call* (Allentown, Pennsylvania), June 14, 2006: 14.

3   Ray Saul, "ASA softball complex impresses PIAA officials and fans," *Standard-Speaker* (Hazleton, Pennsylvania), June 13, 2006: 26.

4   Romy Varghese, "Planners support stadium," *Morning Call*, June 14, 2006: 1.

5   Don Campbell, "'There is no sale agreement,'" *Ottawa Citizen*, June 13, 2006: 28.

6   Ken Warren, "Lynx need fan 'miracle,'" *Ottawa Citizen*, August 25, 2006: 17.

7   Matthew Sekeres, "Lynx sue Ottawa for $10.75M over parking," *Ottawa Citizen*, October 18, 2006: 15.

8   Ken Warren and Vito Pilieci, "Lynx are outta here: Team sold, will move to U.S.," *Ottawa Citizen*, August 29, 2006: 1.

9   Jay Hart, "Grand slam dunk." *Morning Call*, August 29, 2006: 1.

10 Darren Desaulniers, "Lynx affiliation with Phillies hits pitchers," *Ottawa Citizen*, September 28, 2006: 21.

2008 OTTAWA RAPIDZ: A WHITE-KNUCKLE RIDE

BY KURT BLUMENAU

THE WORD "RAPIDS" REFERS TO stretches of river that are fast-flowing, rocky, and turbulent. They're a test of endurance, but some people enjoy them.

"Rapidz" made a good name, then, for the Ottawa baseball team that lasted one scant season, 2008, in the independent Canadian-American Association of Professional Baseball, colloquially known as the Can-Am League. The Rapidz came and went quickly, and the team's existence was rocky and turbulent for some. On the field, the Rapidz finished last in an eight-team league with a 31-63 record, firing their manager midway through the campaign and narrowly dodging the league record for most losses in a season. Off the field, the team went bankrupt, and one of its owners filed a $3-million lawsuit against the city and others.

Despite these travails, those who spent the season in the clubhouse remember it as a largely positive experience. "We had a good group of guys who were fun to play with. We worked hard every day," recalled center fielder Jared Lemieux. "We enjoyed each other's company, and we never got too far down."[1]

Also, in a region that had just lost the Triple-A International League Ottawa Lynx, there were fans for whom the Rapidz represented a relaxing and entertaining—if not always winning—night out at the ballpark. "The Lynx and Rapidz bent over backwards to offer incomparable summertime value to families," fan Neil Kelly wrote to the *Ottawa Citizen* newspaper in 2009. "My two little lads will never forget [Rapidz] coach Ed Nottle's invitations to chat with the players on the field."[2]

Knockabout minor-league manager Nottle became one of the faces of the team during its brief existence. But the man who began the Rapidz' run, so to speak, was Miles Wolff Jr., the veteran minor- and independent-league commissioner and team owner, who was serving in 2007 as commissioner of the Can-Am League.[3]

That season, the Can-Am included a league-owned traveling team called the Grays to bring it to an even number of 10 teams. As reports of the Lynx's pending departure from Ottawa gained momentum, Wolff began talking with city officials, seeing Ottawa as a logical landing spot for the Grays.[4]

Talks began in the summer and continued into the fall, complicated by mutual hostility between former Lynx owner Ray Pecor and the city. Wolff tried to position a Can-Am team as a compromise that would allow both parties to drop their hostile gestures—a lawsuit against the city on Pecor's part, a financial penalty against Pecor on the city's.[5]

Wolff didn't succeed in forging a peace between Pecor and the city.[6] But he got his team on November 28, 2007, when Ottawa city council voted to allow a new Can-Am League franchise to take over the remaining two years of the Lynx's lease on Lynx Stadium, renamed Ottawa Stadium.[7]

By independent league standards, the former Triple-A park was a garden spot. During the 2008 season, Can-Am League managers ranked Ottawa as having the best stadium, field, and amenities in the loop.[8] Catcher Kyle Geiger recalled: "I always tell people one of my favorite places to play was in Ottawa because of the city and how safe and clean it felt. It was also nice to have played in a former Triple-A stadium and have the facilities we did at that time."[9]

The new team, as it turned out, shared no DNA with the Grays. The travel team's players had been scattered a month earlier in a dispersal draft, requiring the new Ottawa ballclub to start from scratch.[10]

The new team vowed to include local and Canadian-born players on its roster, and its earliest signings made good on that promise. The team's first three commitments came from pitcher Mike Kusiewicz, a local native who'd reached the Triple-A level in the Boston Red Sox and Oakland Athletics organizations and represented Canada at the 2004 Summer Olympics; pitcher Fraser Robinson, from North Gower via Northwestern State University in Louisiana; and outfielder Jeremy Ware, an Ontario native who'd played for the 2001 Lynx and also made the 2004 Canadian Olympic baseball team. (Kusiewicz and Robinson played for the Rapidz; Ware did not.)[11]

Two other important blank spaces were filled in in early 2008. As part of a name-that-team contest that drew 1,100 entries, "Rapids" was selected as a tribute to the rivers that had powered the Ottawa area's lumber industry.[12]

The Rapids—or Rapides, to French-speaking fans[13]—also chose an experienced and colorful field manager in 68-year-old Nottle, a pitcher during his playing days. Known as "Singing Ed" for his crooning talent—he'd recorded a self-released album and worked in nightclubs—Nottle had spent a lifetime in baseball but only one season in the majors, serving as the Oakland Athletics' bullpen coach in 1983.[14] He was better known as a manager in the minor leagues and independent ball. After 12 seasons managing as high as Triple-A in the Boston Red Sox and Athletics systems, he'd switched to independent leagues in 1993, spending another 15 seasons in cities like Brockton, Massachusetts, and Sioux City, Iowa.

Nottle promised fans an accessible, community-rooted, and competitive team: "I guarantee people are going to be amazed at the level of baseball. We're asking [fans] to give it a shot."[15] To another writer, he said: "If we're invited to community events, we go. I've had people tell them they've got five years in this community and never met a Lynx. Well, that's changed now."[16]

Baseball backers made a case that independent ball—labeled "professional baseball at its lowest but most lovable form"[17]—would be a good fit for Ottawa. One newspaper columnist pointed out that the Can-Am season didn't start until May 22, which spared the team from having to compete against either the National Hockey League playoffs or unpredictable April weather. And since the team had no affiliation with a major-league organization, manager Nottle would not have to think about player development; he would be free to make decisions with no other goal than winning.[18]

The Rapids continued to sign players, including two of the 34 aspirants who attended an open tryout camp in Ottawa on May 8.[19] The team came together in a hurry. Nottle noted that its preseason training camp would last for just 12 days, and the Rapids would start playing exhibitions five days after the players arrived.[20]

But as the team hustled to prepare for Opening Day, the preseason was marked by upheaval in the front office. New, locally based owners Rick Anderson and Rob Hall—co-founders of movie rental company Zip. ca—bought the team from the league in late April and modified the name, discarding Rapids and Rapides in favor of the language-neutral Rapidz. Anderson emphasized that affordability would be a priority for the new owners: "We're not looking to make money on [the team]. It is not our main business."[21] Ticket prices ranged from $10 for adults to $4 for children under 14. Beer was $4.50 a cup—except when a Rapidz player hit a home run, when it was marked down to half-price for the next inning.[22]

Ten days after they took over, and just 16 days before the season opened, Anderson and Hall fired general manager Don Charrette, a local resident who had been in charge of the Rapidz' day-to-day business operations.[23] It's unclear whether Charrette would have been able to prevent some of the minor issues that arose in the run-up to Opening Day, such as the delayed arrival of the team's uniform pants and caps.[24] In more positive news, the team set up a schedule of 10 local TV broadcasts, as well as French-language radio coverage of games.[25]

The Rapidz began their odyssey with a May 18 exhibition game in which they beat the Quebec Capitales, 7-6, scoring two runs in the bottom of the ninth in front of fewer than 1,000 fans. Pitcher Dallas Strankman got credit for the win; it was

Center fielder Jared Lemieux watches the ball after a hit. Credit: Courtesy Jared Lemieux.

one more victory than he would record in 15 regular-season appearances.[26]

The season proper began on May 22 with a 6-0 home loss to the New Jersey Jackals. Kusiewicz, who doubled as the Rapidz' pitching coach, took the loss as the Rapidz made six errors and mustered only two hits. The best news of the night came from a promising and passionate crowd – 4,246 fans on a rainy evening. "The crowd was loud right to the end. They were still cheering us down by six," Kusiewicz said.[27]

The 2,561 fans who came back the next night saw the Rapidz' first victory, 6-1. Canadian-born starting pitcher Adam Hawes earned the win, and second baseman Jose De Los Santos and first baseman Jabe Bergeron chipped in three hits apiece.[28] De Los Santos, a former Chicago White Sox and Pittsburgh Pirates farmhand, and Bergeron, who'd played in the New York Mets system, went on to become two of the Rapidz' offensive leaders, hitting .288 and .354 respectively. After a loss in the team's third game, Nottle remained optimistic: "I guarantee it right now, we'll be in the playoffs and you can write that."[29]

But the real tone for the Rapidz' season was set on their first road trip, which followed four games at home. The first bus hired to carry the team to Atlantic City, New Jersey, never showed up. The second overheated several times on the highway. (Lemieux recalled, "The A/C went out, and we're going down there with the hatch open and our shirts off."[30]) The sore, sleep-deprived Rapidz arrived two hours late for their game against the Atlantic City Surf. Nottle dubbed it the "road trip from hell" on that first day, and he was prescient. Though some of the games were hard-fought, Ottawa went 1-6 on the road trip and fell into the league's basement with a 2-9 record.[31]

They never made it out. As early as the start of June, Nottle was already shuffling personnel, including the addition of infielder Félix Escalona, the only member of the 2008 Rapidz to have played in the major leagues. Escalona had played 84 games with the Tampa Bay Devil Rays and New York Yankees between 2002 and 2005. Nottle said he was "very happy with the pitching, except the bullpen," and tried to boost his team's confidence with salty pep talks: "Don't give up the ship until your ass hits the water, folks."[32]

The team continued to struggle through June, though. When the bats began to heat up, the pitching went south. After five losses, local favorite Kusiewicz finally earned his first win on June 26, at which point the team's record was 9-23.[33] While team morale stayed positive, Geiger admitted that losing took its toll on him: "It was hard being as competitive as I was to watch the team struggle and not have success. It was new territory for me to lose that much in one season, so the frustrations were there."[34]

It took the Rapidz until July 9 to string together two wins in a row.[35] A few days later, the first half of the Can-Am season ended with the Rapidz in last place at 13-34. Nottle said the team needed "another bat" to be stronger in the second half, while offensive star Bergeron looked on the bright side: "That's the glory of the second half: We have a chance to wipe it clean. Hopefully we'll all get hot at the same time." A local sportswriter took a tougher stance: "If Ottawa Rapidz owners Rob Hall and Rick Anderson viewed their team as any other business venture, mass layoffs would likely be in order."[36]

These difficult weeks were not without their bright spots. Geiger, released by the Minnesota Twins organization a month before the season, stepped up as a solid offensive and defensive contributor; Nottle called him "an absolute delight."[37] And the Rapidz retained a solid core of fan interest, despite their on-field problems and a rainy month of June. At the end of the first half, they ranked fifth in the eight-team league with an average attendance of 2,205 per game.[38]

Two mascots, Trash Monster and Rookie, kept things light at Ottawa Stadium, as did a denim-clad cheer team called the Rapidz Girls. "After the sour departure of the Lynx, we may all have forgotten how pleasant these summer evenings can be," a local columnist wrote. ("There is a *Bad News Bears* quality about the team, which may become endearing," he added.)[39]

Highlights of July included a Montreal Expos tribute night that drew 2,781 fans, with appearances by former Expos Claude Raymond, Warren Cromartie, and Jim Fanning, as well as Montreal organist Fernand Lapierre.[40] On the road, the Rapidz' pitching staff had the satisfaction of holding U.S. Olympic skiing medalist Bode Miller without a hit when Miller made a stunt start for the Nashua (New Hampshire) Pride on July 19. The Rapidz still lost 5-2.[41]

July included an early public hint that the team was financially struggling. It came via a single line in a July 25 column by sports columnist Marty York: "What's this I hear about the new ownership of the Ottawa Rapidz baseball team irking creditors with unpaid bills?"[42] Geiger said that the owners' financial issues did not affect the players: "We were treated very well and compensated for everything in a timely manner. I felt like the owners definitely did a great job in running the team and the day-to-day operations."[43]

That month also ended with an event that left a sour taste in some fans' mouths. On July 23, Nottle left the Rapidz to be with his ailing wife, Patty, in Evansville, Indiana.[44] Under interim manager and hitting coach Tom Carcione, a former catcher in the Athletics organization, the Rapidz rattled off five straight wins. When Nottle returned to Ottawa, the Rapidz' management fired him, handing the reins to Carcione for the rest of the season.[45]

Co-owner Hall acknowledged that the timing looked poor, but said the team had already decided not to bring back Nottle for 2009 and simply chose to make the change earlier than

planned. "Ed was a great ambassador for baseball in Ottawa, he truly was," Hall told reporters. "Unfortunately, a manager's job is measured by what the team does on the field. … The reality is, there's no good time to do it."[46]

Nottle, whose baseball career had begun in 1960 with Pensacola of the Class-D Alabama-Florida League, returned to independent ball as a coach but never managed professionally again. Fan Steve Dolesch of Gatineau put Rapidz management on blast in a letter to the *Ottawa Citizen:* "Rapidz owners and management stink. They will, and I can only hope, lose fans at how they treated Mr. Nottle."[47]

The Rapidz' treatment of their former manager might have raised eyebrows, but judging by numbers, it didn't cut deeply into their fan base. A season-ending home crowd of 5,021 on September 1 gave the Rapidz an average attendance of 2,197 per game for the full season. Not only was that close to their average at the end of the first half, it marked an improvement over the lame-duck Lynx, who drew 1,922 per game in their final season.[48]

The Rapidz' total season attendance reached 101,073. "With Ottawa being a former Triple-A affiliate, I wasn't sure how the fans would react to having independent baseball back in the capital city," Geiger recalled years later. "For the most part, I felt like people enjoyed coming to games and having baseball in Ottawa. The interaction with the fans was always one of my favorite parts about playing professional baseball."[49]

The team continued to play sub-.500 ball under Carcione, going 11-20 under his management. Like the first half, though, the second half was sprinkled with memorable moments and small victories.

In Worcester, Massachusetts, in August, the Rapidz posted a win in front of legendary pitcher Roger Clemens; Clemens was on hand to visit Worcester Tornadoes manager and former teammate Rich Gedman.[50] Infielder Jake Daubert, a former Seattle Mariners draft pick playing for his third independent team of the season, won a game against Brockton that same month with a walk-off two-out single.[51]

Playing for pride, the Rapidz also avoided breaking the league record for losses, held by the 2005 Elmira (New York) Pioneers, who went 28-64. In their third-to-last game of the season, the Rapidz beat Worcester, 7-1, to ensure a finish with no more than 63 losses. "We're staying out of the record books," Carcione said. "That's what we've been looking at for the last two weeks."[52]

A season-ending 8-3 loss to Worcester left the Rapidz with a 31-63 record. In keeping with Nottle's promise of accessibility, Ottawa's players returned to the field after the game and spent 90 minutes signing autographs for fans. "That's the best thing about today. The fans, and sitting here talking," Carcione said. "This is what it's all about in independent ball: getting the fans out. This is awesome and I'm having fun with all these people."[53]

Fans interviewed at the final game returned the praise. "It has been great," Ottawa resident Murray McIntyre said. "Great in-game entertainment and pretty professionally done. The in-between innings stuff for the children is really good. The concessions are more economical than the NHL. It's enjoyable."[54]

Bergeron and Geiger made the league's All-Star team. Bergeron placed in the top five for batting average, doubles, on-base percentage, runs, RBIs, hits, and slugging percentage.[55]

Among pitchers, Hawes (4-13, 6.94), Robinson (4-8, 5.06), and reliever Reid Price (4-0, 2.08 in 20 games) shared the staff lead in wins. Angelo Burrows, a former Atlanta Braves draft pick who began his pro career as an outfielder, led the pitching staff in appearances with 40, posting a tidy 2.76 ERA in 49 innings. Saves were in short supply, but righty Cardoza Tucker—formerly a minor-leaguer with the organizations of the Houston Astros, St. Louis Cardinals, and Mariners—paced the staff with 7.

Planning for 2009 began soon after the season ended. Carcione was to return as manager, while Kusiewicz was hired to serve as pitching coach and director of player personnel.[56] And then, at the end of September 2008, only four weeks after the team's final game, the Rapidz abruptly collapsed.

On September 29, Hall notified the Can-Am League that the Rapidz would fold immediately. According to the team, Ottawa officials told the Rapidz that they planned to raise the annual rent on Ottawa Stadium from $108,000 to $1.1 million after the Lynx's former lease expired in 2009. Having lost $1.4 million in the team's first year, Hall chose not to return for another season just to face a sizable rent increase.[57] The team's creditors included the city, owed $10,415 for water bills, and the local transportation agency, owed $10,500.[58]

City officials characterized their discussions with Hall as preliminary and informal, and said the $1.1 million rent figure was a hypothetical number introduced to make a point during talks about a potential long-term lease.[59] Meanwhile, the league revoked the team's membership and drew down its $200,000 letter of credit, rejecting the Rapidz' request to withdraw from the league because of financial hardship.[60]

In March 2009, Hall filed a $3 million suit against Wolff, the city of Ottawa, the Can-Am League and others, claiming that they knew the team was likely to fail but collectively misled him about its viability. "If given an accurate picture, [Hall] might not have come to the position he found himself in … that he would have thought differently … that this team might not have happened at all," a spokesman for Hall said.[61]

The suit was dismissed by the Superior Court of Justice of Ontario; in January 2010, the city of Ottawa was awarded $12,000 for costs related to the lawsuit.[62] Hall continued to appeal all the way to the Supreme Court of Canada, which closed the book on the suit and the Rapidz by dismissing the appeal in March 2012.[63] Wolff attempted to arrange a new Can-Am team in Ottawa for the 2009 season, to be called the Voyageurs, but plans fell through and the team did not take the field.[64]

Several independent-league teams have since succeeded the Rapidz in Ottawa—and it says something about the city that, despite the Rapidz' struggles, some of those associated with the team have since returned to town. As of this writing in early 2024, Carcione was the pitching coach for the city's current team, the Ottawa Titans of the Frontier League.[65]

Lemieux, too, returned as a coach with the Ottawa Champions, who played in the Can-Am League from 2015 to 2019. "The city's fantastic," he said. "Once I found out there was going to be a new team in Ottawa, I reached out to Miles Wolff and said, 'I love my town up there. Let me know if there's anything I can do to help.'"[66] The 2016 Champions, with Lemieux on staff and former big-leaguer Hal Lanier managing, won the Can-Am's postseason playoffs and brought a league championship to town. Baseball in Ottawa had come a long way from the Rapidz' struggle of eight seasons before.

SOURCES

In addition to the sources cited in the Notes, the author used Baseball-Reference.com for general player, team, and season data, as well as additional coverage of the Rapidz in the *Ottawa Citizen*.

The author thanks former Rapidz players Kyle Geiger and Jared Lemieux for responding to interview requests in January and February 2024, and for contributing photos of their time with the Rapidz.

As of February 2024, amateur footage of the final out in Rapidz history (Geiger popping to second base against the Worcester Tornadoes on September 1, 2008) was available on YouTube:

https://www.youtube.com/watch?v=2H_Ct-qWut4

Amateur footage of several other Rapidz games was also available via the Internet Archive (archive.org), including the team's May 18 exhibition opener against Quebec (https://archive.org/details/Ottawa_Rapidz_VS_Quebec_Capitales_18May2008); the home opener on May 22 against New Jersey (https://archive.org/details/Ottawa_Rapidz_Vs_NJ_Jackels_22May2008/SSA50132.AVI); and August 8, 2008, against Brockton (https://archive.org/details/Ottawa_Rapidz_Vs_Brockton_Rox_09Aug2008/).

A breakdown of the Rapidz' lawsuit, prior to the Supreme Court of Canada hearing the case, can be read here: https://sportlaw.ca/lessons-from-the-ottawa-rapidz-case-contracts-that-help-and-contracts-that-dont/

("Lessons from the Ottawa Rapidz Case: Contracts that Help and Contracts that Don't," *Sport Law*, posted March 1, 2012.)

NOTES

1   Author's interview with Jared Lemieux, January 30, 2024.

2   Neil P. Kelly, "We Shouldn't Rush to Tear Down Stadium" (letter to editor), *Ottawa Citizen*, April 6, 2009: 9.

3   Wolff also owned one of the league's teams, the Quebec Capitales. Darren Desaulniers, "League Makes First Pitch to Councillors Over Lynx Stadium," *Ottawa Citizen*, September 14, 2007: F3.

4   Desaulniers, "League Makes First Pitch to Councillors Over Lynx Stadium."

5 Desaulniers, "League Makes First Pitch to Councillors Over Lynx Stadium."

6 Pecor's ongoing legal action against the city was resolved in the city's favor in March 2011. Joanne Chianello, "City Wins Legal Battle Against Former Lynx Owner Pecor," *Ottawa Citizen*, March 18, 2011: C1.

7 Laura Drake and Don Campbell, "Pro Baseball Will be Back at Lynx Stadium in 2008," *Ottawa Citizen*, November 29, 2007: B1.

8 Don Campbell, "Can-Am League Still Up for Ottawa Challenge," *Ottawa Citizen*, November 20, 2008: B5.

9 Author's email interview with Kyle Geiger, February 5, 2024.

10 Drake and Campbell, "Pro Baseball Will be Back at Lynx Stadium in 2008."

11 Don Campbell, "It All Begins at Home for Rapids," *Ottawa Citizen*, February 20, 2008: B2.

12 Don Campbell, "And Now the Hard Work Begins," *Ottawa Citizen*, February 15, 2008: B1.

13 As of January 2024, the Baseball-Reference page for the 2008 Ottawa team referred to them as the Rapides. https://www.baseball-reference.com/register/team.cgi?id=e74467b2.

14 It's part of the Nottle legend that he was called up to the Chicago White Sox in 1963 but was sent down again without pitching in a game. For what it's worth, a search of *Chicago Tribune* archives on Newspapers.com in January 2024 did not find any mention of an in-season promotion or demotion involving Nottle and the White Sox, although he pitched for the team in spring training in 1963 and 1964. He also pitched for the White Sox's Indianapolis farm club in an in-season exhibition against the parent club on May 23, 1963. Richard Dozer, "Sox Defeat Minor League Indians, 4 to 3," *Chicago Tribune*, May 24, 1963: Section 3: 3.

15 Campbell, "And Now the Hard Work Begins"; Don Campbell. "'Singing Ed' Set to Sign On," *Ottawa Citizen*, February 13, 2008: B2.

16 Don Martin, "Pro Ball, but Low Ball," *National Post* (Toronto, Ontario), May 26, 2008: A3.

17 Martin.

18 Mark Sutcliffe, "How the Rapidz Can Replace Ottawa's Missing Lynx," *Ottawa Citizen*, May 3, 2008: H1.

19 Only one of the two players who drew interest at the tryout, outfielder Greg Dumouchel, played for the 2008 Rapidz. The other, outfielder-catcher Rudy Vallejos, did not make the team. Don Campbell, "Fielders of Dreams," *Ottawa Citizen*, May 9, 2008: B1.

20 Don Campbell, "Can-Am League's Rapids No Place for Field of Dreamers," *Ottawa Citizen*, April 27, 2008: D1.

21 Don Campbell, "Rapid-z Change in Ottawa," *Ottawa Citizen*, April 29, 2008: C2.

22 "Rapidz Announce Ticket Prices for Initial Season," *Ottawa Citizen*, May 15, 2008: B2; "Go Rapidz!!," *The Waffle* (blog), posted July 23, 2008. https://www.thewaffle.ca/index.php/2008/07/23/go-rapidz/.

23 Don Campbell, "Rapidz Fire GM Charrette," *Ottawa Citizen*, May 8, 2008: B2. Charrette's wife Lorraine, a former employee of the Lynx, had also been hired by the Rapidz but resigned her position a day before her husband's dismissal.

24 Don Campbell, "Here's A Uniform, Let's Play," *Ottawa Citizen*, May 18, 2008: D1.

25 "Broadcasts," Ottawa Rapidz website, archived via the Internet Archive and accessed January 2024, https://web.archive.org/web/20080620061530/http://www.ottawarapidz.ca./press-broadcasts.asp; "Ottawa Rapidz on Rogers TV," Rogers TV website, accessed January 2024, https://www.rogerstv.com/show?lid=12&rid=4&sid=2890.

26 Darren Desaulniers, "Baseball Makes a Rapidz Return," *Ottawa Citizen*, May 19, 2008: B2. In his second and last season of independent ball, Strankman went 0-2 with a 7.54 ERA in 2008.

27 Don Campbell, "Nothing Doing in Opener," *Ottawa Citizen*, May 23, 2008: B3.

28 Don Campbell, "Rapidz' Bats Come to Life in Game 2," *Ottawa Citizen*, May 24, 2008: C2.

29 Darren Desaulniers, "Rapidz Short on Offence, but Not Promises," *Ottawa Citizen*, May 25, 2008: D2.

30 Author's interview with Lemieux.

31 Don Campbell, "An Instant 'Road Trip from Hell' for the Rapidz," *Ottawa Citizen*, May 27, 2008: D1; Don Campbell, "Road Trip's a Rough One for Rapidz," *Ottawa Citizen*, June 2, 2008: C1.

32 Darren Desaulniers, "Rapidz Struggle to Get Pitchers Some Run Support," *Ottawa Citizen*, June 6, 2008: B8.

33 Darren Desaulniers, "Kusiewicz Wins First Rapidz Start the Hard Way," *Ottawa Citizen*, June 27, 2008: B6.

34 Author's email interview with Geiger.

35 Darren Desaulniers, "Surf's Up for Modest Rapidz Streak," *Ottawa Citizen*, July 10, 2008: B2.

36 Darren Desaulniers, "Rapidz Slide Out of First Half with Loss to Surf," *Ottawa Citizen*, July 13, 2008: D3.

37 Campbell, "Road Trip's a Rough One for Rapidz."

38 Desaulniers, "Rapidz Slide Out of First Half with Loss to Surf." In an interview with the author, Lemieux pointed out that the Rapidz's crowds of 2,000 to 3,000 people were solid by independent league standards, but they seemed small because Ottawa Stadium could hold 10,000 fans.

39 Kelly Egan, "A Dog and a Beer, the Crack of a Bat and a Giant Man Named Walter," *Ottawa Citizen*, June 27, 2008: F1.

40 Darren Desaulniers, "Hitting Woes Lead to Rapidz Ninth One-Run Loss of Season," *Ottawa Citizen*, July 14, 2008: C3.

41 "Pride Beat Visiting Rapidz," *Ottawa Citizen*, July 19, 2008: C3. Miller signed one-day contracts with the Pride for several years to raise money for charity. "Roundup," *Concord* (New Hampshire) *Monitor*, July 18, 2008: C2.

42 Marty York, "Tillman Bleeds Roughriders Green," *Metro Ottawa*, July 25-27, 2008: 8. https://archive.org/details/metro-ottawa-2008-07-25/page/n7/mode/2up?q=%22ottawa+rapidz%22&view=theater.

43 Author's email interview with Geiger.

44 Darren Desaulniers, "Rapidz Loss Adds to Sad Day for Nottle," *Ottawa Citizen*, July 24, 2008: B4.

45 Don Campbell, "Nottle Fired after Visiting Ailing Wife," *Ottawa Citizen*, July 31, 2008: B1. In his interview with the author, Lemieux said he enjoyed playing for both managers. He described Nottle as "a vibrant personality" who was "all about supporting the guys" and Carcione as "more quiet, but a great guy" with "a wealth of knowledge about the game."

46 Chris Yzerman, "High Praise Follows Nottle Low Note," *Ottawa Citizen,* August 1, 2008: B4.

47 Steve Dolesch, "Disgusting Firing" (letter to the editor), *Ottawa Citizen,* August 6, 2008: A13.

48 Darren Desaulniers, "Rapidz Look on Bright Side," *Ottawa Citizen,* September 2, 2008: B2.

49 Author's email interview with Geiger.

50 "Rapidz Top Tornadoes," *Ottawa Citizen,* August 24, 2008: D7.

51 Mike Beasley, "Late Heroics by Daubert Seals *[sic]* Win for Rapidz," *Ottawa Citizen,* August 11, 2008: B7. Daubert had previously spent time with the York (Pennsylvania) Revolution and Bridgeport (Connecticut) Bluefish of the Atlantic League. The author of this story read several newspaper profiles of Daubert, but none specified whether he was related to Jake Daubert, the star first baseman of major league baseball's Deadball Era.

52 Darren Desaulniers, "Rapids Play to Escape Dubious DIstinction on Last Weekend," *Ottawa Citizen,* August 29, 2008: B1; Darren Desaulniers, "Rapidz Avoid Futility Record with Two to Spare," *Ottawa Citizen,* August 31, 2008: D3.

53 Desaulniers, "Rapidz Look on Bright Side."

54 Darren Desaulniers, "Wait 'Til Next Year: Can-Am Team a Hit with Fans," *Ottawa Citizen,* September 2, 2008: B2. Comparisons between the cost of attending a NHL Ottawa Senators game and a Rapidz game were common in Rapidz news coverage.

55 "Stars Shine on Rapidz Duo," *Ottawa Citizen,* September 4, 2008: B2.

56 Don Campbell, "Rapidz Hand Carcione Manager's Job," *Ottawa Citizen,* September 6, 2008: C4; "Kusiewicz Joins Rapidz Front Office," *Ottawa Citizen,* September 10, 2008: B5.

57 Don Campbell, "Rapidz Out at Home After One Season," *Ottawa Citizen,* September 30, 2008: B1.

58 Campbell, "Rapidz Out at Home After One Season." The Rapidz had arranged for shuttle-bus service to the ballpark to overcome the facility's limited parking. Bob Thomas, "Council Didn't Go to Bat for Pro Baseball" (letter to the editor), *Ottawa Citizen,* April 2, 2009: A11.

59 Don Campbell, "City Would Only Go to Five Years, Rapidz Say," *Ottawa Citizen,* October 1, 2008: B1; CBC News, "Ottawa Rapids Go Under," posted September 30, 2008. https://www.cbc.ca/news/canada/ottawa/ottawa-rapidz-go-under-1.733370.

60 "SCC to Field Arguments Over Baseball Team's Forum Squabble," *Canadian Lawyer* magazine, posted May 19, 2011. https://www.canadianlawyermag.com/news/general/scc-to-field-arguments-over-baseball-teams-forum-squabble/270815.

61 Don Campbell, "Suing Former Owner Claims Rapidz Demise Preordained," *Ottawa Citizen,* March 26, 2008:C6.

62 Chianello, "City Wins Legal Battle Against Former Lynx Owner Pecor"; "City Wins Costs in Baseball Suit," *Ottawa Citizen,* January 11, 2010: C5.

63 Supreme Court of Canada docket for *Momentous.ca Corporation, et al, v. Canadian American Association of Professional Baseball Ltd., et al,* accessed January 29, 2024. https://www.scc-csc.ca/case-dossier/info/dock-regi-eng.aspx?cas=33999.

64 Don Campbell, "Baseball Strikes Out Again in Ottawa," *Ottawa Citizen,* March 31, 2009: B1. The Can-Am League had planned to operate the Voyageurs as a league-owned team. But when a planned sale of the league's Atlantic City franchise fell through, league owners voted to eliminate the Ottawa and Atlantic City teams rather than subsidize and operate them both.

65 "Coaching Staff," OttawaTitans.com, accessed January 31, 2024. https://www.ottawatitans.com/coaching-staff.

66 Author's interview with Lemieux.

THE OTTAWA FAT CATS (2010-2012)

BY LUIS BLANDÓN

PROFESSIONAL BASEBALL IN OTTAWA HAS had a turbulent existence and at times, a bitter heritage. From 1898 to the present, Ottawa professional baseball has been a race between sporadic success and crashing failures, featuring eight professional franchises.[1] As a semiprofessional team, the 2010 arrival of the Ottawa Fat Cats represented a significant departure from the minor-league teams that had stitched together Ottawa's baseball legacy.

The rural sounds of pro baseball were absent from urban Ottawa in 2009.[2] Ottawa considered attracting a minor-league franchise while concurrently examining alternative uses of the Ottawa Stadium ranging from a multi-use facility for events to building a casino and a retail and/or residential complex. However, Duncan MacDonald saw a semiprofessional short-season baseball franchise in the Intercounty Baseball League (IBL) as the path to Ottawa baseball success.[3]

Local tour operator David Butler and MacDonald formed the Ottawa Stadium Group (OSG), developing a plan to bring baseball back with an IBL semipro expansion franchise with all-year events at the stadium. "The stadium's paid for, it's beautiful and kids want to play there. It would be a shame if it did happen to get knocked down and sold off," MacDonald said.[5] They requested the city give them a 10-year lease with renewal options and renovations to the stadium to make the facility attractive to other non-sporting events.

In January 2010, the IBL board voted 6-2 to approve OSG's pitch for a team with a C$30,000 fee.[6] As the team situated furthest from the other IBL teams, Ottawa was required to pay for the visiting teams' travel costs. OSG signed a one-year lease with the city in February with a rent of C$108,000. "People will come," MacDonald bravely predicted. "We understand this is a follow-the-leader-town so we've just got to get the first few people through the turnstiles and once … people are having fun, we think the corporate side will support it."[7] MacDonald warned the team had no commitment beyond 2010: "We have a one-year lease. Let me say that again: We have a one-year lease. And we have a semi-pro franchise."[8]

With MacDonald as general manager, the team hired a former pro player

Duncan MacDonald grew up in Eastern Ontario playing baseball for the Brockville and Waterloo, Ontario youth teams. MacDonald was a player at Ithaca College. He participated in the NCAA Division III College World Series in 1985 and 1986. He was a regional scout for the Toronto Blue Jays from 1990-2002.[4] He tried to make baseball work in Ottawa focusing on the intimacy of semipro baseball over operating a minor-league team. His style was in the tradition of Bill Veeck. He was co-owner of OSG and General Manager of the Fat Cats from its inception until he left the organization after the 2011 season.

with experience in coaching and scouting as manager, Bill Mackenzie.[9] Mackenzie had been in baseball since 1967. Prior to the team's inaugural game against the Guelph Royals on May 8, Mackenzie received a letter from former Montreal Expo general manager and friend, Jim Fanning. Fanning warned Mackenzie "[D]on't manage like I did … Manage more like Connie Mack or Casey Stengel."[10] With seven doubleheaders scheduled and only 11 home dates in a 36-game schedule and a hastily-formed roster, a daunting task was ahead.

The team signed players and held tryouts. A former Blue Jays prospect was the first player signed by Ottawa. Drafted twice by Toronto, pitcher David Steffler was seen as the team's needed mentor to the younger collegiate pitchers and a "veteran arm who can beat anybody in the league," according to Mackenzie.[11] At 34 with a nomadic career including the IBL and Spain, he was vice president of client experience for MD Physician Service.[12] Steffler was unavailable for the team's first game as his wife gave birth to twins.[13] The team was composed of a myriad of players from college and university teams as well as men who had been drafted by major league teams. Several players lived in the Ottawa community, with many employed in real jobs. Mackenzie saw a squad with talent, but he had perspective: "You can win, or you can lose, or it can rain."[14]

MacDonald determined the team moniker. He used focus groups to create a list of 10 potential names but none seemed right. He was inspired by Ottawa's reputation in Canada: "As soon as Fat Cats was on the list, it was the name everyone chose. And I mean everyone. I think we had one vote against it once it was an option."[15] The nickname was a "gentle poke" at Ottawa's role as the seat of power.[16]

The logo, a grinning cat with red-and-black team colors, was unveiled on March 24. The organization promised to focus on the fan experience with reasonable ticket and food prices and fan-friendly entertainment as a means to success. "There isn't going to be a more family-affordable ticket that is going to give people more value and entertainment for their dollar," MacDonald boasted.[17]

The team implemented marketing efforts designed to make the game attractive. Incentives to buy tickets online to avoid long box office lines included free transportation to the ballpark from another site. Current and past members of the Canadian military got in free. "We just want people to come out, have some fun…" MacDonald proclaimed.[18] "We know what not to do. We know what doesn't work.[19]

The Fats Cats' 2010 home schedule began on May 15 with an 8-6 loss against the Mississauga Twins. Paid attendance was 3,724 but estimates were higher. Facing long box-office lines, fans were ushered through the gates for free. The local liquor license regulations allowed fans to buy beer but one could not drink it in the stands or seats, only in the concourse. Instead of watching the game in their seat, one drank a beer and was able to watch the long concession lines grow longer as "no one was prepared for the volume of people that [showed] up for the game."[20] "It's pretty amazing. Overwhelming. It just goes to show you how much the community missed baseball and enjoy family fun entertainment," said MacDonald.[21] According to press accounts, "[F]ans waited in line for up to 30 minutes to get a peanuts or Cracker Jacks, as the old song goes."[22] With a chill in the air, there was a dearth of coffee and hot chocolate. The lack of parking contributed to the long lines to enter the stadium, a familiar problem. MacDonald promised a better performance: "We'll be prepared a little better (Sunday). Nobody expected this crowd. Nobody wants this facility to rot and I think we got that message out there."[23]

In their first season, the Fat Cats went 11-25, in last place in a nine-team league where eight teams made the playoffs. MacDonald was named IBL Executive of the Year. The team led the league with an unheard attendance of 2,328 per date.[24] To make the Fats Cats profitable, the team requested a long-term lease from the city and elimination of the above-noted travel subsidies that the team was required to pay other teams, with no success.

OSG contemplated its future by seeking an affiliated team for Ottawa and asked the city for a lease extension beyond October 2011, preferably five years, to attract a team. Other groups including OSG were interested in having a Toronto Blue Jays farm club in Ottawa. A faction of the public, political leadership and media believed baseball was on the decline and Ottawa was a hockey and football town. The Ottawa City Council published a 51-page report prepared by city employees that recommended selling the stadium parking lots and transforming the stadium into a concert venue.[25] The Council did not act on the report. An air of uncertainty permeated. OSG was committed to operating the stadium and paid its C$108,000 rent for 2010. OSG noted that baseball brought revenue, and social, environmental, and cultural benefits to the community.[26]

In early January 2011, an editorial in the *Ottawa Citizen* was blunt in its assessment: the IBL was a sandlot league, where attendance is secondary. The city must not grant a lease longer than one year for the Fat Cats for a ballpark designed for minor-league baseball: "Maybe the Fat Cats are the best baseball Ottawa fans will support…so the municipality keeps its options open."[27]

On March 10, 2011, the team secured a one-year lease. Mackenzie resigned as manager: "You could say philosophical differences, sure."[28] He remained in the organization in a public relations role. Tim Nelson was named manager. "Tim is local and has a great reputation with Canada's junior team," MacDonald said.[29]

Born in Calgary on May 10, 1978, Tim Nelson was a seventh-round pick out of high school in the 1998 amateur draft as a third baseman by the Baltimore Orioles. A career minor leaguer, he retired in 2005. Nelson was a coach with Ottawa local teams and the Canadian National Junior Team. He managed the Verona Knights in the Italian Premier League. Serving as manager of the Fats Cats in 2011-2012, he worked full-time in finance with the Canadian government at Human Resources and Skills Development Canada while coaching baseball at night. "Being in Ottawa and being able to coach a team like the Fat Cats works out well for me and I enjoy it," Nelson said.[30]

OSG informed the city it had sold 4,200 season ticket packages. It paid the $108,000 rent by the March 14 deadline with a chance for extension for the 2012 campaign. The team announced a partnership with Great River Media who purchased 1,000 season tickets that would be given to employees and advertisers.[31]

The schedule had 17 home dates commencing May 21 against the Kitchener Panthers. The 2011 Fat Cats had three Americans with the remaining players all from the Ottawa region, returning 13 from the 2010 squad. They opened the season with a 7-4 win over the Burlington Twins on May 7. Starting 1-2 before the May 21 home opener, the team anticipated a crowd of over 6,000. "What we have on paper is very good" and "[T]he beer will be flowing and the people will be yelling," Nelson quipped.[32] The team won 5-2 before 4,617.

Though finishing 16-18 and in sixth place, the Fat Cats' second season resulted in astonishing postseason success. All eight teams made the playoffs. It was not enough for Nelson: "Our goal was not just to be in the playoffs, but finish up the season and do well in the playoffs, and hopefully win a couple of rounds and see how far we can go."[33] The playoffs gave fans a chance to root for an underdog.

Ottawa won two playoff best-of-seven series: against the favored London Majors in five games and sweeping the Barrie Baycats. They reached the finals, losing to the more experienced Brantford Red Sox in five games.[34] During the playoff run, fans filled Ottawa Stadium to near capacity, a sight that had not been seen since the early Lynx years. The franchise set a IBL postseason total attendance record, as well as a single game record in Game Three of the finals with 7,355.[35]

The improbable playoff run saw interest in the team escalate. OSG hoped that a long-term lease was in the offing from the city. "Is that the best way to go? No. We weren't thrilled to have a one plus one year lease," MacDonald said.[36] Ottawa needed to determine whether the city wanted affiliated minor-league baseball and whether the stadium had a long-term future. The Fat Cats were important to the equation and could work with a minor-league baseball team. The team provided the opportunity for local players to play at home. "I've never had so much fun playing on a team," said pitcher Josh Soffer, a Kanata native.[37]

As the city pondered a lease extension for 2012, it put out bids to attract a full-season minor-league baseball team. The Fat Cats' lease was set to expire in March 2012. OSG requested a year extension in October but was met with silence. At a November 11, 2011 meeting with the Ottawa City Council finance committee on the future of Ottawa Stadium and recruiting a Double-A team, Fat Cats CEO Brian Carolan said two teams could easily share the stadium. Any concern on the field conditions would be alleviated if astroturf were to be installed as part of any planned upgrade. But the IBL generally played on weekends and the question of scheduling was an issue. Any minor-league team would not willingly give up weekend dates.

Minor League Baseball had the final say on any team moving to an available market.[38] The Massachusetts-based Beacon Sports Capital Partners (Beacon) expressed an interest in bringing a Double-A franchise to Ottawa.

The city government dawdled as it reviewed the bids. A final decision was delayed a few times. Speculation focused on the Binghamton Eastern League franchise. Any recommendation by the city that occurred in early 2012 would be a problem said Eastern League president Joe McEachan. A team needs time to set up shop, establish community roots and develop relationships with the community before a game is played.[39]

On February 9, the city council approved Beacon's bid. On February 22, the city announced that a new team would be lured to Ottawa for 2013. A plan for C$5.7 million in renovations and upgrades in the stadium was put in place. The proposed team and the city would sign a 10-year lease with two five-year options at C$257,000 annual rent. The target team was the Binghamton Mets with an affiliation agreement with the Toronto Blue Jays. There would be no lease extension for the Fat Cats. In fact, with the construction there was no certainty the Fat Cats could play at the stadium in 2012.[40]

Fat Cats catcher Eitan Maoz leaps for a ball. Credit: Michael Gauthier, Freedom Photography

On March 15, the city announced the Fat Cats could play ball after the city developed a construction schedule that meshed with the IBL's schedule. The city still was confident that a Double-A agreement could occur in time for the 2013 season. Nelson returned as manager for the 2012 season. Returning 14 players with 19 home games in a 36-game schedule, Nelson felt great things were in the offing for his team.

Ottawa Mayor Jim Watson on March 25 announced that Double-A ball for 2013 was not occurring, with 2014 still a possibility. Beacon had told the city there was not enough time to move and set up a team in Ottawa. The Fat Cats could play their regular season and the playoffs without having to look for an alternative site.

The players enjoyed playing in Ottawa while hoping for the opportunity to play professional baseball. North Carolina outfielder Kevin Dietrich exemplified this attitude: "Ottawa is great, everything about it. The city is great, the fans are great, I love it up here."[41] They also adjusted to the team's tenuous existence.

During the 2010 and 2011 seasons, OSG had an arrangement with St. Paul University for the players to reside in dorms in exchange for advertising. But the 2012 season saw no such deal, leading to unusual player living arrangements. When not staying at a local hotel, four American Fats Cats became squatters as they slept in the stadium VIP boxes several days a week.[42]

Frustrated with the city's efforts to attract professional baseball and renovate the stadium, the local media became critical. Elizabeth Payne, a member of the *Ottawa Citizen*'s editorial board, questioned the importance of baseball and the need for the stadium: "So why does the same city that has just voted to close a municipal equestrian park still own a white elephant baseball stadium?"[43] Sell the stadium, reduce the stadium to rubble, and stop investing taxpayer funds, she recommended.

A record of 18-18 and a fifth-place tie resulted in a playoff opportunity. However, the postseason magic was gone as Ottawa fell in the first round against the Guelph Royals in six games. Nelson was unable to manage Game Six due to a work commitment. Ace pitcher and 2011 playoff MVP Matt McGovern, with ongoing shoulder issues, pitched only two innings all season and started Game Six with a six-inning four-run effort.[44] Unbeknownst to the players, the last game in Fat Cat history was over.

The Fat Cats became the "latest casualty of the Ottawa Stadium graveyard."[45] The lease expired on September 15. The team "was ordered by the city to have its stuff packed and out of the stadium by 11:59 P.M. Tuesday," September 18.[46] The Fat Cats were caught off guard: "Why not work our schedule around the renovations (next summer)? It's all pretty confusing," Assistant GM Jonathan Trotter said.[47] "A team like us has clearly been successful and we're told to leave. There really is no option for us. A lot of people thought maybe we could play at Heritage (in Orléans). But we'd only be talking about getting a couple of hundred fans and we wouldn't be able to make it work. In my opinion, the city is taking a big risk (with Double-A)."[48]

On December 20, 2012, the IBL released its 2013 schedule. Ottawa was not included. IBL Commissioner Stuart Smith said that with the city's desire for professional baseball, the pending renovations to the stadium and the OSG interest in non-baseball events, it was time to pull the plug and cease operations: "It would almost be a miracle if the Fat Cats were to play in 2013 and we don't do our work based on miracles."[49] The players were to be dispersed to the remaining eight teams.

The Ottawa Fats Cats tweeted their demise on December 22: "Dear Fans: It is our deepest regret to announce that the Fat Cats have ceased operations for the 2013 baseball season."[50]

"It's a tremendous loss for the league. I'm not really (surprised) because these guys basically had to beg to stay on that field every year," said Toronto Maple Leafs owner Jack Dominico who wanted Ottawa to remain in the league.[51] Returning in 2014 was mentioned. Despite being larger in population with more fans than most of the other eight IBL teams, the city wanted the Fat Cats gone. The Fat Cats' existence was an impediment to bringing minor league baseball to Ottawa Stadium. The city was in never-ending talks with Beacon to bring Double-A baseball to Ottawa for 2014. Ottawa desired an affiliated minor-league team in a renovated stadium. It never happened.

Fan support was not the problem, due to the creativity and innovation of the team management. The Fats Cats' popularity was clear, achieving previously unseen league-leading attendance numbers in the IBL. The attendance numbers were aided by the fact that most of the players were local. Despite a limited number of home dates and several scheduled doubleheaders in their initial season, the Fat Cats averaged a better-than-expected 2,328 per home date for a total of 25,611 for the 2010 season. In the 2011 campaign, the Fat Cats made it to the IBL finals only to lose to the Brantford Red Sox. The team drew a total of 38,491 during the regular season. In the playoffs, the Fat Cats averaged 4,120 fans per game and drew a total of 28,483 in only seven home games. A franchise and IBL record crowd of 7,355 attended Game Three of the finals against Brantford. With playoffs included the season attendance total was 67,334. The team led the IBL again in attendance for the 2012 season.[52]

MacDonald was ousted as general manager when his contract was not renewed after the 2011 season. The Fat Cats succeeded and were building a foundation with the short-season summer schedule. As he noted: "You won't find me at the ballpark in April. On Tuesday night, if it's the Senators playing the Bruins, I'm not going to be at the baseball field when it's six degrees outside."[53] He sees baseball as a summer gate attraction with a focus on short-season ball. Selling the innocence of baseball and making the game an event was the right path. MacDonald is still an advocate for Ottawa baseball. In 2019, he proposed a new multi-use stadium at LeBreton Flats in the heart of Ottawa.[54] MacDonald became the director of growth and development for EXIT Realty Eastern Ontario and a licensed real estate agent.

Why has affiliated minor-league baseball failed to return to Ottawa when the game should be as popular as in Toronto? Part of the problem was the indecisiveness of the city. MacDonald strongly asserted it is a multi-dimensional problem stemming from arduous leases and lopsided financial arrangements with the city, the harsh spring weather, and the large number of home games in a minor-league full season. To demonstrate his point, MacDonald recalled a conversation he had with Ottawa Lynx owner Howard Darwin who bought Triple-A ball back to Ottawa in 1993. Darwin stated he would not have bought the team if he knew about the problems he would face dealing with the city: "the revenue-sharing model under which the city received points from parking, concessions, signage, suites, ticket surcharges, naming rights and more made baseball a tough proposition in Ottawa."[55] The Fat Cats combatted these same obstacles, facing a precarious future from the first day.

In June 2013, a person could walk into Ottawa Stadium and be overwhelmed by its decay and nature's immutable reconquest. The pristine infield had been stolen by weeds. The grass grew high. Rodents managed the concourse.[56] Adult summer leagues were scheduled but the games were put on hold until the field was made playable once again. The Fat Cats could have played in 2013. The city's quest for affiliated minor-league baseball has been an illusion.

SOURCES AND ACKNOWLEDGMENTS

Many thanks to the Black Lion Cafe in Travilah, Maryland where I researched, conceived, and wrote several iterations of this article.

In addition to the sources cited in the Notes, the author consulted the National Baseball Hall of Fame Giamatti Research Center, Baseball-Reference.com, the United States Department of the Interior, the Library of Congress, YouTube.com, mlb.com and Dr. Michael L. Lawson of MLL Consulting, LLC.

To my patient wife, Teri, as always for her nonpareil thoughts and input.

NOTES

1   Professional baseball arrived in Ottawa when the Rochester Patriots of the Eastern League moved in early July 1898 and became the Ottawa Senators. The eight professional baseball teams that have called Ottawa home are (a) Ottawa Senators (1898) in the Eastern League, (b) Ottawa Senators (1912-1948 in various incarnations in several leagues), (c) Ottawa Athletics/Giants (1951-1954) in the International League, (d) Ottawa Lynx (1994-2007 in the International League, (e) Ottawa Rapidz (2008 in the Can-Am League, (f) Ottawa Fat Cats (2010-2012 in the Intercounty Baseball League), (g) Ottawa Champions (2015-2020 in the Can-Am League), and (h) Ottawa Titans (2022 to present in the Frontier League)

2   After 15 years, the Triple-A Ottawa Lynx moved to Allentown, Pennsylvania after the conclusion of the 2007 season and the Rapidz folded after one year at the conclusion of the 2008 Can-Am League season.

3   The IBL is the oldest baseball league in Canada formed in 1919. It was previously known as the Intercounty Major Baseball League and the Senior Intercounty Baseball League. Teams compete for the Jack and Lynne Dominico Trophy, which is awarded to the league

champions, named for the late owners of the Toronto Maple Leafs baseball team. A few of the notable players who played in the IBL include Baseball Hall of Famer Ferguson Jenkins, Pete Gray, Jesse Orosco, John Axford, Rob Ducey, Denny McLain, Chris Speier, NHL goalie for the Minnesota North Stars, Ottawa Senators, Toronto Maple Leafs, and Washington Capitals, Don Beaupre, and former Canadian Prime Minister Lester B. Pearson.

4   "Bio for Duncan MacDonald," *Exit Reality*. Accessed April 2, 2024. https://exitrealty.com/agent/Duncan/MacDonald/259168. See https://www.baseball-reference.com/bullpen/Duncan_MacDonald, accessed March 30, 2024.

5   "New Ottawa Baseball Pitch Lands at City," *CBC News*, August 24, 2009. See https://www.cbc.ca/news/canada/ottawa/new-ottawa-baseball-pitch-lands-at-city-1.829101, accessed June 4, 2024.

6   The IBL formerly announced on March 10 that it had awarded its newest franchise to the OSG.

7   Darren Desaulniers, "Fat Cats Dressed for Success," *Ottawa Citizen*, March 25, 2010: B3.

8   Mark Sutcliffe, "Sutcliffe: Incentives to Target Buying Tickets in Advance," *Ottawa Citizen*, March 28, 2010: D4.

9   Mackenzie was born on July 27, 1946 in Pictou, Nova Scotia. He was a catcher in his playing days in the Detroit and Montreal organizations never climbing above Class A. He retired after suffering a broken shoulder. As a scout for the Expos, he signed Tim Raines, Matt Stairs, and Larry Walker.

10 Don Campbell, "Fat Cats Will Try to Manager in Year 1," *Ottawa Citizen*, May 7, 2010: D1.

11 Tracey Tong, "Former Blue Jays prospect becomes first player signed by Ottawa Fat Cats," *Metro US*, April 19, 2010, https://www.metro.us/former-blue-jays-prospect-becomes-first-player-signed-by-ottawa-fat-cats/, accessed on April 24, 2024. Steffler was a 51st-round pick in the 1994 Major League amateur draft and a 67th-round pick in 1997,

12 Martin Cleary, "Fat Cats Signed Veteran Intercounty Arm," *Ottawa Citizen*, April 9, 2010: C4.

13 Don Campbell, "Cats: Perspective Required," *Ottawa Citizen*, May 7, 2010: B2. This was not an uncommon scenario in the IBL.

14 Campbell, "Cats: Perspective Required."

15 Ron Colbert, "Football Moniker Hits the Mark," *Ottawa Sun* (online), December 16, 2012. See https://ottawasun.com/2012/12/16/football-moniker-hits-the-mark, accessed April 3, 2024.

16 Desaulniers, "Fat Cats Dressed for Success."

17 "Fat Cats Aim to Succeed Where Others Have Failed," *Centretown News*, March 26, 2010 (Ottawa, Ontario). See https://capitalcurrent.ca/archive/centretownnews/1997-2016/2010/03/26/fat-cats-aim-to-succeed-where-others-have-failed/, accessed April 3, 2024.

18 Desaulniers, "Fat Cats Dressed for Success."

19 Sutcliffe.

20 Darren Desaulniers, "Fat Cats Draw Mixed Reviews with Opener." *Ottawa Citizen*, May 16, 2010: C6.

21 Desaulniers, "Fat Cats Draw Mixed Reviews with Opener."

22 Desaulniers, "Fat Cats Draw Mixed Reviews with Opener."

23 Desaulniers, "Fat Cats Draw Mixed Reviews with Opener."

24 Don Campbell, "Campbell: Team a Hit with Fans," *Ottawa Citizen*, December 21, 2012: B6.

25 Keith Reichard, "Fat Cats Owners may seek Affiliated Team for Ottawa," *Ballpark Digest*, April 14, 2011. See https://ballparkdigest.

com/201104143748/at-the-ballpark/the-front-office/fats-cats-owners-may-seek-affiliated-team-for-ottawa, accessed February 5, 2024.

26 Reichard, "Fat Cats Owners May Seek Affiliated Team for Ottawa."

27 Our Views, "Editorial: Small League, Big Park," *Ottawa Citizen*, January 15, 2011: B6,

28 Don Campbell and Joanne Chianello, "Fat Cats Lose Manager, Score One-Year Lease," *Ottawa Citizen*, March 11, 2011: B6.

29 Darren Desaulniers, "Fat Cats Ready for 2011," *Ottawa Citizen*, March 17, 2011, B5.

30 Darren Desaulniers, "Nelson Finds Baseball Balance," *Ottawa Citizen*, June 8, 2012: B7.

31 Desaulniers, "Fat Cats Ready for 2011."

32 Desaulniers, "Nelson Finds Baseball Balance."

33 Darren Desaulniers, "Cats Hungry for More," *Ottawa Citizen*, July 27, 2011, B3.

34 The Red Sox had 15 players who played in the minor leagues while the Fats Cats had none.

35 Darren Desaulniers, "Down To Their Last Lives," *Ottawa Citizen*, September 5, 2011: C1.

36 "Fat Cats Hope Playoff Run Leads to Stadium Deal," *CBC News*, August 9, 2011. See https://www.cbc.ca/news/canada/ottawa/fat-cats-hope-playoff-run-leads-to-stadium-deal-1.993346, accessed on April 3, 2024.

37 "Fat Cats Hope Playoff Run Leads to Stadium Deal."

38 Keith Reichard, "Fat Cats: We'd Love to Share Ottawa Stadium with AA Team," *Ballpark Digest*, November 2, 2011. See https://ballparkdigest.com/201111024309/minor-league-baseball/news/fat-cats-wed-love-to-share-ottawa-stadium-with-aa-team, accessed February 5, 2024.

39 David Reevely, "Baseball: Watson 'Very Optimistic,'" *Ottawa Citizen*, January 13, 2012: C4.

40 Neco Cockburn, "OK for Stadium Upgrade Bring Double-A Closer to City," *Ottawa Citizen*, February 23, 2012: C3.

41 Darren Desaulniers, "Capital a Hit with Fat Cats' Dietrich," *Ottawa Citizen*, July 7, 2012: C3.

42 "Fat Cats Players Living Part-time in Ottawa Stadium," *CBC News*, July 9, 2012. See https://www.cbc.ca/news/canada/ottawa/fat-cats-players-living-part-time-in-ottawa-stadium-1.1174057, accessed May 23, 2024.

43 Elizabeth Payne, "Time to Wake Up and Sell Field of Dreams," *Ottawa Citizen*, July 12, 2012: A1.

44 McGovern led the team in 2011 with a 1.83 ERA and striking out 49 while walking 15 in 59 innings of work. McGovern's 2011 postseason pushed the team to another level with five straight nine-inning starts giving up only five earned runs. That season, he led the team in the regular season with three homers in 69 at-bats playing first base when not pitching. McGovern was hoping a major-league team would offer him an opportunity.

45 Baines, "Fat Cats Booted Out of Ottawa Stadium," *Ottawa Sun*, September 18, 2012. See https://ottawasun.com/2012/09/18/fat-cats-booted-out-of-ottawa-stadium, accessed February 5, 2024.

46 Baines, "Fat Cats Booted Out of Ottawa Stadium."

47 Baines, "Fat Cats Booted Out of Ottawa Stadium."

48 Baines, "Fat Cats Booted Out of Ottawa Stadium."

49 Don Campbell, "Fat Cats Won't Play in 2013," *Ottawa Citizen*, December 21, 2012: B1.

50 See https://x.com/ottawafatcats/status/282356122650824707?s=43, accessed March 4, 2024.

51 Mike Koreen, "Ottawa Fat Cats Forced Out of Intercounty Baseball League for 2013 Season," *Ottawa Sun*, December 12, 2012. See https://ottawasun.com/2012/12/21/ottawa-fat-cats-forced-out-of-intercounty-baseball-league-for-2013-season, accessed February 3, 2024.

52 Campbell, "Campbell: Team a Hit with Fans."

53 Tim Baines, "Only Jays Double-A OK in Ottawa," *Ottawa Sun*, February 9, 2012. See https://ottawasun.com/2012/02/09/only-jay-double-a-ok-in-ottawa.

54 Duncan MacDonald, "Op-ed: New Stadium at LeBreton Flats Could be a Ball for Ottawa," *Ottawa Business Journal*, November 20, 2019. See https://obj.ca/op-ed-new-stadium-at-lebreton-flats-could-be-a-ball-for-ottawa/, accessed March 1, 2024.

55 MacDonald, "Op-ed: New Stadium at LeBreton Flats could be a Ball for Ottawa."

56 David Reevely, "Ottawa Stadium in 'Deplorable State,'" *Ottawa Citizen*, June 14, 2013: C2.

REFLECTIONS ON THE OTTAWA CHAMPIONS BASEBALL CLUB

BY DAVID GOURLAY

"The idea of community, the idea of coming together…in baseball, you do that all the time; you can't win alone. You can be the best pitcher…but somebody has to get you a run to win the game. It is a community activity. You need all nine people helping one another. I love bunt plays. I love the idea of the sacrifice. Even the word is good; giving yourself up for the good of the whole. You find your own individual fulfillment in the success of the community."—Mario Cuomo[1]

BASEBALL—A GAME TO BRING US together on any given warm, sunny summer afternoon—brings joy and a sense of belonging. Baseball is a sport for us all, no matter who we are, what we do, or where we live. For an interconnected community like Ottawa, baseball has a natural place and space to thrive. In baseball, the defense initiates play for the offense to respond to, and this is a game with no time limitations. Baseball is rich in strategy—from pitching and batting to field positioning and baserunning and the dynamics between them. But, I have always been most struck by the chemistry and relationships between the players who reflect a community as all nine players are crucial to one another, both for teamwork and the win. This aspect of the game is an analogy for community: belonging, acceptance, cooperation, and mutual support.

Baseball has been a part of who I am from my youngest days as a boy cheering on the Montreal Expos in the late 1970s. I developed a passion for collecting baseball cards with fond memories of hot summer days in Beaverbrook, cycling furiously to the local Mac's Milk to tear open wax packs after scrounging together 50 cents from as many nickels and dimes as I could find around the house. Pulling a 1981 O-Pee-Chee Gary Carter card was my moment. Sitting on the curb with friends and yelling that I had a "Kid" card and to this day, that very card is a part of my over 10,000 baseball card collection as these baseball heroes and their craft helped to build my story and even a part of my identity. When Gary Carter came to Ottawa in 1981 for a promotional tour, and my parents took me to meet my hero, I was swept up by his magnetism, his smile, charisma, and personality. Baseball and Gary Carter, as a role model, gave me a voice at such a young age to be more, do more, and be just like him. Of course, I still couldn't hit a fastball in Little League to save my life!

Thirty years later, it was definitely not my intention to dive into a role in local professional baseball. My story of the Ottawa Champions Baseball Club centers on an awakening that a professional baseball franchise in Ottawa contributes to our community and if done more smartly will foster our collec-tive cohesion, build, memories and provide us some thrilling games at the ballpark at the corner of Coventry Road and the Vanier Parkway.

It started with a Jerry Maguire moment following my reading of Michael Lewis' trailblazing book on baseball, *Moneyball*. As a leadership narrative on behavioral science, Lewis profiles the innovation of Billy Beane with the Oakland Athletics and how Bill James influenced the game to move beyond the scouts' "old school" judgment stereotypes of player evaluation and limit biases and positive favoritisms on the "gut check" into an evidence-based culture of player assessment to value player salaries and performance. The writing engaged my growth mindset with a totally new philosophy on money and winning and inspired me to read more about the game—but not about baseball history or players or stats, but the business strategy of the game and the romantic relationship it has with a community and its people.

I read about detailed business strategies—basic stuff to those in the baseball bubble, but less obvious to fans. It was all about how minor-league franchises build a ballpark culture through in-game promotions, activities, games, and family-friendly engagement for the ballpark to reflect the community it plays in. We want to see ourselves in the ballpark, so we see our neighbors, colleagues, and friends to enjoy a casual evening out and build memories of quality time together. It seemed simple enough—open concourse sections, grassy outfield berms, and more. Other insights piqued my interest on the importance of the five-kilometer radius within a ballpark for walk-up crowds, the value of building business, charitable, and association part-nerships and relationships to bring the community into the ballpark to connect to the community as a whole.

This helps build community and I began connecting the dots in my mind to understand baseball with a generative mindset. I pushed myself to ask difficult questions—with a 10,000-seat ballpark with ample parking, a proven history of success in the past, reasonable proximity to the core with our Trans-Canada Highway next to the ballpark, and lots of resi-dential communities around it, why isn't professional baseball a sustainable and prominent part of our city? Then, I read the City of Ottawa, which owns the ballpark, had tendered a request for proposals seeking a broker to facilitate a Toronto Blue Jays Double-A minor-league franchise moving to Ottawa. It was the epiphany and motivation I was looking for—a city-led procurement process would tremendously benefit from a grassroots presence to support the overall process. My vision was to champion the community assets all around us to give confidence to potential ownership groups that we were ready to fully support this franchise.

I jumped right in, and my main principle was collaboration as we build community together. I formally approached Mayor Jim Watson with a proposal to establish a grassroots organization to champion a new professional Blue Jays franchise in Ottawa to highlight corporate and personal support for a team and a season-ticket deposit drive. At the center of it all was engaging community leaders to voice their commitment by calling ourselves, "The Champions for Ottawa Baseball." The first step was building awareness and securing legitimacy and so I asked former Ottawa Mayor Jim Durrell to act as Honorary Chair of the Champions board. It was Mayor Durrell who put together the resources and talent necessary to attract a Montreal Expos Triple-A franchise to Ottawa in the early 1990s. To listen to Mr. Durrell's stories of that campaign is to understand the complex dynamics of sports business. I was delighted that Mr. Durrell agreed to play a key leadership role, and with that backing, I had the confidence to roll out a vision and strategy to move our agenda forward. My goal was to articulate to the broader Ottawa community that "Baseball Belongs Here" - a vision to foster community support that reflected our aspirations for fans and families to enjoy quality time together at a ball game and provide a new generation of youth role models to emulate for their own future success.

I launched the Champions for Ottawa Baseball on February 16, 2012, as a public delegation at the City of Ottawa's Finance Economic Development Committee at city hall to support the proposed request-for-proposals process and the role that Beacon Sports Capital Partners would undertake to secure a professional baseball franchise. I was one of several delegations supporting the return of affiliated baseball and now, our organization would be an advocate for a new lease arrangement with a potential franchise. We emerged that morning to be a collective voice championing the efforts of the city and the Beacon Group with the promise of a new and exciting era for baseball. The committee and council, led by the leadership of Mayor Jim Watson and Deputy Mayor Bob Monette, delivered the support of their colleagues, and we received significant media interest to get us off the ground to start a season-ticket drive as our first main community engagement. The media coverage was positive, and the calls were starting—there was genuine excitement about a fresh look and new approach for professional baseball.

Sadly, later that very same day, Gary Carter passed away from multiple brain tumor complications. That moment was overwhelming for me, and as I reflected on his life, his legacy, and his presence, it served as deep inspiration to me for the challenges and opportunities ahead. I was now a community advocate for baseball, and everything I did personally to secure collaborative support and help us secure this new franchise was for Gary's legacy.

I questioned how best we could build a board and a series of community engagements that would reflect our community, in order to bring us all together to the ballpark in the summer months to find a collective identity through baseball. I drew a lot of wisdom from an uncle of mine who worked in the game as the general manager for at least three Triple-A franchises in Nashville, Calgary, and Sacramento. His hardest piece of advice—"David, it's about bums in seats and each ticket sold has a monetary value for concessions, merchandise, and more." I will always be a dreamer and I had a vision. It was important for me to recognize a sentiment captured best by author James Kerr in his leadership book, *Legacy,* on the New Zealand All Blacks rugby team—"Vision without action is a dream. Action without vision is a nightmare."[2]

I drew on many points of inspiration to bring the business community together and started a listening tour on the many biases the community had about the past failed baseball franchises. But, we were determined to put a new vision out there and we began to immediately build the board and lay the groundwork for a season-ticket deposit campaign. I wanted the board to reflect our community yet also speak to the business assets a team needs to support the fan experience. So let's talk beer and bats!

Two invaluable relationships were developed that, to this day, are very meaningful to me. I approached Kichesippi Beer Company about the interest of serving local craft beer at future games. Craft beer at the ballpark was a no-brainer and once I met owner and president Paul Meek at Kichesippi, I knew this was the partnership for us. The care and compassion that the Meek family places into every product and customer experience inspired me, and our natural chemistry made Paul a perfect fit for our board. I also called Arlene Anderson, president and co-owner of the iconic SamBat. The story of Sam Holman is fascinating and about our community. Sam learned to make maple bats by borrowing books from the Ottawa Public Library and making them out of his garage just west of downtown. Now based in Carleton Place, SamBat provided great leadership for the Champions franchise.

A good friend and community leader, Doug McLarty, came on board with his team to support the financial administration of a season-ticket deposit drive as it was time for us to test the real support in the community. We launched the season-ticket drive in March 2012 and hosted several community events to drive support, including a business drive to benefit local charities and a Parliament Hill event at the Canadian Brewers Association.

It was a priority that the Champions initiative give back to incredible causes in our city that are on the front line every day, making a difference for us all. To start, we announced corporate packages for local businesses as part of the season-ticket deposit drive to support local charities, but it was not until the moment I met the Desrochers family in July 2012 that I made charitable giving not just the most important part of the Champions initiative, but the legacy of my time in local baseball.

The Miracle League is a US-based charity that collaborates with local communities to establish barrier-free and inclusive sport facilities for children and youth with special needs. On a beautiful Saturday afternoon, I was at Doug Frobel Field in Nepean to observe a Challenger Little League game and I met Michelle and Rolly Desrochers and their son, Bryce, who has cerebral palsy.

Challenger baseball is played on a typical surface that has grass, dirt, gravel, and long, narrow rectangular dugouts. As I listened to the Desrochers explain the barriers for the special needs players, I could see firsthand how the kids were struggling to participate. Michelle and Rolly introduced me to their dream of establishing a Miracle Field in our community. It was a clear gap in our city as a facility of this nature—a baseball field that had a cork/rubberized surface, large box square-shaped dugouts with broken-up benches, and fully accessible washrooms and change rooms—did not exist.

I noticed the kids were really struggling to enjoy the game— walkers and wheelchairs are not meant for grass or gravel sur- faces, plus they could not sit with their friends in the dugout and these barriers prevented enjoyable experiences. As I spoke to Rolly and Michelle about the Miracle League vision, Bryce disappeared with his father into their minivan. Afterward, Rolly told me that Bryce had to go to the bathroom in the van because the washrooms next to the ball field were locked on weekends. I still remember this moment as more than baseball; it was a call to service and an immediate sense of how we can work together to elevate our collective human dignity, especially for these children and youth.

This was a moment to not just help level the playing field, but work with the Desrochers to support hundreds of children in Ottawa with special needs. I served as the volunteer president of the Miracle League of Ottawa with a group of dedicated volunteers and community activists who genuinely believe that human dignity is at the core of who we are as people in Ottawa. Later that winter, we launched a fundraising campaign to secure $2 million to retrofit an existing baseball field at Notre-Dame- des-Champs Park in Orleans. This field was allocated to the Miracle League by the City of Ottawa with Council's support under the Community Partnership Major Capital Program for a 50/50 share of the total project cost to modernize the space to make it fully inclusive. To this day, I remain so grateful to the city staff and leadership who supported the Desrochers. We raised the necessary funds in just two and a half years and in August 2015, the Miracle Field of Ottawa was officially unveiled with our inaugural donors such as the Rotary Clubs Ottawa, the Friends of the Mer Bleue Inc., JaysCare Foundation, Malhotra Family Foundation, Telus Community Fund, Kraft, The Trillium Foundation, Trinity Developments, and more.

On a beautiful summer afternoon in May 2013, we announced a very successful season-ticket deposit drive with 3,100 deposits prior to a Kanata Little League game on Scott Tokessy Field. This leverage fostered our credibility to help the city work on ownership interests to negotiate a lease agreement with the city and ideally, secure local ownership. It was an incredibly interest- ing time to be at the table discussing the business of baseball!

As the discussions evolved with multiple interests, it became apparent that the return of an affiliated franchise was just not tangible due to a variety of factors, namely the public ownership of the ballpark and its aging infrastructure. In the mid 1990s, concrete may have been the norm, but the twenty-first century trend is for open spaces for families and fans and easily acces- sible concourses for more concessions and merchandise sales. Proponents also conducted public opinion polling/surveys in the community to demonstrate knowledge and awareness of a professional baseball team and the level of support for a new Double-A franchise. Not surprisingly, the numbers were low and it deflated our momentum. However, the process meant City of Ottawa commitments to baseball with the new Tremblay Light Rail Station and connecting the LRT station to the ballpark with a brand-new pedestrian bridge over Highway 417 named in honor of the late Max Keeping. In addition, the city had committed to renovations beyond the lifestyle asset requirements.

I commend the city, the Beacon Group and several propo- nents for their engagement and passion to make a deal happen. However, the demands for public investments into modernizing the ballpark were not viable and while we were excited by the many bold visions of a new Ottawa ballpark with Jays AA baseball, the economics did not make sense.

Despite the loss of an affiliated franchise, we attracted the interest of Miles Wolff, the Commissioner of the Canadian- American Association of Professional Baseball, commonly known as the Can-Am League, an independent baseball league with teams in Quebec, New Jersey, and New York State. We believed Miles was a good fit with his past experience in our city, vast relationships in baseball as the "Godfather of Independent Baseball" and former owner of the Durham Bulls and founder of *Baseball America*. By September 2013, we had agreement on a 10-year lease of the Ottawa Baseball Stadium to establish a Can-Am League team for the 2015 season. I sat in the audience as council voted in favor of the lease agreement and it was an honor to speak to councillors one by one in the lead-up to the vote to emphasize the importance of this partnership to make baseball a strong community presence in Ottawa. A 10-year commitment from both sides was a statement for us all—baseball does have a place in the community. I served as the volunteer inaugural president with a small ownership stake and this was exactly the kind of role that I thought was critical for me to transition into following the Champions for Ottawa Baseball. It was essential now to bring all the Champions assets into the new franchise. We also needed a new team name, a cool engaging logo and brand, and time to continue to establish the corporate and community partnerships we'd started and identifying what assets in the ballpark we wanted to improve with the city's funding. It was obvious priority number one was to bring Ottawa baseball into the twenty-first century with a video scoreboard.

Miles and I shared one core value and it was on the importance of the fan experience. My philosophy was that in order to make money, we had to spend money and these investments would not only act to generate profits, but build a positive reputation in the community through fans and our partners. As a volunteer president, I had the responsibility to build a unique and positive reputation in the city. We had to move beyond the status quo and baseball deserved a fresh new look and approach. We named the team the "Ottawa Champions" in June 2014 in recognition of our team culture of celebrating our community, our people, our neighborhood, our businesses, our charities, and our collective identity of being champions of one another. I wanted the ballpark to be transformed into a community gathering space for families, colleagues, and neighbors to enjoy baseball but, more importantly, quality time together. By August, we unveiled our new logo and brand with prominent blues, reds, and whites with a full nostalgic nudge to the Montreal Expos.

The momentum was building for us—we had key wins over 2014 as we prepared for Opening Day on May 22, 2015. We signed business partnerships with SamBat, Kichesippi Beer, Clocktower Brewery, Gabriel Pizza, La Cage Aux Sports, Ottawa Hydro, and a huge win with a naming rights partnership with Raymond Chabot Grant Thornton thanks to Pat Whelan at Extension Marketing. I attended the 2014 Can-Am / American Association All-Star Game in Winnipeg, Manitoba. A success story in independent baseball is Winnipeg under the leadership of former Winnipeg mayor Sam Katz and his general manager, Andrew Collier. Andrew was a valuable source of support and guidance to me as I onboarded into my volunteer presidency role. In Winnipeg, ownership meetings confirmed Ottawa to host the Can-Am / American Association mid-summer classic in 2017 as part of the prominent Canada 150th birthday celebrations. I felt the All-Star game had a place on the roster of key events, and this would be a unique opportunity for us to attract tourism and interest given the markets of teams from Quebec, New York State, and the American Midwest. We were not afraid to put our best foot forward in the community despite the naysayers on the potential we lacked to succeed over the long term.

In November 2014, we introduced our inaugural manager and player in Hal Lanier and Sébastien Boucher, respectively. Seb joined us via a trade with the Quebec Capitales with his unique story as a local youth drafted into major-league baseball by the Seattle Mariners. As a kid, Seb would watch Ottawa Lynx games from Coventry Road, dreaming of becoming a major-league baseball player, and to this day, Seb remains involved in the game and championing youth in sport for their development and leadership.

Hal Lanier played baseball as a member of the San Francisco Giants with such icons as Willie Mays, Juan Marichal, and Willie McCovey. Following his playing career, Hal coached for the St. Louis Cardinals and helped them win the 1982 World Series. As manager of the Houston Astros from 1986 to 1988, he was named National League Manager of the Year in 1986. Meeting Hal and learning about the game was one of the main highlights of my time with the Champions. I spent quality time with Hal behind the batting cage watching players take their cuts, listening to his stories about Roberto Clemente, Yogi Berra, and other stars of the game. But when Hal spoke about his father, another baseball player, Max Lanier, the passion was never as strong. Hal is a close friend to this day and has taught me important leadership lessons. I have long admired the management philosophy of former Expo and recent manager of the Cleveland Guardians, Terry Francona who is well-regarded as a "players manager." I finally developed a sense of that reputation observing Hal who led us with gratitude, patience, and a focus on the wellness of the players. I valued the post-game beer and team performance debrief in Hal's office, learning about the game with his wisdom,

May 22, 2015 will be a date that will be forever in my memory—it was the Ottawa Champions franchise inaugural game in the Can-Am League and despite the cool evening, the community warmed up the atmosphere. Andrew Werner, our Ace, threw the inaugural pitch in Champions history, and we went on to beat the Sussex County Miners, 8-1. It was a night of celebration, humility and I was proud of our success to this point. Werner threw a great game, striking out four while giving up three hits, one earned run, and two walks in five innings before being replaced by reliever and a great guy, Dan Meyer.

Our inaugural season had many exciting highlights, including the engaging series versus the Cuban national team and the Japanese Shikoku Island League team. The international series broke up a monotonous schedule for our fans as there were a lot of repeat visits from the small Can-Am teams, so any new teams from the international leagues or American Association were always of interest to our fans. We saw incredible engagement for the Cuban and Japanese series with their local communities attending and the ambassadors and their embassies hosting the players for receptions.

We finished in fifth place with a 46-50 record, and we saw developing chemistry between our community and the key leaders of our franchise, led by manager Lanier, pitching coach Billy Horn, coach Jared Lemieux, and Sébastien, as well as players like Wilmer Font, Bryce Massanari, Roberto Ramirez, Danny Grauer, Josh Blanco, Alan DeRatt, Chris Winder, Corey Caswell, and Daniel Bick. They all engaged to win baseball games and connect with fans and the community. I felt we were growing a strong internal core to build on for the long term. 2016 proved to be a crucial year for us—when the players arrived for spring training, we gathered at the iconic Chateau Lafayette in the Byward Market with the mayor, players, fans, and our friends at Kichesippi brewery to launch "Champions

Light," a beer made exclusively for sale at the ballpark during the 2016 season.

The season continued the tradition of hosting two international series with the Cubans and the Shikoku Island team. The Cuban series broke our attendance records, and – a fun fact: a young Cuban player who played in Ottawa is now an All-Star slugger with the Chicago White Sox—Luis Robert Jr!

I traveled to St. Paul, Minnesota, with our all-stars Austin Chrismon and Daniel Cordero to enjoy the All-Star Game hosted by the St. Paul Saints and throw out the "last pitch" of the game to transition the annual game to Ottawa in 2017. I was able to observe how meaningful independent baseball is to the Midwest US markets with local ownership, loyal fan bases, and deep corporate support. These were all aspects that we had to have in Ottawa to sustain our franchise over the long term.

During the 2016 season, we had a good sense that we were going to be competitive over the stretch running into the playoffs despite losing ace Wilmer Font to the Toronto Blue Jays. My story of Wilmer Font is one of humility and pride. As an inaugural member of our rotation over a season and a half, Wilmer made an impression. He struck out 142 batters for us over two seasons (2015/16) and was signed by the Jays in 2016 and spent time with the Dodgers, Athletics, and Rays. I caught up with Wilmer in Tampa Bay in April 2019 and as we stood on the field at Tropicana Field, he thanked me for the Champions and credited his time in Ottawa for really improving his game and pitching, and now, he was in "The Show." Later that season, I cheered him on in person in Toronto as he stood on the mound pitching against the mighty New York Yankees in front of 33,903 fans as he got Aaron Judge to fly out and struck out Gary Sanchez and DJ LeMahieu. Talk about a personal bucket list moment where all roads led to that moment of purpose and meaning.

As we continued the 2016 season, we knew our team had the necessary chemistry to win games, have fun, and believe that a Championship was within our reach! While the strategy was simply to mature our fan base, strengthen loyalty, and grow awareness in the community, winning games and watching the players excel was a bonus! Great players like Austin Chrismon, Daniel Cordero, Danny Grauer, Jason Coker, Matt Helms, Miles Moeller, Daniel Bick, Kenny Bryant, Andrew Cooper, Albert Cartwright, and more made the season a thrilling one to follow. By mid-August, Hal and his coaches were focused on September baseball. We qualified for the playoffs and easily beat the New Jersey Jackals three games to one. It was mid-September and a beautiful late summer season as we faced the Rockland Boulders for the Can-Am Championship with two home games to start the best-of-five series. We dropped these two games, and all of the positive momentum from the end of the season and the NJ series was gone. Our team was to travel to Rockland in New York State to play the deciding games in the series. Following our Game Two loss, I took the microphone and spoke to the several thousand fans left and told them to believe in this team and this city. We needed three back-to-back-to-back wins and

with our rotation, bats, and an enduring optimism, we knew we could be the champions our community needed.

We took Games Three and Four, and I traveled to Rockland for the deciding Game Five along with a dedicated group of fans from Ottawa. Game Five was as exciting as you would imagine it. Kenny Bryant got us started in the first inning with a two-run single off the glove of second baseman Pat McKenna, and from there, we had the momentum. As I watched the game (the longest game ever in my life!), I felt that momentum from the early days of 2012 when this journey started. In the eighth inning, Kenny Bryant gave us the insurance run, a monster home run to right field that bounced off the concourse, and with Austin Chrismon pitching a complete game, allowing only one earned run and striking out eight, we became the Champions. Michael Nellis, broadcasting the game live on CKDG-FM, became the official voice of the 2016 Champions with this final out call that has become legend in our community!

A championship brought incredible moments from hoisting the Can-Am Trophy on the field with the team and our coaches, seeing the fans after at the official celebration the day after at the Clocktower Pub and the city hosting a community rally for us with councillors and our fans. It was exhilarating and liberating, and while I was very humbled by the support, I felt a profound sense of validation for all the work that we had done as a community together to deliver a team and then build the necessary resources and support to have a unique moment like this.

Sébastien Boucher and I appeared on CBC's *Our Ottawa* the week following the Championship, and Adrian Harewood posed a question that was on everyone's mind—that this victory was improbable. That was a metaphor for our place in this moment and Ottawa history. Generally, the city did not expect us to survive financially, let alone win a championship against the Rockland Boulders, a Can-Am powerhouse in those days.

This was a crucial time for the franchise—fans were engaged, our brand and identity were growing, our on-field leadership with Hal Lanier was never stronger, we had a championship that fostered legitimacy in the community and across the game, our official charity, the Miracle League of Ottawa, was now open and fully functional, meaning hundreds of kids and youth were enjoying baseball fully, and for the next season, we would host the All-Star Game. We had also won "Can-Am Field of the Year" recognition, and that was due to the incredible work by Guy Vaillancourt and his team of grounds crew that kept the field shining as our impeccable North Star in the community.

With some key pillars in place now, the strategy moved to local ownership. We wanted this momentum to generate discussions on individuals or corporate interests that would invest in making baseball more sustainable and present in our community. However, despite our successes to date, we could not capture the imagination of well-known sport or business leaders to secure ownership. From the moment the team was incorporated, local ownership was the long-term goal, but it was never clearly or coherently planned, managed, or executed. As the 2017 season wore on and we enjoyed the All-Star Game and associated festivities, a repeat playoff run was clearly not in the picture for us. Being the president of the Ottawa Champions was a purely volunteer role, and I was feeling that I had taken my leadership as far as I could following the 2017 season and I wanted to focus my energies on my growing family with my wife, Danielle, and my career. On February 16, 2018, six years to the day after I launched the Champions for Ottawa Baseball organization, I announced my resignation as president. Sadly, the team folded officially following the 2019 season, as did the entire Can-Am League, and now, the Champions are a part of Ottawa baseball and professional sports history. My story of the Ottawa Champions Baseball Club is not one of balls and strikes, wins and losses, or even the 2016 championship. It's not about records set or the size of the crowd at any given game, nor another folded franchise. Instead, this story is about community and the people who enjoyed Champions baseball. I believe to this day the future of professional baseball is affiliated Single-A or Double-A baseball with the parking pushed underground and above the parking surface, a new community "building up" with commercial/retail businesses and a reduced baseball park seat footprint. We don't need 10,000 seats for minor-league affiliated baseball in Ottawa and it takes courage to move forward on a plan to reduce that footprint to meet a more realistic demand for baseball. But, if it puts an end to the endless discussion about crowds and attendance, it will be worth the reward to have sustainable baseball in Ottawa.

My gratitude to every person who bought a ticket, a hot dog, a t-shirt or cap, cheered on a home run or stolen base, and took a moment to enjoy Ottawa Champions baseball. I am humbled by all those who worked with me on a vision to bring the community to the ballpark and, in turn, the ballpark into all of our neighborhoods. I am proud of the small wins. We did them as a team and showed how when we all work together, we can succeed.

NOTES

1   Ken Burns, *Baseball* (New York: PBS, 1994), episode 5.
2   James Kerr, *Legacy: What The All Blacks Can Teach Us About The Business Of Life* (London: Constable & Robinson, 2013).

OTTAWA TITANS

BY JORDAN PRESS

THE FIRST WEATHER ALERT WENT out about two hours before the Ottawa Titans of the Frontier League were to play their 2024 home opener. The warning to residents of Canada's capital from Environment Canada was grim: prepare for heavy rains and wind gusts of over 100 kilometres per hour.[1]

An hour before game time, torrential rain and heavy winds struck.[2] A crowd of 3,000 huddled on the covered concourse.[3] The first pitch was delayed by an hour.[4]

"We're planning to play," said a post on the team's account on X, the platform formerly known as Twitter.[5] Added to the post was, "#HereToStay."

The Titans are the latest iteration of professional baseball in Canada's capital, hoping to capture something that eluded its predecessors: long-term, sustained success.

"Clearly there has been a demand" for baseball in Ottawa, says team general manager Martin Boyce.[6] "I feel like it would be a little bit naive to believe that that demand just doesn't exist anymore."

The Frontier League announced in September 2020 that it would add a team in Ottawa, with baseball set to return in 2021.[7] At the time, league commissioner Bill Lee called Ottawa "a major league city that deserves professional baseball."[8]

When the Frontier and Can-Am leagues merged in 2019, Ottawa appeared destined to join the new outfit. But the city's team, the Champions, were left out of the merger.

In autumn 2019, the Champions' owner, Miles Wolff, had two groups looking to purchase the franchise and its assets. One group included three local investors. A second ownership group had experience with independent-league baseball and local sports teams:[9]

- Ottawa Sports and Entertainment Group (OSEG), which owns the Ottawa RedBlacks of the Canadian Football League and the Ottawa 67's of the Ontario Hockey League.[10]
- Sam Katz, a former Winnipeg mayor who has owned the Winnipeg Goldeyes of the American Association of Independent Professional Baseball since 1994.[11]

Any deal to buy the Champions was contingent on signing a lease with the municipal government for use of Ottawa's ballpark and the city recouping a debt of nearly half-a-million-dollars from the Champions.

"We're trying to minimize our loss and get our money back. It's been part of the negotiations," then-city manager Steve Kanellakos told local councilors in September 2019.[12]

"We feel now that we have two viable, legitimate owners' groups who are interested in the team [and] who have the financial means to be able to deal with that outstanding debt."

At the time, local officials had already signaled their support for Katz and OSEG, even though Wolff said an agreement-in-principle had been reached with the group of local investors.[13] By December, city staff presented a plan to municipal politicians to negotiate a lease with Katz and OSEG.[14] The final 10-year lease included:

- an annual base rent for three years of $125,000[15]
- annual increases in the base rent starting in the fourth year, with each increase tied to the rate of inflation
- a designation that exempts the stadium from municipal taxes so long as "business activities taking place at the stadium are related to baseball and other related events"
- a provision that Katz and OSEG accepted the stadium as-is and without any additional work by the city
- an agreement that the ownership group would pay the Champions' debt of more than $473,000
- an effective date of January 1, 2021[16]

Katz believed baseball could thrive in Ottawa just as the Goldeyes had in Winnipeg for years. The cities shared some traits: Both are cold weather cities, where playing baseball outside is an option for only a few months of the year. Local sports fans have been built around National Hockey League teams—the Senators in Ottawa, the Jets in Winnipeg—and CFL teams.

And both had large populations that sustained a variety of minor-league sports teams.

"Ottawa is a city of a million people, so the other teams in our league are successful in markets that are 100,000 people," Boyce said in 2024. "There's just so much to draw from that how could (the team) not be a success?"[17]

In autumn 2019, Katz had also noted something else that could help the team succeed: Ottawa's economy and high per-capita income.[18]

Being the national capital, Ottawa is home to a large, educated workforce. The City of Ottawa's website notes that the region is the largest hub of federal workers in the country, has a median family income of $102,000 (which is one of the highest in the country), and has a workforce with more PhDs per capita than any other major region in Canada.[19] Those conditions suggest that local residents have more disposable income than residents of other Canadian cities.[20] A study of attendance[21] at Carolina League games found that a team being located in a region with a higher per capita income can help increase attendance at games.[22]

But that high per capita income could have less of an impact on attendance in large cities: A 2009 study[23] found that attendance in the South Atlantic League declined as per capita incomes and populations grew. The authors suggested that populations in larger cities with more disposable income had more options on where to spend their entertainment dollars. Baseball was competing with everything else.

Ottawa's stadium itself was also a source of potential. The ballpark was built for the Ottawa Lynx, a one-time Triple-A affiliate of the Montreal Expos (and, later, the Baltimore Orioles and Philadelphia Phillies). It could host baseball games and other events from a location easily accessible by car or transit. Notably, a pedestrian bridge over Ottawa's key thoroughfare, Highway 417, connects the stadium to a station on the city's recently opened light-rail transit system, which is being expanded to connect more parts of the national capital.[24]

"Ottawa is a no-brainer. It fits all the criteria for having a successful sports franchise," Katz told the *Ottawa Sun* in September 2020.[25] "Saying all that, it doesn't mean it happens automatically just because, 'Hey, we're here, hello, come on down.' You have to motivate and inspire people to come, you have to keep them coming back and you have to work hard to do that."

The home-opener for the 2024 season may have done just that.

The home team got out to an early lead, but fell behind in the top of the ninth when the Tri-City ValleyCats took a 6-5 lead. The home side drew even in their half of the inning before newly-named captain Jason Dicochea pulled one inside the bag at third for a walk-off hit.[26] Maybe this team would live up to its name.

The team got its name through a contest the organization ran in autumn of 2020. In all, the contest yielded 700 unique names across 1,200 submissions and engaged local residents. The organization selected the name Titans from those submissions. Aside from the connection to Greek mythology, the name had another advantage for any team in Canada's bilingual capital: it was the same in English and French.[27]

With that challenge complete, the team prepared for its inaugural season with another challenge: the COVID-19 pandemic.

Canada entered 2021 battling a resurgent second wave of COVID-19. Renewed government restrictions, including stay-at-home orders implemented by Ontario's provincial government, aimed to curb the spread of the virus. The country then faced a third wave that peaked in April, followed by a fourth wave later in the summer.[28] Public health measures aimed to curb the virus's spread through physical distancing, mask mandates, reduced capacity at sporting events, and restrictions on international travel.[29]

The 14-day mandatory quarantine for incoming travelers posed a significant challenge for professional sports leagues.[30] Visiting teams couldn't fulfill their game schedules while isolating for such an extended period. Uncertain about the full reopening of the Canada-US border, the Frontier League presented its three Canadian teams—including the Titans—with the tough choice of playing all their games in the United States until at least July 1 (Canada Day).

In April 2021, the Titans and their fellow Canadian teams decided against playing south of the border.[31] Ottawa would have to wait another year for baseball in the capital.

"This was not an easy decision, but we believe it is the right decision," Titans vice-president Regan Katz said in a release.[32] "We thank our staff, players, coaches and manager for their commitment to the Ottawa Titans and look forward to seeing them on our field next May."

The decision meant the team spent its first year covering its operating expenses without a key source of revenue: ticket sales. The upside was that the organization gained time to renovate its home stadium.

The Titans' lease agreement with the city required them to accept the stadium as-is. When the team moved in, they found a venue that was in rougher shape than the front office originally believed.[33]

Originally built in 1993, the stadium had a seating capacity of 10,332 and had been home to a series of ball clubs. After the Lynx left Ottawa following the 2007 season, the city leased the stadium to the Rapidz of the Can-Am League for one year in 2008, then the Fat Cats of the Intercounty Baseball League between 2010 and 2012, and the Champions between 2015 and 2019. In between teams, the stadium sat largely idle.[34]

The Titans encountered delays in getting the venue ready. Some work stretched into the preseason. Among the issues that fans noticed when they arrived at the ballpark were seats that weren't bolted to the concrete stands and signage that still had the Champions' logo.[35] One fan described the venue as "below average" but thought that improvements could attract more people to games.[36]

Issues persisted well beyond the inaugural opening day. In 2023, the team had to reschedule games early in the season when a faulty transformer caused intermittent blackouts in the stadium.[37] As Boyce described it, a facility that is over 30 years old will likely always have some maintenance issue that needs addressing.[38] One reason is that something that wasn't an issue one year may become an issue further down the line.

Despite all the bumps in the road, the Titans played their first official home game on May 24, 2022—a 2-0 win against the visiting Evansville Otters.[39]

The victory boded well for the team's inaugural season.

The Titans were hot early in the season, but fell out of a playoff spot in early August. Ottawa earned itself a playoff spot with a furious end to the season as the Titans won nine of their final 10 games. After winning a wild card game on the road, the Titans fell in a best-of-three division series to the eventual champions, the Quebec Capitales.

"We didn't know what to expect, in a new league, starting from scratch," Regan Katz told the *Ottawa Sun* shortly after the season ended.[40] "Competing in the playoffs is one thing, but we were able to put up a really good battle against probably the best team in the league and come really close."

The 2023 campaign was, from a baseball perspective, not as successful as the 2022 season. After posting a 56–39 record in their first season, the Titans finished their second season at 48-48 and failed to make the playoffs.

Heading into the 2024 season, the Titans looked like a competitive team on paper. After a slow start, the Titans went on a roll over June and into early July, winning two-thirds of their games through that stretch before stumbling into the all-star break with a four-game losing streak. Still, that was good enough for third place in the division, four games back of the Quebec Capitales. Beating the Capitales would be high on the team's on-field to-do list. Off the field, the team had another to-do item: forge a distinct identity among the growing number of sports teams in Ottawa.[41] What the Titans wanted to do was solidify a brand as a fun, social experience—more than just a baseball team—that everyone in Ottawa could recognize.[42]

From the moment the league awarded Ottawa an expansion team, the ownership group had framed the business case for drawing fans around creating a welcoming venue, providing an entertaining time and making an outing to the ballpark affordable and family-friendly. Yes, the goal of any sports team is to sell out a venue, whether that goal is realistic or not, Sam Katz said.[43] But selling Ottawa residents on the baseball was secondary to selling them on the team's brand.[44] The Titans wanted to make sure that potential fans knew they could come to the ballpark with a family of four and get in the door for far less money than to see other teams in town.

"Every city is a bit different, but the one thing you know people are always looking for is quality, affordable family entertainment—there's never enough of that to go around," Sam Katz told the *Ottawa Sun* in September 2020.[45] "We intend to have lots of fun, win lots of games and the ultimate goal is to win a championship."

The idea of affordable family fun that the Titans have promoted has a long tradition in independent baseball leagues.[46] Selling local fans on the Titans was based on the idea that a trip to the ballpark was more like going to dinner theatre than a ballgame, as Lee, the Frontier League's former commissioner, once described it.[47]

Promotions like fireworks and creative marketing have been shown to help boost attendance at minor league games, but a successful marketing strategy in one year won't necessarily work in subsequent years.[48] A whole host of changes—demographics and economic conditions, for example—could affect how residents decide to spend their entertainment dollars.

From Boyce's perspective, the organization is getting the hang of creating new, fun experiences at games, evolving their

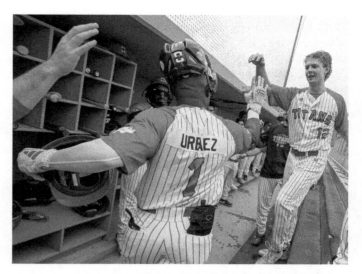

Jackie Urbaez congratulates a teammate during a Frontier League game. Credit: Courtesy Timothy Austen.

promotions to capitalize on things happening in the national capital to draw fans.[49] For instance, the team held a theme night for Canadian singer Shania Twain when she performed at the city's annual Bluesfest music festival in 2023, even going so far as to hire an impersonator to belt out songs for fans. For the 2024 season, the concept got a revival with a night dedicated to Canadian rock band Nickelback when it performed at Bluesfest.

The team continues to reshape the ballpark to create more social spots as part of a 10-year renovation plan aimed at attracting more fans to games and hosting more non-baseball events like concerts and festivals.

Work started before the first season when the organization renovated suites that overlook the field from the stadium's second and third floors. Demand from the first season led the team to add more furnishings to the suites in the second season. The team hoped that some of those attendees would enjoy the atmosphere and come back to watch games on their own, with family or with friends.

Along with the suites—which were finished for the team's third season—the Titans worked on a grassy area down the left-field line with a stand selling local beer. Families can hang out at picnic tables, children can run around on the grass and fans can stroll down the knoll to field-level and interact with players in the bullpen. That gave fans two spots to socialize in groups.[50]

What followed was work on a third-floor space that at one time was home to a restaurant. That area has been turned into a large group space that the team hopes will be used by corporate groups—which helps with attendance and revenues.

Other plans include creating patio decks where fans can hang out with a group of people instead of in seats.

"The goal, essentially, with all of these plans would be just to make the ballpark more lively," Boyce said.[51]

The work in Ottawa will require removing some seats. Depending on which seats are removed, the ballpark may feel like a more intimate setting to watch baseball and a game with 2,000 fans may feel like 5,000—and 5,000 fans may feel like 10,000.[52]

Club officials have spoken about how 10,000 seats are far too many for the team's needs. According to a list maintained by BaseballPilgrimages.com, Ottawa's stadium is the second largest for any professional baseball team in Canada, behind only the Rogers Centre in Toronto, and second largest of any independent league team on the list.[53] The stadium's capacity is also more than double those of the stadiums that are home to the other two Canadian teams in the Frontier League.[54]

"Having 10,000 seats is far too many for baseball at nearly every level, and certainly more seats than we need as is," Regan Katz said in late 2023.[55] "So these plans will actually start removing seats and converting them into mingling spaces instead."

Teams in the Frontier League require an average attendance of 2,000 fans per game to meet expenses.[56] That number may fluctuate based on market conditions, other sources of revenue, the size of any one-time expenses and annual increases in the cost of living.

Fans didn't initially flock to Titans games in great numbers. Some of that may have been lingering impacts from the first two years of the Covid-19 pandemic, which included rounds of public health restrictions and lockdowns. In the summer of 2022, Regan Katz said that cautiousness around the pandemic had kept some fans at home early in the season, leaving the gate numbers below where the front office wanted them to be.[57] But the numbers would turn around, just as they did at other sporting venues through 2022.

Attendance at sporting events in Canada jumped in 2022 after public health restrictions were lifted and vaccination rates rose. A 2024 report from Statistics Canada noted that spectator sports, as an industry, witnessed a massive rebound in 2022 with operating revenues rebounding that year to pre-pandemic levels.[58]

Attendance at the ballpark reflected that growth.

The Titans' regular-season finale in 2022 drew a crowd of over 3,500.[59] More fans than that—3,777 to be precise—showed up for opening day in 2023.[60] Attendance dropped off after the 2023 opener, and fell closer to the team's per-game average in 2022 by the end of the homestand.[61] By the end of the year, attendance rose. The Titans reported that fan appreciation day in 2023 set an attendance record with more than 4,600 people in the stands. Overall, average attendance increased by just over 27% between seasons one and two, rising from a per-game average of 1,211 fans in 2022 to 1,540 in 2023 but still under the league average of 2,148.[62]

At the end of the 2024 season, average per-game attendance had gone up again from the previous season, rising just under 29% to 1,982.[63] But the attendance boost didn't boost the Titans' playoff fortunes in 2024. The Titans advanced to their second ever East Division series after beating the Tri-City ValleyCats 5-2 on the road in the East Division Wild Card game.[64] In the first game of the series, the Titans rode some timely offence to walk-off the Quebec Capitales at home in extra innings to take an early lead in the best-of-three playoff.[65] But the next two games didn't go as the Titans hoped, first falling 10-6 and then losing the deciding match 8-7–leaving the tying run in scoring position in the ninth–to drop the series to the eventual league champions.[66]

There's always next year. And likely years beyond that from the team's perspective.

Sam Katz and the rest of the front office have repeatedly said that they are in it for the long haul in Ottawa, and that the Titans can succeed where others have not. Hence the hashtag in the team's social media posts: #HereToStay.

To do so, the organization understands it has a few obstacles to overcome: baseball isn't the most popular professional sport in Ottawa, and players transition faster out of the Frontier League than minor league teams, for example. So for Boyce, the primary focus isn't necessarily baseball unlike past teams that may have focused less on creating a social experience for fans.[67]

"Our goal is to approach this differently than teams have in the past and the common denominator with most of the teams, not all, was that fun wasn't necessarily the focus and baseball was at times the primary focus," Boyce said ahead of the 2024 season.[68]

"We're confident in what we do but we hope that it's the successful magic potion that makes baseball successful very long term in Ottawa."

NOTES

1　Andrew Osmand, "Severe thunderstorm warnings dropped but not before clouds darkened Ottawa skies," *CityNews Ottawa*, May 21, 2024, https://ottawa.citynews.ca/2024/05/21/ottawa-rain-wind-thunderstorm-warning/. Accessed July 21, 2024.

2　Kiersten Vuorimaki, "The Ottawa Titans are coming in hot this weekend," Apt613.ca, May 30, 2024, https://apt613.ca/the-ottawa-titans-are-coming-in-hot-this-weekend/. Accessed July 21, 2024.

3　"The Ottawa Titans are coming in hot this weekend."

4　"The Ottawa Titans are coming in hot this weekend."

5　The post can be accessed through https://x.com/ottawa_titans/status/1792988274459324758.

6　Martin Boyce, telephone interview, April 11, 2024.

7　"Ottawa Gets Frontier League Baseball Team for 2021," CBC News, September 25, 2020, (https://www.cbc.ca/news/canada/ottawa/frontier-league-ottawa-baseball-new-team-1.5739965). Accessed May 7, 2024.

8　Gordon Engelhardt, "Ottawa Becomes Third Canadian Team to Join Frontier League," *Evansville Courier & Press*, September 25, 2020 (https://www.courierpress.com/story/sports/2020/09/25/ottawa-becomes-third-canadian-team-join-frontier-league/3532130001/). Accessed May 7, 2024.

9　Ottawa Titans Baseball Club Inc., "Ottawa Titans Expand Ownership Group Ahead of 2021 Season," December 14, 2020 (https://www.ottawatitans.com/ottawa-titans-expand-ownership-group-ahead-of-2021-season). Accessed May 7, 2024.

10 Ottawa Sports and Entertainment Group. For more information, see the website for TD Place Stadium: https://www.tdplace.ca/oseg/. Accessed May 7, 2024.

11 Winnipeg Goldeyes. More details are available on the "History" page of the team's website at https://www.goldeyes.com/about/history. May 7, 2024.

12 "Ottawa Champions Left Off New League's 2020 Roster," CBC News, October 16, 2019. https://www.cbc.ca/news/canada/ottawa/ottawa-champions-left-off-2020-roster-1.5323308. Accessed May 7, 2024.

13 "Ottawa Champions Left Off New League's 2020 Roster."

14 Jon Willing, "Analysis: With OSEG Involved, Is the Ottawa Baseball Stadium Ripe for a Mini-Lansdowne Transformation?," *Ottawa Citizen*, December 2, 2019 (https://ottawacitizen.com/news/local-news/analysis-with-oseg-involved-is-ottawa-stadium-ripe-for-a-mini-lansdowne-transformation/). Accessed May 7, 2024.

15 All dollar figures in this article are in Canadian dollars unless otherwise noted.

16 Lease Agreement. Details about the lease agreement can be found in Tim Baines, "Play Ball! Sam Katz Confident Baseball Will Be a Hit in Ottawa When It Returns Next Year," *Ottawa Sun*, September 23, 2020. https://ottawasun.com/sports/baseball/play-ball-sam-katz-confident-baseball-will-be-a-hit-in-ottawa-when-it-returns-next-year. Accessed April 8, 2024 ; Kevin Reichard, "Frontier League Returns to Ottawa in 2021," BallparkDigest.com, September 25, 2020. https://ballparkdigest.com/2020/09/25/frontier-league-returns-to-ottawa-in-2021/. Accessed May 7, 2024; and David Sali, "New Ownership Group Confident It Can Reverse Ottawa's Pro Baseball Curse," *Ottawa Business Journal*, September 25, 2020. https://obj.ca/new-ownership-group-confident-it-can-reverse-ottawas-pro-baseball-curse/. Accessed April 8, 2024.

17 Boyce interview.

18 "New Ownership Group Confident It Can Reverse Ottawa's Pro Baseball Curse."

19 City of Ottawa, "Statistics and Demographics," https://ottawa.ca/en/living-ottawa/statistics-and-demographics#section-2224a97d-596c-47b0-bad5-dbd36957830b. Accessed May 7, 2024.

20 Institut de la statistique du Québec, "Per Capita Disposable Income Continued To Grow in Québec and in All Administrative Regions in 2022" (press release, April 25, 2024), https://statistique.quebec.ca/en/communique/per-capita-disposable-income-continued-to-grow-quebec-administrative-regions-2022. Accessed May 7, 2024.

21 Richard J. Cebula, Michael Toma, and Jay Carmichael. 2009. "Attendance and Promotions in Minor League Baseball: The Carolina League," *Applied Economics* 41: 3209–3214.

22 David Quiring and Andrew Zimbalist, "Attendance and Promotions in Minor League Baseball: The Carolina League," ResearchGate, https://www.researchgate.net/publication/46528525_Attendance_and_promotions_in_minor_league_baseball_The_Carolina_League. Accessed May 7, 2024.

23 Rodney J. Paul, Michael Toma, and Andrew P. Weinbach, "The Minor League Experience: What Drives Attendance at South Atlantic League Baseball Games?" *Coastal Business Journal* 8(1): 70–84. https://digitalcommons.coastal.edu/cgi/viewcontent.cgi?article=1052&context=cbj. Last accessed May 9, 2024.

24 Ottawa Titans Baseball Club Inc., "Ottawa Titans Announce Ongoing Ballpark Enhancements, Seek Stadium Naming Rights" (press release, September 12, 2023), https://www.ottawatitans.com/ottawa-titans-announce-ongoing-ballpark-enhancements-seek-stadium-naming-rights. Accessed May 7, 2024.

25 Tim Baines, "Play Ball! Sam Katz Confident Baseball Will Be a Hit in Ottawa When It Returns Next Year," *Ottawa Sun*, September 23, 2020. https://ottawasun.com/sports/baseball/play-ball-sam-katz-confident-baseball-will-be-a-hit-in-ottawa-when-it-returns-next-year. Accessed April 8, 2024.

26 Ottawa Titans Baseball Club Inc., "Walk-Off Heroics Headline Titans Home-Opening Victory," May 22, 2024, https://www.ottawatitans.com/walk-off-heroics-headline-titans-home-opening-victory. Accessed July 21, 2024.

27 Tim Baines, "Remember The Titans: Ottawa's New Pro Baseball Team Gets a Name," *Ottawa Sun*, December 3, 2020. https://ottawasun.com/sports/baseball/remember-the-titans-ottawas-new-pro-baseball-team-gets-a-name. Accessed April 8, 2024.

28 Christopher J. Rutty, "COVID-19 Pandemic in Canada," *The Canadian Encyclopedia*, https://www.thecanadianencyclopedia.ca/en/article/covid-19-pandemic. Accessed May 7, 2024.

29 Canadian Institute for Health Information, "Canadian COVID-19 Intervention Timeline," https://www.cihi.ca/en/canadian-covid-19-intervention-timeline. Accessed May 7, 2024.

30 U.S. Embassy and Consulates in Canada, "Message to U.S. Citizens in Canada: Update on Canadian International Travel Restrictions," February 12, 2021. https://ca.usembassy.gov/message-to-u-s-citizens-in-canada%E2%80%AF-update-on-canadian-entry-restrictions/. Accessed May 7, 2024; Public Health Agency of Canada, "Government of Canada To Remove COVID-19 Border and Travel Measures Effective October 1" (press release, September 26, 2022), https://www.canada.ca/en/public-health/news/2022/09/government-of-canada-to-remove-covid-19-border-and-travel-measures-effective-october-1.html. Accessed May 7, 2024.

31 The Québec Capitales and Trois-Rivières Aigles merged for the 2021 season, calling themselves Équipe Québec. The merged team played exclusively as a road team until August when it returned to the province of Quebec for home games. For more, see Paul Caputo, "Frontier League merges two teams into Team Quebec for 2021," *SportsLogos.Net*, April 27, 2021, https://news.sportslogos.net/2021/04/27/frontier-league-merges-two-teams-into-team-quebec-for-2021/baseball/; and Jessica Lapinski, "La triste fin d'une belle épopée," *Journal de Québec*, September 19, 2021, https://www.journaldequebec.com/2021/09/19/equipe-quebec-eliminee-par-les-wild-things. Both accessed August 12, 2024."

32 "Canadian Teams Opt Out of Frontier League Season," *Observer-Reporter*, April 17, 2021, https://www.observer-reporter.com/sports/2021/apr/17/canadian-teams-opt-out-of-frontier-league-season/. Accessed May 7, 2024.

33 Frankie Benvenuti, "Here To Stay: Regan Katz Committed To Baseball In Ottawa," 13th Man Sports, July 11, 2022, https://13thmansports.ca/2022/07/11/here-to-stay-regan-katz-committed-to-baseball-in-ottawa/. Accessed May 7, 2024.

34 City of Ottawa, "The Ottawa Stadium - Community Visioning" (last updated November 15, 2023), https://engage.ottawa.ca/the-ottawa-stadium-community-visioning?tool=story_telling_tool#tool_tab. Accessed April 8, 2024.

35 "Here To Stay: Regan Katz Committed To Baseball In Ottawa."

36 Michael Vavaroutsos, "Ottawa Titans Plan Further Changes To Make Baseball Park a More Social Space," *Capital Current*, October

11, 2023, https://capitalcurrent.ca/ottawa-titans-plan-further-changes-to-make-baseball-park-a-more-social-space/. Accessed May 9, 2024.

37 Ken Warren, "Powering Up: City Fixes Problem That Forced Re-scheduling of Ottawa Titans Games," *Ottawa Sun*, May 25, 2023, https://ottawasun.com/sports/baseball/titans-forced-to-play-morning-and-afternoon-games-due-to-power-issues. Accessed May 9, 2024.

38 Boyce interview.

39 Jackie Perez, "Play Ball! Ottawa Titans Mark Their Home Debut at RCGT Park," CTV News Ottawa, May 11, 2022, https://ottawa.ctvnews.ca/play-ball-ottawa-titans-mark-their-home-debut-at-rcgt-park-1.5898087. Accessed May 9, 2024.

40 Ken Warren, "Ottawa Titans Talk About Positive Future Amid the Frustration of Losing Divisional Final," *Ottawa Sun*, September 12, 2022, https://ottawasun.com/sports/baseball/ottawa-titans-talk-about-positive-future-amid-the-frustra-tion-of-losing-divisional-final. Accessed May 9, 2024.

41 Mario Carlucci, "What will it take for all of Ottawa's pro sports teams to thrive?" *CBC News*, March 10, 2024, https://www.cbc.ca/news/canada/ottawa/what-does-it-take-for-ottawa-sports-teams-to-thrive-1.7138764. Accessed September 13, 2024.

42 Boyce interview.

43 "Play Ball! Sam Katz Confident Baseball Will Be a Hit in Ottawa When It Returns Next Year."

44 Ken Warren, "The Search for Fans: Ottawa's Minor Pro Squads Look To Fill More Seats," *Ottawa Sun*, May 19, 2023, https://ottawasun.com/sports/the-search-for-fans-ottawas-minor-pro-squads-look-to-fill-more-seats. Accessed May 9, 2024.

45 "Play Ball! Sam Katz Confident Baseball Will Be a Hit in Ottawa When It Returns Next Year."

46 Paul, Rodney J., Michael Toma, and Andrew P. Weinbach. 2009. "The Minor League Experience: What Drives Attendance at South Atlantic League Baseball Games?" *Coastal Business Journal* 8(1): 70–84. https://digitalcommons.coastal.edu/cgi/viewcontent.cgi?article=1052&context=cbj. Last accessed May 9, 2024.

47 Hamza Ali, "New Stadium Lease Brings Hope of a Successful Revival of Professional Baseball in Ottawa," *Capital Current*, October 20, 2020, https://capitalcurrent.ca/new-stadium-lease-brings-hope-of-a-successful-revival-of-profes-sional-baseball-in-ottawa/. Accessed May 9, 2024.

48 Richard J. Cebula, Michael Toma, and Jay Carmichael. 2009. "Attendance and Promotions in Minor League Baseball: The Carolina League," *Applied Economics* 41: 3209–3214.

49 Boyce interview.

50 Ottawa Titans Baseball Club Inc., "Ottawa Titans Announce Ongoing Ballpark Enhancements, Seek Stadium Naming Rights" (press release, September 12, 2023); and David Sali, "Titans Pitching New Uses for Ottawa Stadium as Renovations at City-Owned Ballpark Continue," *Ottawa Business Journal*, September 21, 2023, https://obj.ca/ottawa-titans-pitching-new-uses-for-stadium/. Accessed May 9, 2024.

51 Boyce interview.

52 Boyce interview.

53 Baseball Pilgrimages, "Current Ballparks," https://www.baseballpil-grimages.com/ballparks/current.html. Accessed May 9, 2024.

54 Canac Stadium in Quebec City has a capacity of 4,300 (for more, see "Sports facilities and competition venues," Quebec City Business Destination, https://meetings.quebec-cite.com/en/sports-events-quebec-city/sports-facilities-competition-venues). Quillorama Stadium in Trois-Rivieres has seating for 4,000 and standing room for 500 (see "Stade Quillorama," Tourisme Trois-Rivieres, https://www.tourismetroisrivieres.com/en/sports/facilities-and-equipment/stade-quillorama).

55 Michael Vavaroutsos, "Ottawa Titans Plan Further Changes To Make Baseball Park a More Social Space," *Capital Current*, October 11, 2023. https://capitalcurrent.ca/ottawa-titans-plan-further-changes-to-make-baseball-park-a-more-social-space/. Accessed April 8, 2024.

56 Ken Warren, "Powering Up: City Fixes Problem That Forced Re-scheduling of Ottawa Titans Games," *Ottawa Sun*, May 25, 2023.https://ottawasun.com/sports/baseball/titans-forced-to-play-morning-and-afternoon-games-due-to-power-issues. Accessed May 7, 2024; and Martin Boyce, telephone interview, April 11, 2024.

57 "Here To Stay: Regan Katz Committed To Baseball In Ottawa."

58 Statistics Canada, *The Daily – Spectator sports, event promoters, artists*, February 14, 2024. https://www150.statcan.gc.ca/n1/daily-quotidi-en/240214/dq240214c-eng.htm. Accessed May 7, 2024.

59 Ottawa Titans Baseball Club, "History," https://www.ottawatitans.com/history.

60 Ken Warren, "Ottawa Titans Talk About Positive Future Amid the Frustration of Losing Divisional Final," *Ottawa Sun*, September 12, 2022. https://ottawasun.com/sports/baseball/ottawa-titans-talk-about-positive-future-amid-the-frustra-tion-of-losing-divisional-final. Accessed May 7, 2024.

61 Ken Warren, "The Search for Fans: Ottawa's Minor Pro Squads Look To Fill More Seats," *Ottawa Sun*, May 19, 2023. https://ottawasun.com/sports/the-search-for-fans-ottawas-minor-pro-squads-look-to-fill-more-seats. Accessed April 8, 2024.

62 Frontier League website: "2022 Individual Statistics - Ottawa Titans - Ottawa Titans," https://www.frontierleague.com/sports/bsb/2021-22/teams/ottawatitans; "2022-23 Baseball Statistics - Ottawa Titans," https://www.frontierleague.com/sports/bsb/2022-23/teams/ottawatitans; "2023 Season Attendance," https://www.frontierleague.com/sports/bsb/2022-23/attendance/atten-dance?sort=ata&r=0&pos=att (all accessed May 10, 2024).

63 Frontier League, "All Frontier League Teams Increased Average Attendance in 2024," September 18, 2024, https://www.frontier-league.com/sports/bsb/2023-24/releases/20240918hly9wt. Accessed September 23, 2024.

64 Mark Singelais, "ValleyCats end season with wildcard loss to Ottawa," *Times Union*, September 3, 2024, https://www.timesunion.com/sports/article/valleycats-end-season-wildcard-loss-otta-wa-19739360.php. Accessed September 13, 2024.

65 Ottawa Titans Baseball Club, "Titans Strike First in Division Series with Walk-Off Win," September 6, 2024, https://www.ottawati-tans.com/titans-strike-first-in-division-series-with-walk-off-win, Accessed September 13, 2024.

66 Kevin Dubé, "Contre vents et marées, les Capitales de retour en finale: «Perdre n'était pas une option pour nous ce soir,»" *Journal de Québec*, September 8, 2024.

67 Boyce interview.

68 Boyce interview.

AN ALL-TIME OTTAWA ALL-STAR TEAM

BY DAVID MCDONALD

THERE ARE A NUMBER OF approaches one could take to choosing an all-star team from the passing parade of professional ballplayers—some on their way up, some on their way down, most of them going nowhere in particular—who have represented an on-and-off minor-league city like Ottawa since the late 1800s.

What we've tried to do is to identify the best players to have worn Ottawa uniforms, based not on what they did during their typically brief, often statistically unrepresentative stopovers in the city, but on their overall professional careers. We considered a player's major-league performance the primary criterion for selection, but we have also made allowances for those players whose careers were delayed, disrupted, or derailed by racial segregation and/or by military service. Longevity and a colorful personal backstory didn't hurt, either.

Here then is a fickle baseball town's all-time all-star team.

CATCHER

Wally Schang - Ottawa Senators, Can-Am League, 1939
Philadelphia Athletics, Boston Red Sox, New York Yankees, St. Louis Browns, Detroit Tigers, 1913-31.

Historian Bill James rates him the top catcher in baseball for the decade 1910-19 and the 20th-best catcher of all-time. In 19 years in the major leagues, from 1913 to 1931, the indestructible Schang batted .284/.393/.401 in 1842 games. A switch-hitter, he was the first player to homer from both sides of the plate in the same game. His on-base percentage (OBP) is second among major-league catchers all-time. Schang played on seven pennant winners and was a member of four World Series-winning teams.

In 1939 Schang came to Ottawa as playing manager of the Senators. It was the summer of his 50th birthday, and he batted .327/.484./.439. He last played professionally for Utica of the Eastern League in 1943. He was 53 years old.

FIRST BASE

Luke Easter - Ottawa A's, International League, 1954
Homestead Grays, 1947-48; Cleveland Indians, 1949-54.

"[T]hirty-four years for a rookie is starting with one
foot in the grave."[1]
—Bernard Malamud, *The Natural.*

A victim of baseball apartheid and a world war, the charismatic 6-foot-4, 240-to-250-pound Easter didn't make his American League debut, with the Cleveland Indians, until August 11, 1949, a week after his 34th birthday. Still, in his first three full seasons, he whacked 86 homers and drove in 307 runs. In 1952 *The Sporting News* named him Most Outstanding Player in the American League. Easter, often hobbled due to a series of foot, ankle, and knee injuries, batted .276/.356/.481 with 104 home runs over eight major league seasons.

Bill James ranks Easter the second-best first baseman in Negro League history, behind only Buck Leonard. And this despite the fact Easter didn't begin his Negro League career until 1947, when he was already 31. He played only two seasons, but it was enough to establish a near-mythical reputation as a Bunyanesque slugger.

In 1948, while with the pennant-winning Grays, he became the first player ever to hit a home run into the center-field bleachers at New York's Polo Grounds. The drive was estimated at 490 feet. Wrote James, "If you could clone him and bring him back, you'd have the greatest power hitter in baseball today, if not ever."[2]

In 1954, Easter—then 38—played 66 games for Ottawa, batting .348/.448/.587, with 15 home runs. He went on to play Triple-A ball for another decade. All told, Easter played 18 seasons of professional baseball and hit 351 home runs. He retired in 1964, aged 48. In 1979, he was shot to death during a robbery in Euclid, Ohio.

SECOND BASE

Mark Grudzielanek - Ottawa Lynx, International League, 1995
Montreal Expos, Los Angeles Dodgers, Chicago Cubs, St. Louis Cardinals, Kansas City Royals, Cleveland Indians, 1995-2010.

Grudzielanek batted .298 in 49 games at shortstop for the Lynx in 1995, earning him a call-up to the Expos. In his first full season, 1996, he was selected to the National League All-Star team en route to accumulating 201 hits, which places him behind only Vladimir Guerrero Sr. and Al Oliver on the Expos single-season hit list. In his second full season with the Expos, he knocked a major league-leading 54 doubles.

Five times during his 15-year major league career, Grudzielanek batted over .300, with a high of .326 for the Dodgers in 1999, when he set an NL record by hitting safely in 35 straight home games. In 2003 he slashed .314/.366/.416 for the Cubs and won an NL Silver Slugger Award for second basemen. At age 36 he was an AL Gold Glove winner at second base, for the Royals in 2006. During a 15-year career he batted .289 and was selected to the 1996 NL All-Star Team.

THIRD BASE

Bill "Wagon Tongue" Keister - Rochester Patriots-Ottawa Senators, Eastern League, 1898
Boston Beaneaters, St. Louis Cardinals, Baltimore Orioles (NL and AL), Washington Senators, Philadelphia Phillies. 1896, 1898-1903.

The speedy fireplug (5-foot-5, 168 pounds) Keister was dubbed "Wagon Tongue", not due to some anatomical anomaly, but from the practice in the 1800s of recycling the hard, seasoned wood of wagon tongues into baseball bats. So maybe the nickname was a nod to Keister's undeniable talent for hitting a baseball. But the moniker may also have been a play on "waggin' tongue" – signifying someone who had trouble keeping his mouth shut. That may have been a factor in Keister's inability to stick with any team for more than one season, but the fact he was also a dreadful fielder probably trumped other considerations.[3]

He sure could hit, though. Playing mostly third base for the Ottawa (née Rochester) club in 1898, Keister batted a typical .322. In each of his five full seasons (1899-1903) in the majors, he hit .300 or better, and he made the top 10 in slugging three times. In 1901 with his hometown Orioles, he tied with teammate Jimmy Williams for the AL lead in triples, with 21. In 1902 while with Washington, he became the second player in American League history to homer in four straight games.

Keister's major-league career ended in 1903 in rather puzzling fashion. Despite a .320 batting average he was not picked up for the following year. Overall, he batted .312/.349/.440.

SHORTSTOP

Orlando Cabrera - Ottawa Lynx, International League, 1997-1998, 2000
Montreal Expos, Boston Red Sox, Los Angeles Angels, Chicago White Sox, Oakland A's, Minnesota Twins, Cincinnati Reds, Cleveland Indians, San Francisco Giants, 1997-2011.

The Colombia-born Cabrera batted .248 with two home runs and 28 stolen bases over parts of three seasons with the Lynx. In 1999 he became the Expos regular shortstop, a position he held until being traded to the Red Sox in 2004. His best offensive season came with the Expos in 2003, when he slashed .297/.347/.460 with 17 home runs (the most ever by an Expos shortstop), 80 RBIs, and 24 stolen bases. In 2006 for the Angels he reached base in 63 consecutive games, the fourth longest streak in major-league history. But Cabrera's biggest asset was his glove. He won Gold Gloves for the Expos in 2001 and the Angels in 2007. With the White Sox in 2008, he was named Defensive Player of the Year by mlb.com.

Cabrera appeared nine times in the postseason. He won his only World Series in 2004, as the Red Sox broke the "Curse of the Bambino" and swept the Cardinals. Over 15 major-league

seasons, with nine teams, Cabrera batted .272/.317/.390 with 123 home runs, 854 RBIs, and 216 stolen bases.

OUTFIELD

Willard "Home Run" Brown - Ottawa Nationals, Border League, 1950
Kansas City Monarchs, 1937-1948; St. Louis Browns, 1947. National Baseball Hall of Fame, 2006.

Buck O'Neil called the Louisiana-born Brown "the most natural ballplayer I ever saw." Between 1937 and 1948, the Kansas City Monarchs star led the Negro American League in hits eight times, in RBIs seven times and in slugging six times. Brown and his fellow Monarchs—featuring Blackball greats like O'Neil, Satchel Paige, Double Duty Radcliffe, Bullet Rogan, Turkey Stearnes, and Elston Howard—captured eight pennants in his 11 seasons with the club. They also won the Negro Leagues World Series in 1942.

During those years he out-slugged the legendary Josh Gibson, the man who gave Brown his "Home Run" nickname. Brown captured the Negro American League batting crown with a .377 average in 1947. Three times he finished second. Eight times he led the league in RBI. His Negro Leagues batting line over 11 seasons, as per Baseball Reference, is .358/.407/.592 with an OPS+ of 185 (Ruth clocks in at 206, Ted Williams 191, and Barry Bonds 182).

On August 13, 1947, Brown became the first African American to hit a home run in the AL, an inside-the-park shot off future Hall of Famer Hal Newhouser. However, Brown, then 32, struggled to adapt to the newly-integrated environment and played just 21 games before being released and returning to the Monarchs.

Brown joined Ottawa for the 1950 pennant run and helped the club to its third Border League title in four years. In 30 games for the Nationals, the 35-year-old batted a typical .352. He continued playing minor-league ball until 1957, when he was 42. Brown died of Alzheimer's in 1996, aged 81.

Tim Raines Sr. - Ottawa Lynx, International League, 2001
Montreal Expos, Chicago White Sox, New York Yankees, Oakland A's, Baltimore Orioles, Florida Marlins, 1979-2002. National Baseball Hall of Fame, 2017.

His connection with Ottawa is pretty tenuous, having played just two games with the Lynx, on a rehab stint in 2001. It was, however, a memorable experience for Raines, as it gave him an opportunity to play a doubleheader against 21-year-old Tim Raines Jr., of the Rochester Red Wings. (Later that season the Raineses played the outfield together for the Orioles in a game against the Red Sox, becoming, after the Ken Griffeys, the only father-son combo to play in the majors at the same time.)

Raines compiled a .294/.385/.425 batting line over 23 major-league seasons, with 170 home runs and 980 RBIs. He won the NL batting title in 1986 with a .334 average. The speedy switch-hitter was a seven-time All-Star and a four-time NL stolen base leader. His 808 stolen bases place him fifth on the all-time list, just behind Ty Cobb. He was a member of the Yankees Series-winning teams of 1996 and 1998.

Taft "Taffy" Wright - Ottawa A's, International League, 1953-54
Washington Nationals, Chicago White Sox, Philadelphia Athletics, 1938-1942, 1946-49.

As a 26-year-old rookie with Washington in 1938, Wright, a left-handed contact hitter, led the AL with a .350 batting average. The batting crown, however, was awarded to future Hall of Famer Jimmie Foxx of the Red Sox, who batted .349. Although Wright managed to meet the then-minimum requirement for a batting title, namely 100 games played, many of his appearances came as a pinch-hitter. Wright played only 60 games *in the field*, and under what became known as the "Taffy Wright Rule", the league arbitrarily awarded the title to Foxx, the league MVP.

The ruling served, even in those pre-sabermetric days, to highlight the fundamental absurdity of crowning the player with the highest average but in limited action over a player who batted one percentage point less, but hit 50 home runs, drove in 175, and compiled a 1.166 OPS in 149 games—all in the field.

While Wright was no Jimmie Foxx, he was a consistent offensive threat. Despite losing more than three years to World War II in the middle of his career, he managed a .311 batting average over nine big-league seasons. Six times he hit over .300. Four times he finished in the AL top 10 for batting average. Three times he received MVP votes.

After 1949, Wright played and managed in the minors—and continued to hit. As a 41-year-old with the Ottawa A's in 1953, he led the International League in batting with a .354 average. The next season he also managed the club, which featured Luke Easter. Wright's final season came in 1956, when, as a 44-year-old, he again batted .354, this time for Orlando in the Florida State League. The man could always hit.

UTILITY PLAYER

Jamey Carroll - Ottawa Lynx, International League, 2000-2002
Montreal Expos, Washington Nationals, Colorado Rockies, Cleveland Indians, Los Angeles Dodgers, Minnesota Twins, Kansas City Royals, 2002-13.

This is perhaps the most potentially fraught selection in a city with an abiding affection for baseball grinders in the mold of Héctor López, F.P. Santangelo, Geoff Blum, and Jamey Carroll. Santangelo and Carroll, in fact, are the only two Lynx players to have had their numbers retired. All are worthy candidates in the utility category, but based on the fact Carroll played every position except first base and catcher during his 12-year big-league career while cobbling together a 17.0 WAR, we've chosen him as our all-star utility man.

A former college All-American Carroll didn't hit for much power—only 13 homers in the major leagues—but he was adept at getting on base, compiling a .349 career OBP. And in 2006 he led NL second basemen in fielding percentage and range factor. His best offensive years came in 2006, when he batted .300/.377/.404 in 136 games for the Rockies, and in 2010, when he got into 133 games for the Dodgers and batted .291/.379/.339. In 2007 he played on the Rockies' team that lost the Series to the Red Sox. On October 3, 2004, Carroll scored the last-ever run for the Expos and was in the on-deck circle when Endy Chávez turned out the lights on the franchise.

Carroll played 291 games over three seasons for the Lynx, batting .269. For his major-league career, he batted .272/.349/.338.

DESIGNATED HITTER

Matt Stairs - Ottawa Lynx, International League, 1993
Montreal Expos, Boston Red Sox, Oakland A's, Chicago Cubs, Milwaukee Brewers, Pittsburgh Pirates, Kansas City Royals, Texas Rangers, Detroit Tigers, Toronto Blue Jays, Philadelphia Phillies, San Diego Padres, 1992-2011.

Matt Stairs is the best bench player of all time. Bill James said so.[4] And he also said that if Stairs's talent had been recognized earlier and managed properly, he might well have put up Hall of Fame numbers. Per at-bat, he hit more home runs and drove in more runs than Hall of Fame sluggers Orlando Cepeda, Billy Williams, and Eddie Murray, and more than power-hitting contemporaries like Jack Clark and Joe Carter. By James's reckoning, Stairs's career numbers are better than Roger Maris's, comparable to those of Reggie Jackson, Frank Howard, Dale Murphy, and Greg Luzinski.

Despite his potent bat the Saint John, New Brunswick-born Stairs didn't get 400 at-bats in a major-league season until he was 30, and he only managed that four times in his career. His best season came in 1999, when the then-31-year-old slashed .258/.366/.533 with 38 home runs as designated hitter for Billy Beane's "Moneyball" A's. Part of Stairs' chronic shortage of playing time is attributable to the fact he wasn't a great defensive player. But a lot of it was no doubt an image problem. He just didn't look the part. At 5-foot-9, 200-something pounds, Stairs looked more like a slo-pitch softballer than professional baseball player.

Instead of being remembered in elite baseball company Stairs has had to settle for the distinction of holding the major-league record for pinch-hit home runs—23—over a 19-year career, which lasted until he was 43. In 2008, a Stairs pinch-hit blast produced the winning runs for the eventual World Series champion Phillies in their NLCS win over the Dodgers. All told he hit 265 major-league home runs, 294 doubles, and drove in 899 runs.

For the Lynx in 1993, Stairs batted .280 with three homers in 34 games, before moving on to the Chunichi Dragons of the Japanese Central League, then finishing up the year in Montreal.

RIGHT-HANDED STARTER

Urban Shocker - Ottawa Senators, Canadian League, 1914-15
New York Yankees, St. Louis Browns, 1916-28.

In April 1914 Senators center fielder/manager/part-owner Frank Shaughnessy embarked on one of his regular spring cross-border shopping trips and came back with a 23-year-old catcher-turned-pitcher with just 16 Class-D professional appearances under his belt and a tabloid headline for a name. He was Urban Shocker (born Urbain Jacques Shockcor, in Cleveland, Ohio), but in Ottawa everyone called him Herbie.

Ottawa marked a crucial stage in Shocker's development as a pitcher. It was here he learned his go-to pitch – the spitball – from a fellow Senator. Shocker led the Senators with 20 wins in 1914, including a pennant-clinching victory on the final afternoon of the season. He won 19 more in 1915, as the Senators won their fourth consecutive title. That fall the Yankees shelled out $750 to draft him from the Senators.

Pitching for the Toronto Maple Leafs of the International League in 1916, Shocker pitched an 11-inning no-hitter. It came in the midst of a 54 1/3-inning scoreless streak (the major league record is 59, set by the Dodgers' Orel Hershiser in 1988). In 1918 he was drafted again, this time into the U.S. Army, serving in France.

When the major leagues banned the spitter in 1920, Shocker and 16 others were grandfathered for the remainder of their careers. The ill-fated hurler turned out to be the best player the Canadian League (1912-15) ever produced. He would go on to win 187 big-league games for the Browns and the Yankees, including a tie for the major-league lead with 27 for the Browns in 1921. He won 20 games or more in four straight seasons, 1920-23. In 1927 he was 18-6 for the Murderers' Row Yankees. A year later he was dead of a congenital heart ailment. He was 37.

LEFT-HANDED STARTER

Ted Lilly - Ottawa Lynx, International League, 1998-99
Montreal Expos, New York Yankees, Oakland A's, Toronto Blue Jays, Chicago Cubs, Los Angeles Dodgers, 1999-2013.

Our closest battle for a spot on the All-Time Ottawa All-Star team comes down to a choice between three eerily similar Lynx southpaws – Lilly, J.A. Happ (2007), and fan favorite Kirk Rueter (1993-96).

Lilly made 23 starts, Happ 24 for the Lynx. Both had 15-year big-league careers. Rueter by comparison made 31 Lynx starts and went on to pitch 13 years in the majors.

Rueter started 336 major-league games, Lilly 331, Happ 328. Lilly and Happ both averaged 35 games and 33 starts per 162 team games, Reuter 34 games and 34 starts.

Happ gave up 1822 career hits, Lilly 1827, Rueter 2092. Lilly and Happ surrendered an identical .421 slugging percentage, Rueter .435.

Happ won 133 major-league games, Rueter and Lilly 130. All three averaged 13 wins per 162 games played by their teams. For their careers, Happ had a 4.13 career ERA, Lilly 4.14, and Rueter 4.27.

It's hardly surprising then that the most similar pitcher in major-league history to Ted Lilly, as ranked by Baseball Reference's Bill James-inspired Similarity Scores, is none other than J.A. Happ. And Lilly and Happ, in turn, are two of the 10 most similar pitchers to Kirk Rueter. In statistical terms all three are virtually the same player.

To determine which one of these copycat southpaws ultimately deserves our all-star nod, we consulted some of the advanced sabermetrics intended to lessen statistical noise and produce context-neutral comparisons. By ERA+ Lilly, at 106, has a slight edge over Happ (100) and Rueter (97). In Wins Above Replacement (WAR), a measure of how many wins a particular player provides his team over some imaginary fringe major leaguer, Lilly is credited with 27.1, while Happ and Rueter lag behind at 21.1 and 16.0 respectively. By the Jaffe WAR Score (JAWS), which measures a player's Hall of Fame worthiness by comparing him to the players at his position who are already in Cooperstown, Lilly scores 25.8, Happ 20.8, and Rueter 15.5. In Win Probability Added (WPA), Lilly is at 7.1, Happ 3.5, and Rueter 0.1.

By these metrics, Ted Lilly emerges by a slight margin as the best of the southpaw starters to have come through Ottawa. He was an All-Star in both major leagues, for the Blue Jays in 2004 and the Cubs in 2009. Four times he finished in the top 10 in his league in strikeouts per nine innings and in WHIP. Probably his best year came with the Cubs in 2008, when he started a league-leading 34 games and won 17. He pitched five times in the postseason, but failed to make it to the Series. In 2015 Lilly was convicted of insurance fraud in California related to a claim on a damaged RV.

SHORT RELIEF

Ugueth Urbina - Ottawa Lynx, International League, 1995-96
Montreal Expos, Boston Red Sox, Texas Rangers, Florida Marlins, Detroit Tigers, Philadelphia Phillies, 1995-2005.

Strangely for a pitcher who led the NL with 41 saves in 1999 and recorded 237 during an 11-year big-league career, the memorably-monikered Ugueth Urtain Urbina, brother of Ulmer Ulysses Urbina, never recorded a save in the minors. Urbina, in fact, started 16 games for the Lynx over parts of two seasons, winning eight and losing two. He was part of the of the 1995 squad that won the city's only Governor's Cup. He started 17 games for the Expos in 1996, before becoming a full-time reliever the following year.

A two-time all-star, Urbina was the losing pitcher for the NL in the 1998 classic. In 2003, he appeared in 10 postseason games for the World Series-champion Florida Marlins, winning one and saving four more, including two in the final. In 2005, his final major-league season, he appeared in a career-high 81 games for the Tigers and Phils.

Urbina's career came to an ignominious end when he was charged later that year in his native Venezuela with attempting to kill five farm laborers on his ranch. He was convicted and sentenced to 14 years in prison. He was released in 2012 after serving half of his sentence.

LONG RELIEF

Greg A. Harris - Ottawa Lynx, International League, 1995
New York Mets, Cincinnati Reds, Montreal Expos, San Diego Padres, Texas Rangers, Philadelphia Phillies, Boston Red Sox, New York Yankees, 1981-1995

Harris was 3-0 with a 1.06 ERA in 11 games for the '95 International League champions. A durable journeyman, he tossed 1,467 innings for eight teams over 15 major league seasons. In 1984 he threw a scoreless 5 1/3 innings for the Padres in their World Series loss to the Tigers. In 1993 he led the AL in games pitched, with 80.

But the ambidextrous Harris is perhaps best remembered for a switch-pitching performance—the first in the majors in baseball's modern era—in 1995. The 40-year-old Harris, then the oldest player in the NL and in the penultimate game of his career, threw both right- and left-handed in a hitless ninth inning for the Expos against the Cincinnati Reds. His major-league totals: a 74-90 record with a 3.69 ERA and 54 saves in 1,467 innings of work.

CLOSER

Eric Gagné - Ottawa Champions, Can-Am League, 2016
Los Angeles Dodgers, Texas Rangers, Boston Red Sox, Milwaukee Brewers, 1999-2008.

OK, so the 2003 NL Cy Young winner and three-time All-Star has an even flimsier connection with Ottawa than Tim Raines. Gagné's came in 2016 as a late-season promotional stunt for the Champions: two hits and one run allowed over five innings of work as a starter. But these are our rules, so we'll take both of them.

In three seasons between 2002 and 2004 the Montreal-born Gagné made 224 appearances and recorded 152 saves for the Dodgers, including a major-league-leading 55 in his Cy Young season. He made the NL All-Star team all three seasons during that stretch, as he recorded ERAs of 1.97, 1.20 and 2.19. But the heavy workload exacted a physical toll, and he threw only 15 1/3 innings for the Dodgers over the next two years.

Gagné had one more decent season in "The Show", recording 16 saves in 54 games for Texas and Boston in 2007. That year he made his only World Series appearance, a hitless inning for the Red Sox as they swept the Rockies four games to none. Over his injury-shortened 10-year career Gagné totaled 187 saves and a 3.47 ERA.

NOTES

1   Bernard Malamud. *The Natural*. (New York: Farrar, Straus and Giroux, 2003, 43.)

2   Bill James. *The New Bill James Historical Baseball Abstract*. (New York: Free Press, 2001, 181.)

3   How bad was he? Playing shortstop for Baltimore in 1901, Keister committed an AL-record 97 errors in 112 games and established the major-league record for lowest fielding average for a shortstop (minimum 100 games), .851. However, in equal time as a major-league second baseman Keister fared much better, managing a respectable career .936 fielding average.

4   Bill James, "The Greatest Bench Players of All Time." https://www.billjamesonline.com/the_greatest_bench_players_of_all_time/, October 3, 2014.

HOMETOWN HEROES: OTTAWA'S MAJOR LEAGUERS, EACH WITH A STORY TO TELL

BY CHRISTOPHER SAILUS

As a national capital, the City of Ottawa and its environs attract some of the best and brightest of our country. It's not uncommon to be having dinner with coworkers or acquaintances and meet people who hail from Quebec City, Vancouver, Newfoundland, or the far north.

Ottawa and the federal government tend to be such a magnet that it is a little more rare to see the reverse. In baseball terms, that means seeing Ottawa's best ballplayers make it big further afield—in Toronto, the United States, or perhaps Japan or South Korea—and represent the national capital region on baseball's greatest stages. This chapter will help you get better acquainted with those lucky and hard-working few who have been able to turn their passion for the game they loved into a major-league career.

While there may not be an extensive roster to pull from, the region has contributed ballplayers that fit virtually every traditional mold—and some even a little less traditional. These include colorful figures from some of baseball's earliest days as an organized professional sport, like North Gower's Jack Humphries. They include career relievers with enough talent to get to "The Show" but not quite enough to stay there, like George Korince and Chris Mears. They include rangy, hard-hitting outfielders like Doug Frobel, and towering, flame-throwing journeymen relievers like Philippe Aumont. And they even include top of the card talent like Orioles and Mariners staff ace Érik Bédard or All-Star catcher Russell Martin.

Ottawa may not be a baseball hotbed like the deserts of Arizona or the plains of the American south but, as one can see, it has still turned out plenty of players who brought with them their distinctly Ottawa character.

JACK HUMPHRIES

BY DAVID MCDONALD

Remember Mathewson, Ames, and Donlin,
Buck Ewing, Rusie, Smiling Mickey Welch?
Remember a left–handed catcher named Jack Humphries,
Who sometimes played the outfield, in '83?

—From Rolfe Humphries, "Polo Grounds."[1]

BY THE USUAL BASEBALL BENCHMARKS, Jack Humphries' major-league career was the definition of forgettable: a puny .143 batting average in 98 games as a backup catcher with the New York Gothams and Washington Nationals in the 1880s.

But that's not to say Humphries' life and career weren't noteworthy. He was, after all, the first native of the Ottawa area, the first graduate of Cornell, and the first Phi Beta Kappa to make it to the major leagues. And after his brief fling with big-time baseball ended, he became a minor-league manager, an educator, and a mentor to an eminent American poet, classicist, and translator, his son Rolfe.

John Henry Humphries was born in 1861[2] in North Gower[3], then a bustling lumber town of five boot and shoe shops, four general stores, three churches, two wagon shops and a post office, located just south of Ottawa. Humphries' father, possibly a bookkeeper, came from England in the 1850s and married a local girl of Irish descent. In 1866 the family moved to Syracuse, New York, where young Jack developed into a star athlete and student. Despite throwing left-handed, he insisted on catching.[4]

In 1879 Humphries won a scholarship to study Science and Letters at Cornell College[5], in Ithaca, New York, where he became captain of the varsity baseball team. He was known to have the strongest throwing arm at Cornell, twice capturing the baseball-throwing

Jack Humphries Credit: Courtesy David McDonald.

event at the school's spring athletic meet. But most of all Jack Humphries was tough, perhaps the prime requisite for a catcher in those days of minimal protective gear. He was once ordered to sit out a college game because of a hand injury, but refused. "When he got through," said one report, "his hand looked as though encased in a boxing glove."[6]

During his senior year at Cornell, 1883, Humphries was recruited to play for the National League's fledgling New York franchise, the Gothams.[7] According to his future wife, Florence Yost, Jack was "much criticized, not to say berated"[8] by his university-educated peers for his choice of career. But Jack insisted baseball would be a pleasant way to earn a living. And, early on, that was probably the case.

A week or two after graduation, the 21-year-old Humphries found himself behind the plate in the Polo Grounds catching future Hall of Famer "Smiling Mickey" Welch. It was a debut that earned a thumb's-up from the *New York Times:* "The position of catcher was filled up to the mark by Humphries … He supported Welch in fine style, and threw to the bases very accurately."[9]

The strapping, 6-foot, 185-pound rookie also earned favorable notice from the New York fans. One young woman described the youngest Gotham as being "as good looking as a real oil painting."[10]

On July 13, 1883, Humphries partnered with James "Tip" O'Neill, the

"Woodstock Wonder," to form the first Canadian-born battery in big-league history.

Despite the presence of O'Neill and four future Hall of Famers in the lineup—Welch, catcher Buck Ewing, slugging first baseman Roger Connor, and pitcher John Montgomery Ward—the Gothams finished a dismal sixth in 1883, 16 games behind the pennant-winning Beaneaters of Boston.

Humphries batted just .112 in 29 games, but the Gothams were happy with his defensive work and made him one of 11 players reserved for 1884. During the offseason, Humphries obtained his release from New York—the reason why is unclear—to accept an offer from the Minneapolis Millers of the Northwestern League. However, at the last minute, he changed his mind and signed with the Washington Nationals, aka Statesmen, of the major-league American Association.

As the first-string catcher for the sad-sack Nationals, Humphries was batting .176 when the club folded on August 2, 1884, having won just 12 of 63 games. He immediately re-upped with the Gothams, but batted only .094 for the rest of the National League season.

In the spring of 1885 Humphries, uncertain of his future at baseball's top level, accepted an offer to captain the Syracuse Stars of the newly-organized New York State League. His big-league career was over.

For Humphries, playing in his adopted hometown was mostly a positive experience. Highlights included catching a no-hitter thrown by Guelph, Ontario's Bob Emslie, against Oneida, and a 5-0 exhibition victory over Cap Anson's National League champion Chicago White Stockings before 10,000 fans in Syracuse. He was widely considered the best catcher in the league.

In September Stars manager Henry Ormsbee resigned[11], and 23-year-old Jack Humphries replaced him. Under his leadership the Stars coasted to the pennant. "Humphries has worked hard this season, and to him is to a large extent due the success of the Stars," wrote the *Syracuse Standard*.[12]

The Stars, however, dithered in signing players for the following season, and Humphries accepted an offer as player-manager of the Toronto Canucks of the newly formed International League. "Base ball is booming," wrote *Sporting Life*, "and so is Toronto."[13] The Canucks, unsettled by the death in a swimming accident of their leading hitter, 26-year-old third baseman Billy Smith, performed poorly in the second half of the season and slid from first to third place.

At season's end, anxious to escape the negativity surrounding the team, Humphries reportedly shelled out $200 to secure his own release. He then signed a pre-ar-

ranged $1,800 deal to play for and manage the rival Rochester Maroons.

Wrote *Sporting Life*'s Rochester correspondent, "In Mr. Humphries they have an educated, gentlemanly manager, who is well up in base ball and fully capable of taking complete charge of the team for 1887..."[14]

But the 1887 Maroons were an unruly bunch, even by the standards of the day, and Humphries, as he had been in Toronto, was soon under fire from the Rochester press.

"Jack Humphries, catcher-manager, had little control over off-diamond activities of this aggregation," says a 1950 history of Rochester baseball. "Rollicking Rochesters flirted with hops and barley, and were the drinkingest fish yet spawned in International pool. Always in hock to management and town bar-keeps, they were known as the good-time Charleys of a riotous league."[15]

The Charleys stumbled home in seventh place. Humphries batted .276 in 28 games. He was released in October.

For Humphries, baseball seemed further away than ever from the "pleasant way to make a living" he'd envisioned when he left Cornell five years before. That fall he decided he'd had enough of life in the professional trenches and went to work at a Syracuse insurance firm, while playing semipro ball on the side.

On June 30, 1890, Humphries married fellow Cornell Phi Beta Kappa Florence Yost, the daughter of George W. N. Yost, the eccentric genius behind the invention of some of the most popular early typewriters. The Humphries moved to Philadelphia and both pursued careers in education. Jack became principal in charge of 2,000 students at the venerable Philadelphia High School for Girls. In 1912 the Humphries and their five children, including future poet Rolfe, moved to California, where Jack taught Latin and math for the rest of his career.

Jack Humphries, the classically educated left-handed catcher, died in Salinas, California, in 1933.

A longer profile of Jack Humphries can be found at https://sabr.org/bioproj/person/jack-humphries/

NOTES

1   First published in *The New Yorker*, August 22, 1942: 22.

2   Major baseball reference works invariably give Humphries' birthdate as November 12. However, John Humphries Jr. told Hall of Fame historian Lee Allen in 1962 that his father's actual birthdate was November 15.

3   North Gower is now part of the City of Ottawa.

4   Only 30 left-handers have ever caught a big-league game. Humphries modest 75 appearances behind the plate still

rank him seventh all-time. The last southpaw to catch a major-league game was the Pittsburgh Pirates' Benny Distefano in 1989.

5 Now Cornell University.

6 Quoted by Peter Morris in *Catcher: How the Man Behind the Plate Became an American Folk Hero* (Chicago: Ivan R. Dee, 2009), 52.

7 Later the New York Giants, now the San Francisco Giants.

8 Quoted in Richard Gillman and Michael Paul Novak, editors, *Poets, Poetics, and Politics: America's Literary Community Viewed From the Letters of Rolfe Humphries, 1910-1969* (Lawrence, Kansas: University Press of Kansas, 1992), 11.

9 "Base-Ball," *New York Times*, July 8, 1883.

10 "Luck, Pluck and Muscle," *Syracuse Standard*, August 2, 1883.

11 Stars manager Henry Ormsbee, a veteran performer and stage manager, left to prepare for an opera he was mounting in the offseason.

12 "Two Games To-Day, Humphries Made Manager of the Stars in Place of Mr. Ormsbee," *Syracuse Standard*, September 18, 1885.

13 "The Canadians," *Sporting Life*, April 14, 1886.

14 "Base Ball," *Sporting Life*, January 12, 1887.

15 Jim Mandelaro and Scott Pitoniak, *Silver Seasons: The Story of the Rochester Red Wings* (Syracuse, New York: Syracuse University Press, 1996), 7.

DOUG FROBEL

BY JOHN FREDLAND

Nepean's doug frobel started in right field for the Pittsburgh Pirates on Opening Day 1984, seven years after signing out of a Utica, New York, tryout camp. Offensive struggles limited his big-league career to five seasons, but the 6-foot-4, lefty-swinging Frobel was part of a small group of Canadians to reach the majors in the years before the country's amateurs became subject to the major-league draft in 1991.[1]

Born in Ottawa on June 6, 1959,[2] Doug Frobel was the son of Frank "Chummy" Frobel, a distinguished fast-pitch softball pitcher,[3] and Helen Warwick. He was the youngest of seven siblings.[4] In 1972 Doug's brother Tim, also a star athlete in Nepean, died of a heart attack at the age of 16. "Timmy was probably the biggest driving force I had," Doug Frobel said in 1981. "I've always been trying to be better than what I thought Timmy would be."[5]

Frobel attended Merivale High School, where he played football and hockey.[6] In the summer, he pitched and played third base for the amateur Ottawa Canadians at both the Connie Mack (ages 16-18) and North Eastern States Baseball League (no age limit) levels.[7] He led the Canadians to the North Eastern States Baseball League championship at the Nepean Sportsplex in August 1977, hitting three home runs and earning tournament MVP honors.[8]

Frobel's play with the Canadians resulted in an invitation to a Pirates' tryout camp.[9] He signed with Pittsburgh after impressing scouts with 400-foot home runs and sub-6.8-second 60-yard sprints.[10] In 1980, his third professional season, he emerged as a prospect with 20 homers at Class A.[11]

Climbing to Double A and Triple A in the next two seasons, Frobel shifted to right field,[12] hit a combined 51 home runs, and debuted with Pittsburgh in September 1982 as just the third-ever Ottawa Valley area native to reach the big leagues.[13]

Frobel grew up as a Montreal Expos fan,[14] and many of his early major-league milestones involved Canadian foes. His first hit was a single off Hall of Fame-bound Fergie Jenkins.[15] His first start was against the Expos at Olympic Stadium.[16] He hit his first two home runs off Montreal's Charlie Lea and Bill Gullickson in Pittsburgh.[17]

The Pirates returned Frobel to Triple A in 1983.[18] He was batting .304 with 24 home runs in August when a thumb injury sidelined left fielder Mike Easler.[19] With Pittsburgh in a four-team National League East Division race, Frobel started regularly against right-handed pitching during Easler's three-week absence. In his first game up, he hit a tie-breaking double against Expos star Steve Rogers; later, he homered in back-to-back wins over the New York Mets.[20]

Pittsburgh was in transition after two World Series championships and five division titles in the 1970s. When future Hall of Famer Willie Stargell singled in his final game before retiring in 1982, Frobel was the pinch-runner.[21] In December 1983, right fielder Dave Parker—a four-time All-Star, two-time batting champ, and the 1978 NL MVP as a Pirate—signed with the Cincinnati Reds, creating an opening for Frobel.[22]

One of only two Canadians in the majors in 1984—along with Saskatchewan-born Houston Astros outfielder Terry Puhl—Frobel was in right field when the Pirates opened in San Diego on April 3. He went hitless, striking out on three pitches against Rich Gossage, a high-profile free agent making his Padres debut.[23] Newspapers around the league pitilessly described Gossage's dominance.[24] By May 19 Frobel was batting just .139. He became an infrequent presence in Pittsburgh's box scores, making scattered starts or appearing as a defensive replacement.

Still, Frobel had a handful of 1984 highlights: breaking up rookie phenom Dwight Gooden's no-hitter; slugging two homers, including a tape-measure shot, in a game at Wrigley Field; and beating Gossage with an 11th-inning RBI double.[25] He finished with 12 home runs in 276 at-bats, but he struck out 84 times and had a .203 batting average.

Frobel dropped on the depth chart when the Pirates, who finished last in the division in 1984, acquired three veteran outfielders during the 1984-85 offseason.[26] An injury to one of the newcomers, Steve Kemp, led to Frobel starting in left field on Opening Day 1985,[27] but his playing time diminished when Kemp returned. The Pirates sold Frobel to the Expos in August 1985.[28] He appeared in 12 games with the Expos, who traded him to the Mets in April 1986.[29] He spent the entire '86 season in Triple-A Tidewater.

The Cleveland Indians gave Frobel another shot in the majors in 1987. In his second plate appearance, he pinch-hit a walk-off home run against Chicago White Sox reliever Bob James.[30] But Frobel hit only .100 in 40 at-bats with Cleveland. He spent the next two seasons trying to catch on with the Expos and White Sox organizations until tearing ligaments in his thumb in 1989, which ended his career.[31]

Frobel became a batting instructor after his retirement, hosting youth clinics.[32] He was inducted into the Nepean Sports Wall of Fame, Ottawa Sport Hall of Fame, and Ottawa Nepean Canadians Hall of Fame. In 2000, Nepean named a city park in his honor.[33]

NOTES

1   There are only eight players who attended high school in Canada; signed with major-league teams as amateur free agents between 1965, when the draft was instituted, and 1991; and appeared in 100 or more big-league games: Reggie Cleveland (signed with St. Louis Cardinals in 1965, 428 games), Dave McKay (signed with Minnesota Twins in 1971, 645 games), Terry Puhl (signed with Houston Astros in 1973, 1,531 games), Frobel (signed with Pirates in 1977, 268 games), Rob Ducey (signed with Toronto Blue Jays in 1984, 703 games), Larry Walker (signed with Montreal Expos in 1984, 1,988 games), Matt Stairs (signed with Expos in 1989, 1,895 games), and Rob Butler (signed with Blue Jays in 1990, 109 games). Two other Canadian natives during this period attended colleges in the United States, were drafted by major-league teams, and appeared in 100 or more games: Steve Wilson (drafted by Texas Rangers in 1985, 205 games) and Rheal Cormier (drafted by Cardinals in 1988, 683 games).

2   Nepean was a separate municipality outside of Ottawa until 2001, when it became part of the city.

3   Eddie MacCabe, "Fastball Great Enters the Hall," *Ottawa Citizen*, May 10, 1984: 51.

4   Bob Elliott, "From Nepean to Pittsburgh on Memories and a Big Bat," *Ottawa Citizen*, January 17, 1981: 17.

5   Elliott, "From Nepean to Pittsburgh on Memories And a Big Bat"

6   Gerry Dulac, "Bucs Singing Praises of Ex-Iceman Frobel," *Pittsburgh Press*, August 17, 1983: B-12.

7   "Frobel Spins 3-Hitter," *Ottawa Journal,* July 19, 1977: 18; Bob Elliott, "Pirates Snatch Frobel," *Ottawa Journal*, August 25, 1977: 15.

8   "A Frobel Finish," *Ottawa Journal*, August 15, 1977: 14; Elliott, "Pirates Snatch Frobel." The Canadians beat teams from three cities in New York – Rome, Kingston, and Utica – in the tournament.

9   Elliott, "From Nepean to Pittsburgh on Memories and a Big Bat."

10   Elliott, "From Nepean to Pittsburgh on Memories And a Big Bat"; Dan Turner, "Still Living The Dream: Unlike Roy Hobbs, Frobel Works for Everything," *Ottawa Citizen*, August 14, 1987: B1.

11   Dan Donovan, "Here's Rundown on Young Bucs," *Pittsburgh Press*, March 10, 1981: C-1.

12   "Pirates Must Make Move in Drive for Division Title," *Pittsburgh Press*, September 3, 1982: C-1.

13   Catcher Jack Humphries appeared in 98 games with the National League's New York franchise (later the Giants) and American Association's Washington Nationals in 1883 and 1884, and George Korince pitched in 11 games with the Detroit Tigers in 1966 and 1967.

14   Bob Elliott, "A Long Way to Major Ball," *Ottawa Citizen*, September 28, 1982: 17.

15   United Press International, "First Hit for Pride of Nepean," *Ottawa Citizen*, September 16, 1982: 21.

16   Russ Franke, "Bucs Exit Quietly in 9-4 Loss to Expos," *Pittsburgh Press*, September 25, 1982: D-4.

17   Bob Elliott, "Fanning's Exit Doesn't Guarantee Expos '83 Title," *Ottawa Citizen*, October 5, 1982: 19.

18   Russ Franke, "Bucs Deep in Vets, Somebody Must Go," *Pittsburgh Press*, March 6, 1983: D-2.

19   "Easler 'Disabled,' Frobel Called Up," *Pittsburgh Post-Gazette*, August 11, 1983: 22; Bob Elliott, "Frobel Finally Gets Chance to Show Stuff," *Ottawa Citizen*, August 13, 1983: 63.

20   Ian MacDonald, "Pena, Canadian Frobel Help Bucs Creep Up on Expo [sic]," *Montreal Gazette*, August 13, 1983: H-1; Dan Donovan, "Rookies Major Factors in Pirates' 4th Straight Victory: DeLeon, Frobel Overpower Mets," *Pittsburgh Press*, August 16, 1983: D-1; Helene Elliott, "Frobel's Bat Hurts Mets Again," *Newsday* (New York, Suffolk), August 17, 1983: 106.

21   Paul Jayes, "He Pops One: Stargell Singles in Last Time at Bat as Pirate," *Pittsburgh Post-Gazette*, October 4, 1982: 1.

22   Bob Hertzel, "Parker Makes His Move, Signs 2-Year, $1.6 Million Deal with Reds," *Pittsburgh Press*, December 8, 1983: D-4.

23   Bob Smizik, "Pirates Discover Gossage Can Still Cook Their Goose," *Pittsburgh Press*, April 4, 1984: B1; Bud Shaw, "Goose's Fast Start Heats Things up," *San Diego Tribune*, April 4, 1984: C-1.

24   Tracy Ringolsby, "Down-the-Middle Players are up the Creek on 1st and 15th," *Kansas City Star*, April 8, 1984: SPORTS, 4; Chris Mortensen, "Goose Having Fun Again," *Atlanta Journal-Constitution*, April 1, 1984: 7-D.

25   Associated Press, "Frobel Stops Gooden's No-Hitter," *Ottawa Citizen*, June 7, 1984: 43; Bob Hertzel, "Frobel Breaks Tape with Long Home Run," *Pittsburgh Press*, June 27, 1984: D3; Bob Hertzel, "Frobel's Payback Against Gossage Prevents Sweep," *Pittsburgh Press*, July 23, 1984: C5.

26   The Pirates acquired George Hendrick in a trade with the St. Louis Cardinals and Steve Kemp in a trade with the New York Yankees. They also signed Sixto Lezcano, formerly of the Philadelphia Phillies, as a free agent. Bob Hertzel, "Mum's the Word: Hendrick's a Pirate," *Pittsburgh Press*, December 13, 1984: D1; Bob Hertzel, "Ueberroth Reportedly OKs

Kemp-Berra Deal," *Pittsburgh Press*, December 20, 1984: D1; Bruce Keidan, "Lezcano Signs With Bucs: Power Hitter Accepts Deal for Two Years," *Pittsburgh Post-Gazette*, January 23, 1985: 13.

27 Bob Hertzel, "Frobel Won't Be Left Out," *Pittsburgh Press*, April 8, 1985: D2.

28 Charley Feeney, "Pirates Sell Frobel to Expos," *Pittsburgh Post-Gazette*, August 12, 1985: 9.

29 Bob Elliott, "Expos Trade Frobel to Mets' Organization for 2 Players," *Ottawa Citizen*, April 8, 1986: D2.

30 Paul Hoynes, "Indians Win on Frobel's HR in 9th," *Cleveland Plain Dealer*, April 30, 1987: 1-E.

31 Bob Smizik, "Frobel's Opportunity for a Big Hit Went Foul," *Pittsburgh Press*, April 9, 1990: B2.

32 Don Campbell, "Frobel Takes Show on the Road," *Ottawa Citizen*, April 28, 1990: E3.

33 Jocelyn Bell, "Nepean Plans to Rename Park After Early Settlers: Council Also Plans to Rename Park After Baseball Player," *Ottawa Citizen*, August 26, 2000: C3.

CHRIS MEARS

BY JORDAN PRESS

CHRIS MEARS IS USED TO traveling for work.

But in June 2010, the Boston Red Sox sent Mears somewhere he hadn't expected: the Major League Baseball Network studios in Secaucus, New Jersey.[1] The reason? The team wanted him to fill in for Hall of Famer Jim Rice as the person who would announce which players the team was selecting in that month's draft.[2]

Mears, as a scout, had a role in choosing those players, some of whom were coming out of high school like he once did.

"We're trying to find out, particularly with the high school kids being drafted, that they know what lies ahead and determine whether they're ready to make the commitment necessary to play professionally," Mears told *The Province* newspaper in British Columbia just after the draft.[3]

"I know I had no idea what I'd go through when I was drafted, and I try to use my story to help them understand."

Christopher Peter Mears was born in Ottawa on January 20, 1978.[4] He didn't live in Ottawa for very long, as his family moved to Toronto while he was in elementary school.

He spent his teenage years at Lord Byng Secondary School in Vancouver's west side, where he caught the attention of scouts. In 1996, the Seattle Mariners took Mears in the fifth round of the draft.[5]

Mears made stops with 11 minor-league teams over 10 seasons.[6] Some of those places he visited more than once. And he showed promise on more than one occasion.

With the Wisconsin Timber Rattlers in 1999, Mears went 10–1 and was selected to play in the Midwest League's all-star game and in the first Futures Game.[7]

The Mariners released Mears after the 2002 season and he signed with the Detroit Tigers.

In 2003, the 25-year-old Mears caught the eye of the big-league squad, going 5–1 with a 2.78 ERA for the Toledo Mud Hens.[8]

"In all the years I've been in baseball, I've never seen someone so excited to be going up," Mud Hens pitching coach Jeff Jones said at the time.[9]

Mears made his major-league debut on June 29, 2003. By early July, he had retired 21 of 23 batters that he faced, and had picked up three saves en route to five in total that season, which tied him for the team lead that year.[10]

"He's tall, and all arms and legs out there when he throws," Alan Trammell, then Detroit's manager, said that July.[11] "That can make it tough for hitters to pick up his pitches."

On September 25, the playoff-bound Minnesota Twins came to town as the Tigers, at 118 losses with four games to play, were closing in on the 1962 New York Mets' record of 120 regular-season losses.

A late Detroit rally sent the game into extra innings. Mears came out of the bullpen and set down six straight batters, striking out three, in the 10th and 11th innings.[12] With two outs in the bottom of the 11th, Shane Halter hit a solo home run to give the Tigers a 5–4 win. One of the game balls from that victory resides in Mears' home office—a reminder of his first, and only, major-league win.[13]

Mears pitched one more inning—a shutout seventh—three days later on the last day of the regular season. That inning was his last in the majors. He played for two more years in the minors and pitched for Team Canada at the 2004 Olympics before retiring in 2005.

Mears moved far from the diamond in retirement, working two years in banking before pining for a job in baseball.[14] He turned to folks he knew, including Gord Ash, former general manager of the Toronto Blue Jays, for ways to get involved in scouting and developing talent.[15] In 2008, the Red Sox hired him as an amateur scout.

"Getting out there and trying to find the next great player is an exciting proposition," Mears said at the time.[16]

"It's a good feeling to bring a good person into an organization and watch them contribute and get to the next level and ultimately to where they're making an impact in the big leagues."

Mears told *The Province* that he was interested in moving into the front office of a baseball club, possibly as an assistant to the general manager.[17] He may yet get the chance: the Red Sox made him a pitching crosschecker in 2015, promoted him to a pitching coordinator in 2020 and then moved him to cover the upper levels of the organization before the 2023 season.[18] [19]

NOTES

1   Tony Gallagher, "Mears making career of it in baseball," *The Province*, June 17, 2010.

2   "Jim Rice," National Baseball Hall of Fame and Museum. Accessed July 7, 2024, https://baseballhall.org/hall-of-famers/rice-jim.

3   "Mears making career of it in baseball."

4   "Chris Mears Stats, Age, Position, Height, Weight, Fantasy & News," MLB.com. Accessed July 4, 2024, https://www.mlb.com/player/chris-mears-277407.

5   "Chris Mears Stats, Height, Weight, Position, Rookie Status & More," Baseball-Reference.com. Accessed July 4, 2024, https://www.baseball-reference.com/players/m/mearsch01.shtml.

6   "Chris Mears Minor League Statistics," Baseball-Reference.com. Accessed July 4, 2024, https://www.baseball-reference.com/register/player.fcgi?id=mears-001chr.

7   "#12: Chris Mears - 1999," MiLB.com, https://www.milb.com/news/gcs-253618. Last accessed: July 8, 2024; "1999 Futures Game," Baseball-Reference.com. Accessed July 8, 2024, https://www.baseball-reference.com/bullpen/1999_Futures_Game.

8   "Chris Mears Minor League Statistics," Baseball-Reference.com. Accessed July 4, 2024, https://www.baseball-reference.com/register/player.fcgi?id=mears-001chr; *Huron Daily Tribune*, "Tigers Buy Mears' Contract From Toledo," June 28, 2003. Accessed July 8, 2024, https://www.michigansthumb.com/news/article/Tigers-Buy-Mears-Contract-From-Toledo-7333051.php.

9   Gene Guidi, "Bonderman and Ledezma limited," *Detroit Free Press*, July 11, 2003. Accessed July 9, 2024, Via Internet Archive: https://web.archive.org/web/20030713132015/https://www.freep.com/sports/tigers/tcorn11_20030711.htm/.

10   "Bonderman and Ledezma limited."

11   "Bonderman and Ledezma limited."

12   "Tigers 5-4 Twins (Sep 25, 2003) Play-by-Play," ESPN.com. Accessed July 9, 2024, https://www.espn.com/mlb/playbyplay/_/gameId/230925106.

13   Stephen J. Nesbitt and Cody Stavenhagen, "How the '03 Tigers stared down infamy — and won: 'We may be the worst team to ever play,'" *New York Times*, September 7, 2023.

14   Tony Gallagher, "Mears loves the life of a pro baseball scout," *The Province*, September 12, 2008.

15   "Mears loves the life of a pro baseball scout."

16   "Mears loves the life of a pro baseball scout."

17   "Mears loves the life of a pro baseball scout."

18   MLB.com, "Red Sox announce personnel moves in player development and Minor League field staffs," press release, January 16, 2020. Accessed July 6, 2024, https://www.mlb.com/press-release/press-release-red-sox-announce-personnel-moves-in-player-development-and-minor-l.

19   Chris Cotillo, "Red Sox lose both female minor league coaches in organization, announce full staffs," MassLive.com, January 27, 2023. Accessed July 10, 2024, https://www.masslive.com/redsox/2023/01/red-sox-lose-both-female-minor-league-coaches-in-organization-announce-full-staffs.html.

ÉRIK BÉDARD

BY JONATHON SYMONS

OPENING DAY OF THE 2007 season held special attention for Ottawa baseball fans—one of their own took the mound for his team's opening game for the first time.

Pitching for the Baltimore Orioles at the Metrodome, Érik Bédard fired a fastball down the middle to Twins leadoff man Luis Castillo for a called strike, the first pitch of a career year for the 28-year-old hurler.

Bédard was born on March 5, 1979 in Navan, Ontario, a suburb of Ottawa, to parents Normand and Nicole.[1] He was small and thin in his days with Orléans Little League, but a growth spurt in his senior year of high school resulted in a successful tryout with a community college in Connecticut. "I was five foot four and one hundred twenty pounds," Bédard told MLB.com journalist Spencer Fording in 2007. "That summer, I grew to 5-foot-11 and 150 pounds and went to college, where I gained about 30 pounds in four months."[2]

In his two-year stint at Norwalk Community College, Bédard led his club to a Junior College National Championship, while twice being named a JUCO All-American. This success led to the Orioles taking him in the sixth round of the 1999 major-league amateur draft.[3]

He quickly signed and, using his fastball, a devastating, late-breaking curve, and a developing sinker,[4] Bédard climbed a level every season. He was called up on April 17, 2002, and had his first taste of MLB action in that hallowed of ballparks, Yankee Stadium. Bédard entered in the bottom of the eighth and recorded his first strikeout by catching Robin Ventura swinging. He would appear in one more game that season before being sent back to Double A. Unfortunately, Bédard's rapid rise took a toll on his arm, and he was shut down in September 2002 with the dreaded UCL tear, requiring Tommy John surgery.

After sitting out most of the 2003 season, Bédard made the O's out of spring training in 2004. He would acquaint himself well in his rookie season, and by 2006 emerged as the staff ace in Baltimore, leading the club in all major pitching categories.

His breakout campaign led to that Opening Day start in 2007, a season that would arguably be the high point of his MLB career. On July 7, Bédard spun a two-hit, 15-strikeout complete game victory over the Texas Rangers and contin-

ued to dazzle throughout the year, sitting among American League leaders in ERA, strikeouts, and K/9, before a rib injury sidelined him in September, ending his season. He finished the year fifth in AL Cy Young Award voting while leading the AL with a 10.9 K/9 rate.

In a *Sports Illustrated* article published in the 2008 off-season, Ben Reiter painted a portrait of Bédard the person, rather than a player who would soon become a coveted trade piece. "He sleeps in his folks' basement, in a lair fit for a college student. A poster of Bruce Lee hangs above a rumpled bed. A Molson kegerator sits in a corner. Trophies commemorating past athletic glories cover nearly every flat surface."[5] Bédard was, in essence, the quintessential Canadian boy.

Bédard's career season led to a franchise-altering move for the Orioles. With 28 wins, a 3.47 ERA and 392 strikeouts over two seasons, Bédard was on the radar of several major league teams. Facing salary arbitration in the 2008 offseason and an expected raise,[6] Baltimore dealt their ace to the Seattle Mariners on February 8. Going back to the Orioles was a package of five players, including outfielder Adam Jones, who became a mainstay in Charm City for 11 seasons.

Bédard earned his second consecutive Opening Day start, opening his Mariners tenure by going five innings in his new club's 5–2 victory over Texas. Unfortunately, arm injuries took their toll and he only started 30 games over two full seasons with the Mariners, quickly being supplanted in the pecking order by emerging superstar Félix Hernández.

Bédard embarked on a nomadic back half of his career, plagued by injuries and never staying more than one season at five different MLB clubs, but still showing flashes of the early success that granted him "ace" status in Baltimore.

In 2012, Bédard made the third Opening Day start of his career for his third different team, his Pirates going up against the Phillies. Bédard pitched well, going seven innings and surrendering just one run, but that first start would be the best that year for Bédard and he was released by the club before the season ended, his ERA over five and leading the NL in losses at the time.

His 2013 tenure with the Houston Astros led to Bédard coming out of the bullpen for the first time since his rookie season, but in a July 20 start against old club Seattle, Bédard had a pitching line of 6 1/3 innings, five walks, 10 strikeouts—and zero hits—before the left-hander removed himself from the game for precautionary reasons. "I've had three shoulder surgeries," Bédard told the press pool following the game. "I'm not going over 110 [pitches]. I'd rather pitch a couple more years than face another batter."[7]

His sound bite proved prescient. During a minor-league start with the Dodgers, Bédard's shoulder once again gave out. He told a reporter in 2021 that "it felt like someone was stabbing a knife into his shoulder when he threw the ball that day."[8] He retired on June 11, 2015 with a 71–82 record and a 3.99 ERA with 1,246 strikeouts in his career.

Those 2006-2007 seasons in Baltimore will always be remembered by Ottawa baseball fans as a time when one of their own was amongst the best in the game, and surely that run will be enough to one day warrant Bédard a place in the Canadian Baseball Hall of Fame.

SOURCES

In addition to sources shown in the Notes, the author referred to Baseball-Reference.com and MLB.com for statistical information.

NOTES

1   Tim Baines, "Erik Bédard of Navan gets one more shot to prove he belongs," *Ottawa Sun*, February 9, 2013. Accessed February 18, 2024, https://ottawasun.com/2013/02/09/erik-Bédard-of-navan-gets-one-more-shot-to-prove-he-belongs

2   Spencer Fordin, "Bédard arrives on a road less traveled," *MLB.com*, July 30, 2007. Accessed February 18, 2024, https://web.archive.org/web/20110928012711/http://baltimore.orioles.mlb.com/news/article.jsp?ymd=20070730&content_id=2118847&vkey=news_bal&fext=.jsp&c_id=bal.

3   "Bédard arrives on a road less traveled."

4   Ben Reiter, "The Real Steal," *Sports Illustrated* 108 (5): 56–60. Accessed March 18, 2024. https://vault.si.com/vault/2008/02/11/the-real-steal.

5   "The Real Steal."

6   "Orioles trade Bédard to Mariners for five prospects," *ESPN.com*, February 8, 2008. Accessed February 2, 2024. https://www.espn.com/mlb/news/story?id=3237189.

7   "Astros' Erik Bédard halts own no-no," *ESPN.com*, July 21, 2013. Accessed March 14, 2024. https://www.espn.com/mlb/story/_/id/9496259/erik-Bédard-houston-astros-asked-leave-no-hit-bid-7th-inning.

8   Tim Baines, "Life Beyond Pitching: So many What Ifs in MLB career, but Navan's Erik Bédard enjoying retired life," *Ottawa Sun*, March 20, 2021. Accessed March 18, 2024. https://ottawasun.com/sports/baseball/life-beyond-pitching-so-many-what-ifs-in-mlb-career-but-navans-erik-Bédard-enjoying-retired-life.

PHILLIPPE AUMONT

BY CLAYTON TRUTOR

PHILLIPPE AUMONT PITCHED IN 46 big-league games over the course of four seasons for the Philadelphia Phillies (2012-2015). A tall (6'7"), powerfully-built (265 pounds), and hard-throwing (fastball in the high 90s) right-hander, Aumont is the most highly selected player from Quebec in the history of the major-league draft. The Seattle Mariners made the 18-year-old hurler from Gatineau the 11th overall selection in the first round of the 2007 amateur draft. Aumont pitched professionally for 13 years, spending time in the Mariners, Detroit Tigers, Toronto Blue Jays, and Chicago White Sox organizations as well as for the Philadelphia club where he completed the entirety of his major-league service. He worked almost exclusively as a relief pitcher for the Phillies, starting just one game in his career. Aumont posted a 1-6 career record with an ERA of 6.80 during an MLB career highlighted not only by his status as an important milestone holder in Canadian baseball history but also the 2012 and 2013 campaigns where he served as a key stopper in Philadelphia's bullpen.

Aumont was born on January 7, 1989 in Gatineau, Quebec, just across the Ottawa River from Canada's capital city. The future major leaguer grew up in a working-class Francophone neighborhood and was raised primarily by his father, Jean-Pierre Aumont, who worked for a moving company.[1]

Phillipe spent most of his time as a young man outside, playing with other children from his neighborhood. At age 11, he started playing baseball competitively and soon joined up with Canada's national baseball program. As Aumont grew during his adolescence, the baseball-mad teenager started to draw interest from baseball scouts.

"My style of pitching was more power pitching than anything else. I never wanted you to touch the ball. All I was shooting for was a strikeout. Period," Aumont said.[2] His size and strength made his approach to pitching highly successful. As a junior in high school, he first realized that scouts were following his games closely. Mariners scout Dave May marveled at the velocity of both Aumont's fastball and slider, describing him as having "one of the highest ceilings" of the era's pitching prospects.[3]

When the Mariners made Aumont their first-round pick in 2007, it was a significant milestone in the baseball history of Quebec. Never before had a native son of «La belle province" been selected so highly in the first round. Aumont progressed rapidly through the Mariners' system. At age 20, Aumont advanced to Double A spending much of the summer of 2009 with the West Tennessee Diamond Jaxx of the Southern League. The trajectory of Aumont's career changed in December 2009 when he was one of three players (the other two being minor-league outfielder Tyson Gillies and pitcher J. C. Ramírez) sent to the Philadelphia Phillies in exchange for 2008 Cy Young Award winner Cliff Lee. For the next three seasons, Aumont bounced around the Philadelphia organization before debuting for the Phillies on August 23, 2012. He pitched a scoreless eighth inning against the Cincinnati Reds, which presaged a strong rookie campaign. Over the next two months, Aumont made 18 appearances for Philadelphia, earning 2 saves and garnering a 3.68 ERA as a middle reliever.

He split 2013 between AAA Lehigh Valley of the International League and Philadelphia. He again performed admirably for the Phillies, making a career-high 22 appearances, all in relief. In 2013, Aumont had a 4.19 ERA for the season and a 1-3 overall record.

For whatever reason, Aumont could never break out of his status as a borderline big-league pitcher in the Philadelphia organization. Both at the major- and minor-league levels, Aumont had a tendency to give up walks and give up home runs—both were certainly a product of his power pitching approach to the game. 2014 and 2015 proved to be particularly frustrating seasons for Aumont. During both campaigns, he pitched well for Lehigh Valley but struggled in his rare appearances at the major-league level.

In all, Aumont made just five appearances for the Phillies in 2014, posting an ERA of 19.06 for the season. In 2015, he made just one MLB appearance.

On June 19, 2015, Aumont started his first major-league game. He surrendered six earned runs to the St. Louis Cardinals in just four innings, taking the loss in a 12-4 Cards win. The defeat proved to be not only Aumont's first career start but also his final MLB appearance and his only appearance of the 2015 season. The Phillies released Aumont shortly thereafter, thus beginning a more than half-decade odyssey throughout organized baseball. He spent time in the Toronto Blue Jays, Chicago White Sox, and Detroit Tigers organizations for the next three seasons.

Following his release by the Tigers, Aumont re-signed with Ottawa of the Canadian-American Association in 2019 and enjoyed a renaissance season. Working exclusively as a starter, Aumont was named Pitcher of the Year in the Canadian-American Association, going 8-4 for the season with a 2.65 ERA. His production in 2019 earned Aumont another opportunity to make it back to the big leagues.

In December 2019, he signed on with the Blue Jays and gave it another shot in spring training. Before Major League Baseball shut down in mid-March 2020, Aumont made two appearances for the Blue Jays in spring training. Amidst the COVID-19 shutdown, Aumont decided to retire from baseball and pursue family farming on a farmstead just outside Gatineau, Quebec.

Looking back on his big-league career, Aumont feels a great sense of pride.

"From where I come from to where I am now, not many people in the world can say they did and experienced what I did. I'm proud to be part of that." [4]

NOTES

1   Phillippe Aumont, interview by the author, June 14, 2021.

2   Phillippe Aumont, interview by the author, June 14, 2021.

3   Scott Hanson, "M's Pick Up Aumont at No. 11," *Seattle Times*, June 8, 2007. Accessed on September 14, 2020: https://www.seattletimes.com/sports/ms-pick-up-aumont-at-no-11/.

4   Phillippe Aumont, interview by the author, June 14, 2021.

GEORGE KORINCE

BY JERRY NECHAL

GEORGE KORINCE'S PATH TO THE big leagues started by throwing stones in a pond. "My mother saw me and suggested that I go out for baseball."[1] With early success in his native Canada, he became a much-acclaimed professional prospect. Unfortunately, Korince's major-league career was very brief.

Korince was born to George Sr. and Simone Korince, on January 10, 1946 in Ottawa. His father was an autoworker with five children. Korince moved at age four to St. Catharines, Ontario.

In youth sports, Korince was a physically dominating persona known as "Moose." He reached 6-foot-2 and 200 pounds by age 18. Korince's pitching helped his teams win four Ontario provincial baseball championships. Former batboy Pat Leahy recalled "he would strikeout 11–14 without even thinking about it."[2] At Merritton High School, Korince was also on the track and basketball teams. He held district records in shot put and javelin.

In 1964, Tigers scout Bob Prentice watched Korince hurl a no-hitter in a game between the Merritton Juniors and the Toronto Columbus Boys Club. Korince soon signed with Detroit for a $1,500 bonus.

In 1965, when Korince reported to spring training, Canadian professional baseball players were still a novelty. Korince's journey generated a lot of attention. CBC aired a TV special following his first steps in professional baseball, *The Tigers That Bloom in the Spring*.[3] Korince was assigned to Single-A Jamestown. He finished with a record 7–11 and a 3.38 ERA. Most impressive were his 151 strikeouts, but he exhibited control issues with 96 walks and 13 wild pitches.

In the 1960s it was generally acknowledged that Canadian prospects were about two years behind their US counterparts in skill development. Korince and future Detroit pitcher John Hiller, a fellow Canadian, discussed the disadvantage in a 1967 *Calgary Herald* interview. Korince confirmed, "I always thought I could throw a curve when I was at home. Hell I didn't even know how to hold the ball."[4] Hiller added, "I remember my coaches…always somebody's father, a nice guy…But all they could tell you, really, was to pick up the ball and throw it…The first time I pitched on a mound was after I turned pro."[5]

Given these handicaps, Korince's progress was remarkable. In 1966, he moved up to Double-A Montgomery. He again dominated batters, leading the Southern League with 183 strikeouts. He was labeled a "can't miss" prospect. By September, Korince was in the big leagues. He made his first major-league appearance pitching a scoreless eighth inning against Kansas City on September 10. He made one more appearance that season, pitching two scoreless innings.

In the spring of 1967, the *Detroit Free Press* referred to Korince as "the golden boy of the organization."[6] Korince did not disappoint, finishing the preseason with a 1.21 ERA which vaulted him onto the opening day major-league roster. The 21-year-old Korince was the youngest player on the Tigers team.

Korince started the season strong. In his first two appearances, he yielded no runs and no hits with four strikeouts. Then on May 13 at Fenway Park, with the Tigers trailing Boston, Korince pitched the eighth inning. He held the Red Sox scoreless. Detroit rallied to score six runs and post a victory. Korince was the winning pitcher in what ultimately would be his only big-league decision. Unfortunately, his fortunes quickly changed. On May 28, Korince was optioned to Triple-A Toledo. In 14 innings, Korince had an ERA of 5.14, with 11 strikeouts and 11 walks.

Korince continued in the minors for four years. In 1968, he led the Southern League in strikeouts and complete games. Korince's last season was in 1970. With Toledo, his ERA skyrocketed to 10.80. He also played three games with the Winnipeg Whips. Years later, he stated "I had chips in my elbow and my arm was hurting really bad."[7] At the age of 24, Korince's career was finished. He would look back at this time as "probably the best five years of my life."[8]

After baseball, Korince worked in the cleaning business and for General Motors. He was inducted into the St. Catharines Sports Hall of Fame. As of 2024, he lives in North Fort Myers, Florida.

SOURCES

In addition to sources shown in the Notes, the author used Baseball-Reference.com.

For a more complete biography of George Korince, please see the author's work on BioProject: George Korince. The biography was also included in the SABR book, *One-Win Wonders*. https://sabr.org/latest/sabr-digital-library-one-win-wonders/

NOTES

1 "Korince Is Happy To Be In Majors," *Beckley Post-Herald*, May 4, 1967: 2.

2 Pat Leahy, telephone interview, February 7, 2022.

3 "The TV Journal," *Ottawa Journal*, April 17, 1965: 15.

4 Paul Rimstead, "In big league ball, the American kid has a two-year break," *Calgary Herald*, April 29, 1967: 27.

5 "In big league ball, the American kid has a two-year break."

6 "4 Rookie Hurlers Rate Tiger Shot," *Detroit Free Press*, February 22, 1967: 3-D.

7 Bernie Puchalski, "Merritton's Moose Joins St. Catharine's Sport Hall," *St. Catharine's Standard*, May 4, 2012: B2.

8 Puchalski.

PETE LAFOREST

BY JORDAN PRESS

PIERRE-LUC "PETE" LAFOREST'S FIRST SPRING training with the Tampa Bay Devil Rays was a much different experience than ballplayers envision, for somewhat unusual reasons.

Rather than walking under the sun in St. Petersburg, Florida, with players trying to earn a spot on the big-league roster, Laforest was trudging through the snow and cold in Ottawa.

"It's a dream. You get your first big-league spring training, you get a chance to make the team, all the opportunities are right there and all of a sudden everything is, well, not thrown away. I mean the chance is still there," Laforest said at the time.[1]

The native of Hull, Quebec, didn't initially dream of playing for a big-league team. But his father introduced him to the game and it grew on him. (Another factor in his decision: the cost of competitive hockey, which was more than his family could afford.[2])

While in high school, he joined the Baseball Academy of Canada, a high-performance training program for elite players from Quebec. At the time, the academy also developed young players for Canada's national teams.[3]

Laforest got his first chance to represent the country at the age of 17 when he played on the under-18 junior national team.[4] He would have more chances to represent Canada in international competition, including at the Olympics in Athens in 2004 and the first World Baseball Classic in 2006.

Then, in 1995, a break. The Montreal Expos drafted Laforest in the 16th round of that year's draft—two rounds before the Expos drafted a catcher named Tom Brady, who ultimately decided to pursue football and went on to win seven Super Bowls.[5][6] But what seemed a dream opportunity turned into another bump on the road to the big leagues when the Expos voided Laforest's contract for what the *Tampa Bay Times* described as "a supposed back problem."[7]

So Laforest left Canada to attend Fort Scott Community College, which is more than 2,000 kilometers from Canada's national capital in a Kansas town of about 7,800 people—a far cry from the francophone communities Laforest was used to.[8]

In 1997, he signed with the expansion Tampa Bay Devil Rays after one year in Fort Scott.[9] After working his way up from rookie ball to Triple A, where he played with the Durham Bulls, Laforest got an invite to spring training in 2003.[10] But he ran into bureaucratic hurdles trying to renew his work visa so he could play ball in the United States.

"Papers were lost, everything was going wrong. The FBI was doing background checks for three months; I don't have a criminal record. It was just a mess," Laforest said.[11] "Even the lawyer told me he'd been doing this stuff for years and years and he'd never seen anything as messed up as this."

So he spent most of spring training in a batting cage in Ottawa, hitting and doing defensive drills until the first week of May when he finally made it down south.[12] He didn't make the big-league roster, but got called up in September and played in 19 games.

He played in 25 games for Tampa Bay in 2005, then played 10 games for the San Diego Padres in 2007 before the Philadelphia Phillies picked him off waivers and used him as a pinch-hitter in 14 games that September.[13]

He returned to Canada in 2009 to play for the Quebec Capitales of the Can-Am League. He earned the league's MVP award in his first season as the Capitales won the first of five consecutive league championships.[14]

Injuries ended his playing career in 2012.[15] But his coaching career was just starting.

He had served as the Capitales' hitting coach in 2011 and 2012 while still playing, and he was unveiled in 2013 as the manager of the Trois-Rivières Aigles, the newest team in the Can-Am League.[16]

"It reminds me a little of my career. Each year I started from scratch," Laforest said of coaching the Aigles.[17] "The Capitales were my second family. I had a lot of fun in Quebec (City), but I have now moved on. And being the underdog, I like that."

After two seasons in which the Aigles finished with more losses than wins, Laforest's squad took a big jump in 2015 when it captured the Can-Am League title for the first time.[18] The Aigles regressed the next year, and the club fired Laforest in early July 2016.[19]

In the spring of 2017, Laforest launched the B45 Academy in Kalamazoo, Michigan, which provides coaching and training for baseball players.[20] He lives in nearby Portage, Michigan, with his wife Cara and their two sons.[21]

NOTES

1   Mike Readling, "LaForest rues missed shot," *Tampa Bay Tribune*, May 14, 2003. Accessed May 12, 2024, https://www.tampabay.com/archive/2003/05/14/laforest-rues-missed-shot/.

2   Marc Topkin, "Rays Tales," *Tampa Bay Times*, September 14, 2003.

3   Académie de baseball, *À propos de l'ABC*. Accessed May 12, 2024, https://abc.baseballquebec.com/fr/page/programme/historique.html.

4   "Pete Laforest," B45 Academy. Accessed May 12, 2024, https://www.b45academy.com/about-us/.

5   "Pete Laforest," Baseball-Almanac.com. Accessed May 12, 2024, https://www.baseball-almanac.com/players/player.php?p=laforpe01.

6   The Expos selected Tom Brady in the 18th round of the 1995 June amateur draft. A complete list of the Expos' picks from that draft is available at Baseball-Reference.com: https://www.baseball-reference.com/draft/?team_ID=WSN&year_ID=1995&draft_type=junreg&query_type=franch_year&from_type_jc=0&from_type_hs=0&from_type_4y=0&from_type_unk=0.

7   "Rays Tales."

8   "Rays Tales"; City of Fort Scott, *Demographics*. Accessed May 12, 2024, https://www.fscity.org/319/Demographics.

9   Mike Readling, "LaForest rues missed shot," *Tampa Bay Tribune*, May 14, 2003. A history of the Tampa Bay Rays is available on the team's website: https://www.mlb.com/rays/history/timeline.

10   For a complete history of Laforest's major- and minor-league careers, see his page on Baseball-Reference.com. Accessed May 12, 2024, https://www.baseball-reference.com/register/player.fcgi?id=lafore001pie.

11   "LaForest rues missed shot."

12   "LaForest rues missed shot."

13   Matt Veasy, "Phillies 50: Forgotten 2007 – Pete LaForest," MattVeasy.com, April 30, 2020. Accessed May 12, 2024, https://mattveasey.com/2020/04/30/philadelphia-phillies-50-forgotten-2007-pete-laforest/.

14   "Can-Am League (2005-2019)," Fun While It Lasted. Accessed May 12, 2024, https://funwhileitlasted.net/can-am-league-baseball/.

15   "Pleins feux sur le nouvel entraîneur des Aigles de Trois-Rivières," *Radio-Canada*, March 12, 2013. Accessed May 12, 2024, https://ici.radio-canada.ca/nouvelle/604171/entraineur-chef-aigles-pierre-luc-laforest.

16   Kevin Reichard, "Trois-Rivieres Aigles unveil branding, logo," *BallparkDigest.com*, November 15, 2012. Accessed May 12, 2024, https://ballparkdigest.com/201211155847/independent-baseball/news/trois-rivieres-aigles-unveil-branding-logos.

17   This quote has been translated from French. For the original, see Carl Tardif, "Le premier match des Aigles de Trois-Rivières inspire Pierre-Luc Laforest," *Le Soleil*, May 16, 2013. Accessed May 12, 2024, https://www.lesoleil.com/2013/05/16/le-premier-match-des-aigles-de-trois-rivieres-inspire-pierre-luc-laforest-c76ccb94c88c9e7d3c7c2ecb87cccd14/.

18   "Can-Am League (2005-2019)," Fun While It Lasted. https://funwhileitlasted.net/can-am-league-baseball/. For more, see Baseball-Reference.com: https://www.baseball-reference.com/bullpen/Canadian-American_Association#League_Champions.

19   "Les Aigles de Trois-Rivières congédient leur gérant Pierre-Luc Laforest," *Radio-Canada*, July 12, 2016. Accessed May 12, 2024, https://ici.radio-canada.ca/nouvelle/792311/aigles-trois-rivieres-baseball-pierre-luc-laforest-gerant-congediement.

20   Marc-Antoine Gariépy, "Pete Laforest Launches B45 Academy," b45baseball.com, May 3, 2017. accessed May 12, 2024, Ahttps://www.b45baseball.com/blogs/news/pete-laforest-launches-b45-academy.

21   "Pete Laforest," B45 Academy. Accessed May 12, 2024, https://www.b45academy.com/about-us/.

RUSSELL MARTIN

BY MARK S. STERNMAN

BORN IN EAST YORK (NOW part of the city of Toronto) in 1983, a four-year Blue Jays backstop, and a Canadian Baseball Hall of Famer, four-time All-Star catcher Russell Martin has lasting links to Ontario.

Quebec can also claim Martin: as he recalled after Chelsea—about a half-hour drive from Ottawa—named a field after him, "I grew up in Chelsea (but) I really didn't play much baseball there ..."[1] Martin's family situation explains his provincial ties. "Martin's parents split when he was a boy, and Little Russ lived in Ottawa with his mother during the school year while spending summers in Quebec with his dad."[2]

Like all good Canadians, Martin played hockey. He fondly remembers his first goal, a thrilling breakaway—though it unfortunately went into his own net.[3]

After graduating from Polyvalente Edouard-Montpetit, a high school in Montreal with a strong emphasis on athletics, Martin aspired to attend a university in the United States. However, his college coach at Chipola College in Florida advised professional scouts that Martin's best chance to reach the major leagues might be to transition to the catcher position.[4]

Martin made his major-league debut with the Dodgers on May 5, 2006. He hit a two-run double in a 4–3 win.

Martin successfully transitioned from playing multiple positions in college to becoming a highly regarded catcher in the major leagues. His former high school teammate, Eric Gagné, praised Martin's exceptional skills, comparing him to the legendary Pudge Rodriguez.[5]

Martin's OPS dipped from .843 in 2007, to .781 in 2008, to .680 in 2009 and to .679 in 2010. On August 3, 2010, in what was his last game in his first LA stint, "Martin refused to leave, catching five innings after tearing his hip, departing only after the Dodgers brought in Hong-Chih Kuo and Martin made a confession. 'I can't move enough to block his slider,' he told [Dodger manager Joe] Torre."[6]

With Jorge Posada turning 40 in 2010, the Yankees signed Martin as a free agent. He played two New York seasons and received his third All-Star selection in 2011. Pittsburgh signed Martin as a free agent; in 2014, he had a career-high 5.7 WAR and finished 13th in NL MVP voting. Martin returned to Canada in 2015 and starred on the AL East champion Blue Jays. Early that year, "Russell Martin Sr. played 'O Canada' on a saxophone before a Jays-Reds exhibition game in Montreal. 'That was the dream as a kid,' said Martin, 'to play some professional games at Olympic Stadium. To get to do that in the major leagues and to have my dad out there, that's going to go into the memory banks for the rest of my days.'"[7]

"Martin, who broke down several times while paying tribute to parents Suzanne Jeanson and Russell Martin Sr.,"[8] at his Hall of Fame induction ceremony, also noted, "I wished I could have ended up playing with [the Expos]; maybe they would still be around – who knows?"[9]

Toronto made the playoffs twice with Martin. Cathal Kelly, a columnist for the *Globe and Mail* (Toronto), observed, "Those Jays teams had a lot of big egos and loud talkers, but no one carried himself more like a future Hall of Famer than Martin. It's like he got what he was meant to do - be in charge, but subtly. There was a kind of forcefield around his locker. Nobody approached unless invited."[10]

Russell Martin at the Canadian Baseball Hall of Fame and Museum induction ceremony on June 15, 2024, in St. Marys, Ontario. Credit: Courtesy Mark S. Sternman

Longtime Toronto beat writer Richard Griffin asserted, "Nothing was more important than the signing of Russell Martin to creating a winner and to going to the postseason and almost to the World Series like [the Blue Jays] did."[11]

Toronto traded Martin back to the Dodgers for minor leaguers. On September 28, 2019, he singled and caught a 2–0 win in his final game.

As of June 2024, Martin and his wife Élisabeth Chicoine have three daughters; his wife is pregnant with their fourth child, a boy.

NOTES

1   "Blue Jays' Russell Martin honoured with baseball field in Chelsea," *Montreal Gazette*, March 31, 2017, montrealgazette.com/sports/baseball/blue-jays-russell-martin-honoured-with-baseball-field-in-chelsea (accessed July 19, 2024).

2   Jerry Crasnick, "Martin grows through experience," *Baseball America*, October 23-November 5, 2006: 4.

3   Steve Serby, "Serby's Sunday Q&A with … Russell Martin," *New York Post*, April 10, 2011: 89.

4   Everett Cook, "Pirates' Russell Martin endures long road to become catcher," *Pittsburgh Post-Gazette*, August 6, 2013. Unpaginated article from the National Baseball Hall of Fame and Museum's file on Martin. Thanks to Hall Reference Librarian Rachel Wells for scanning the file.

5   Michael Farber, "The Backstop Of Notre-Dame-de-Grâce," *Sports Illustrated*, July 2, 2007: 42.

6   Bill Plaschke, "Russell Martin might be through in blue," *Los Angeles Times*, August 5, 2010. Unpaginated article from the National Baseball Hall of Fame and Museum's file on Martin.

7   Mike Wilner, "Russell Martin. Ashley Stephenson. Jimmy Key. Canadian Baseball Hall of Fame class covers a lot of bases," *[Toronto] Star*, February 6, 2024, www.thestar.com/sports/blue-jays/russell-martin-ashley-stephenson-jimmy-key-canadian-baseball-hall-of-fame-class-covers-a-lot/article_ab4b758e-c450-11ee-b4ce-f3ce3b311fd5.html (accessed July 19, 2024).

8   Mike Wilner, "Russell Martin and Ashley Stephenson add star power to Canadian Baseball Hall of Fame, where induction day is a chance to set the record straight," *[Toronto] Star*, June 15, 2024, www.thestar.com/sports/blue-jays/russell-martin-and-ashley-stephenson-add-star-power-to-canadian-baseball-hall-of-fame-where/article_4a4945d4-2b27-11ef-b580-1f7c9badf942.html (accessed July 19, 2024).

9   The author attended the June 15, 2024 ceremony in St. Marys, Ontario.

10 Cathal Kelly email to Mark S. Sternman, February 11, 2024.

11 Rich Griffin and Scott MacArthur, "S2E5 - The O's-Jays Verdict," *Exit Philosophy with Griff and Scotty Mac*, February 6, 2024, podcasts.apple.com/us/podcast/s2e5-the-os-jays-verdict/id1688792600?i=1000644405282 (accessed February 16, 2024).

EPILOGUE

BY CHARLES GORDON

FOR A FEW YEARS IN the early to mid-'90s Ottawa fans thought pro baseball would prosper forever in their city. Sadly, they were wrong. Baseball had a brief period of glory here, then faded. There have been continual stirrings, a series of new beginnings, but the glory days have not returned. Can they?

First, we need to look at what made the Ottawa Lynx so successful. With the benefit of hindsight, we can see that a perfect storm of factors worked in their favor. Novelty was one thing, but novelty alone cannot explain the phenomenon. The lack of competition would be a partial explanation: When the Ottawa Lynx first appeared, the Ottawa Senators were just one year into their existence and losing all the time in a cramped and outdated arena. Their fancy new home, then called the Palladium, was not built until 1996.

Other distractions were yet to come. There was no Netflix. Phones were just phones. Video games were in their infancy.

Cultural factors played in. We were in the midst of what I like to call the Thrill of the Grass period—a time when baseball was romanticized within an inch of its life. W.P. Kinsella's baseball novels (*Shoeless Joe*, *The Iowa Baseball Confederacy* and, yes, *The Thrill of the Grass*) were all the rage. The movie version of *Shoeless Joe*, *Field of Dreams*, came out in 1989. Kinsella's notion of all the world somehow being in fair territory resonated deeply.

A League of Their Own, another affecting baseball movie, came out in 1992. Perhaps most important was the nostalgic Ken Burns documentary series, *Baseball*, which first aired in 1994. Baseball, the sport, was fashionable. The Lynx Stadium was the place to be.

Your friends were at the stadium—friends you didn't even know were baseball fans. They talked about it at work. They bought season tickets, or shares of season tickets. You had to be there, too.

And a good stadium it was, to give it credit. There was lots of parking, good seating, good sight lines, an abundance of concessions, real grass (the better to be thrilled by). It was a well-run, locally-owned operation.

Another important factor in the success of the Lynx was the success of the Montreal Expos. The Expos had many fans in Ottawa, some who regularly made the trek down Highway 417 to catch games at the Big O, many others who watched the games on television or tuned in to Duke and Dave on the country music FM station CKBY. The Lynx affiliation with the Expos was part of the draw: we could see Expos stars of the future, on their way up; we could see Expos stars of the past on their way down; we could see Expos stars of the present on rehab assignments. We could see Rondell White, Cliff Floyd, Chris Nabholz, Sean Berry, even Charlie Montoyo, a light-hitting shortstop before he became an ill-fated manager in the American League. We could see visiting stars, such as Carlos Delgado, then a catcher for the Syracuse Chiefs. And we could create fan favorites of our own, such as the versatile F.P. Santangelo and the hearing-impaired outfielder, Curtis Pride.

Finally, the Lynx existed in an ideal media situation. The *Ottawa Citizen* was engaged in a newspaper war with the upstart *Ottawa Sun*. Much of that war took place on the sports pages. The Lynx got lots and lots of coverage—profiles, advance stories, and game stories complete with box scores.

You have only to look at today's media situation to get an idea of how the perfect storm plays out in reverse. Newspapers have tiny sports sections and tiny staffs. Today's professional baseball iteration, the Titans, receive almost no coverage. If you want to find out when a game is, you have to look for the team website. The same with finding out who won. The Titans' predecessors—the Champions, Fat Cats, and Rapidz—received a similar fate.

There is no link to the Expos because there are no Expos. Even when there were Expos, they dropped their Lynx affiliation in 2002. Local fans were less interested in seeing the farmhands of the Baltimore Orioles and, later, the Philadelphia Phillies. Some of the less committed of the fans discovered that watching a baseball game in Ottawa in April, and even May, could be a cold experience.

The ballpark still has the grass, but it has less parking, fewer concessions. Its location, something which never bothered folks during the height of Lynx popularity, is now seen as a disadvantage. Like its ill-fated cousin, Montreal's Olympic Stadium, it is walking distance to nothing. Ottawa's sometimes chill spring weather, which didn't bother anyone in the initial glow of the early Lynx years, now keeps people away.

Baseball itself may not have helped. Although the Lynx survived past the 1994 strike, they would, like all of baseball, have been hurt by the general souring of public attitudes toward the game as the result of the steroid revelations. The corporatization of the sport, where players earn millions and stadiums are named after banks, has put it at a remove from everyday life. Some people began to suspect they lived in foul territory after all.

The perfect storm rages on. Spectator sports are expensive and people have only so much. Today's discretionary sports spending in Ottawa goes to the Senators and, to a lesser extent, football's

RedBlacks, both of which have occasional ups to go with their downs and both of which receive ample media coverage.

Baseball's role in daily life has diminished. Neighborhood little leagues have shrunk or disappeared altogether. Fields that once held baseball games now hold soccer games, or dogs. Soccer is seen by parents as more fitness-enhancing than baseball, and it probably is. Basketball has grown in popularity.

And of course many kids do not want to play anything, at least out of the house. They want to stay home and play video games, encouraged by their helicopter parents, who don't want their child exposed to such dangers as bats and balls may pose. Participation in baseball, like participation in other sports, has been hurt by the high cost of training at the elite level.

This is not good. If kids are not playing a game, they have less interest in watching it.

So, who *is* watching it? Who are those few hundred folks out there at the stadium? Perhaps they hold the key to survival.

Who are they? Well, you can only guess. Some of them will be families looking for something to do on a sunny afternoon or a warm evening. And some of them, perhaps the majority, will be die-hard baseball fans. They will go to a game no matter what. They are unaffected by the parking situation, by the presence or absence of between innings entertainment, craft beer, mascots, loud music between pitches and the playing of "YMCA" or "Sweet Caroline." On the face of it, at least judging by the Ottawa experience, there are not enough of these to make a franchise profitable over the long run.

Certainly baseball owners the world over sense this, sense that baseball alone is not enough to put seats in the seats. At the major-league level there is so much entertainment happening—on the scoreboard, on the public address system, in the stands, on top of the dugout—that the game sometime seems an afterthought. Does this work? Hard to know, because no one has tried to do without it. Certainly, it would please the die-hards, who would like to be left in peace, the better to hear the infield chatter and the occasional bird, but no serious attempt has been made, to my knowledge, to have a silent baseball game.

The assumption is that there are not enough die-hards, not enough true baseball fans, to support a distraction-free free baseball experience. The Ottawa experience neither proves nor disproves this theory, since the stadium keeps pumping out the oldies, running various mascot suits through the stands and bringing fans onto the field between innings to humiliate themselves in wacky competitions. On the one hand, there are few fans. On the other hand, maybe there would be fewer.

The Saint of Second Chances, a 2023 documentary about the baseball entrepreneur Mike Veeck suggests that more and more stadium wackiness can be the salvation of minor-league baseball. Veeck, son of the legendary St. Louis Browns owner Bill Veeck, and author of the infamous disco demolition promotion at Chicago's Comiskey in 1979, is shown to have resurrected a number of minor-league franchises by going all-in on crazy stunts and promotions.

Could that be the answer for Ottawa? Perhaps not, given the capital city's buttoned-up reputation. Similarly, it is unlikely that Ottawa baseball would go the route of the Savannah Bananas, a team whose recent successes have more to do with comedy than baseball prowess.

A more relevant place to look would be Winnipeg, home of the Goldeyes, also an independent league franchise, also owned by the owner of the Ottawa Titans, Sam Katz. Playing in an independent league similar to the one hosting the Ottawa Titans, and playing in a city with challenges similar to Ottawa's, the Goldeyes averaged 3,641 fans per game in 2023[1], compared to the Titans, who averaged 1,540.[2] The Goldeyes were third in attendance in a 12-team league, the Titans 13th in a 15-team league.

The comparison is not entirely fair, since the Goldeyes have been around long enough to be a local institution, while the Titans were in their second year of existence. But if you are optimistic you can see the potential for Ottawa. Winnipeg's population is similar to Ottawa's, a bit smaller actually. Winnipeg also has National Hockey League and Canadian Football League competition. Winnipeg also has challenging weather in the spring. Winnipeg's Blue Cross Stadium is similar to Ottawa's ballpark.

Where Winnipeg has a huge advantage over Ottawa is in the location of that stadium. It is in the Forks, a hugely popular and well-designed area of parks, museums, restaurants and trails. Going to the baseball game can be part of larger excursions. Contrast this to Ottawa's stadium, whose closest nearby attraction is the train station.

And then there is the unmeasurable issue of civic pride, which Winnipeg has in spades and Ottawa may lack. Winnipeggers, perhaps because of geographical isolation, perhaps because of enlightened leadership, have always supported local endeavors. Professional theatre thrives, as do museums and ballet. Ottawa, where so many residents come from somewhere else, needs the federal presence to provide a cultural imprint. And, of course, the attractions of Montreal and Toronto are not that far away.

Still, Winnipeg's example shows that it can be done, that good baseball, coupled with intelligent management, is viable in a city of this size. In Ottawa, there have been some variations over the years, but the quality of ball, has never been the issue. You could always take your grandchildren to the stadium to show them the game played at a high level. And if you're of a certain age, you can remember when that stadium was rocking.

Times have changed but maybe they can change back. At the professional level, the potential exists. If Major League Baseball returned to Montreal, a remote possibility at the moment, a positive spinoff would be felt here. Similarly, if Ottawa could succeed in landing a Toronto Blue Jays minor-league affiliate, as has been discussed in the past, the impact on local baseball would be dramatic.

All of this assumes that baseball itself will continue to hold an appeal. Its player base is shrinking at the youth level[3], never a good sign. At the major-league level, the sport is showing signs of lack of confidence, evidenced most recently in continued tinkering with the rules. Still, those rule changes have been well received.

In many ways, Ottawa's baseball future is tied to the future of baseball itself. We live in a world of rapid change. Both the smartphone and the pitch clock were unknown 20 years ago. Perhaps baseball's reassuring sameness, in a world of rapid change, will be the key to its endurance. Whether professional baseball exists in town or not, there will always be kids—and their parents and even grandparents—out in a field, throwing the ball around.

NOTES

1   Mike McIntyre, "Goldeyes swing and miss in 2023," *Winnipeg Free Press*, September 5, 2023, https://www.winnipegfreepress.com/sports/2023/09/05/goldeyes-swing-and-miss-in-2023. Accessed June 11, 2024.

2   Kevin Reichard, "2023 MLB Partner League Attendance by Average," *Ballpark Digest*, September 19, 2023, https://ballparkdigest.com/2023/09/19/2023-mlb-partner-league-attendance-by-average/. Accessed June 11, 2024.

3   Statista, "Share of Children Aged 6 to 12 Who Participate in Baseball on a Regular Basis in the United States from 2008 to 2021," https://www.statista.com/statistics/982278/participation-kids-baseball/ . Accessed June 11, 2024.

ACKNOWLEDGEMENTS

WRITING A BOOK ABOUT BASEBALL history is a daunting task—especially when that history is tied to your hometown. As someone who has lived in Ottawa for most of my life, I felt a real duty to tell the city's baseball history honestly and accurately. Thankfully, I had plenty of help. This project would not have been possible without the support and contributions of many people, to whom I am deeply indebted

I want to first thank the Society for American Baseball Research (SABR) for agreeing to take on this project. Ottawa's baseball history may not be as storied as other places, but I think it's a story that deserves to be told. I'm thankful to SABR—particularly Publications Director Cecilia Tan and the rest of the editorial board—for the chance to tell it.

This book might have come together without Bill Nowlin, but likely not as smoothly and definitely not as quickly. Bill is a world-class editor with an uncanny ability to juggle multiple SABR projects at once without making you feel like you had anything less than his full attention. I hope that I get to work with him again someday.

To everyone who contributed their time and effort to this book, either as an author, fact-checker, or copy editor: thank you. You brought more than 150 years of history to life with an admirable commitment to accuracy and a true passion for storytelling. The end result is a remarkable collaboration that extends beyond SABR members to include journalists and researchers. I'm grateful for your help in bringing this project to life.

I also want to thank Ottawa Mayor Mark Sutcliffe for writing the foreword to this book. Mark has so many demands on his time, but he still made the effort to be part of this project.

He is a lifelong baseball fan who has made so many contributions to this city, and I'm thankful that he shared his story with us.

Thanks also to the City of Ottawa Archives, Library and Archives Canada, the Bytown Museum, and the National Baseball Hall of Fame and Museum for providing access to their archival photographs and documents for this book.

I am grateful to the Centre for Canadian Baseball Research—notably Andrew North, Martin Lacoste, and Bill Humber—for their encouragement and support, and for indulging me as I bombarded them with newspaper accounts of nineteenth century games from Ottawa and Eastern Ontario.

I could not write a list of acknowledgements without including my parents, Mike and Sue, for always supporting me in everything I have done. I hope I am making you proud.

The world of baseball writing feels incomplete without Don McCormick. I wish I could share this book with him.

My children, Caleb and Viola, bring me more joy than they could ever know. I love you both so much.

Finally, I want to thank my wife, Joanna, for her unwavering support and love. She is my rock, my inspiration, and my best friend. Without her, none of this would have been possible. Je t'aime.

I would also like to take a moment to address the use of American spelling throughout this book. While the content focuses on Ottawa, we opted for American spelling conventions since this book is being published by SABR, which is based in the United States. To our Canadian readers: thank you for your understanding.

— Steve Rennie

CONTRIBUTORS

GARY BELLEVILLE is a retired Information Technology professional living in Victoria, British Columbia. He grew up in Ottawa and graduated from the University of Waterloo with a Bachelor of Mathematics (Computer Science) degree. Gary has written a variety of articles for the *Baseball Research Journal*, Games Project, and Baseball BioProject. He has also contributed to several SABR books, including *Our Game, Too: Influential Figures and Milestones in Canadian Baseball*. Gary was the 2024 winner of the McFarland-SABR Baseball Research Award for his article "The Trailblazing Canadian Trio That Powered the Rockford Peaches Dynasty of 1948-50," which was published in the *Journal of Canadian Baseball*.

LUIS BLANDÓN, a Washington, DC native, is a producer, writer and researcher in video and documentary film production and in archival, manuscript, historical, film and image research. His creative storytelling has garnered numerous awards, including three regional Emmys®, regional and national Edward R. Murrow Awards, two TELLY awards and a New York Festival World Medal. His writing has been published in several platforms. He was Senior Researcher and Manager of the Story Development Team for two national television programs. He served as the principal researcher for several authors including for *The League of Wives* by Heath Hardage Lee and her current biography project *The Mysterious Mrs. Nixon: The Life and Times of Washington's Most Private First Lady*. Luis has a Masters of Arts in International Affairs from George Washington University.

KURT BLUMENAU grew up in the Rochester, New York, area, following the Mets and the Triple-A Rochester Red Wings. He works in corporate communications in the Boston area. He has a strong interest in the minor leagues, particularly the New York-Penn League, and also enjoys watching college games.

WARREN CAMPBELL is a Canadian-based entertainment industry executive who once lived in a suburb of Ottawa, but not at a time when professional baseball was in the area. For 30 years, he has avoided being on a stage and spends his free time searching through old publications for curious baseball stories. He still has dreams of owning an independent team.

PHILIPPE COUSINEAU was a long-time fan of the Montreal Expos. He worked for the Canadian Foreign Service for more than three decades and is now retired in Gatineau, Quebec, across the Ottawa River from Ottawa.

ANDREW FORBES is the author of three books on baseball: *The Utility of Boredom: Baseball Essays* (Invisible Publishing, 2016*); The Only Way is the Steady Way: Essays on Baseball, Ichiro, and How We Watch the Game* (2021); *Field Work: Essays on Baseball and Making a Living* (Assembly Press, April 2025). He is also the author of two collections of short fiction, a novel, and *McCurdle's Arm* (2024), a novella about 1890s semipro baseball in southern Ontario. Born and raised, mostly, in Ottawa, Forbes now lives in Peterborough, Ontario.

JOHN FREDLAND is an attorney and retired Air Force officer. As an undergraduate at Rice University, he covered the school's nationally ranked baseball teams for the school newspaper, the *Rice Thresher*. John received his law degree at Vanderbilt University, then served as an active-duty attorney in the Air Force's Judge Advocate General's Corps for 20 years. He lives in San Antonio, Texas, and chairs SABR's Baseball Games Project Research Committee.

CHARLES GORDON is a former journalist (*Ottawa Citizen, Maclean's*), author (*At The Cottage, How To Be Not Too Bad*) and third baseman in the Ottawa Regional Softball League.

DAVID GOURLAY is the Chief Executive Officer of the Shepherds of Good Hope Foundation, having joined in 2020. David's role fits a career that is characterized by a passion for people, relationships and building the community he was born, raised and lives in—Ottawa. David had a 10+ year career in the private sector following a 15-year career in the Government of Canada and the City of Ottawa. He has served on the Board of Directors for the Ottawa Public Library, the Ottawa Community Housing Foundation and the Ottawa Sport Council. David established the Ottawa Champions Baseball Club and proudly co-founded the Miracle League of Ottawa to provide children with special needs a fully accessible and inclusive baseball facility in Orléans. In June 2009, David received an Ottawa Business Journal "40Under40" Award and in 2014, he became a Member of the Order of Ottawa. In 2022, he was recognized as AFP

Ottawa's Outstanding Fundraising Executive. David lives in Kanata with his wife Danielle and their two children.

SHARON HAMILTON is the chair of the Society for American Baseball Research's (SABR) Century Research Committee, which celebrates important milestones in baseball history. She served as project manager for the special 100th anniversary SABR Century 1921 project at SABR.org and for the web project on Jackie Robinson and the 75th anniversary of baseball's re-integration.

TIM HARPER interspersed baseball coverage with a long career as a political reporter at the *Ottawa Citizen* and *Toronto Star*, reporting on the Montreal Expos, the Toronto Blue Jays and the birth of the Washington Nationals, successor to his beloved Expos. He covered postseason series in New York, Los Angeles, St. Louis and Kansas City and traveled to the Dominican Republic to chronicle the roots of Dominican stars for the Jays. Labour strife book-ended his baseball writing, beginning with a trip to West Palm Beach to cover the Expos' training camp for the second half of the 1981 season divided by a strike, then becoming the *Star's* Jays beat writer in 1994 when he was dealt the ultimate bad hop—the premature end of the season and the cancellation of that year's World Series due to a players' strike. Tim lives in Toronto.

MARTIN LACOSTE recently retired as a high school music educator and is excited to have more time to devote to some of his interests, including baseball. Once an avid Montreal Expos fan, since their relocation he has refocused his passion for the sport towards its history, notably nineteenth-century Canadian baseball. He has presented papers at the Canadian Baseball History Conference, written biographies for SABR, and contributed articles for the 2022 SABR publication on the development of Canadian baseball, entitled *Our Game, Too*.

Long-time SABR member **DAVID MCDONALD** is a writer, filmmaker and broadcaster with a particular interest in Ottawa baseball history. He has contributed to a number of SABR publications, including *Our Game Too, Boston's First Nine: The 1871–75 Boston Red Stockings*, and *The Babe*, as well as *The Baseball Research Journal, The National Pastime*, and SABR's Bio Project. Other baseball writings have appeared in the *Ottawa Citizen*, the *Globe and Mail*, and the Canadian anthology *All I Dreamed About Was Baseball*. He has also presented papers on left-handed catcher Jack Humphries and on communications guru Marshall McLuhan at the Canadian Baseball History Conference.

FRANK MCDONALD lives in Ottawa and is a retired public servant. He has been a SABR member since 2007 and takes a particular interest in the activities of the Deadball Era and Games and Simulation committees.

JERRY NECHAL is a retired former administrator at Wayne State University, residing in Sylvan Lake, Michigan. He has previously written about "The Worst Team Ever" in the *Baseball Research Journal* as well as making several contributions to both the SABR Biography Project and the Games Project. Other interests include hiking, architecture, theater and gardening. He still longs for a bleacher seat in old Tiger Stadium.

BILL NOWLIN is from Boston, a fan of the hometown team. After a dozen years as a professor of political science and more than 50 years in the music business, he spends most of his time researching, writing, and helping edit baseball articles and books.

JORDAN PRESS is a former journalist who now works as an editor at Canada's central bank. He is married to a spectacular woman and a father to two wonderful daughters who love taking batting practice at the local park.

STEVE RENNIE is a former journalist now working in the Canadian government. He grew up in the village of Osgoode, which is now part of the city, and got to see the Ottawa Lynx in their heyday. His baseball writing includes articles for the SABR Team Ownership Histories Project and an upcoming piece on the short-lived Eastern International League of 1888. In the spring of 2024, he presented on Ottawa's early baseball history at the Frederick Ivor-Campbell 19th Century Base Ball Conference in Cooperstown, New York. He is the president of SABR's Ottawa-Gatineau and Eastern Ontario chapter. He has a particular interest in nineteenth-century baseball in Canada and enjoys unearthing forgotten games and teams from the sport's early history for the Centre for Canadian Baseball Research and Protoball. He lives in Ottawa with his wife Joanna and their two children.

CARL RIECHERS retired from United Parcel Service in 2012 after 35 years of service. With more free time, he became a SABR member that same year. Born and raised in the suburbs of St. Louis, he became a big fan of the Cardinals. He and his wife Janet have three children and is the proud grandpa of two.

CHRISTOPHER SAILUS is a Michigan-born, Canadian public servant and history instructor. He holds an M.A. in British history from Louisiana State University, and his varied research interests include early colonialism, religion during the Reformation era and, of course, baseball and early sport in general. He is based in Ottawa, Ontario, where he lives with his wife, Jennifer, and their two children.

A fan of the New York Yankees who owns a partial season ticket plan for the Boston Red Sox, **MARK S. STERNMAN** enjoys visiting Ottawa. In attending the 2013 World Women's Ice

Hockey Championship he learned the difference and distance between Kanata and downtown. He looks forward to returning to one of his two favourite bookstores in Canada (Perfect Books; Shelf Life Books in Calgary is the other). Sternman appreciated the chance to profile Russell Martin since he fondly recalls longtime radio announcer John Sterling's homer call for the backstop ("Russell! Shows Muscle!").

JONATHON SYMONS grew up in the Canadian Prairies where exposure to Whitaker, Trammell, Morris and Tanana on WDIV formed his love of the Detroit Tigers, alongside his Mom's beloved Toronto Blue Jays. The long winters were broken every year when *The Sporting News* Baseball Yearbook hit the stands. Dog-eared copies still exist, amongst boxes and boxes of late 80s and early 90s-era Topps and Donruss cards in his childhood basement. He lives in Winnipeg and can often be found walking through West Broadway with his lovely wife.

After failing to achieve his childhood dream of becoming the starting centerfielder for the San Francisco Giants, **MIKE TRICKEY** turned his attention to covering sports for radio stations and newspapers in British Columbia. Later, as a foreign correspondent for Southam News, he sought out opportu-nities to cover events connected to baseball. He covered the 1991 Hot Dog Summit between U.S. President George Bush and Canadian Prime Minister Brian Mulroney, at which they met int the bowels of Toronto's SkyDome to discuss how to support Mikhail Gorbachev's efforts to democratize the Soviet Union and how to end apartheid prior to watching the All-Star game. He was in Havana in March 1999 when the Baltimore Orioles met the Cuban national team, marking the first time an American professional team had played in Cuba since the 1959 revolution. He also has a remarkably poor record in far too many fantasy baseball leagues.

CHRISTIAN TRUDEAU is a professor of economics at the University of Windsor. He is a game theory specialist by day, and a historian of Quebec baseball by night.

CLAYTON TRUTOR holds a PhD in history from Boston College, teaches at Norwich University, and chairs the SABR-Vermont chapter. He is the author of *Loserville: How Professional Sports Remade Atlanta—and How Atlanta Remade Professional Sports* and *Boston Ball: Rick Pitino, Jim Calhoun, Gary Williams & the Forgotten Cradle of Basketball Coaches.* Twitter: @ClaytonTrutor IG: @ctrutor

Our Game, Too: Influential Figures and Milestones in Canadian Baseball

Canadian baseball has a rich, diverse, and deeply rooted history, one that spans fully two centuries. As was true in the United States, the stories reflect the competitive and entrepreneurial spirits of a rapidly changing time. Arranged chronologically, the essays in his volume tell the tales of the influential figures and milestone events that defined and directed the game's growth in Canada. The articles shine a spotlight on the movers and shakers, the pioneers, the leagues and games and tournaments, and the regions all across the country that hosted them.

Edited by Andrew North
Associate Editors: Len Levin, Bill Nowlin, and Carl Riechers
ISBN (ebook): 978-1-970159-81-3, $9.99
ISBN (paperback): 978-1-970159-82-0, $34.95 US / $44.99 CDN
8.5″ x 11″, 460 pages

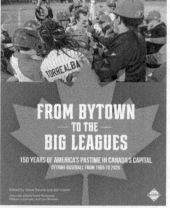

From Bytown to the Big Leagues: Ottawa baseball 1865-2025

The thrilling journey through 150 years of America's pastime in Canada's capital, including Ottawa's earliest baseball teams' remarkable face-offs against the famed Boston Red Stockings, the rise and fall of professional franchises like the Ottawa Giants, the Ottawa Lynx, and the current Ottawa Titans, and the stories of local heroes who have graced the diamond, including Jack Humphries, Frank "Shag" Shaughnessy, Érik Bédard, and Philippe Aumont.

Edited by Steve Rennie and Bill Nowlin
Associate editors Frank McDonald, Philippe Cousineau, and Carl Riechers
978-1-960819-32-1 (ebook) $9.99
978-1-960819-33-8 (paperback) $24.95 US/ $34.95 CDN
8.5"X11", 168 pages

We Are, We Can, We Will: The 1992 World Champion Toronto Blue Jays

This book features biographies of every player who played for the 1992 Toronto Blue Jays including Hall of Famers Dave Winfield, Jack Morris, and Roberto Alomar. Manager Cito Gaston, Hall of Fame general manager Pat Gillick, and radio broadcaster Tom Cheek are also included, as well as a "ballpark biography" of SkyDome, and ten significant games from the 1992 season, and concludes with an essay on the Blue Jays celebratory visits to Washington, DC, and Ottawa.

Edited by Adrian Fung and Bill Nowlin
Associate Editors: Len Levin and Carl Riechers
Forewords by Buck Martinez and Dave Winfield
ISBN (ebook): 978-1-970159-83-7, $9.99
ISBN (paperback): 978-1-970159-84-4, $34.95 US / $41.95 CDN
8.5″ x 11″, 394 pages

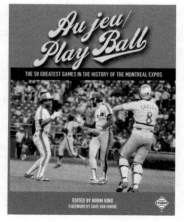

Au jeu/Play Ball: The 50 Greatest Games in the History of the Montreal Expos

The book details games from the earliest days of the franchise, to the glory years of 1979-81, the what-might-have-been years of the early 1990s, and the sad, final days, from the famous first game at Shea Stadium on April 8, 1969. It also details the first regular season game ever played outside the United States, when fans jammed little Jarry Park and began a love affair with the team. These game summaries don't just retell the runs, hits, and errors. They give a context to the times and individuals involved. The article about Dennis Martinez's perfect game also describes how he overcame his struggle with alcohol to resurrect his career. The piece about Curtis Pride recounts how he reached the major leagues despite the disadvantages of deafness, and what it felt like when 45,000 fans cheered as Expos coach Jerry Manuel spurred him through gestures to acknowledge the crowd.

Edited by Norm King
Foreword by Dave Van Horne
ISBN (paperback): 978-1-9438-1615-6, $19.95 US / $19.95 CDN
ISBN (ebook): 978-1-9438-1614-9, $5.99
150 pages, 8.5″ x 11″

Society for American Baseball Research

Become a SABR member today!

If you're interested in baseball — writing about it, reading about it, talking about it — there's a place for you in the Society for American Baseball Research.

SABR members include everyone from academics to professional sportswriters to amateur historians and statisticians to students and casual fans who merely enjoy reading about baseball history and gathering online or in person with other members to talk baseball.

We hope you'll join the most passionate international community of baseball fans!

Check us out online at SABR.org/join

SABR Membership Benefits

- Receive two e-book editions (spring and fall) of the Baseball Research Journal, our flagship publication
- Receive e-book edition of The National Pastime, our annual convention journal
- New e-books published by the SABR Digital Library, FREE to all members
- "This Week in SABR" e-newsletter, sent every Friday
- Regional chapter meetings, which can include guest speakers, presentations, and trips to ballgames
- Participate in research committees and online discussion groups

- Contribute to books, the Baseball Biography Project, and the SABR Games Project
- Collaborate with SABR researchers and experts
- Publish your research in peer-reviewed SABR journals
- Discount on registration to our annual conferences and National Convention
- FREE online access to Historical Black Newspapers Collection via ProQuest, the Newspapers.com World Collection, and The Sporting News via Paper of Record
- Discounts with other partners in the baseball community

- -

SABR MEMBERSHIP FORM

Name _____

Email _____

Address _____

City _____ State _____ Zip _____

Phone _____

If you wish to pay by credit card, please contact the SABR office at (602) 496-1460 or sign up securely online at SABR.org/join.

We accept Visa, Mastercard & Discover.

	Standard	Young Pro.	Student
Annual:	❑$80	❑$55	❑$25
3 Year:	❑$215		
Monthly:	❑$7.95	❑$5.95	

Members who wish to be mailed a printed copy of the Baseball Research Journal should add $7 per issue (U.S.) or $11 per issue (international). Two (2) issues of the BRJ are delivered each year.

SABR memberships are available on an annual, multi-year, or monthly subscription basis. Memberships auto-renew for your convenience. Young Professional memberships are for ages 30 and under. Student memberships are available to currently enrolled middle/high school or full-time college/university students. Monthly subscription members are eligible for SABR event discounts after 12 months.

Mail to: SABR, PO Box 1715, Milwaukee, WI 53201

www.ingramcontent.com/pod-product-compliance
Lightning Source LLC
LaVergne TN
LVHW081156240125
801920LV00009B/61

9781960819338